T-SQL Window Functions, Second Edition

For data analysis and beyond

Itzik Ben-Gan

Published with the authorization of Microsoft Corporation by:

Pearson Education, Inc.

Copyright © 2020 by Itzik Ben-Gan.

ISBN-13: 978-0-13-586144-8

ISBN-10: 0-13-586144-6

Library of Congress Control Number: 2019949146

1 2019

Trademarks

Microsoft and the trademarks listed at on the "Trademarks" webpage are trademarks of the Microsoft group of companies. All other marks are property of their respective owners.

Warning and Disclaimer

Every effort has been made to make this book as complete and as accurate as possible, but no warranty or fitness is implied. The information provided is on an "as is" basis. The author, the publisher, and Microsoft Corporation shall have neither liability nor responsibility to any person or entity with respect to any loss or damages arising from the information contained in this book.

Special Sales

For information about buying this title in bulk quantities, or for special sales opportunities (which may include electronic versions; custom cover designs; and content particular to your business, training goals, marketing focus, or branding interests), please contact our corporate sales department at corpsales@pearsoned.com or (800) 382-3419.

For government sales inquiries, please contact governmentsales@pearsoned.com.

For questions about sales outside the U.S., please contact intlcs@pearson.com.

EDITOR-IN-CHIEF

Brett Bartow

EXECUTIVE EDITOR

Loretta Yates

DEVELOPMENT EDITOR

Rick Kughen

MANAGING EDITOR

Sandra Schroeder

SENIOR PROJECT EDITOR

Tracey Croom

COPY EDITOR

Rick Kughen

INDEXER

Erika Millen

PROOFREADER

Gill Editorial Services

TECHNICAL EDITOR

Adam Machanic

ASSISTANT SPONSORING EDITOR

Charvi Arora

COVER DESIGNER

Twist Creative, Seattle

COMPOSITOR

codeMantra

In loving memory of my parents, Mila and Gabi Ben-Gan.

Contents at a Glance

Contents

About the Author

Itzik Ben-Gan is a mentor and co-founder of SolidQ and has been a data platform Microsoft MVP (Most Valuable Professional) since 1999. Itzik has delivered numerous training events around the world focused on T-SQL Querying, Query Tuning, and Programming. Itzik is the author of several books including *T-SQL Fundamentals* and *T-SQL Querying*. He has written articles for SentryOne's sqlperformance.com, ITProToday, and SolidQ. Itzik's speaking activities include PASS Summit, SQLBits, and various events and user groups around the world. Itzik is the author of SolidQ's Advanced T-SQL Querying, Programming, and Tuning and T-SQL Fundamentals courses, and he is a primary resource within the company for their T-SQL–related activities.

Introduction

To me, Window functions are the most profound feature supported by both the SQL standard and Microsoft SQL Server's dialect—T-SQL. They allow you to perform calculations against sets of rows in a flexible, clear, and efficient manner. The design of window functions is ingenious and overcomes a number of shortcomings of the traditional alternatives. The range of tasks that window functions help solve is so wide that it is well worth investing your time in learning those. Window functions have evolved quite substantially since their inception in SQL Server over the different versions, as well as in the SQL standard. This book covers both the SQL Server–specific support for window functions as well as the SQL standard's support, including elements that were not yet implemented in SQL Server.

Who Should Read This Book

This book is intended for SQL Server developers, database administrators (DBAs), data scientists, business intelligence (BI) specialists, and those who need to write queries and develop code using T-SQL. The book assumes that you already have at least six months to a year of experience writing and tuning T-SQL queries.

Organization of This Book

The book covers both the logical aspects of window functions as well as their optimization and practical usage aspects.

- Chapter 1, "SQL Windowing," explains the standard SQL windowing concepts. It describes the design of window functions, the types of window functions, and the elements involved in a window specification, such as partitioning, ordering, and framing.

- Chapter 2, "A Detailed Look at Window Functions," gets into the details and specifics of the different window functions. It describes window aggregate functions, window ranking functions, window offset functions, and window statistical (distribution) functions.

- Chapter 3, "Ordered Set Functions," describes the support that T-SQL and the SQL standard have for ordered set functions, including string concatenation, hypothetical set functions, inverse distribution functions, and others. For standard functions that are not yet available in T-SQL, the chapter provides working solutions.

- Chapter 4, "Row-Pattern Recognition in SQL," describes a profound standard concept for data analysis called row-pattern recognition (RPR) that you could think of as the next step in the evolution of window functions. This concept is not available yet in T-SQL, but as mentioned, this book does cover important standard analytical features even if not available yet in T-SQL.

- Chapter 5, "Optimization of Window Functions," covers in detail the optimization of window functions in SQL Server and Azure SQL Database. It provides indexing guidelines for optimal performance, explains how parallelism is handled and how to improve it, row-mode processing versus batch mode processing, and more.

- Chapter 6, "T-SQL Solutions Using Window Functions," covers practical uses of window functions to address common business tasks.

System Requirements

Window functions are part of the core database engine of Microsoft SQL Server and Azure SQL Database; hence, all editions of the product support this feature. To run the code samples in this book, you need access to an instance of the SQL Server 2019 database engine or later (any edition), or Azure SQL Database with the target database set to compatibility level 150 or above. You will also need to have the book's sample database TSQLV5 installed. If you don't have access to an existing instance, Microsoft provides trial versions. You can find details at *https://www.microsoft.com/en-us/sql-server/ sql-server-downloads*.

As the client tool for connecting to the database engine and submitting code against it, you can use either SQL Server Management Studio (SSMS) or Azure Data Studio. I used the former to generate the graphical query execution plans that I cover in this book. You can download SSMS at *https://docs.microsoft.com/en-us/sql/ssms/ download-sql-server-management-studio-ssms*.

You can download Azure Data Studio at *https://docs.microsoft.com/en-us/sql/ azure-data-studio/download*.

Code Samples

This book features a companion website that makes available to you all the code used in the book, sample data, the errata, additional resources, and more, at the following page:

MicrosoftPressStore.com/TSQLWindowFunctions/downloads

The book's page has a link to download a compressed file with the book's source code, including a file called TSQLV5.sql that creates and populates the book's sample database, TSQLV5.

Acknowledgments

A number of people contributed to making this book a reality, whether directly or indirectly, and deserve thanks and recognition.

To Lilach, for giving reason to everything I do, and for helping review the text.

To members of the Microsoft SQL Server development team (past and present): Conor Cunningham, Joe Sack, Vassilis Papadimos, Marc Friedman, Craig Freedman, Milan Ruzic, Milan Stojic, Jovan Popovic, Borko Novakovic, Tobias Ternström, Lubor Kollar, Umachandar Jayachandran, Pedro Lopes, Argenis Fernandez, and I'm sure many others. Thanks for the great effort in the ongoing improvement of window functions in SQL Server, and thanks for all the time you spent meeting with me and responding to my emails, addressing my questions, and answering my requests for clarification.

To the editorial team at Pearson. Loretta Yates, many thanks for believing in this project and making it happen! Thanks to Charvi Arora for all your hard work and effort. Also, thanks to Rick Kughen and Tracey Croom. Thanks to Aswini Kumar and her team for working on the book's PDFs.

To Adam Machanic: Thanks for agreeing to be the technical editor of the book. There aren't many people who understand SQL Server development as well as you do. You were the natural choice for me to fill this role for this book.

To "Q2," "Q3," and "Q4": It's great to be able to share ideas with people who understand SQL as well as you do and who are such good friends who take life lightly. I feel that I can share everything with you without worrying about any boundaries or consequences.

To SolidQ, my company for the past two decades: It's gratifying to be part of such a great company that evolved to what it is today. The members of this company are much more than colleagues to me; they are partners, friends, and family. Thanks to Fernando G. Guerrero, Antonio Soto, and so many others.

To Aaron Bertrand and Greg Gonzales: I love having my column in sqlperformance. com. SentryOne is a great company with great products and service to the community.

To SQL Server MVPs—Alejandro Mesa, Erland Sommarskog, Aaron Bertrand, Paul White, and many others: This is a great program that I'm grateful and proud to be part of. The level of expertise of this group is amazing, and I'm always excited when we all get to meet, both to share ideas and just to catch up at a personal level over beer. I believe that, in great part, Microsoft's decision to provide more complete support for window functions in SQL Server is thanks to the efforts of SQL Server MVPs and, more generally, the SQL Server community. It is great to see this synergy yielding such meaningful and important results.

Finally, to my students: Teaching SQL is what drives me. It's my passion. Thanks for allowing me to fulfill my calling and for all the great questions that make me seek more knowledge.

Errata & Book Support

We've made every effort to ensure the accuracy of this book and its companion content. You can access updates to this book—in the form of a list of submitted errata and their related corrections—at:

MicrosoftPressStore.com/TSQLWindowFunctions/errata

If you discover an error that is not already listed, please submit it to us at the same page.

For additional book support and information, please visit *http://www.MicrosoftPressStore.com/Support*.

Please note that product support for Microsoft software and hardware is not offered through the previous addresses. For help with Microsoft software or hardware, go to http://support.microsoft.com.

Stay in Touch

Let's keep the conversation going! We're on Twitter: *http://twitter.com/MicrosoftPress*

CHAPTER 1

SQL Windowing

Window functions can help solve a wide variety of querying tasks by helping you express set calculations more easily, intuitively, and efficiently than ever before. Window functions are functions applied to sets of rows defined by a clause called *OVER*. They are used mainly for analytical purposes, allowing you to calculate running totals, calculate moving averages, identify gaps and islands in your data, handle intervals, and perform many other computations. These functions are based on an amazingly profound concept in the ISO/IEC SQL standard—the concept of *windowing*. The idea behind windowing is to allow you to apply various calculations to a set, or *window*, of rows and return a single value.

Window functions have evolved quite substantially in SQL Server and Azure SQL Database since their inception in SQL Server 2005. I'll describe their evolution shortly. There's still some standard functionality missing, but with the enhancements added over the years, the support is quite extensive. In this book, I cover both the functionality SQL Server implements as well as standard functionality that is still missing. When I describe a feature for the first time in the book, I also mention whether it is supported in SQL Server.

From the time SQL Server introduced support for window functions, I found myself using those functions more frequently to improve my solutions. I keep replacing older solutions that rely on more classic, traditional language constructs with the newer window functions. And the results I'm getting are usually simpler and more efficient. This happens to such an extent that the majority of my querying solutions nowadays make use of window functions. Also, the SQL standard, relational database management systems (RDBMSs), and the data industry in general, are moving toward analytical solutions, and window functions are an important part of this trend. The online transactional processing (OLTP) focus of the 90s is gone. Therefore, I think window functions are the future in terms of SQL querying solutions; the time you take to learn them is time well spent.

This book provides extensive coverage of window functions, their optimization, and querying solutions implementing them. This chapter starts by explaining the concept, and it provides

- A background of window functions
- A glimpse of solutions using windows functions
- Coverage of the elements involved in window specifications
- An account of the query elements supporting window functions
- A description of the standard's solution for reusing window definitions

Evolution of Window Functions

As mentioned, window functions evolved quite extensively since their inception in SQL Server, and there's still potential for further enhancements in the future. Figure 1-1 illustrates the major milestones when SQL Server introduced features related to window functions, including unsupported major features that hopefully will be added in the future.

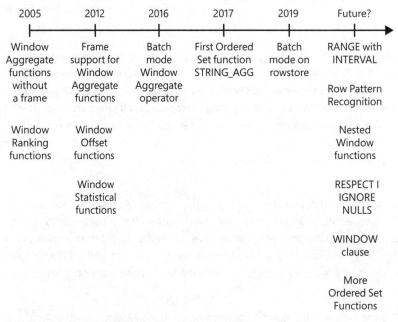

FIGURE 1-1 Evolution of window functions.

At this stage of the book, some of these features may not mean much to you yet. This timeline is provided mainly for reference purposes. Rest assured that by the time you're done reading the book, they will all be meaningful to you. Here's a brief description of the milestones from Figure 1-1:

- SQL Server 2005 introduced support for window aggregate functions—but without a window frame yet—as well as full support for window ranking functions (*ROW_NUMBER, RANK, DENSE_RANK, and NTILE*).

- SQL Server 2008 and 2008 R2 did not introduce windowing capabilities.

- SQL Server 2012 introduced support for window aggregate functions with a frame, window offset functions (*LAG, LEAD, FIRST_VALUE, and LAST_VALUE*), and window statistical functions (*PERCENT_RANK, CUME_DIST, PERCENTILE_CONT, and PERCENTILE_DISC*).

- SQL Server 2014 did not introduce windowing capabilities.

- SQL Server 2016 introduced optimization improvements for window functions with an entirely new batch-mode Window Aggregate operator. However, in order to benefit from this improvement, there has to be a *columnstore* index present on at least one of the tables participating in the query.

- SQL Server 2017 introduced support for the first ordered set function *STRING_AGG*, which applies string concatenation as an aggregate grouped function.

- SQL Server 2019 introduces support for batch mode on *rowstore*, enabling the use of batch mode operators on *rowstore* data, and lifting the previous requirement to have a *columnstore* index present on the queried data.

- A few major windowing capabilities are not yet supported in SQL Server at the date of this writing. Those include the *RANGE* window frame unit with an *INTERVAL* type, row pattern recognition, nested window functions, the ability to indicate the *RESPECT* | *IGNORE NULLS* option, the *WINDOW* clause to reuse window definitions, more ordered set functions, and others.

Background of Window Functions

Before you learn the specifics of window functions, it can be helpful to understand the context and background of those functions, which is explained in this section. It explains the difference between set-based and cursor/iterative approaches to addressing querying tasks and how window functions bridge the gap between the two. Finally, this section explains the drawbacks of alternatives to window functions and why window functions are often a better choice than the alternatives.

Window Functions Described

A window function is a function applied to a set of rows. A *window* is the term the SQL standard uses to describe the context for the function to operate in. SQL uses a clause called *OVER* in which you provide the window specification. Consider the following query as an example:

```
USE TSQLV5;

SELECT orderid, orderdate, val,
  RANK() OVER(ORDER BY val DESC) AS rnk
FROM Sales.OrderValues
ORDER BY rnk;
```

 Note See the book's Introduction for information about the sample database TSQLV5 and companion content.

Here's abbreviated output for this query:

```
orderid   orderdate   val        rnk
--------  ----------  ---------  ----
10865     2019-02-02  16387.50   1
10981     2019-03-27  15810.00   2
11030     2019-04-17  12615.05   3
10889     2019-02-16  11380.00   4
10417     2018-01-16  11188.40   5
```

```
10817      2019-01-06 10952.85   6
10897      2019-02-19 10835.24   7
10479      2018-03-19 10495.60   8
10540      2018-05-19 10191.70   9
10691      2018-10-03 10164.80  10
. . .
```

The function used in this example is *RANK*. For ranking purposes, ordering is naturally required. In this example, it is based on the column *val* ranked in descending order. This function calculates the rank of the current row with respect to a specific set of rows and a sort order. When using descending order in the ordering specification—as in this case—the rank of a given row is computed as one more than the number of rows in the relevant set that have a greater ordering value than the current row. So, pick a row in the output of the sample query—say, the one that got rank 5. This rank was computed as *5* because based on the indicated ordering (by *val* descending), there are 4 rows in the final result set of the query that have a greater value in the *val* attribute than the current value (*11188.40*), and the rank is that number plus 1.

The *OVER* clause is where you provide the specification that defines the exact set of rows that the current row relates to, the ordering specification, if relevant, and other elements. Absent any elements that restrict the set of rows in the window—as is the case in this example, the set of rows in the window is the final result set of the query.

> **Note**   More precisely, the window is the set of rows—or relation—given as input to the logical query processing phase where the window function appears. However, this explanation probably doesn't make much sense yet. So, to keep things simple, for now, I'll just refer to the final result set of the query, and I'll provide the more precise explanation later.

What's most important to note is that conceptually the *OVER* clause defines a window for the function with respect to the current row. And this is true for all rows in the result set of the query. In other words, with respect to each row, the *OVER* clause defines a window independent of the window defined for other rows. This idea is really profound and takes some getting used to. Once you get this, you get closer to a true understanding of the windowing concept, its magnitude, and its depth. If this doesn't mean much to you yet, don't worry about it for now. I wanted to throw it out there to plant the seed.

The first time the SQL standard introduced support for window functions was in an extension document to SQL:1999 that covered what they called "OLAP functions" back then. Since then, the revisions to the standard continued to enhance support for window functions. So far, the revisions have been SQL:2003, SQL:2008, SQL:2011, and SQL:2016. The latest SQL standard has very rich and extensive coverage of window functions. It also has related analytical features like row pattern recognition, which shows the standard committee's belief in the concept. This trend seems to be to keep enhancing the standard's support with more window functions and more analytical capabilities.

The SQL standard supports several types of window functions: aggregate, ranking, distribution (statistical), and offset. But remember that windowing is a concept; therefore, we might see new types emerging in future revisions of the standard.

Aggregate window functions are the all-familiar aggregate functions you already know—like *SUM*, *COUNT*, *MIN*, *MAX*, and others—though traditionally, you're probably used to using them in the context of grouped queries. An aggregate function needs to operate on a set, be it a set defined by a grouped query or a window specification.

Ranking functions are *RANK*, *DENSE_RANK*, *ROW_NUMBER*, and *NTILE*. The standard actually puts the first two and the last two in different categories, and I'll explain why later. I prefer to put all four functions in the same category for simplicity, just like the official SQL Server documentation does.

Distribution, or statistical, functions are *PERCENTILE_CONT*, *PERCENTILE_DISC*, *PERCENT_RANK*, and *CUME_DIST*. These functions apply statistical computations like percentiles, percentile ranks, and cumulative distribution.

Offset functions are *LAG*, *LEAD*, *FIRST_VALUE*, *LAST_VALUE*, and *NTH_VALUE*. SQL Server supports the first four. As of SQL Server 2019, there's no support for the *NTH_VALUE* function.

Note Chapter 2, "A Detailed Look at Window Functions," provides the meaning, the purpose, and details about the different functions.

With every new idea, device, and tool—even if the tool is better and simpler to use and implement than what you're used to—typically, there's a barrier. New stuff often seems hard. So, if window functions are new to you and you're looking for motivation to justify making the investment in learning about them and making the leap to using them, here are a few things I can mention from my experience:

- Window functions help address a wide variety of querying tasks. I can't emphasize this enough. As mentioned, I now use window functions in most of my query solutions. After you've had a chance to learn about the concept and the optimization of the functions, the last chapter in the book (Chapter 6) shows some practical applications of window functions. To give you a sense of how they are used, the following querying tasks can be solved with window functions:

  - Paging
  - De-duplicating data
  - Returning top *n* rows per group
  - Computing running totals

- Performing operations on intervals such as packing intervals, and calculating the maximum number of concurrent intervals
- Identifying gaps and islands
- Computing percentiles
- Computing the mode of the distribution
- Sorting hierarchies
- Pivoting
- Computing recency

- I've been writing SQL queries for almost three decades and have been using window functions extensively for several years now. I can say that even though it took a bit to get used to the concept of windowing, today, I find window functions both simpler and more intuitive in many cases than alternative methods.

- Window functions lend themselves to good optimization. You'll see exactly why this is so in later chapters.

Declarative Language and Optimization

You might wonder why in a declarative language such as SQL, where you logically declare your request as opposed to describing how to achieve it, two different forms of the same request—say, one with window functions and the other without—can get different performance? Why is it that an implementation of SQL such as SQL Server, with its T-SQL dialect, doesn't always figure out that the two forms really represent the same thing, and hence produce the same query execution plan for both?

There are several reasons for this. For one, SQL Server's optimizer is not perfect. I don't want to sound unappreciative—SQL Server's optimizer is truly a marvel when you think of what this software component can achieve. But it's a fact that it doesn't have all possible optimization rules encoded within it. Secondly, the optimizer must limit the amount of time spent on optimization; otherwise, it could spend a much longer time optimizing a query than the amount of time the optimization shaves off the runtime of the query. There can be millions of possible plans for a given query, and it could take hours to consider every possible path. Based on factors like the sizes of the tables involved in the query, SQL Server calculates two values. One is a cost considered *good enough* for the query, and the other is the maximum amount of time to spend on optimization before stopping. If either threshold is reached, optimization stops, and SQL Server uses the best plan found at that point.

The design of window functions, which we will get to later, often lends itself to better optimization than alternative methods of achieving the same thing.

What's important to understand from all this is that you need to make a conscious effort to make the switch from traditional SQL to using SQL windowing because it's a different idea. But you do this in order to reap the benefits. SQL windowing takes some getting used to. But once the switch is made, SQL windowing is simple and intuitive to use; think of any gadget you can't live without today and how it seemed like a difficult thing to learn at first.

Set-Based versus Iterative/Cursor Programming

People often characterize T-SQL solutions to querying tasks as either declarative/set-based or iterative/cursor-based solutions. The general consensus among T-SQL developers is to try to stick to a declarative/set-based approach. However, there's wide use of iterative/cursor-based solutions. There are several interesting questions here. Why is the set-based approach the recommended one? And if the declarative/set-based approach is the recommended one, why do so many developers use the iterative approach? What are the obstacles that prevent people from adopting the recommended approach?

To get to the bottom of this, one first needs to understand the foundations of T-SQL and what the set-based approach truly is. When you do, you realize that the set-based approach is nonintuitive for many people, whereas the iterative approach is intuitive. It's just the way our brains are programmed, and I will try to clarify this shortly. The gap between iterative and set-based thinking is quite big. The gap can be closed, though it certainly isn't easy to do so. And this is where window functions can play an important role. I find window functions to be a great tool that can help bridge the gap between the two approaches and allow a more gradual transition to set-based thinking.

First, I'll explain what the set-based approach to addressing T-SQL querying tasks is. T-SQL is a dialect of standard SQL (both ISO/IEC and ANSI SQL standards). SQL is based (or attempts to be based) on the relational model. The relational model is a mathematical model for data management and manipulation formulated and proposed initially by E. F. Codd in the late 1960s. The relational model is based on two mathematical foundations: set-theory and predicate logic. Many aspects of computing were developed based on intuition, and they keep changing very rapidly—to a degree that sometimes makes you feel that you're chasing your tail. The relational model is an island in this world of computing because it is based on much stronger foundations—mathematics. Some think of mathematics as the ultimate truth. Being based on such strong mathematical foundations, the relational model is very sound and stable. The relational model keeps evolving but not as fast as many other aspects of computing. For several decades now, the relational model has held strong, and it's still the basis for the leading database platforms—what we call *relational database management systems (RDBMSs)*.

SQL is an attempt to create a language based on the relational model. SQL is not perfect and actually deviates from the relational model in a number of ways. However, at the same time, it provides enough tools that, if you understand the relational model, you can use SQL relationally. SQL is doubtless the leading, de facto language of data.

However, as mentioned, thinking in a relational way is not intuitive for many people. Part of what makes thinking in relational terms difficult are the key differences between the iterative and set-based approaches. It is especially difficult for people who have a procedural programming background, where interaction with data in files is handled in an iterative way, as the following pseudocode demonstrates:

```
open file
fetch first record
while not end of file
begin
  process record
  fetch next record
end
```

Data in files (or, more precisely, data in the indexed sequential access method, or ISAM, files) is stored in a specific order. And you are guaranteed to fetch the records from the file in that order. Also, you fetch the records one at a time. So, your mind is programmed to think of data in such terms: ordered and manipulated one record at a time. This is similar to cursor manipulation in T-SQL; hence, for developers with a procedural programming background, using cursors or any other form of iterative processing feels like an extension to what they already know.

A relational, set-based approach to data manipulation is quite different. To try to get a sense of this, let's start with the definition of a *set* by the creator of set theory—Georg Cantor:

> By a "set" we mean any collection M into a whole of definite, distinct objects m (which are called the "elements" of M) of our perception or of our thought.
>
> —Joseph W. Dauben, Georg Cantor (Princeton University Press, 1990)

There's so much in this definition of a set that I could spend pages and pages just trying to interpret the meaning of this sentence. However, for the purposes of our discussion, I'll focus on two key aspects—one that appears explicitly in this definition and one that is implied:

- **Whole**   Observe the use of the term *whole*. A set should be perceived and manipulated as a whole. Your attention should focus on the set as a whole and not on the individual elements of the set. With iterative processing, this idea is violated because records of a file or a cursor are manipulated one at a time. A table in SQL represents (albeit not completely successfully) a relation from the relational model; a relation is a set of elements that are alike (that is, have the same attributes). When you interact with tables using set-based queries, you interact with tables as whole, as opposed to interacting with the individual rows (the tuples of the relations)—both in terms of how you phrase your declarative SQL requests and in terms of your mind-set and attention. This type of thinking is very hard for many to truly adopt.

- **Absence of Order**   Notice there is no mention of the order of elements in the definition of a set. That's for a good reason—there is no order to the elements of a set. That's another thing that many have a hard time getting used to. Files and cursors *do* have a specific order to their records, and when you fetch the records one at a time, you can rely on this order. A table has no order to its rows because a table is a set. People who don't realize this often confuse the logical layer of the data model and the language with the physical layer of the implementation.

They assume that if there's a certain index on the table, you get an implied guarantee that the data will always be accessed in index order when they query the table. Sometimes, even the correctness of the solution will rely on this assumption. Of course, SQL Server doesn't provide any such guarantees. For example, the only way to guarantee that the rows in a result will be presented in a certain order is to add a presentation ORDER BY clause to the outer query. And if you do add one, you need to realize that what you get back is not relational because the result has a guaranteed order.

If you need to write SQL queries and you want to understand the language you're dealing with, you need to think in set-based terms. And this is where window functions can help bridge the gap between iterative thinking (one row at a time, in a certain order) and set-based thinking (seeing the set as a whole, with no order). The ingenious design of window functions can help you transition from one type of thinking to the other.

For one, window functions support a *window order clause* (*ORDER BY*) when relevant and where you specify the order. However, note that just because the function has an order specified doesn't mean it violates relational concepts. The input to the query is relational with no ordering expectations, and the output of the query is relational with no ordering guarantees. It's just that there's ordering as part of the specification of the calculation, producing a result attribute in the resulting relation. There's no assurance that the result rows will be returned in the same order used by the window function; in fact, different window functions in the same query can specify different ordering. Window ordering has nothing to do—at least conceptually—with the query's presentation ordering. Figure 1-2 tries to illustrate the idea that both the input to a query with a window function and the output are relational, even though the window function has ordering as part of its specification. By using ovals in the illustration—and having the positions of the rows look different in the input and the output—I'm trying to express the fact that the order of the rows does not matter.

There's another aspect of window functions that helps you gradually transition from thinking in iterative, ordered terms to thinking in set-based terms. When teaching a new topic, teachers sometimes have to "lie" a little bit when explaining it. Suppose that you, as a teacher, know the student's mind might not be ready to comprehend a certain idea if you explain it in full depth. You can sometimes get better results if you initially explain the idea in simpler, albeit not completely correct, terms to allow the student's mind to start processing the idea. Later, when the student's mind is ready for the "truth," you can provide the deeper, more correct meaning.

Such is the case with understanding how window functions are conceptually calculated. There's a basic way to explain the idea, although it's not really conceptually correct, but it's one that leads to the correct result. The basic way uses a row-at-a-time, ordered approach. And then there's the deeper, conceptually correct way to explain the idea, but one's mind needs to be in a state of maturity to comprehend it. The deep way uses a set-based approach.

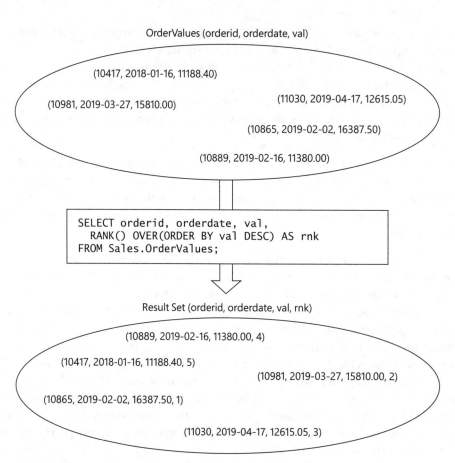

FIGURE 1-2 Input and output of a query with a window function.

To demonstrate what I mean, consider the following query:

```
SELECT orderid, orderdate, val,
  RANK() OVER(ORDER BY val DESC) AS rnk
FROM Sales.OrderValues;
```

Following is an abbreviated output of this query. (Note there's no guarantee of presentation ordering here.)

```
orderid  orderdate  val       rnk
-------- ---------- --------- ----
10865    2019-02-02 16387.50  1
10981    2019-03-27 15810.00  2
11030    2019-04-17 12615.05  3
10889    2019-02-16 11380.00  4
10417    2018-01-16 11188.40  5
...
```

The following example, which is expressed in pseudocode, shows the basic way to think of how the rank values are calculated conceptually:

```
arrange the rows sorted by val, descending
iterate through the rows
for each row
    if the current row is the first row in the partition emit 1 (absent explicit
partitioning, treat the entire result as one partition)
        else if val is equal to previous val emit previous rank
        else emit count of rows so far
```

Figure 1-3 shows a graphical depiction of this type of thinking.

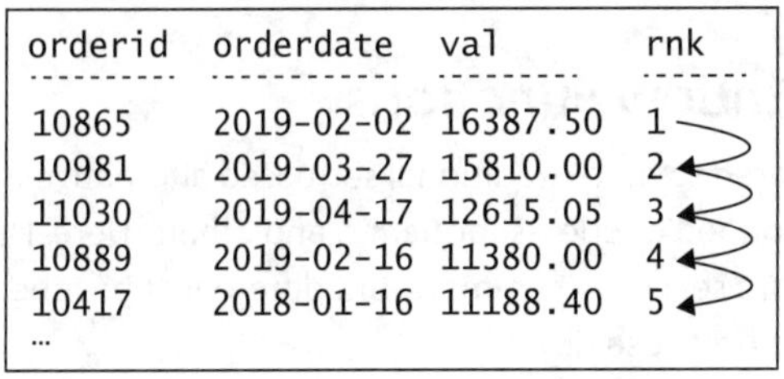

```
orderid   orderdate    val         rnk
--------- ------------ ----------- -------
10865     2019-02-02   16387.50    1
10981     2019-03-27   15810.00    2
11030     2019-04-17   12615.05    3
10889     2019-02-16   11380.00    4
10417     2018-01-16   11188.40    5
...
```

FIGURE 1-3 Basic understanding of the calculation of rank values.

Again, although this type of thinking leads to the correct result, it's not entirely correct. In fact, making my point is even more difficult because the process I just described is actually very similar to how SQL Server physically handles the rank calculation. However, my focus at this point is not the physical implementation but rather the conceptual layer—the language and the logical model. When I discuss the "incorrect type of thinking," I mean conceptually, from a language perspective, the calculation is thought of differently, in a set-based manner—not iterative. Remember that the language is not concerned with the physical implementation in the database engine. The physical layer's responsibility is to figure out how to handle the logical request and both produce a correct result and produce it as fast as possible.

So, let me attempt to explain what I mean by the deeper, more correct understanding of how the language thinks of window functions. The function logically defines—for each row in the result set of the query—a separate, independent window. Absent any restrictions in the window specification, each window consists of the set of all rows from the result set of the query as the starting point. However, you can add elements to the window specification (for example, partitioning, framing, and so on) that will further restrict the set of rows in each window. (I'll discuss partitioning and framing in more detail later.) Figure 1-4 shows a graphical depiction of this idea as it applies to our query with the RANK function.

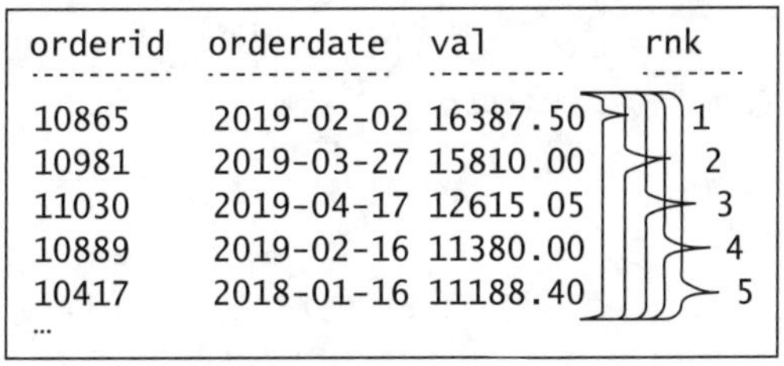

```
orderid   orderdate    val         rnk
--------- ------------ ----------- -------
10865     2019-02-02   16387.50    1
10981     2019-03-27   15810.00    2
11030     2019-04-17   12615.05    3
10889     2019-02-16   11380.00    4
10417     2018-01-16   11188.40    5
...
```

FIGURE 1-4 Deep understanding of the calculation of rank values.

With respect to each window function and row in the result set of the query, the *OVER* clause conceptually creates a separate window. In our query, we have not restricted the window specification in any way; we just defined the ordering specification for the calculation. So, in our case, all windows are made of all rows in the result set. They all coexist at the same time. In each, the rank is calculated as one more than the number of rows that have a greater value in the *val* attribute than the current value.

As you might realize, it's more intuitive for many to think in the basic terms of the data being in an order and a process iterating through the rows one at a time. That's okay when you're starting out with window functions because you get to write your queries—or at least the simple ones—correctly. As time goes by, you can gradually transition to the deeper understanding of the window functions' conceptual design and start thinking in a set-based manner.

Drawbacks of Alternatives to Window Functions

Window functions have several advantages compared to more traditional set-based alternative ways to achieve the same calculations—for example, grouped queries, subqueries, and others. Here, I'll provide a couple of straightforward examples. There are several other important differences beyond the advantages I'll show here, but it's premature to discuss those now.

I'll start with traditional grouped queries. Those do give you insight into new information in the form of aggregates, but you also lose something—the detail.

Once you group data, you're forced to apply all calculations in the context of the group. But what if you need to apply calculations that involve both detail and aggregates? For example, suppose that you need to query the *Sales.OrderValues* view and calculate for each order the percentage of the current order value of the customer total, as well as the difference from the customer average. The current order value is a detail element, and the customer total and average are aggregates. If you group the data by customer, you don't have access to the individual order values. One way to handle this need with traditional grouped queries is to have a query that groups the data by customer, define a table expression based on this query, and then join the table expression with the base table to match the detail with the aggregates. Listing 1-1 shows a query that implements this approach.

LISTING 1-1 Mixing Detail and the Result of a Grouped Query

```
WITH Aggregates AS
(
  SELECT custid, SUM(val) AS sumval, AVG(val) AS avgval
  FROM Sales.OrderValues
  GROUP BY custid
)
SELECT O.orderid, O.custid, O.val,
  CAST(100. * O.val / A.sumval AS NUMERIC(5, 2)) AS pctcust,
  O.val - A.avgval AS diffcust
FROM Sales.OrderValues AS O
  INNER JOIN Aggregates AS A
    ON O.custid = A.custid;
```

Here's the abbreviated output generated by the query shown in Listing 1-1:

```
orderid  custid  val      pctcust  diffcust
-------- ------- -------  -------- ------------
10835    1       845.80   19.79    133.633334
10952    1       471.20   11.03    -240.966666
10643    1       814.50   19.06    102.333334
10692    1       878.00   20.55    165.833334
11011    1       933.50   21.85    221.333334
10702    1       330.00   7.72     -382.166666
10625    2       479.75   34.20    129.012500
10759    2       320.00   22.81    -30.737500
10308    2       88.80    6.33     -261.937500
10926    2       514.40   36.67    163.662500
...
```

Now imagine needing to also involve the percentage from the grand total and the difference from the grand average. To do this, you need to add another table expression, as shown in Listing 1-2.

LISTING 1-2 Mixing Detail and the Results of Two Grouped Queries

```
WITH CustAggregates AS
(
  SELECT custid, SUM(val) AS sumval, AVG(val) AS avgval
  FROM Sales.OrderValues
  GROUP BY custid
),
GrandAggregates AS
(
  SELECT SUM(val) AS sumval, AVG(val) AS avgval
  FROM Sales.OrderValues
)
SELECT O.orderid, O.custid, O.val,
  CAST(100. * O.val / CA.sumval AS NUMERIC(5, 2)) AS pctcust,
  O.val - CA.avgval AS diffcust,
  CAST(100. * O.val / GA.sumval AS NUMERIC(5, 2)) AS pctall,
  O.val - GA.avgval AS diffall
FROM Sales.OrderValues AS O
  INNER JOIN CustAggregates AS CA
    ON O.custid = CA.custid
  CROSS JOIN GrandAggregates AS GA;
```

Here's the output of the query shown in Listing 1-2:

```
orderid  custid  val      pctcust  diffcust     pctall  diffall
-------- ------- -------  -------- ------------ ------- -------------
10835    1       845.80   19.79    133.633334   0.07    -679.252072
10952    1       471.20   11.03    -240.966666  0.04    -1053.852072
10643    1       814.50   19.06    102.333334   0.06    -710.552072
10692    1       878.00   20.55    165.833334   0.07    -647.052072
11011    1       933.50   21.85    221.333334   0.07    -591.552072
10702    1       330.00   7.72     -382.166666  0.03    -1195.052072
10625    2       479.75   34.20    129.012500   0.04    -1045.302072
```

10759	2	320.00	22.81	-30.737500	0.03	-1205.052072
10308	2	88.80	6.33	-261.937500	0.01	-1436.252072
10926	2	514.40	36.67	163.662500	0.04	-1010.652072
...						

You can see how the query gets more and more complicated, involving more table expressions and more joins.

Another way to perform similar calculations is to use a separate subquery for each calculation. Listing 1-3 shows the alternatives, using subqueries to the last two grouped queries.

LISTING 1-3 Mixing Detail and the Results of Scalar Aggregate Subqueries

```
-- subqueries, detail and cust aggregates
SELECT orderid, custid, val,
  CAST(100. * val /
        (SELECT SUM(O2.val)
         FROM Sales.OrderValues AS O2
         WHERE O2.custid = O1.custid) AS NUMERIC(5, 2)) AS pctcust,
  val - (SELECT AVG(O2.val)
         FROM Sales.OrderValues AS O2
         WHERE O2.custid = O1.custid) AS diffcust
FROM Sales.OrderValues AS O1;

-- subqueries, detail, customer and grand aggregates
SELECT orderid, custid, val,
  CAST(100. * val /
        (SELECT SUM(O2.val)
         FROM Sales.OrderValues AS O2
         WHERE O2.custid = O1.custid) AS NUMERIC(5, 2)) AS pctcust,
  val - (SELECT AVG(O2.val)
         FROM Sales.OrderValues AS O2
         WHERE O2.custid = O1.custid) AS diffcust,
  CAST(100. * val /
        (SELECT SUM(O2.val)
         FROM Sales.OrderValues AS O2) AS NUMERIC(5, 2)) AS pctall,
  val - (SELECT AVG(O2.val)
         FROM Sales.OrderValues AS O2) AS diffall
FROM Sales.OrderValues AS O1;
```

There are two main problems with the subquery approach. First, you end up with lengthy complex code. Second, SQL Server's optimizer is not coded at the moment to identify cases where multiple subqueries need to access the same set of rows; hence, it will use separate visits to the data for each subquery. This means that the more subqueries you have, the more visits to the data you get. Unlike the previous problem, this one is not a problem with the language, but rather with the specific optimization you get for subqueries in SQL Server.

Remember that the idea behind a window function is to define a window, or a set, of rows for the function to operate on. Aggregate functions are supposed to be applied to a set of rows; therefore, the concept of windowing can work well with those as an alternative to using grouping or subqueries. And when calculating the aggregate window function, you don't lose the detail. You use the *OVER* clause to define the window for the function. For example, to calculate the sum of all values from the result set of the query, simply use the following expression:

```
SUM(val) OVER()
```

If you do not restrict the window (empty parentheses), your starting point is the result set of the query.

To calculate the sum of all values from the result set of the query where the customer ID is the same as in the current row, use the partitioning capabilities of window functions (which I'll say more about later) and partition the window by *custid*, as follows:

```
SUM(val) OVER(PARTITION BY custid)
```

Note that within window functions, the term *partitioning* suggests a filter because it limits the rows that the function operates on compared to the complete, nonpartitioned, window.

Using window functions, here's how you address the request involving the detail and customer aggregates, returning the percentage of the current order value of the customer total as well as the difference from the average (with window functions in bold):

```
SELECT orderid, custid, val,
    CAST(100. * val / SUM(val) OVER(PARTITION BY custid) AS NUMERIC(5, 2)) AS pctcust,
    val - AVG(val) OVER(PARTITION BY custid) AS diffcust
FROM Sales.OrderValues;
```

And here's another query where you also add the percentage of the grand total and the difference from the grand average:

```
SELECT orderid, custid, val,
    CAST(100. * val / SUM(val) OVER(PARTITION BY custid) AS NUMERIC(5, 2)) AS pctcust,
    val - AVG(val) OVER(PARTITION BY custid) AS diffcust,
    CAST(100. * val / SUM(val) OVER() AS NUMERIC(5, 2)) AS pctall,
    val - AVG(val) OVER() AS diffall
FROM Sales.OrderValues;
```

Observe how much simpler and more concise the versions with the window functions are. Also, in terms of optimization, note that SQL Server's optimizer was coded with the logic to look for multiple functions with the same window specification. If any are found, SQL Server will use the same visit to the data for those. For example, in the last query, SQL Server will use one visit to the data to calculate the first two functions (the sum and average that are partitioned by *custid*), and it will use one other visit to calculate the last two functions (the sum and average that are nonpartitioned). I will demonstrate this concept of optimization in Chapter 5, "Optimization of Window Functions."

Another advantage window functions have over subqueries is that the initial window prior to applying restrictions is the result set of the query. This means that it's the result set after applying table operators (for example, joins), row filters (the *WHERE* clause), grouping, and group filtering (the *HAVING* clause). You get this result set because of the phase of logical query processing in which window functions get evaluated. (I'll say more about this later in this chapter.) Conversely, a subquery starts from scratch—not from the result set of the underlying query. This means that if you want the subquery to operate on the same set as the result of the underlying query, it will need to repeat all query constructs used by the underlying query. As an example, suppose that you want our calculations of the percentage of the total and the difference from the average to apply only to orders placed in the year 2018. With the solution using window functions, all you need to do is add one filter to the query, like so:

```
SELECT orderid, custid, val,
  CAST(100. * val / SUM(val) OVER(PARTITION BY custid) AS NUMERIC(5, 2)) AS pctcust,
  val - AVG(val) OVER(PARTITION BY custid) AS diffcust,
  CAST(100. * val / SUM(val) OVER() AS NUMERIC(5, 2)) AS pctall,
  val - AVG(val) OVER() AS diffall
FROM Sales.OrderValues
WHERE orderdate >= '20180101'
  AND orderdate < '20190101';
```

The starting point for all window functions is the set after applying the filter. But with subqueries, you start from scratch; therefore, you need to repeat the filter in all of your subqueries, as shown in Listing 1-4.

LISTING 1-4 Repeating Filter in All Subqueries

```
SELECT orderid, custid, val,
  CAST(100. * val /
        (SELECT SUM(O2.val)
         FROM Sales.OrderValues AS O2
         WHERE O2.custid = O1.custid
           AND orderdate >= '20180101'
           AND orderdate < '20190101') AS NUMERIC(5, 2)) AS pctcust,
  val - (SELECT AVG(O2.val)
         FROM Sales.OrderValues AS O2
         WHERE O2.custid = O1.custid
           AND orderdate >= '20180101'
           AND orderdate < '20190101') AS diffcust,
  CAST(100. * val /
        (SELECT SUM(O2.val)
         FROM Sales.OrderValues AS O2
         WHERE orderdate >= '20180101'
           AND orderdate < '20190101') AS NUMERIC(5, 2)) AS pctall,
  val - (SELECT AVG(O2.val)
         FROM Sales.OrderValues AS O2
         WHERE orderdate >= '20180101'
           AND orderdate < '20190101') AS diffall
FROM Sales.OrderValues AS O1
WHERE orderdate >= '20180101'
  AND orderdate < '20190101';
```

Of course, you could use workarounds, such as first defining a common table expression (CTE) based on a query that performs the filter, and then have both the outer query and the subqueries refer to the CTE. However, my point is that with window functions, you don't need any workarounds because they operate on the result of the query. I will provide more details about this aspect in the design of window functions later in the chapter (see "Window Functions").

As mentioned earlier, window functions also lend themselves to good optimization, and often, alternatives to window functions don't get optimized as well, to say the least. Of course, there are cases where the inverse is also true. I explain the optimization of window functions in Chapter 5 and provide plenty of examples for using them efficiently in Chapter 6.

A Glimpse of Solutions Using Window Functions

The first five chapters of the book describe window functions, their optimization, and related analytical features. The material is very technical, and even though I find it fascinating, I can see how some might find it a bit dry. What's usually much more interesting for people to read about is the use of the functions to solve practical problems, which is what this book gets to in the final chapter. When you see how window functions are used in problem solving, you truly realize their value. So, how can I convince you it's worth your while to go through the more technical parts and not give up reading before you get to the more interesting part later? What if I give you a glimpse of a solution using window functions right now?

The querying task I will address here involves querying a table holding a sequence of values in some column and identifying the consecutive ranges of existing values. This problem is also known as the *islands problem*. The sequence can be a numeric one, a temporal one (which is more common), or any data type that supports *total ordering*. The sequence can have unique values or allow duplicates. The interval can be any fixed interval that complies with the column's type (for example, the integer 1, the integer 7, the temporal interval 1 day, the temporal interval 2 weeks, and so on). In Chapter 6, I will get to the different variations of the problem. Here, I'll just use a simple case to give you a sense of how it works—using a numeric sequence with the integer 1 as the interval. Use the following code to generate the sample data for this task:

```
SET NOCOUNT ON;
USE TSQLV5;

DROP TABLE IF EXISTS dbo.T1;
GO

CREATE TABLE dbo.T1
(
  col1 INT NOT NULL
    CONSTRAINT PK_T1 PRIMARY KEY
);

INSERT INTO dbo.T1(col1)
  VALUES(2),(3),(11),(12),(13),(27),(33),(34),(35),(42);
```

As you can see, there are some gaps in the col1 sequence in T1. Your task is to identify the consecutive ranges of existing values (also known as *islands*) and return the start and end of each island. Here's what the desired result should look like:

```
startrange  endrange
----------- -----------
2           3
11          13
27          27
33          35
42          42
```

If you're curious as to the practicality of this problem, there are numerous production examples. Examples include producing availability reports, identifying periods of activity (for example, sales), identifying consecutive periods in which a certain criterion is met (for example, periods where a stock value was above or below a certain threshold), identifying ranges of license plates in use, and so on. The current example is very simplistic on purpose so that we can focus on the techniques used to solve it. The technique you will use to solve a more complicated case requires minor adjustments to the one you use to address the simple case. So, consider it a challenge to come up with an efficient, set-based solution to this task. Try to first come up with a solution that works against the small set of sample data. Then repopulate the table with a decent number of rows—say, 10,000,000—and try your technique again. See how it performs. Only then take a look at my solutions.

Before showing the solution using window functions, I'll show one of the many possible solutions that use more traditional language constructs. In particular, I'll show one that uses subqueries. To explain the strategy of the first solution, examine the values in the *T1.col1* sequence, where I added a conceptual attribute that doesn't exist at the moment and that I think of as a group identifier:

```
col1 grp
----- ---
2     a
3     a
11    b
12    b
13    b
27    c
33    d
34    d
35    d
42    e
```

The *grp* attribute doesn't exist yet. Conceptually, it is a value that uniquely identifies an island. This means that it must be the same for all members of the same island and different from the values generated for other islands. If you manage to calculate such a group identifier, you can then group the result by this *grp* attribute and return the minimum and maximum *col1* values in each group (island). One way to produce this group identifier using traditional language constructs is to calculate, for each current *col1* value, the minimum *col1* value that is greater than or equal to the current one, and that has no following value.

As an example, following this logic, try to identify with respect to the value *2* what the minimum *col1* value is that is greater than or equal to 2 and that appears before a missing value. It's *3*. Now try to do the same with respect to *3*. You also get *3*. So, *3* is the group identifier of the island that starts with *2* and ends with *3*. For the island that starts with *11* and ends with *13*, the group identifier for all members is *13*. As you can see, the group identifier for all members of a given island is actually the last member of that island.

Here's the T-SQL code required to implement this concept:

```
SELECT col1,
  (SELECT MIN(B.col1)
    FROM dbo.T1 AS B
    WHERE B.col1 >= A.col1
      -- is this row the last in its group?
      AND NOT EXISTS
        (SELECT *
         FROM dbo.T1 AS C
         WHERE C.col1 = B.col1 + 1)) AS grp
FROM dbo.T1 AS A;
```

This query generates the following output:

```
col1          grp
-----------   -----------
2             3
3             3
11            13
12            13
13            13
27            27
33            35
34            35
35            35
42            42
```

The next part is pretty straightforward—define a table expression based on the last query, and in the outer query, group by the group identifier and return the minimum and maximum *col1* values for each group, like so:

```
SELECT MIN(col1) AS startrange, MAX(col1) AS endrange
FROM (SELECT col1,
        (SELECT MIN(B.col1)
          FROM dbo.T1 AS B
          WHERE B.col1 >= A.col1
            AND NOT EXISTS
              (SELECT *
               FROM dbo.T1 AS C
               WHERE C.col1 = B.col1 + 1)) AS grp
      FROM dbo.T1 AS A) AS D
GROUP BY grp;
```

There are two main problems with this solution. First, it's a bit complicated to follow the logic here. Second, it's horribly slow. I don't want to start going over query execution plans yet—there will be plenty of this later in the book—but I can tell you that for each row in the table, SQL Server will perform almost two complete scans of the data. Now think of a sequence of 10,000,000 rows and try to translate it to the amount of work involved. The total number of rows that will need to be processed is simply enormous, and the scaling of the solution is quadratic.

The next solution is also one that calculates a group identifier but using window functions. The first step in the solution is to use the *ROW_NUMBER* function to calculate row numbers based on *col1* ordering. I will provide the gory details about the *ROW_NUMBER* function later in the book; for now, it suffices to say that it computes unique integers within the partition starting with 1 and incrementing by 1 based on the given ordering.

With this in mind, the following query returns the *col1* values and row numbers based on *col1* ordering, followed by its output:

```
SELECT col1, ROW_NUMBER() OVER(ORDER BY col1) AS rownum
FROM dbo.T1;
```

```
col1          rownum
-----------   --------------------
2             1
3             2
11            3
12            4
13            5
27            6
33            7
34            8
35            9
42            10
```

Now focus your attention on the two sequences. One (*col1*) is a sequence with gaps, and the other (*rownum*) is a sequence without gaps. With this in mind, try to figure out what's unique to the relationship between the two sequences in the context of an island. Within an island, both sequences keep incrementing by a fixed interval. Therefore, the difference between the two is constant. For instance, consider the island that starts with *11* and ends with *13*. The *col1* values in this island are *11*, *12*, and *13*, and the respective row numbers are *3*, *4*, and *5*. The difference between the *col1* values and the respective row numbers is the constant *8* throughout this island. For the next island, *col1* increases by more than 1, whereas *rownum* increases just by 1, so the difference keeps growing. In other words, the difference between the two is constant and unique for each island. Run the following query to calculate this difference:

```
SELECT col1, col1 - ROW_NUMBER() OVER(ORDER BY col1) AS diff
FROM dbo.T1;
```

col1	diff
2	1
3	1
11	8
12	8
13	8
27	21
33	26
34	26
35	26
42	32

You can see that this difference satisfies the two requirements of our group identifier (being constant and unique per island); therefore, you can use it as such. The rest is the same as in the previous solution; namely, you group the rows by the group identifier and return the minimum and maximum *col1* values in each group, like so:

```
WITH C AS
(
  SELECT col1,
    -- the difference is constant and unique per island
    col1 - ROW_NUMBER() OVER(ORDER BY col1) AS grp
  FROM dbo.T1
)
SELECT MIN(col1) AS startrange, MAX(col1) AS endrange
FROM C
GROUP BY grp;
```

Observe how concise and simple the solution is. Of course, it's always a good idea to add comments to help those who see the solution for the first time better understand it.

The solution is also highly efficient, and with the right indexing, scales linearly. The work involved in assigning the row numbers is negligible compared to the previous solution. It's just a single ordered scan of the index on *col1* and an operator that keeps incrementing a counter. In a performance test I ran with a sequence with 10,000,000 rows, this query finished in 3 seconds. Other solutions ran for a much longer time.

I hope that this glimpse to solutions using window functions was enough to intrigue you and help you see that they contain immense power. Now we'll get back to studying the technicalities of window functions. Later in the book, you will have a chance to see many more examples.

Elements of Window Functions

The specification of a window function appears in the function's *OVER* clause and involves multiple elements. The three core elements are window partitioning, ordering, and framing. Not all window functions support all elements. As I describe each element, I'll also indicate which functions support it.

Window Partitioning

The optional window partitioning element is implemented with a *PARTITION BY* clause and is supported by all window functions. It restricts the window of the current calculation to only those rows from the result set of the query that have the same values in the partitioning columns as in the current row. For example, if your function uses *PARTITION BY custid* and the *custid* value in the current row is *1*, the window partition with respect to the current row is all rows from the result set of the query that have a *custid* value of *1*. If the *custid* value of the current row is *2*, the window partition with respect to the current row is all rows with a *custid* of *2*.

If a *PARTITION BY* clause is not specified, the window is not restricted. Another way to look at it is that in case explicit partitioning wasn't specified, the default partitioning is to consider the entire result set of the query as one partition.

If it wasn't obvious, let me point out that different functions in the same query can have different partitioning specifications. Consider the query in Listing 1-5 as an example.

LISTING 1-5 Query with Two RANK Calculations

```
SELECT custid, orderid, val,
  RANK() OVER(ORDER BY val DESC) AS rnkall,
  RANK() OVER(PARTITION BY custid
              ORDER BY val DESC) AS rnkcust
FROM Sales.OrderValues;
```

Observe that the first *RANK* function (which generates the attribute *rnkall*) relies on the implied partitioning, and the second *RANK* function (which generates *rnkcust*) uses explicit partitioning by *custid*. Figure 1-5 illustrates the partitions defined for a sample of three results of calculations in the query: one *rnkall* value and two *rnkcust* values.

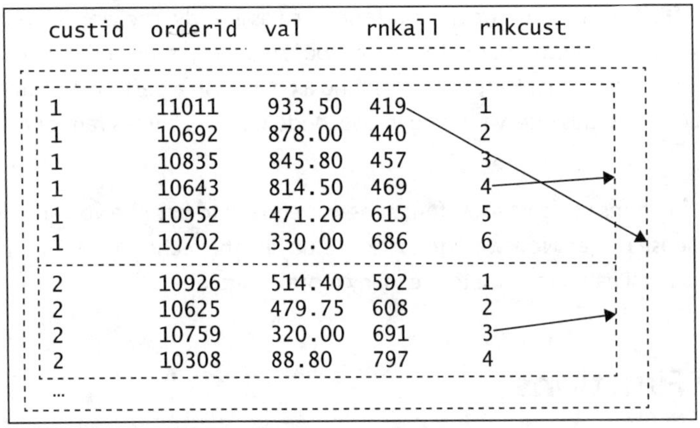

custid	orderid	val	rnkall	rnkcust
1	11011	933.50	419	1
1	10692	878.00	440	2
1	10835	845.80	457	3
1	10643	814.50	469	4
1	10952	471.20	615	5
1	10702	330.00	686	6
2	10926	514.40	592	1
2	10625	479.75	608	2
2	10759	320.00	691	3
2	10308	88.80	797	4
...				

FIGURE 1-5 Window partitioning.

The arrows point from the result values of the functions to the window partitions that were used to compute them.

Window Ordering

The window ordering clause defines the ordering for the calculation, if relevant, within the partition. Interestingly, this clause has a slightly different meaning for different function categories. With ranking functions, ordering is intuitive. For example, when using descending ordering, the *RANK* function returns one more than the number of rows in your respective partition that have a greater ordering value than yours. When using ascending ordering, the function returns one more than the number of rows in the partition with a lower ordering value than yours. Figure 1-6 illustrates the rank calculations from Listing 1-5 shown earlier—this time including the interpretation of the ordering element.

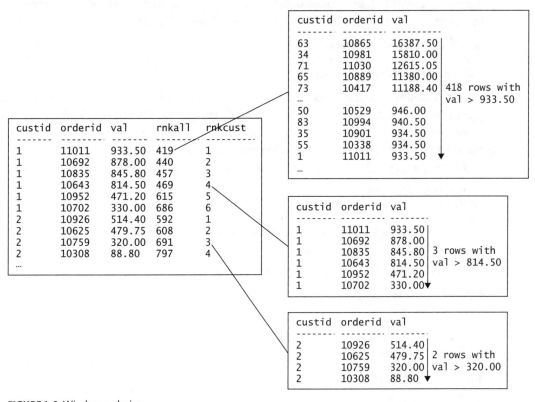

FIGURE 1-6 Window ordering.

Figure 1-6 depicts the windows of only three of the rank calculations. Of course, there are many more—1,660, to be precise. That's because there are 830 rows involved, and for each row, two rank calculations are made. What's interesting to note here is that conceptually it's as if all those windows coexist simultaneously.

Aggregate window functions have a slightly different meaning for *window ordering*, when specified, compared to *ranking* window functions. With aggregates, contrary to what some might think, ordering has nothing to do with the order in which the aggregate is applied; rather, the ordering element gives meaning to the framing options that I will describe next. In other words, the ordering element is an aid as part of defining which rows to restrict in the window.

NULL Ordering

If the ordering element supports NULLs, the SQL standard leaves it to the implementation to choose whether to sort NULLs before or after non-NULLs. Microsoft chose to sort NULLs first when using ascending order. The SQL standard supports adding an option to the ordering clause indicating *NULLS FIRST or NULLS LAST. This is relevant for window ordering as well as presentation ordering. For example, suppose that you want to query the Sales.Orders table, returning order IDs and shipped dates of orders, sorted by shipped date, ascending, but with unshipped orders last. Unshipped orders have a NULL shipped date. According to the SQL Standard, you are supposed to use the *NULLS LAST* option, like so:

```
SELECT orderid, shippeddate
FROM Sales.Orders
ORDER BY shippeddate NULLS LAST;
```

Unfortunately, SQL Server doesn't support specifying the *NULLS LAST* option. It just uses *NULLS FIRST* implicitly. If you want to order NULLs last, you need to come up with your own programmatic solution. For example, one way to achieve this is to have an ordering element preceding the *shippeddate* attribute in the window order clause, based on a *CASE* expression that returns a lower ordering value for non-NULLs (say 1) compared to NULLs (say 2), like so:

```
SELECT orderid, shippeddate
FROM Sales.Orders
ORDER  BY
  CASE WHEN shippeddate IS NOT NULL THEN 1 ELSE 2 END,
  shippeddate;
```

This query generates the following output (abbreviated):

```
orderid      shippeddate
-----------  -----------
10249        2017-07-10
10252        2017-07-11
10250        2017-07-12
10251        2017-07-15
10255        2017-07-15
...
11050        2019-05-05
11055        2019-05-05
11063        2019-05-06
11067        2019-05-06
11069        2019-05-06
11008        NULL
11019        NULL
11039        NULL
11040        NULL
...
```

Unfortunately, this trick has a performance downside in SQL Server: it prevents the ability to rely on index ordering and forces explicit sorting in the query plan. I'll provide more details on this including a workaround in Chapter 5.

Window Framing

Earlier, I referred to window partitioning as serving a filtering role. Window framing is essentially another filter that further restricts the rows in the window partition. It is applicable to aggregate window functions as well as to three of the offset functions: *FIRST_VALUE*, *LAST_VALUE*, and *NTH_VALUE*. As a reminder, the last is unsupported in SQL Server. Think of this windowing element as defining two end points, or delimiters, in the current row's partition based on the given ordering, framing the rows that the calculation will apply to.

The framing specification in the standard includes a *ROWS*, *GROUPS* or *RANGE* option that defines the starting row and ending row of the frame, as well as a window frame-exclusion option. SQL Server supports framing, with full implementation of the *ROWS* option, partial implementation of the RANGE option, and no implementation of the *GROUPS* and window frame-exclusion options.

The *ROWS* option allows you to indicate the points in the frame as an offset in terms of the number of rows with respect to the current row, based on the window ordering. The *GROUPS* option is similar to *ROWS*, but you specify an offset in terms of the number of distinct groups with respect to the current group, based on the window ordering. The *RANGE* option is more dynamic, defining the offsets in terms of a difference between the ordering value of the frame point and the current row's ordering value. The window frame-exclusion option specifies what to do with the current row and its peers in case of ties. This explanation might seem far from clear or sufficient, but I don't want to get into the details just yet. There will be plenty of that later. For now, I just want to introduce the concept and provide a simple example. Following is a query against the *EmpOrders* view, calculating the running total quantity for each employee and order month:

```
SELECT empid, ordermonth, qty,
  SUM(qty) OVER(PARTITION BY empid
               ORDER BY ordermonth
               ROWS BETWEEN UNBOUNDED PRECEDING
                        AND CURRENT ROW) AS runqty
FROM Sales.EmpOrders;
```

Observe that the window function applies the *SUM* aggregate function to the *qty* attribute, partitions the window by *empid*, orders the partition rows by *ordermonth*, and frames the partition rows based on the given ordering between unbounded preceding (no low boundary point) and the current row. In other words, the result will be the sum of all prior rows in the frame, inclusive of the current row. This query generates the following output, shown here in abbreviated form:

```
empid  ordermonth  qty   runqty
------ ----------- ----  -------
1       2017-07-01 121   121
1       2017-08-01 247   368
1       2017-09-01 255   623
1       2017-10-01 143   766
1       2017-11-01 318   1084
...
2       2017-07-01 50    50
2       2017-08-01 94    144
2       2017-09-01 137   281
2       2017-10-01 248   529
2       2017-11-01 237   766
...
```

Observe how the window specification is as easy to read as plain English. I will provide much more detail about the framing options in Chapter 2.

Query Elements Supporting Window Functions

Window functions aren't supported in all query clauses; rather, they're supported only in the *SELECT* and *ORDER BY* clauses. To help you understand the reason for this restriction, I first need to explain a concept called *logical query processing*. Then I'll get to the clauses that support window functions, and finally I'll explain how to circumvent the restriction with the other clauses.

Logical Query Processing

Logical query processing describes the conceptual way in which a *SELECT* query is evaluated according to the logical language design. It describes a process made of a series of steps, or phases, that proceed from the query's input tables to the query's final result set. Note that by "logical query processing," I mean the conceptual way in which the query is evaluated—not necessarily the physical way SQL Server processes the query. As part of the optimization, SQL Server can make shortcuts, rearrange the order of some steps, and pretty much do whatever it likes. But that's as long as it guarantees that it will produce the same output as the one defined by logical query processing applied to the declarative query request.

Each step in logical query processing operates on one or more virtual tables (sets of rows) that serve as its input and return a virtual table as its output. The output virtual table of one step then becomes the input virtual table for the next step.

Figure 1-7 is a flow diagram illustrating the logical query processing flow in SQL Server.

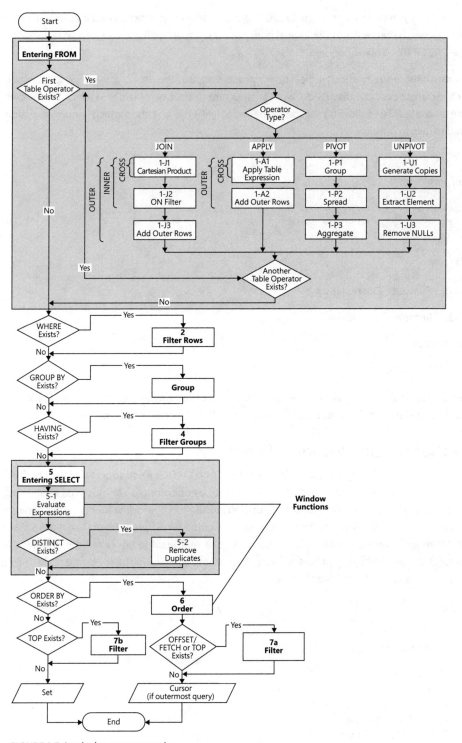

FIGURE 1-7 Logical query processing.

Note that when you write a query, the *SELECT* clause appears first in terms of the keyed-in, or typed, order, but observe that in terms of the logical query processing order, it appears almost last—just before the *ORDER BY* clause is handled.

There's much more to say about logical query processing, but the details are a topic for another book. For the purposes of our discussion, what's important to note is the order in which the various clauses are evaluated. The following list shows the order (with the phases in which window functions are allowed shown in bold):

1. *FROM*

2. *WHERE*

3. *GROUP BY*

4. *HAVING*

5. *SELECT*

    5-1. **Evaluate Expressions**

    5-2. Remove Duplicates

6. ***ORDER BY***

7. *OFFSET-FETCH/TOP*

Understanding logical query processing and the logical query processing order enables you to understand the necessity behind restricting window functions to only specific clauses.

Clauses Supporting Window Functions

As illustrated in Figure 1-7, only the query clauses *SELECT* and *ORDER BY* support window functions directly. The reason for the limitation is to avoid ambiguity by operating on (almost) the final result set of the query as the starting point for the windowed calculation. If window functions are allowed in phases previous to the *SELECT* phase, their initial window could be different from that in the *SELECT* phase, and therefore, with some query forms, it could be very difficult to figure out the right result. I'll try to demonstrate the ambiguity problem through an example. First run the following code to create the table T1 and populate it with sample data:

```
SET NOCOUNT ON;
USE TSQLV5;

DROP TABLE IF EXISTS dbo.T1;
GO

CREATE TABLE dbo.T1
(
  col1 VARCHAR(10) NOT NULL
    CONSTRAINT PK_T1 PRIMARY KEY
);
```

```
INSERT INTO dbo.T1(col1)
  VALUES('A'),('B'),('C'),('D'),('E'),('F');
```

Suppose that window functions were allowed in phases prior to the *SELECT*—for example, in the *WHERE* phase. Consider then the following query, and try to figure out which *col1* values should appear in the result:

```
SELECT col1
FROM dbo.T1
WHERE col1 > 'B'
  AND ROW_NUMBER() OVER(ORDER BY col1) <= 3;
```

Before you assume that the answer should obviously be the values C, D, and E, consider the all-at-once concept in SQL. The concept of *all-at-once* means that all expressions that appear in the same logical phase are conceptually evaluated at the same point in time. This means that the order in which the expressions are evaluated shouldn't matter. With this in mind, the following query should be semantically equivalent to the previous one:

```
SELECT col1
FROM dbo.T1
WHERE ROW_NUMBER() OVER(ORDER BY col1) <= 3
  AND col1 > 'B';
```

Now can you figure out what the right answer is? Is it C, D, and E, or is it just C?

That's an example of the ambiguity I was talking about. By restricting window functions to only the *SELECT* and *ORDER BY* clauses of a query, this ambiguity is eliminated.

Looking at Figure 1-7, you might have noticed that within the *SELECT* phase, it's step 5-1 (Evaluate Expressions) that supports window functions, and this step is evaluated before step 5-2 (Remove Duplicates). If you wonder why it is important to know such subtleties, I'll demonstrate why.

Following is a query returning the *empid* and *country* attributes of all employees from the Employees table, followed by its output:

```
SELECT empid, country
FROM HR.Employees;
```

```
empid        country
-----------  ----------------
1            USA
2            USA
3            USA
4            USA
5            UK
6            UK
7            UK
8            USA
9            UK
```

Next, examine the following query and see if you can guess what its output is before executing it:

```
SELECT DISTINCT country, ROW_NUMBER() OVER(ORDER BY country) AS rownum
FROM HR.Employees;
```

Some expect to get the following output:

```
country           rownum
--------------- --------------------
UK                1
USA               2
```

But in reality, you get this:

```
country   rownum
-------- -------
UK       1
UK       2
UK       3
UK       4
USA      5
USA      6
USA      7
USA      8
USA      9
```

Now consider that the *ROW_NUMBER* function in this query is evaluated in step 5-1 where the *SELECT* list expressions are evaluated—prior to the removal of the duplicates in step 5-2. The *ROW_NUMBER* function assigns nine unique row numbers to the nine employee rows, and then the *DISTINCT* clause has no duplicates left to remove.

When you realize this and understand that it has to do with the logical query processing order of the different elements, you can think of a solution. For example, you can have a table expression defined based on a query that just returns distinct countries and have the outer query assign the row numbers after duplicates are removed, like so:

```
WITH EmpCountries AS
(
  SELECT DISTINCT country FROM HR.Employees
)
SELECT country, ROW_NUMBER() OVER(ORDER BY country) AS rownum
FROM EmpCountries;

country   rownum
-------- -------
UK       1
USA      2
```

Can you think of other ways to solve the problem, perhaps even simpler ways than this one?

The fact that window functions are evaluated in the *SELECT* or *ORDER BY* phase means that the window defined for the calculation—before applying further restrictions—is the intermediate form of rows of the query after all previous phases. This means that window functions are evaluated after applying the *FROM* with all of its table operators (for example, joins), and after the *WHERE* filtering, the grouping, and the filtering of the groups. Consider the following query as an example:

```
SELECT O.empid,
  SUM(OD.qty) AS qty,
  RANK() OVER(ORDER BY SUM(OD.qty) DESC) AS rnk
FROM Sales.Orders AS O
  INNER JOIN Sales.OrderDetails AS OD
    ON O.orderid = OD.orderid
WHERE O.orderdate >= '20180101'
  AND O.orderdate < '20190101'
GROUP BY O.empid;
```

```
empid  qty    rnk
------ ------ ----
4      5273   1
3      4436   2
1      3877   3
8      2843   4
2      2604   5
7      2292   6
6      1738   7
5      1471   8
9      955    9
```

First the FROM clause is evaluated and the join is performed. Then, because of the filter, only the rows where the order year is 2018 remain. Then the remaining rows are grouped by employee ID. Only then are the expressions in the *SELECT* list evaluated, including the *RANK* function, which is calculated based on ordering by the total quantity descending. If there were other window functions in the *SELECT* list, they would all use the same result set as their starting point. Recall from earlier discussions about alternative options to window functions (for example, subqueries) that they start their view of the data from scratch—meaning that you have to repeat all the logic you have in the outer query in each of your subqueries, leading to much more verbose code.

Now back to my question of whether you can think of a simpler way to assign row numbers to distinct employee countries compared to the solution with the CTE; here's a simpler solution:

```
SELECT country, ROW_NUMBER() OVER(ORDER BY country) AS rownum
FROM HR.Employees
GROUP BY country;
```

There are nine employees initially, but within them, there are two distinct countries; therefore, the grouping phase defines two groups. The expressions in the *SELECT* clause, including the *ROW_NUMBER* calculation, are then applied to the grouped data, producing the two expected result rows:

```
country   rownum
--------  -------
UK        1
USA       2
```

Circumventing the Limitations

I explained the reasoning behind disallowing the use of window functions in logical query processing phases that are evaluated prior to the *SELECT* clause. But what if you need to filter by or group by a calculation based on window functions? The solution is to use a table expression such as a CTE or a derived table. Have a query invoke the window function in its *SELECT* list, assigning the calculation an alias. Define a table expression based on that query, and then have the outer query refer to that alias where you need it.

Here's an example showing how you can filter by the result of a window function using a CTE:

```
WITH C AS
(
  SELECT orderid, orderdate, val,
    RANK() OVER(ORDER BY val DESC) AS rnk
  FROM Sales.OrderValues
)
SELECT *
FROM C
WHERE rnk <= 5;
```

```
orderid  orderdate  val        rnk
-------- ---------- ---------- ----
10865    2019-02-02 16387.50   1
10981    2019-03-27 15810.00   2
11030    2019-04-17 12615.05   3
10889    2019-02-16 11380.00   4
10417    2018-01-16 11188.40   5
```

With modification statements, window functions are disallowed altogether because those don't support *SELECT* and *ORDER BY* clauses. But there are cases where involving window functions in modification statements is needed. Table expressions can be used to address this need as well because T-SQL supports modifying data through table expressions. I'll demonstrate this capability with an *UPDATE* example. First, run the following code to create a table called T1 with columns *col1* and *col2* and populate it with sample data:

```
SET NOCOUNT ON;
USE TSQLV5;

DROP TABLE IF EXISTS dbo.T1;
GO

CREATE TABLE dbo.T1
(
  col1 INT NULL,
  col2 VARCHAR(10) NOT NULL
);

INSERT INTO dbo.T1(col2)
  VALUES('C'),('A'),('B'),('A'),('C'),('B');
```

Explicit values were provided in *col2*, and NULLs were used as defaults in *col1*.

Suppose this table represents a situation with data-quality problems. A key wasn't enforced in this table; therefore, it is not possible to uniquely identify rows. You want to assign unique *col1* values in all rows. You're thinking of using the *ROW_NUMBER* function in an *UPDATE* statement, like so:

```
UPDATE dbo.T1
  SET col1 = ROW_NUMBER() OVER(ORDER BY col2);
```

However, remember that this is not allowed. The workaround is to write a query against T1 returning *col1* and an expression based on the *ROW_NUMBER* function (call it *rownum*); define a table expression based on this query; finally, have an outer *UPDATE* statement against the CTE assign *rownum* to *col1*, like so:

```
WITH C AS
(
  SELECT col1, col2,
      ROW_NUMBER() OVER(ORDER BY col2) AS rownum
  FROM dbo.T1
)
UPDATE C
  SET col1 = rownum;
```

Query T1, and observe that all rows got unique *col1* values:

```
SELECT col1, col2
FROM dbo.T1;

col1  col2
----- -----
5     C
1     A
3     B
2     A
6     C
4     B
```

Potential for Additional Filters

I provided a workaround in T-SQL that allows you to use window functions indirectly in query elements that don't support those directly. The workaround is a table expression in the form of a CTE or derived table. It's nice to have a workaround, but a table expression adds an extra layer to the query and complicates it a bit. The examples I showed are quite simple, but think about long and complex queries to begin with. Can you have a simpler solution that doesn't require this extra layer?

With window functions, SQL Server doesn't have a solution at the moment. It's interesting, though, to see how others coped with this problem. For example, Teradata created a filtering clause it calls

QUALIFY that is conceptually evaluated after the *SELECT* clause. This means that it can refer to window functions directly, as in the following example:

```
SELECT orderid, orderdate, val
FROM Sales.OrderValues
QUALIFY RANK() OVER(ORDER BY val DESC) <= 5;
```

Furthermore, you can refer to column aliases defined in the *SELECT* list, like so:

```
SELECT orderid, orderdate, val,
  RANK() OVER(ORDER BY val DESC) AS rnk
FROM Sales.OrderValues
QUALIFY rnk <= 5;
```

The QUALIFY clause isn't defined in the SQL standard; rather, it's a Teradata-specific feature. However, it seems like a very interesting solution, and it would be nice to see both the standard and SQL Server providing a solution to this need.

Reuse of Window Definitions

Suppose that you need to invoke multiple window functions in the same query and part of the window specification (or all of it) is common to multiple functions. If you indicate the complete window specifications in all functions, the code can quickly get lengthy. Here's an example illustrating the problem:

```
SELECT empid, ordermonth, qty,
  SUM(qty) OVER (PARTITION BY empid
                 ORDER BY ordermonth
                 ROWS BETWEEN UNBOUNDED PRECEDING
                            AND CURRENT ROW) AS runsumqty,
  AVG(qty) OVER (PARTITION BY empid
                 ORDER BY ordermonth
                 ROWS BETWEEN UNBOUNDED PRECEDING
                            AND CURRENT ROW) AS runavgqty,
  MIN(qty) OVER (PARTITION BY empid
                 ORDER BY ordermonth
                 ROWS BETWEEN UNBOUNDED PRECEDING
                            AND CURRENT ROW) AS runminqty,
  MAX(qty) OVER (PARTITION BY empid
                 ORDER BY ordermonth
                 ROWS BETWEEN UNBOUNDED PRECEDING
                            AND CURRENT ROW) AS runmaxqty
FROM Sales.EmpOrders;
```

The SQL standard has an answer to this problem in the form of a clause called *WINDOW* that allows naming a window specification or part of it; then you can refer to that name in other window definitions—ones used by window functions or even by a definition of another window name. This clause is conceptually evaluated after the *HAVING* clause and before the *SELECT* clause.

SQL Server doesn't yet support the *WINDOW* clause. But according to the SQL standard, you can abbreviate the preceding query using the *WINDOW* clause like so:

```
SELECT empid, ordermonth, qty,
  SUM(qty) OVER W1 AS runsumqty,
  AVG(qty) OVER W1 AS runavgqty,
  MIN(qty) OVER W1 AS runminqty,
  MAX(qty) OVER W1 AS runmaxqty
FROM Sales.EmpOrders
WINDOW W1 AS ( PARTITION BY empid
               ORDER BY ordermonth
               ROWS BETWEEN UNBOUNDED PRECEDING
                   AND CURRENT ROW );
```

That's quite a difference, as you can see. In this case, the *WINDOW* clause assigns the name W1 to a complete window specification with partitioning, ordering, and framing options. Then all four functions refer to W1 as their window specification. The *WINDOW* clause is actually quite sophisticated. As mentioned, it doesn't have to name a complete window specification; rather, it can even name only part of it. Then a window definition can include a mix of named parts plus explicit parts. As an aside, the coverage of the SQL standard for the *WINDOW* clause is a striking length of 10 pages! And trying to decipher the details is no picnic.

There are a few platforms that already support the *WINDOW* clause, including PostgreSQL, MariaDB, MySQL, and SQLite. It would be great to see SQL Server add such support in the future, especially now that it has extensive support for window functions and people are likely to end up with lengthy window specifications.

Summary

This chapter introduced the concept of windowing in SQL. It provided the background to window functions, explaining the motivation for their use. The chapter then provided a glimpse of solving querying tasks using window functions by addressing the task of identifying ranges of existing values in a sequence—a problem also known as *identifying islands*. The chapter then proceeded to explain the design of window functions, covering the elements involved in window specifications: partitioning, ordering, and framing. Finally, this chapter explained how the SQL standard addresses the need to reuse a window specification or part of it. The next chapter provides a breakdown of window functions and gets into more detail.

CHAPTER 2

A Detailed Look at Window Functions

This chapter looks at the various types of window functions and gets into the details of each. Still, this chapter focuses on the logical aspects of the functions. Optimization will be covered separately in Chapter 5, "Optimization of Window Functions."

The main reason for separating the discussion of the two layers into different chapters is that the SQL standard deals only with the logical layer. And because Microsoft SQL Server implements the functions based on the standard, the coverage of the logical aspects of the functions in this book could be interesting for readers who use database platforms other than SQL Server as well. Chapter 5 focuses on the optimization of the functions—namely, the physical layer, which is very platform-specific—and will be of interest mainly to readers who use SQL Server and Azure SQL Database.

This chapter is organized in sections based on the function categories: window aggregate functions, rank functions, statistical (distribution) functions, and offset functions. With each category of functions, I first explain the windowing elements supported by the category, and then I explain the specifics of each function.

Window Aggregate Functions

This section covers window aggregate functions. I first explain how the windowing concept works with aggregate functions; then I describe the supported elements in the specification of window aggregate functions and their meaning in detail. Then I get to more specialized aspects such as further windowing ideas and nested group aggregates within window aggregates.

Window Aggregate Functions Described

Window aggregate functions are the same functions as grouped aggregate functions (for example, *COUNT, MIN, MAX, SUM,* and so on); only instead of applying them to groups in grouped queries, you apply them to windows defined by the *OVER* clause. An aggregate function is supposed to be applied to a set of rows, and it shouldn't matter to the function which language mechanism defines the set.

Supported Windowing Elements

In the SQL standard, window aggregate functions support three main elements: partitioning, ordering, and framing. The general form of a window aggregate function is as follows:

```
function_name(<arguments>) OVER(
  [ <window partition clause> ]
  [ <window order clause> [ <window frame clause> ] ] )
```

The purpose of all three elements is to filter the rows in the window. When you don't apply any restrictions to the window—namely, when you use empty parentheses in the *OVER* clause—the window consists of all rows in the result set of the underlying query. More precisely, the initial window consists of the set of rows in the virtual table provided as input to the logical query processing phase where the window function appears. This means that if the window function appears in the query's *SELECT* list, it is the virtual table provided as input to phase 5-1. (See Figure 1-7 in Chapter 1, "SQL Windowing.") This phase appears after processing the *FROM, WHERE, GROUP BY*, and *HAVING* clauses, and before the removal of duplicate rows if a DISTINCT clause was specified (phase 5-2). But that's the initial window prior to applying restrictions. The next sections explain how to further restrict the window.

Window Partitioning

The window partitioning element allows you to restrict the window to only those rows that have the same values in the partitioning attributes as the current row. Some think of the partitioning element like grouping, and some think of it like correlated subqueries, but it's actually different from both. Unlike grouping, partitioning is specific to one function's window and can be different for different functions in the same query. Unlike correlated subqueries, partitioning filters rows from the virtual table provided to the *SELECT* phase as input, as opposed to starting with a fresh view of the data and needing to repeat all constructs that appear in the outer query.

As the first partitioning example, the following query invokes two window *SUM* aggregate functions—one without partitioning and another partitioned by *custid*:

```
USE TSQLV5;

SELECT orderid, custid, val,
  SUM(val) OVER() AS sumall,
  SUM(val) OVER(PARTITION BY custid) AS sumcust
FROM Sales.OrderValues AS O1;
```

```
orderid  custid  val      sumall       sumcust
-------- ------- ------- ----------- ---------
10643    1       814.50  1265793.22  4273.00
10692    1       878.00  1265793.22  4273.00
10702    1       330.00  1265793.22  4273.00
10835    1       845.80  1265793.22  4273.00
10952    1       471.20  1265793.22  4273.00
11011    1       933.50  1265793.22  4273.00
10926    2       514.40  1265793.22  1402.95
```

```
10759    2          320.00  1265793.22  1402.95
10625    2          479.75  1265793.22  1402.95
10308    2          88.80   1265793.22  1402.95
...
```

The first window function calculates for each row the grand total *val* (the *sumall* attribute). The second function calculates the customer total *val* (the *sumcust* attribute). Figure 2-1 highlights three arbitrary sums with braces just as examples and illustrates the windows used to calculate those.

```
orderid  custid  val       sumall       sumcust
-------  ------  --------  -----------  ---------
10643    1       814.50    1265793.22   4273.00
10692    1       878.00    1265793.22   4273.00
10702    1       330.00    1265793.22   4273.00
10835    1       845.80    1265793.22   4273.00
10952    1       471.20    1265793.22   4273.00
11011    1       933.50    1265793.22   4273.00
10926    2       514.40    1265793.22   1402.95
10759    2       320.00    1265793.22   1402.95
10625    2       479.75    1265793.22   1402.95
10308    2       88.80     1265793.22   1402.95
...
```

FIGURE 2-1 The first partitioning example.

Observe that in the case of the *sumall* attribute calculated for order *10692* (the second row in the output), the respective window consists of all rows from the result set of the underlying query, because an explicit partitioning element wasn't specified. Therefore, the grand total *val* for this row is *1,265,793.22*, as is the case for all other rows. As for the *sumcust* attribute, the window function calculating it is partitioned by *custid*; therefore, rows with different *custid* values have different, disjoint, subsets of rows in their respective windows. That's the case with the two orders that were highlighted in the figure with braces, just as a couple of examples: *10643* and *10926*. The former was placed by customer 1; hence, the respective window consists of the rows with customer ID 1, yielding *4,273.00* as the customer total. The latter was placed by customer 2; therefore, its respective window consists of the rows with customer ID 2, yielding *1,402.95* as the customer total. Like their sibling orders, these two orders are each part of a window partition for their respective customers; therefore, they get the sum total of order volume for those customers.

As the second partitioning example, the following query mixes detail elements and window aggregate functions to calculate the percent of the current order value out of the grand total, as well as out of the customer total:

```
SELECT orderid, custid, val,
  CAST(100. * val / SUM(val) OVER() AS NUMERIC(5, 2)) AS pctall,
  CAST(100. * val / SUM(val) OVER(PARTITION BY custid) AS NUMERIC(5, 2)) AS pctcust
FROM Sales.OrderValues AS O1;
```

```
orderid   custid  val      pctall  pctcust
--------  ------  -------  ------  --------
10643     1       814.50   0.06    19.06
10692     1       878.00   0.07    20.55
10702     1       330.00   0.03    7.72
10835     1       845.80   0.07    19.79
10952     1       471.20   0.04    11.03
11011     1       933.50   0.07    21.85
10926     2       514.40   0.04    36.67
10759     2       320.00   0.03    22.81
10625     2       479.75   0.04    34.20
10308     2       88.80    0.01    6.33
...
```

Figure 2-2 illustrates the applicable window partitions used by the three calculations that are highlighted.

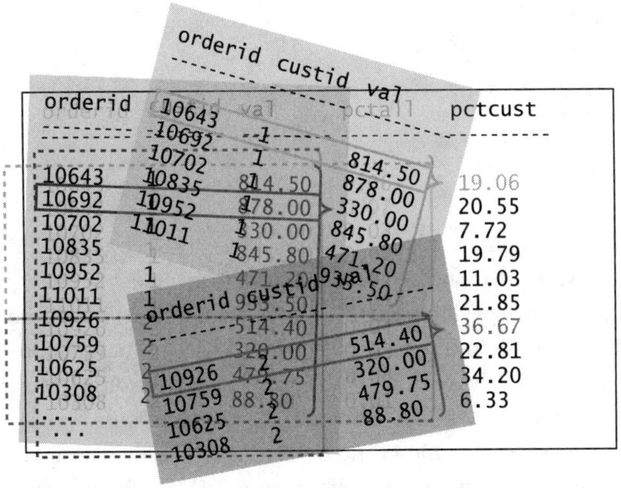

FIGURE 2-2 The second partitioning example.

The figure also attempts to visually express the idea that all windows conceptually coexist at the same time. Each rectangle highlights a window for one sample underlying row and calculation. The largest rectangle at the back is an example for a window generated for one of the rows when using the *OVER* clause with empty parentheses. The two smaller rectangles represent the windows for two sample rows when using the *OVER* clause with *PARTITION BY custid*. The top rectangle is generated for a row with a *custid* value of *1*, and the bottom rectangle for a row with a *custid* value of *2*.

Window Ordering and Framing

Framing is another option that enables you to further restrict the rows in the window partition. The ordering element plays a different role for window aggregate functions than for ranking, statistical, and the LAG and LEAD offset functions. With aggregate functions, ordering just gives meaning to the framing option. Once ordering is defined, framing identifies two bounds, or endpoints, in the window partition, and only the rows between those two bounds are filtered.

Earlier, I provided the general form of a window aggregate function. Here it is again as a reminder:

```
function_name(<arguments>) OVER(
  [ <window partition clause> ]
  [ <window order clause> [ <window frame clause> ] ] )
```

The window frame clause can include three parts and takes the following form:

```
<window frame units> <window frame extent> [ <window frame exclusion> ]
```

In the *window frame units* part, you indicate *ROWS, GROUPS,* or *RANGE*. With the *ROWS* option you specify the endpoints of the frame as offsets in terms of the number of rows of difference from the current row. The *GROUPS* option is similar to the *ROWS* option, only you specify offsets as a number of distinct groups of difference from the current group, based on the ordering element. With the *RANGE* option the offsets are more dynamic, and you express them as a logical value difference from the current row's (only) ordering attribute value. This part will become clearer in the upcoming examples.

The *window frame extent* part is where you indicate the offsets of the bounds with respect to the current row.

SQL Server supports the *ROWS* option with all related *window frame extent* options, doesn't support the *GROUPS* option at all, and supports the *RANGE* option with a partial implementation of the related *window frame extent* options.

Finally, the *window frame exclusion* part allows you to specify whether to exclude the current row, its peers, or both. The *window frame exclusion* part isn't implemented in SQL Server.

The ROWS Option

I'll start with examples for using the *ROWS* clause. As mentioned, using *ROWS* as the *window frame units* part means that you indicate the frame bounds as offsets in terms of the number of rows with respect to the current row. The standard *ROWS* clause supports the following options, all of which are implemented in SQL Server:

```
ROWS BETWEEN UNBOUNDED PRECEDING |
             <n> PRECEDING       |
             <n> FOLLOWING       |
             CURRENT ROW
        AND
             UNBOUNDED FOLLOWING |
             <n> PRECEDING       |
             <n> FOLLOWING       |
             CURRENT ROW
```

These options are probably straightforward, but just in case they're not, I'll provide a brief explanation. For the low bound of the frame, *UNBOUNDED PRECEDING* means there is no low boundary point; *<n> preceding* and *<n> following* specifies a number of rows before and after the current one, respectively; and *CURRENT ROW*, obviously, means that the starting row is the current row.

As for the high bound of the frame, you can see the options are quite similar, except that if you don't want a high boundary point, you indicate *UNBOUNDED FOLLOWING*, naturally.

As an example, consider the following frame:

```
PARTITION BY custid
ORDER BY ordermonth
ROWS BETWEEN UNBOUNDED PRECEDING
  AND CURRENT ROW
```

The window frame created for each row contains all rows from the first order month through the current row. Note that you can use *ROWS UNBOUNDED PRECEDING* as a shorthand way of saying "ROWS BETWEEN UNBOUNDED PRECEDING AND CURRENT ROW." However, if you omit the *window frame unit* part altogether, just leaving the partitioning and ordering parts, you get something a bit different by default. I'll get to this later when discussing the *RANGE* option.

As the first example using the *ROWS* option, consider the following query against the *Sales.EmpOrders* view, followed by its output shown here in abbreviated form:

```
SELECT empid, ordermonth, qty,
  SUM(qty) OVER(PARTITION BY empid
                ORDER BY ordermonth
                ROWS BETWEEN UNBOUNDED PRECEDING
                      AND CURRENT ROW) AS runqty
FROM Sales.EmpOrders;
```

```
empid  ordermonth   qty   runqty
------ -----------  ----  -------
1      2017-07-01   121   121
1      2017-08-01   247   368
1      2017-09-01   255   623
1      2017-10-01   143   766
1      2017-11-01   318   1084
...
2      2017-07-01   50    50
2      2017-08-01   94    144
2      2017-09-01   137   281
2      2017-10-01   248   529
2      2017-11-01   237   766
...
```

This query uses the aforementioned frame specification to calculate a running total quantity for each employee and order month. Recall that you can use a more concise form to indicate the frame while retaining the same meaning:

```
SELECT empid, ordermonth, qty,
  SUM(qty) OVER(PARTITION BY empid
                ORDER BY ordermonth
                ROWS UNBOUNDED PRECEDING) AS runqty
FROM Sales.EmpOrders;
```

Figure 2-3 provides an illustration that depicts the applicable frame with respect to each row using arrows.

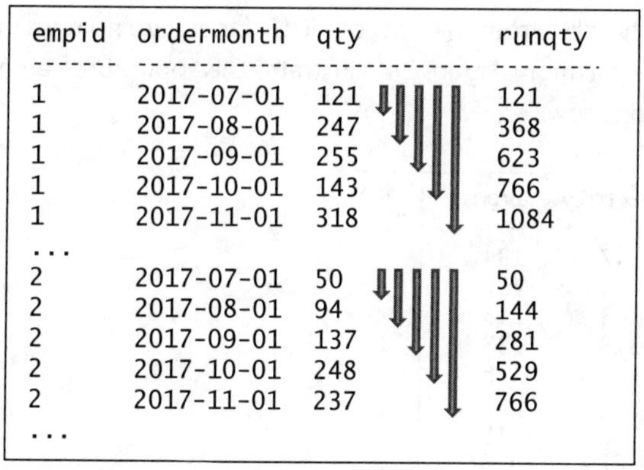

```
empid   ordermonth    qty              runqty
------  ------------  --------------   --------
1       2017-07-01    121              121
1       2017-08-01    247              368
1       2017-09-01    255              623
1       2017-10-01    143              766
1       2017-11-01    318              1084
...
2       2017-07-01    50               50
2       2017-08-01    94               144
2       2017-09-01    137              281
2       2017-10-01    248              529
2       2017-11-01    237              766
...
```

FIGURE 2-3 Frame example: ROWS UNBOUNDED PRECEDING.

As a second example for using the *ROWS* option, the following query invokes three window functions with three different frame specifications:

```
SELECT empid, ordermonth,
  MAX(qty) OVER(PARTITION BY empid
                ORDER BY ordermonth
                ROWS BETWEEN 1 PRECEDING
                         AND 1 PRECEDING) AS prvqty,
  qty AS curqty,
  MAX(qty) OVER(PARTITION BY empid
                ORDER BY ordermonth
                ROWS BETWEEN 1 FOLLOWING
                         AND 1 FOLLOWING) AS nxtqty,
  AVG(qty) OVER(PARTITION BY empid
                ORDER BY ordermonth
                ROWS BETWEEN 1 PRECEDING
                         AND 1 FOLLOWING) AS avgqty
FROM Sales.EmpOrders;
```

```
empid   ordermonth   prvqty   curqty   nxtqty   avgqty
------  -----------  -------  -------  -------  -------
1       2017-07-01   NULL     121      247      184
1       2017-08-01   121      247      255      207
1       2017-09-01   247      255      143      215
1       2017-10-01   255      143      318      238
1       2017-11-01   143      318      536      332
...
1       2019-01-01   583      397      566      515
1       2019-02-01   397      566      467      476
1       2019-03-01   566      467      586      539
1       2019-04-01   467      586      299      450
1       2019-05-01   586      299      NULL     442
...
```

The calculation that generates the attribute *prvqty* defines a frame in terms of rows between 1 preceding and 1 preceding. This means that the frame includes just the previous row in the partition. The *MAX* aggregate applied to the *qty* attribute is artificial here because, at most, there will be just one row in the frame. The maximum *qty* value is the *qty* value from that row or *NULL* if there are no rows in the frame (if the current row is the first one in the partition). Figure 2-4 illustrates the applicable frame with respect to each row, containing at most just one row.

```
empid   ordermonth   prvqty   curqty   nxtqty   avgqty
-------  -----------  -------  -------  -------  -------
1        2017-07-01   NULL     121      247      184
1        2017-08-01   121      247      255      207
1        2017-09-01   247      255      143      215
1        2017-10-01   255      143      318      238
1        2017-11-01   143      318      536      332
...
1        2019-01-01   583      397      566      515
1        2019-02-01   397      566      467      476
1        2019-03-01   566      467      586      539
1        2019-04-01   467      586      299      450
1        2019-05-01   586      299      NULL     442
...
```

FIGURE 2-4 Frame example: ROWS BETWEEN 1 PRECEDING AND 1 PRECEDING.

Note that there's no previous row with respect to the first one in the partition; therefore, the *prvqty* value in the first row in the partition is *NULL*.

Similarly, the calculation that generates the attribute *nxtqty* defines a frame in terms of rows between 1 following and 1 following, meaning that the frame includes just the next row. Then the *MAX(qty)* aggregate returns the *qty* value from the next row. Figure 2-5 illustrates the applicable frame with respect to each row.

```
empid   ordermonth   prvqty   curqty   nxtqty   avgqty
-------  -----------  -------  -------  -------  -------
1        2017-07-01   NULL     121      247      184
1        2017-08-01   121      247      255      207
1        2017-09-01   247      255      143      215
1        2017-10-01   255      143      318      238
1        2017-11-01   143      318      536      332
...
1        2019-01-01   583      397      566      515
1        2019-02-01   397      566      467      476
1        2019-03-01   566      467      586      539
1        2019-04-01   467      586      299      450
1        2019-05-01   586      299      NULL     442
...
```

FIGURE 2-5 Frame example: ROWS BETWEEN 1 FOLLOWING AND 1 FOLLOWING.

Just like there's no previous row with respect to the first one in the partition, there's no next row with respect to the last one in the partition; therefore, the *nxtqty* value in the last row in the partition is *NULL*.

Note Later in this chapter in the section describing offset functions, you will see alternative, more concise ways to obtain a value from a single row that is in a certain offset from the current one. For example, you will see how to get a value from the previous row using the *LAG* function and from the next row using the *LEAD* function.

The calculation that generates the result attribute *avgqty* defines a frame of rows between 1 preceding and 1 following, meaning that the frame consists of up to three rows. Figure 2-6 illustrates the applicable frame with respect to two arbitrary rows just as an example.

```
empid  ordermonth   prvqty  curqty  nxtqty  avgqty
------ ------------ ------- -------- ------- --------
1      2017-07-01   NULL     121      247     184
1      2017-08-01   121      247      255     207
1      2017-09-01   247      255      143     215
1      2017-10-01   255      143      318     238
1      2017-11-01   143      318      536     332
...
1      2019-01-01   583      397      566     515
1      2019-02-01   397      566      467     476
1      2019-03-01   566      467      586     539
1      2019-04-01   467      586      299     450
1      2019-05-01   586      299      NULL    442
...
```

FIGURE 2-6 Frame example: ROWS BETWEEN 1 PRECEDING AND 1 FOLLOWING.

As with the other calculations, there's no row preceding the first one in the partition and no row following the last one; hence, the frame in this case can consist of fewer than, but no more than, three rows. The *AVG* function correctly divides the sum by the actual count of rows in the frame.

Combined, the partitioning and ordering elements in the *EmpOrders* view are unique. This means that the same combination of *empid* and *ordermonth* values cannot repeat itself in the view. And this, in turn, means that the three calculations used in our query are deterministic—in other words, the query has only one possible correct result for a given state of the input.

Things are different, though, when the combination of partitioning and ordering elements isn't unique. Then calculations using the *ROWS* option might be nondeterministic. I'll demonstrate this with an example. Run the code in Listing 2-1 to create and populate a table called T1.

LISTING 2-1 DDL and Sample Data for Table T1

```
SET NOCOUNT ON;
USE TSQLV5;

DROP TABLE IF EXISTS dbo.T1;
GO
CREATE TABLE dbo.T1
```

```
(
  keycol INT          NOT NULL CONSTRAINT PK_T1 PRIMARY KEY,
  col1   VARCHAR(10) NOT NULL
);
INSERT INTO dbo.T1 VALUES
  (2, 'A'),(3, 'A'),
  (5, 'B'),(7, 'B'),(11, 'B'),
  (13, 'C'),(17, 'C'),(19, 'C'),(23, 'C');
```

Consider the following query, which is followed by its output:

```
SELECT keycol, col1,
  COUNT(*) OVER(ORDER BY col1
                ROWS BETWEEN UNBOUNDED PRECEDING
                AND CURRENT ROW) AS cnt
FROM dbo.T1;
```

keycol	col1	cnt
2	A	1
3	A	2
5	B	3
7	B	4
11	B	5
13	C	6
17	C	7
19	C	8
23	C	9

Observe that different rows that share the same implicit partitioning and explicit ordering values (peers) get different counts. In SQL Server, the order of access between such peers depends on optimization. For example, I created the following index:

```
CREATE UNIQUE INDEX idx_col1D_keycol ON dbo.T1(col1 DESC, keycol);
```

Then I ran the query again, and the second time I got the following output:

keycol	fcol1	cnt
3	A	1
2	A	2
5	B	3
11	B	4
7	B	5
23	C	6
19	C	7
17	C	8
13	C	9

Technically, as far as the standard is concerned, this output is just as correct as the previous output.

If you need a deterministic order—namely, guaranteed repeatable results—you should make sure that the combination of partitioning and ordering elements is unique. You can achieve this by adding a tiebreaker to the ordering specification—in our case, by adding the primary key column, like so:

```
SELECT keycol, col1,
  COUNT(*) OVER(ORDER BY col1, keycol
                ROWS BETWEEN UNBOUNDED PRECEDING
                         AND CURRENT ROW) AS cnt
FROM dbo.T1;
```

```
keycol       col1        cnt
-----------  ----------  -----------
2            A           1
3            A           2
5            B           3
7            B           4
11           B           5
13           C           6
17           C           7
19           C           8
23           C           9
```

Now the query is deterministic, meaning that there's only one correct result, and it's guaranteed to be repeatable as long as the underlying data doesn't change.

The GROUPS Option

As mentioned, the *GROUPS* option is similar to *ROWS*, only instead of specifying how many rows to go backward or forward with respect to the current row, you specify how many distinct window ordering groups (based on the sort key) to go backward or forward with respect to the window ordering group containing the current row. At the date of this writing, this option is not supported in SQL Server. The only platform that I know of that supports it is PostgreSQL.

As an example, suppose that you need to query the *Sales.Orders* table, and return per order, the number of orders placed in the last three days of activity. The challenge here is that the order date isn't unique. Obviously, you can have multiple orders placed on the same date.

Using the standard *GROUPS* option, you would achieve this task easily like so:

```
SELECT orderid, orderdate,
  COUNT(*) OVER(ORDER BY orderdate
                GROUPS BETWEEN 2 PRECEDING AND CURRENT ROW) AS numordersinlast3days
FROM Sales.Orders;
```

Here's the expected output of this query:

```
orderid  orderdate   numordersinlast3days
-------- ----------  --------------------
10248    2017-07-04  1
10249    2017-07-05  2
10250    2017-07-08  4
```

```
10251      2017-07-08 4
10252      2017-07-09 4
10253      2017-07-10 4
10254      2017-07-11 3
10255      2017-07-12 3
10256      2017-07-15 3
10257      2017-07-16 3
...
11067      2019-05-04 10
11068      2019-05-04 10
11069      2019-05-04 10
11070      2019-05-05 10
11071      2019-05-05 10
11072      2019-05-05 10
11073      2019-05-05 10
11074      2019-05-06 11
11075      2019-05-06 11
11076      2019-05-06 11
11077      2019-05-06 11
```

The workaround in SQL Server involves a few steps. You apply preliminary grouping (in our case, by order date) and compute the relevant group aggregate (in our case, *COUNT*). You then apply a windowed aggregate on top of the group aggregate, using the ROWS option with the relevant delimiters (in our case, *ROWS BETWEEN 2 PRECEDING AND CURRENT ROW*). You then define a CTE based on the last query, and finally in the outer query, join the table with the detail rows with the CTE holding the aggregates. Here's the complete solution's code:

```
WITH C AS
(
  SELECT orderdate,
    SUM(COUNT(*))
      OVER(ORDER BY orderdate
            ROWS BETWEEN 2 PRECEDING
                    AND CURRENT ROW) AS numordersinlast3days
  FROM Sales.Orders
  GROUP BY orderdate
)
SELECT O.orderid, O.orderdate, C.numordersinlast3days
FROM Sales.Orders AS O
  INNER JOIN C
    ON O.orderdate = C.orderdate;
```

As you can see, grouping and windowing are not mutually exclusive. Grouping happens in phase 3 of logical query processing (*GROUP BY*), and windowing happens in phase 5-1 (evaluate expressions in the *SELECT* list). Hence, window functions can use group functions as their inputs and as part of their specification. If you see this capability for the first time, it could be a bit hard to digest initially. Later in the chapter, I provide more details under "Nesting Group Functions within Window Functions."

The logic could be more elaborate, involving computations that mix detail and aggregate elements. For instance, suppose you need to query the *Sales.OrderValues* view and return for each order the percent that the current order value represents out of the total of all orders placed in the last three days of activity. Here's how you would achieve this with the standard *GROUPS* option:

```
SELECT orderid, orderdate, val,
  CAST( 100.00 * val /
          SUM(val) OVER(ORDER BY orderdate
                          GROUPS BETWEEN 2 PRECEDING
                                     AND CURRENT ROW)
        AS NUMERIC(5, 2) ) AS pctoflast3days
FROM Sales.OrderValues;
```

Here's the expected output of this query:

```
orderid  orderdate   val       pctoflast3days
-------- ----------  --------   --------------
10248    2017-07-04  440.00     100.00
10249    2017-07-05  1863.40    80.90
10250    2017-07-08  1552.60    34.43
10251    2017-07-08  654.06     14.50
10252    2017-07-09  3597.90    46.92
10253    2017-07-10  1444.80    19.93
10254    2017-07-11  556.62     9.94
10255    2017-07-12  2490.50    55.44
10256    2017-07-15  517.80     14.52
10257    2017-07-16  1119.90    27.13
...
11067    2019-05-04  86.85      0.83
11068    2019-05-04  2027.08    19.40
11069    2019-05-04  360.00     3.45
11070    2019-05-05  1629.98    10.48
11071    2019-05-05  484.50     3.11
11072    2019-05-05  5218.00    33.55
11073    2019-05-05  300.00     1.93
11074    2019-05-06  232.09     1.80
11075    2019-05-06  498.10     3.87
11076    2019-05-06  792.75     6.15
11077    2019-05-06  1255.72    9.75
```

Here's a supported workaround that does work in SQL Server, using a similar technique to the one shown in the count task:

```
WITH C AS
(
  SELECT orderdate,
    SUM(SUM(val))
      OVER(ORDER BY orderdate
             ROWS BETWEEN 2 PRECEDING
                      AND CURRENT ROW) AS sumval
  FROM Sales.OrderValues
  GROUP BY orderdate
)
```

```
SELECT O.orderid, O.orderdate,
  CAST( 100.00 * O.val / C.sumval AS NUMERIC(5, 2) ) AS pctoflast3days
FROM Sales.OrderValues AS O
  INNER JOIN C
    ON O.orderdate = C.orderdate;
```

The RANGE Option

The SQL standard also supports specifying the *RANGE* option as the *window frame unit*. Here are the possibilities for the low and high bounds—or endpoints—of the frame:

```
RANGE BETWEEN UNBOUNDED PRECEDING  |
              <val> PRECEDING      |
              <val> FOLLOWING      |
              CURRENT ROW
        AND
              UNBOUNDED FOLLOWING  |
              <val> PRECEDING      |
              <val> FOLLOWING      |
              CURRENT ROW
```

This option is supposed to enable you to specify the low and high bounds of the frame more dynamically—as a logical difference between the current row's ordering value and the bound's value. Think about the difference between saying "Give me the total quantities for the last three points of activity," versus saying "Give me the total quantities for the period starting two months before the current period and until the current period." The former concept is what *ROWS* was designed to provide, and the latter concept is what *RANGE* was designed to provide. (I'll say more about this example shortly.)

At the date of this writing, *RANGE* is not implemented fully in SQL Server. It is currently supported only with *UNBOUNDED* and *CURRENT ROW* window-frame delimiters. What's also still missing is support for a temporal *INTERVAL* type that, combined with full support for the *RANGE* option, would provide a lot of flexibility in the frame definition. As an example, the following query defines a frame based on a range between two months before the current month and the current month (and this query doesn't run in SQL Server):

```
SELECT empid, ordermonth, qty,
  SUM(qty) OVER(PARTITION BY empid
                ORDER BY ordermonth
                RANGE BETWEEN INTERVAL '2' MONTH PRECEDING
                          AND CURRENT ROW) AS sum3month
FROM Sales.EmpOrders;
```

This is different than using *ROWS BETWEEN 2 PRECEDING AND CURRENT ROW* even when the order month is unique for each employee. Consider the possibility that an employee can be inactive in certain months. With the ROWS option, the frame simply starts two rows before the current one, which might be more than two months before the current one. With *RANGE*, the frame is more dynamic, starting two months before the current one—whatever number of rows this translates to. Figure 2-7 illustrates the applicable frame of rows for some of the rows in the underlying query.

```
empid    ordermonth  qty                 sum3month
-------  ----------  ------------------  ------------
...
9        2017-07-01  294 ↓               294
9        2017-10-01  256   ↓             256
9        2017-12-01  25                  281
9        2018-01-01  74                  99
9        2018-03-01  137                 211
9        2018-04-01  52                  189
9        2018-05-01  8                   197
9        2018-06-01  161                 221
9        2018-07-01  4                   173
9        2018-08-01  98                  263
...
```

FIGURE 2-7 Frame example: RANGE INTERVAL '2' MONTH PRECEDING.

Observe that the number of rows in the different frames varies between 1, 2, and 3. This happens because, in some cases, there aren't three consecutive months of activity for the same employee.

Just like with the *ROWS* option, the *RANGE* option also supports more concise ways to express what you want. If you don't specify an upper bound, *CURRENT ROW* is assumed. So, in our example, instead of using *RANGE BETWEEN INTERVAL '2' MONTH PRECEDING AND CURRENT ROW*, you can use just *RANGE INTERVAL '2' MONTH PRECEDING*. But as mentioned, this query won't run in SQL Server because of the incomplete support for the RANGE option and the lack of support for the *INTERVAL* type. For now, you need to use alternative methods.

It's possible to handle the task with the existing support for window functions, but the solution is quite elaborate. Step 1 is to produce the set of all months between the minimum and maximum in the *EmpOrders* view. This can be achieved using a helper table function I made available in the database TSQLV5 called *GetNums*, which returns a sequence of integers in a desired range. Here's the query using the *GetNums* function to achieve this step:

```
SELECT
  DATEADD(month, N.n,
    (SELECT MIN(ordermonth) FROM Sales.EmpOrders)) AS ordermonth
FROM dbo.GetNums(0,
  DATEDIFF(month,
    (SELECT MIN(ordermonth) FROM Sales.EmpOrders),
    (SELECT MAX(ordermonth) FROM Sales.EmpOrders))) AS N;
```

This query generates the following output:

```
ordermonth
----------
2017-07-01
2017-08-01
2017-09-01
2017-10-01
2017-11-01
...
```

```
2019-01-01
2019-02-01
2019-03-01
2019-04-01
2019-05-01

(23 rows affected)
```

Step 2 is to produce all combinations of months and employees by applying a cross join between the result of Step 1 and the Employees table, like so:

```
WITH M AS
(
  SELECT
    DATEADD(month, N.n,
      (SELECT MIN(ordermonth) FROM Sales.EmpOrders)) AS ordermonth
  FROM dbo.GetNums(0,
    DATEDIFF(month,
      (SELECT MIN(ordermonth) FROM Sales.EmpOrders),
      (SELECT MAX(ordermonth) FROM Sales.EmpOrders))) AS N
)
SELECT E.empid, M.ordermonth
FROM HR.Employees AS E
  CROSS JOIN M;
```

Step 3 then left joins the result of Step 2 with the EmpOrders view, resulting in both employee-month combinations that have matches, and ones that don't (marked with NULLs in the nonpreserved side of the join). Here's the query implementing this step:

```
WITH M AS
(
  SELECT
    DATEADD(month, N.n,
      (SELECT MIN(ordermonth) FROM Sales.EmpOrders)) AS ordermonth
  FROM dbo.GetNums(0,
    DATEDIFF(month,
      (SELECT MIN(ordermonth) FROM Sales.EmpOrders),
      (SELECT MAX(ordermonth) FROM Sales.EmpOrders))) AS N
)
SELECT E.empid, M.ordermonth, EO.qty,
  SUM(EO.qty) OVER(PARTITION BY E.empid
                   ORDER BY M.ordermonth
                   ROWS 2 PRECEDING) AS sum3month
FROM HR.Employees AS E
  CROSS JOIN M
  LEFT OUTER JOIN Sales.EmpOrders AS EO
    ON E.empid = EO.empid
    AND M.ordermonth = EO.ordermonth;
```

Here's a partial output of this query for employee 9:

```
empid   ordermonth   qty    sum3month
------  -----------  -----  -----------
...
9       2017-07-01   294    294
9       2017-08-01   NULL   294
9       2017-09-01   NULL   294
9       2017-10-01   256    256
9       2017-11-01   NULL   256
9       2017-12-01   25     281
9       2018-01-01   74     99
9       2018-02-01   NULL   99
9       2018-03-01   137    211
9       2018-04-01   52     189
9       2018-05-01   8      197
9       2018-06-01   161    221
9       2018-07-01   4      173
9       2018-08-01   98     263
...
```

Finally, the last step is to remove inapplicable rows by filtering only result rows from Step 3 where the *qty* attribute is not NULL, like so:

```
WITH M AS
(
  SELECT
    DATEADD(month, N.n,
      (SELECT MIN(ordermonth) FROM Sales.EmpOrders)) AS ordermonth
  FROM dbo.GetNums(0,
    DATEDIFF(month,
      (SELECT MIN(ordermonth) FROM Sales.EmpOrders),
      (SELECT MAX(ordermonth) FROM Sales.EmpOrders))) AS N
),
C AS
(
  SELECT E.empid, M.ordermonth, EO.qty,
    SUM(EO.qty) OVER(PARTITION BY E.empid
                     ORDER BY M.ordermonth
                     ROWS 2 PRECEDING) AS sum3month
  FROM HR.Employees AS E
    CROSS JOIN M
    LEFT OUTER JOIN Sales.EmpOrders AS EO
      ON E.empid = EO.empid
      AND M.ordermonth = EO.ordermonth
)
SELECT empid, ordermonth, qty, sum3month
FROM C
WHERE qty IS NOT NULL;
```

Another option is to rely on more traditional constructs such as subqueries, as the following example shows:

```
SELECT empid, ordermonth, qty,
  (SELECT SUM(qty)
   FROM Sales.EmpOrders AS O2
   WHERE O2.empid = O1.empid
     AND O2.ordermonth BETWEEN DATEADD(month, -2, O1.ordermonth)
                           AND O1.ordermonth) AS sum3month
FROM Sales.EmpOrders AS O1;
```

As mentioned, SQL Server does support the RANGE option with UNBOUNDED and CURRENT ROW as delimiters. For example, the window function in the following query calculates the running total quantity from the beginning of the employee activity until the current month:

```
SELECT empid, ordermonth, qty,
  SUM(qty) OVER(PARTITION BY empid
                ORDER BY ordermonth
                RANGE BETWEEN UNBOUNDED PRECEDING
                          AND CURRENT ROW) AS runqty
FROM Sales.EmpOrders;

empid       ordermonth  qty         runqty
----------- ----------- ----------- -----------
1           2017-07-01  121         121
1           2017-08-01  247         368
1           2017-09-01  255         623
1           2017-10-01  143         766
1           2017-11-01  318         1084
...
2           2017-07-01  50          50
2           2017-08-01  94          144
2           2017-09-01  137         281
2           2017-10-01  248         529
2           2017-11-01  237         766
...
```

Figure 2-8 illustrates the applicable frame with respect to each row in the underlying query.

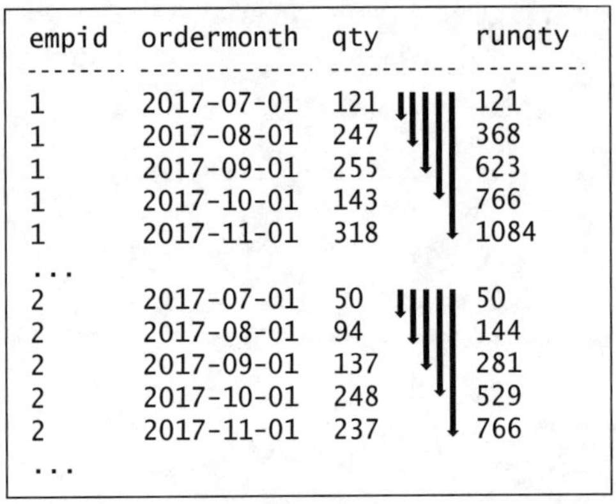

empid	ordermonth	qty	runqty
1	2017-07-01	121	121
1	2017-08-01	247	368
1	2017-09-01	255	623
1	2017-10-01	143	766
1	2017-11-01	318	1084
...			
2	2017-07-01	50	50
2	2017-08-01	94	144
2	2017-09-01	137	281
2	2017-10-01	248	529
2	2017-11-01	237	766
...			

FIGURE 2-8 Frame example: RANGE UNBOUNDED PRECEDING.

As mentioned, if you don't indicate the upper bound, the default is *CURRENT ROW*. So instead of using *RANGE BETWEEN UNBOUNDED PRECEDING AND CURRENT ROW*, you can use the shorter form of *RANGE UNBOUNDED PRECEDING*, like so:

```
SELECT empid, ordermonth, qty,
  SUM(qty) OVER(PARTITION BY empid
               ORDER BY ordermonth
               RANGE UNBOUNDED PRECEDING) AS runqty
FROM Sales.EmpOrders;
```

RANGE UNBOUNDED PRECEDING, as it turns out, is also the default when you indicate window ordering without an explicit *window frame unit* with its related window frame extent specification. So, the following query is logically equivalent to the last two:

```
SELECT empid, ordermonth, qty,
  SUM(qty) OVER(PARTITION BY empid
               ORDER BY ordermonth) AS runqty
FROM Sales.EmpOrders;
```

That's quite a significant savings in the amount of code.

If you carefully followed the examples with both the *ROWS* and the *RANGE* options, at this point you might wonder whether there's any difference between the two when using only *UNBOUNDED* and *CURRENT ROW* as delimiters. For example, when comparing Figure 2-3 (which shows the frames defined with *ROWS UNBOUNDED PRECEDING*) and Figure 2-8 (which shows the frames defined with *RANGE UNBOUNDED PRECEDING*), they seem identical. Indeed, the two specifications have the same logical meaning when the combination of partitioning plus ordering elements is unique. Querying the *EmpOrders* view, with *empid* as the partitioning element and *ordermonth* as the ordering element, you do get a unique combination. So, in this case, both options are logically equivalent. There is a difference between the meanings of the two when the combination of partitioning and ordering elements isn't unique, meaning that there is potential for ties.

To demonstrate the difference, I'll use the table T1 you created and populated earlier by running the code in Listing 2-1. As a reminder, the option *ROWS BETWEEN UNBOUNDED PRECEDING AND CURRENT ROW* (or the equivalent *ROWS UNBOUNDED PRECEDING*) ends the frame at the current row and doesn't include further peers:

```
SELECT keycol, col1,
  COUNT(*) OVER(ORDER BY col1
               ROWS BETWEEN UNBOUNDED PRECEDING
                        AND CURRENT ROW) AS cnt
FROM dbo.T1;

keycol      col1       cnt
----------- ---------- -----------
2           A          1
3           A          2
5           B          3
7           B          4
11          B          5
```

13	C	6
17	C	7
19	C	8
23	C	9

Here's a similar query, only this one uses *RANGE* instead of *ROWS*:

```
SELECT keycol, col1,
  COUNT(*) OVER(ORDER BY col1
                RANGE BETWEEN UNBOUNDED PRECEDING
                          AND CURRENT ROW) AS cnt
FROM dbo.T1;
```

keycol	col1	cnt
2	A	2
3	A	2
5	B	5
7	B	5
11	B	5
13	C	9
17	C	9
19	C	9
23	C	9

With RANGE, when the upper bound is *CURRENT ROW*, by default peers are included. Even though the terminology is *CURRENT ROW*, it actually means *current ordering value*. For example, notice that all three rows in which the *col1* value is *B* get a count of *5*. Conceptually, expressed as a predicate, it means *<frame_row>.ordermonth <= <current_row>.ordermonth*. In practice, though, it's not common that you will want to order by something that isn't unique and want to include peers. Typically, you do one of two alternative things. One is to break ties, like so:

```
SELECT keycol, col1,
  COUNT(*) OVER(ORDER BY col1, keycol
                ROWS BETWEEN UNBOUNDED PRECEDING
                          AND CURRENT ROW) AS cnt
FROM dbo.T1;
```

The ordering is now deterministic, and there's only one correct result:

keycol	col1	cnt
2	A	1
3	A	2
5	B	3
7	B	4
11	B	5
13	C	6
17	C	7
19	C	8
23	C	9

Another common thing to do is preliminary grouping, and then nest the group aggregate within the window aggregate as explained earlier, like so:

```
SELECT col1,
  SUM(COUNT(*)) OVER(ORDER BY col1
                      ROWS BETWEEN UNBOUNDED PRECEDING
                                AND CURRENT ROW) AS cnt
FROM dbo.T1
GROUP BY col1;
```

This query is deterministic as well, meaning that it has only one correct result:

```
col1        cnt
----------  -----------
A           2
B           5
C           9
```

With both workarounds, you do get total order (unique order in the combination of partitioning and ordering); therefore, the *ROWS* and *RANGE* options have the same semantics when using the same *window frame extent* specification.

> **Note** Later in the book, I'll also get into the performance differences between these two options, and I will explain why you will want to be very conscious about your choice.

Again, I provide more details on nesting group functions within window functions later in the chapter.

Window Frame Exclusion

Window functions in the SQL standard support an option called *window frame exclusion* that is part of the framing specification. This option controls whether to include the current row and its peers in case of ties in the ordering element's values. At the date of this writing, this option is not supported in SQL Server. The only platform that I know of that supports it is PostgreSQL.

The standard supports four window frame exclusion possibilities, listed here with a short description:

- **EXCLUDE CURRENT ROW** Exclude the current row.

- **EXCLUDE GROUP** Exclude the current row as well as its peers.

- **EXCLUDE TIES** Keep the current row but exclude its peers.

- **EXCLUDE NO OTHERS (default)** Don't exclude further rows.

Note that the window frame exclusion option can only further remove rows from the frame; it won't return a row if the previous framing options (window frame unit and window frame extent) removed it.

I'll use the table T1 created and populated with the code provided earlier in Listing 2-1 to demonstrate the concept of window frame exclusion through examples. Listing 2-2 shows four queries with the different window frame exclusion possibilities, each followed by what would be its desired output.

LISTING 2-2 Queries with Different Window Frame Exclusion Options

```
-- EXCLUDE NO OTHERS (don't exclude rows)
SELECT keycol, col1,
  COUNT(*) OVER(ORDER BY col1
                RANGE BETWEEN UNBOUNDED PRECEDING
                          AND CURRENT ROW
                EXCLUDE NO OTHERS) AS cnt
FROM dbo.T1;
```

keycol	col1	cnt
2	A	2
3	A	2
5	B	5
7	B	5
11	B	5
13	C	9
17	C	9
19	C	9
23	C	9

```
-- EXCLUDE CURRENT ROW (exclude current row)
SELECT keycol, col1,
  COUNT(*) OVER(ORDER BY col1
                RANGE BETWEEN UNBOUNDED PRECEDING
                          AND CURRENT ROW
                EXCLUDE CURRENT ROW) AS cnt
FROM dbo.T1;
```

keycol	col1	cnt
2	A	1
3	A	1
5	B	4
7	B	4
11	B	4
13	C	8
17	C	8
19	C	8
23	C	8

```
-- EXCLUDE GROUP (exclude current row and its peers)
SELECT keycol, col1,
  COUNT(*) OVER(ORDER BY col1
                RANGE BETWEEN UNBOUNDED PRECEDING
                          AND CURRENT ROW
                EXCLUDE GROUP) AS cnt
FROM dbo.T1;
```

```
keycol      col1       cnt
----------- ---------- -----------
2           A          0
3           A          0
5           B          2
7           B          2
11          B          2
13          C          5
17          C          5
19          C          5
23          C          5
```

```
-- EXCLUDE TIES (keep current row, exclude peers)
SELECT keycol, col1,
   COUNT(*) OVER(ORDER BY col1
                  RANGE BETWEEN UNBOUNDED PRECEDING
                            AND CURRENT ROW
                EXCLUDE TIES) AS cnt
FROM dbo.T1;
```

```
keycol      col1       cnt
----------- ---------- -----------
2           A          1
3           A          1
5           B          3
7           B          3
11          B          3
13          C          6
17          C          6
19          C          6
23          C          6
```

Further Windowing Ideas

There are a few additional ideas related to window aggregate functions, and in some cases also applicable to other kinds of window functions, that SQL Server doesn't support yet. Some of those ideas are standard and some are proprietary inventions in other database platforms. I find them interesting and useful; therefore, I thought I'd mention them here to give you a sense of what's out there. Here I'll cover the standard *FILTER* clause, the standard nested window functions, and the Teradata-specific *RESET WHEN* clause.

FILTER Clause

Recall that the various elements in the window specification (partitioning, ordering, and framing) are essentially different filtering options. There are additional filtering needs that the aforementioned options don't address. Some of those needs are addressed by the standard with a clause called *FILTER*. You specify this clause after an aggregate function to filter the set of rows that the aggregate applies to using a predicate. The form of this clause is as follows:

```
<aggregate_function>(<input_expression>) FILTER (WHERE <search_condition>)
```

As an example, the following query calculates the difference between the current quantity and the employee monthly average up to three months before the present date (not the current row's month):

```
SELECT empid, ordermonth, qty,
  qty - AVG(qty)
          FILTER (WHERE ordermonth <=
                     DATEADD(month, -3, CURRENT_TIMESTAMP))
          OVER(PARTITION BY empid) AS diff
FROM Sales.EmpOrders;
```

The workaround that is supported in SQL Server is to use a *CASE* expression as input to the aggregate function, like so:

```
<aggregate_function>(CASE WHEN <search_condition> THEN <input_expression> END)
```

Here's the complete query that addresses the last example:

```
SELECT empid, ordermonth, qty,
  qty - AVG(CASE WHEN ordermonth <=
                 DATEADD(month, -3, CURRENT_TIMESTAMP)
                 THEN qty
             END)
          OVER(PARTITION BY empid) AS diff
FROM Sales.EmpOrders;
```

 Note With *NULL* inputs, the standard *FILTER* clause can have a different meaning from the alternative that uses a *CASE* expression. For some functions, the former does not process NULL inputs at all, whereas the latter processes every input row. This difference isn't relevant in the examples above.

Nested Window Functions

According to the SQL Standard, you can nest two kinds of window functions as an aggregated argument of a window aggregate function. This capability allows you to refer to strategic (important) positions, or markers, of window elements like the first or last row in the partition or to the value of an expression at such markers. The two standard nested window functions are *nested row number function* (not to confuse with a regular windowed row number function I cover later under "Ranking Functions"), and *nested value_of expression at row* function.

The *nested row number function* uses the same function name *ROW_NUMBER* like the regular windowed row number function, but you nest it in a window aggregate function to get the row number of a strategic marker of a window element. The syntax of this function is:

```
<aggregate_function>(<argument with
  ROW_NUMBER(<row marker>)
    >) OVER(<over_specification>)
```

Following are the standard row markers and their descriptions:

- **BEGIN_PARTITION**   First row of window partition

- **BEGIN_FRAME**   First row of window frame

- **CURRENT_ROW**   Current outer or underlying row

- **FRAME_ROW**   Current inner window frame row

- **END_FRAME**   Last row of window frame

- **END_PARTITION**   Last row of window partition

As an example, suppose that you need to query the *Sales.OrderValues* view, and for each order show the current order value, as well as the difference from *the employee average excluding the very first and last employee's orders*. Here's how you would achieve this task using nested row number functions:

```
SELECT orderid, orderdate, empid, custid, val,
  val - AVG(CASE
              WHEN  ROW_NUMBER(FRAME_ROW) > ROW_NUMBER(BEGIN_PARTITION)
                AND ROW_NUMBER(FRAME_ROW) < ROW_NUMBER(END_PARTITION)
                  THEN val
            END)
          OVER(PARTITION BY empid
              ORDER BY orderdate, orderid
              ROWS BETWEEN UNBOUNDED PRECEDING
                        AND UNBOUNDED FOLLOWING) AS diff
FROM Sales.OrderValues;
```

The *nested value_of expression at row* function allows you to refer to a value of an expression at a given row marker. Here's the syntax of this function:

```
<aggregate_function>(< argument with
  VALUE OF <expression> AT <row marker> [<delta>] [, <default>]
    >) OVER(<over_specification>)
```

As you can see, you can specify a certain negative or positive delta with respect to the row marker, and optionally provide a default value in case a row doesn't exist at the specified position.

For example, suppose that you need to calculate for each order the difference between the current order value and the employee average for customers other than the current one. You would use the following query to achieve this task:

```
SELECT orderid, orderdate, empid, custid, val,
  val - AVG(CASE
              WHEN custid <> VALUE OF custid AT CURRENT_ROW
                THEN val
            END)
          OVER(PARTITION BY empid) AS diff
FROM Sales.OrderValues;
```

Curiously, if SQL Server had support for nested window functions, it would have been easy to emulate the *RANGE* option with the *INTERVAL* type even without such options. For example, recall the standard query shown earlier with a range between two months before the current month and the current month:

```
SELECT empid, ordermonth, qty,
   SUM(qty) OVER(PARTITION BY empid
              ORDER BY ordermonth
              RANGE BETWEEN INTERVAL '2' MONTH PRECEDING
                        AND CURRENT ROW) AS sum3month
FROM Sales.EmpOrders;
```

Using nested window functions, the following query has the same meaning:

```
SELECT empid, ordermonth, qty,
   SUM(CASE
         WHEN ordermonth BETWEEN DATEADD(month, -2,
                                 VALUE OF ordermonth AT CURRENT_ROW)
                             AND VALUE OF ordermonth AT CURRENT_ROW
         THEN qty
       END)
     OVER(PARTITION BY empid
              ORDER BY ordermonth
              RANGE UNBOUNDED PRECEDING) AS sum3month
FROM Sales.EmpOrders;
```

Nested window functions seem like a powerful tool, and it would certainly be good to see them supported in SQL Server someday. At the date of this writing, I do not know of a single platform that implements nested window functions.

> **Note** Nested window functions shouldn't be confused with nesting group functions within window functions. This section focused on the former. I cover the latter a bit later in the chapter.
>
> You can also find a feedback item with a request to improve SQL Server by adding this feature here: *https://feedback.azure.com/forums/908035-sql-server/suggestions/37966075*.

RESET WHEN

The *RESET WHEN* clause is a proprietary feature in Teradata that allows you to reset a window partition based on a predicate. You specify this clause as part of a window specification in the *OVER* clause, followed by a predicate. As soon as the predicate is true, a new window partition starts. What's powerful about this feature is that in the predicate you can use a window function.

Among many challenges that you can handle with this feature, a classic group of tasks involves computing capped sums. You have quantities that you need to add up based on some order to fulfill some need, like filling a container, and you need to stop as soon as the total reaches or exceeds a certain capacity.

To demonstrate capped sums, I'll use a table called T2. Use the code in Listing 2-3 to create T2 and populate it with sample data.

LISTING 2-3 Code to Create and Populate T2

```
SET NOCOUNT ON;
USE TSQLV5;

DROP TABLE IF EXISTS dbo.T2;

CREATE TABLE dbo.T2
(
  ordcol  INT NOT NULL,
  datacol INT NOT NULL,
  CONSTRAINT PK_T2
    PRIMARY KEY(ordcol)
);

INSERT INTO dbo.T2 VALUES
  (1,   10),
  (4,   15),
  (5,    5),
  (6,   10),
  (8,   15),
  (10,  20),
  (17,  10),
  (18,  10),
  (20,  30),
  (31,  20);
```

Suppose that you need to compute a running sum of the *datacol* values based on *ordcol* ordering, and stop before the sum exceeds 50. In other words, you want to start a new partition when the sum exceeds 50. Here's how you would achieve this task with the *RESET WHEN* clause:

```
SELECT ordcol, datacol,
  SUM(datacol)
    OVER(ORDER BY ordcol
         RESET WHEN
           SUM(qty) OVER(ORDER BY ordcol
                         ROWS UNBOUNDED PRECEDING) > 50
         ROWS UNBOUNDED PRECEDING) AS runsum
FROM dbo.T2;
```

Here's the expected output of this query:

ordcol	datacol	runsum
1	10	10
4	15	25
5	5	30
6	10	40
8	15	15

10	20	35
17	10	45
18	10	10
20	30	40
31	20	20

As a variation of this task, suppose that you need to stop when the sum reaches or exceeds 50 for the first time. You would use a similar query, only start a new partition when the sum up to the previous row reaches or exceeds 50, like so:

```
SELECT ordcol, datacol,
  SUM(datacol)
    OVER(ORDER BY ordcol
         RESET WHEN
           SUM(qty) OVER(ORDER BY txid
                         ROWS BETWEEN UNBOUNDED PRECEDING
                                 AND 1 PRECEDING) >= 50
         ROWS UNBOUNDED PRECEDING) AS runsum
FROM dbo.T2;
```

Here's the expected output of this query:

ordcol	datacol	runsum
1	10	10
4	15	25
5	5	30
6	10	40
8	15	55
10	20	20
17	10	30
18	10	40
20	30	70
31	20	20

Note You can find more information about the *RESET WHEN* clause in the following article: *https://www.itprotoday.com/programming-languages/t-sql-feature-request-add-reset-when-clause-reset-window-partition*. You can also find a feedback item with a request to improve SQL Server by adding this feature here: *https://feedback.azure.com/forums/908035-sql-server/suggestions/32901541-add-reset-when-clause-like-in-teradata-to-restart*.

Note that many of the challenges that you can solve using the Teradata-specific *RESET WHEN* clause, you can also solve with a standard concept called row pattern recognition. This concept is so big and profound that it really deserves a whole chapter of its own. I cover it in Chapter 4, "Row-Pattern Recognition in SQL," and demonstrate using it to handle capped sums as well as other tasks.

Distinct Aggregates

SQL Server doesn't support using the *DISTINCT* option with window aggregate functions. For example, suppose that you need to query the *Sales.OrderValues* view and return with each order the number of distinct customers that were handled by the current employee up to, and including, the current date. Intuitively, you would expect to run the following query:

```
SELECT empid, orderdate, orderid, val,
  COUNT(DISTINCT custid) OVER(PARTITION BY empid
                              ORDER BY orderdate) AS numcusts
FROM Sales.OrderValues;
```

But because this query is not supported, you need a workaround. One way to address this need is with the help of the *ROW_NUMBER* function. I will describe this function in more detail later in this chapter. For now, it suffices to say that it returns a unique integer for each row in the partition, starting with 1 and incrementing by 1 based on the window ordering specification. Using the *ROW_NUMBER* function, you can assign row numbers partitioned by *empid* and *custid*, and ordered by *orderdate*. This means that the rows marked with row number 1 represent the first occurrence of a customer for each employee based on order-date ordering. Using a *CASE* expression, you can return the *custid* value only when the row number is equal to *1* and use *NULL* otherwise. Listing 2-4 shows a query implementing the logic described so far, followed by an abbreviated form of its output.

LISTING 2-4 Emulating Distinct Aggregate with ROW_NUMBER, Step 1

```
SELECT empid, orderdate, orderid, custid, val,
  CASE
    WHEN ROW_NUMBER() OVER(PARTITION BY empid, custid
                           ORDER BY orderdate) = 1
      THEN custid
  END AS distinct_custid
FROM Sales.OrderValues;
```

empid	orderdate	orderid	custid	val	distinct_custid
1	2019-01-15	10835	1	845.80	1
1	2019-03-16	10952	1	471.20	NULL
1	2018-09-22	10677	3	813.37	3
1	2018-02-21	10453	4	407.70	4
1	2018-06-04	10558	4	2142.90	NULL
1	2018-11-17	10743	4	319.20	NULL
1	2018-05-01	10524	5	3192.65	5
1	2018-08-11	10626	5	1503.60	NULL
1	2018-10-01	10689	5	472.50	NULL
1	2018-11-07	10733	5	1459.00	NULL
1	2017-10-29	10340	9	2436.18	9
1	2018-05-02	10525	9	818.40	NULL
1	2019-01-12	10827	9	843.00	NULL
1	2019-03-25	10975	10	717.50	10
1	2019-04-16	11027	10	877.73	NULL
1	2019-04-14	11023	11	1500.00	11

```
1      2018-11-19 10746    14      2311.70   14
1      2019-03-23 10969    15      108.00    15
1      2019-01-09 10825    17      1030.76   17
1      2019-05-04 11067    17      86.85     NULL
1      2017-09-20 10311    18      268.80    18
1      2017-11-26 10364    19      950.00    19
1      2018-01-01 10400    19      3063.00   NULL
1      2017-07-17 10258    20      1614.88   20
1      2017-11-11 10351    20      5398.73   NULL
1      2018-12-11 10773    20      2030.40   NULL
1      2018-12-15 10776    20      6635.28   NULL
1      2019-03-23 10968    20      1408.00   NULL
...
```

Observe that only the first occurrence of each *custid* value for each employee based on order-date ordering is returned, and *NULLs* are returned instead of the subsequent occurrences. The next step is to define a CTE based on the previous query and then apply a running count aggregate to the result of the *CASE* expression, as shown in Listing 2-5.

LISTING 2-5 Emulating Distinct Aggregate with ROW_NUMBER, Complete Solution

```
WITH C AS
(
  SELECT empid, orderdate, orderid, custid, val,
    CASE
      WHEN ROW_NUMBER() OVER(PARTITION BY empid, custid
                             ORDER BY orderdate) = 1
        THEN custid
    END AS distinct_custid
  FROM Sales.OrderValues
)
SELECT empid, orderdate, orderid, val,
  COUNT(distinct_custid) OVER(PARTITION BY empid
                              ORDER BY orderdate) AS numcusts
FROM C;

empid  orderdate    orderid   val       numcusts
------ -----------  --------  --------  ---------
1      2017-07-17   10258     1614.88   1
1      2017-08-01   10270     1376.00   2
1      2017-08-07   10275     291.84    3
1      2017-08-20   10285     1743.36   4
1      2017-08-28   10292     1296.00   5
1      2017-08-29   10293     848.70    6
1      2017-09-12   10304     954.40    6
1      2017-09-16   10306     498.50    7
1      2017-09-20   10311     268.80    8
1      2017-09-25   10314     2094.30   9
1      2017-09-27   10316     2835.00   9
1      2017-10-09   10325     1497.00   10
1      2017-10-29   10340     2436.18   11
1      2017-11-11   10351     5398.73   11
```

1	2017-11-19	10357	1167.68	12
1	2017-11-22	10361	2046.24	12
1	2017-11-26	10364	950.00	13
1	2017-12-03	10371	72.96	14
1	2017-12-05	10374	459.00	15
1	2017-12-09	10377	863.60	17
1	2017-12-09	10376	399.00	17
1	2017-12-17	10385	691.20	18
1	2017-12-18	10387	1058.40	19
1	2017-12-25	10393	2556.95	21
1	2017-12-25	10394	442.00	21
1	2017-12-27	10396	1903.80	22
1	2018-01-01	10400	3063.00	22
1	2018-01-01	10401	3868.60	22

. . .

> **Note**   You can find more information on distinct windowed calculations in the following article: *https://www.itprotoday.com/sql-server/what-you-need-know-about-distinct-windowed-aggregate-calculations.*

Nesting Group Functions within Window Functions

By now, you know that there are grouped aggregates and window aggregates. As mentioned, the functions themselves are the same, but the context is different. Grouped aggregates operate on groups of rows defined by the *GROUP BY* clause and return one value per group. Window aggregates operate on windows of rows and return one value for each row in the underlying query. Recall the discussion about logical query processing from Chapter 1. As a reminder, here's the order in which the various query clauses are conceptually evaluated:

1. *FROM*

2. *WHERE*

3. *GROUP BY*

4. *HAVING*

5. *SELECT*

6. *ORDER BY*

Grouped aggregates are used when the query is a grouped query, and they are allowed in phases that are evaluated after the groups have been defined—namely, from phase 4 and on. Keep in mind that each group is represented by only one row in the result. Window aggregates are allowed from phase 5 and on because they are supposed to operate on rows from the underlying query—after the *HAVING* phase.

The two types of aggregates—even though they share the same function names and calculation logic—operate in different contexts. And to the point I want to make in this section: What if you want to sum a value grouped by employee ID and, at the same time, aggregate those sums across all employees?

It's perfectly valid, albeit strange at first sight, to apply a window aggregate to a window that contains rows with attributes produced by grouped aggregates. I say strange because at first sight an expression like *SUM(SUM(val))* in a query usually doesn't seem right. But it could very well be. Consider the following query, which addresses the task at hand, followed by its output:

```
SELECT empid,
  SUM(val) AS emptotal,
  SUM(val) / SUM(SUM(val)) OVER() * 100. AS pct
FROM Sales.OrderValues
GROUP BY empid;
```

```
empid  emptotal    pct
------ ----------- -----------
3      202812.88   16.022500
6      73913.15    5.839200
9      77308.08    6.107400
7      124568.24   9.841100
1      192107.65   15.176800
4      232890.87   18.398800
2      166537.76   13.156700
5      68792.30    5.434700
8      126862.29   10.022300
```

To distinguish between the two types of aggregates, the grouped *SUM* aggregate is italicized, and the window **SUM** aggregate is bolded. The grouped aggregate *SUM(val)* calculates the total values of all orders for each employee. This means that the result of the underlying query has a row for each employee, with that total. Then the window aggregate calculates the total of all employee totals—in other words, the grand total—and divides the grouped aggregate by the window aggregate to calculate the percentage of the employee total out of the grand total.

It can be easier to see the logic behind this capability if you think of the query in two steps. The first step calculates the grouped aggregate, like so:

```
SELECT empid,
  SUM(val) AS emptotal
FROM Sales.OrderValues
GROUP BY empid;
```

```
empid  emptotal
------ -----------
3      202812.88
6      73913.15
9      77308.08
7      124568.24
```

```
1         192107.65
4         232890.87
2         166537.76
5          68792.30
8         126862.29
```

You can think of this result as being the starting point for further window aggregation. So, you can apply a window *SUM* aggregate to the expression that the alias *emptotal* represents. Unfortunately, you cannot apply it directly to the alias for reasons discussed in Chapter 1. (Remember the all-at-once concept?) But you can apply it to the underlying expression, as in *SUM(SUM(val)) OVER(…)*, and in your mind, think of it as *SUM(emptotal) OVER(…)*. And thus, you get the following:

```
SELECT empid,
   SUM(val) AS emptotal,
   SUM(val) / SUM(SUM(val)) OVER() * 100. AS pct
FROM Sales.OrderValues
GROUP BY empid;
```

> **Note** Nesting a group aggregate function within a window function shouldn't be confused with *nested window functions*, which I discussed earlier in the chapter.

If you wish, you can avoid the complexity of direct nesting of group functions within window functions by using table expressions such as CTEs. You can define a CTE based on the query that computes the grouped aggregate and have the outer query compute the windowed aggregate, like so:

```
WITH C AS
(
  SELECT empid,
     SUM(val) AS emptotal
  FROM Sales.OrderValues
  GROUP BY empid
)
SELECT empid, emptotal,
  emptotal / SUM(emptotal) OVER() * 100. AS pct
FROM C;
```

Consider another example for complexities related to windowed and grouped functions. You get a request that is a variation of an earlier request in this chapter. Query the *Sales.Orders* table, and return for each employee the distinct order dates along with the count of distinct customers handled by the current employee up to, and including, the current date. You make the following attempt:

```
WITH C AS
(
  SELECT empid, orderdate,
    CASE
      WHEN ROW_NUMBER() OVER(PARTITION BY empid, custid
                             ORDER BY orderdate) = 1
        THEN custid
```

```
      END AS distinct_custid
   FROM Sales.Orders
)
SELECT empid, orderdate,
   COUNT(distinct_custid) OVER(PARTITION BY empid
                               ORDER BY orderdate) AS numcusts
FROM C
GROUP BY empid, orderdate;
```

But when you run this query, you get the following error:

```
Msg 8120, Level 16, State 1, Line 12
Column 'C.distinct_custid' is invalid in the select list because it is not
contained in either an aggregate function or the GROUP BY clause.
```

The outer *COUNT* isn't a grouped aggregate; rather, it's a window aggregate. As such, it can operate only on elements that would have been valid if they were specified alone—namely, not as input to the window aggregate. Now ask yourself, absent the window aggregate, is the following a valid query (with the CTE definition removed for brevity)?

```
SELECT empid, orderdate, distinct_custid
FROM C
GROUP BY empid, orderdate;
```

It's clear that the answer is no. The attribute *distinct_custid* is invalid in the select list because it is not contained in either an aggregate function or the *GROUP BY* clause, which is pretty much what the error message says. What you need to do is apply a window *SUM* aggregate with a frame implementing a running total to a grouped *COUNT* aggregate that counts distinct occurrences, as shown in Listing 2-6.

LISTING 2-6 Nesting a Group Function within a Window Function

```
WITH C AS
(
  SELECT empid, orderdate,
    CASE
      WHEN ROW_NUMBER() OVER(PARTITION BY empid, custid
                             ORDER BY orderdate) = 1
        THEN custid
    END AS distinct_custid
  FROM Sales.Orders
)
SELECT empid, orderdate,
  SUM(COUNT(distinct_custid)) OVER(PARTITION BY empid
                                   ORDER BY orderdate) AS numcusts
FROM C
GROUP BY empid, orderdate;

empid       orderdate   numcusts
----------- ----------- -----------
1           2017-07-17  1
1           2017-08-01  2
1           2017-08-07  3
```

```
1                  2017-08-20   4
1                  2017-08-28   5
1                  2017-08-29   6
1                  2017-09-12   6
1                  2017-09-16   7
1                  2017-09-20   8
1                  2017-09-25   9
1                  2017-09-27   9
1                  2017-10-09   10
1                  2017-10-29   11
1                  2017-11-11   11
1                  2017-11-19   12
1                  2017-11-22   12
1                  2017-11-26   13
1                  2017-12-03   14
1                  2017-12-05   15
1                  2017-12-09   17
1                  2017-12-17   18
1                  2017-12-18   19
1                  2017-12-25   21
1                  2017-12-27   22
1                  2018-01-01   22
...
```

Of course, this is not the only way to achieve this desired result, and some of the other forms could be much more easily readable. The point was to illustrate examples for the concept of nesting a grouped aggregate within a window aggregate. Remember that according to logical query processing, window functions are evaluated in the *SELECT* or *ORDER BY* phase—after the *GROUP BY* phase. For this reason, grouped aggregates are visible as input expressions to window aggregates. Also recall that if the code becomes complex to follow, you can always use table expressions to avoid nesting the functions directly, and in this way make the code more readable.

Ranking Functions

The standard supports four window functions that deal with ranking calculations. Those are *ROW_NUMBER, NTILE, RANK*, and *DENSE_RANK*. The standard covers the first two as one category and the last two as another, probably due to determinism-related differences. I will provide more details shortly when describing the functions.

The easiest way to apply ranking calculations in T-SQL is using window ranking functions. Still, I will show alternative standard, set-based methods to achieve the same result for two reasons: one, because it can be an interesting exercise; two, I believe that it can help you understand the functions and their subtleties better. Note, though, that in practice it is strongly recommended that you stick to using the window functions because they are both much simpler and more efficient than the alternatives. I will get to the optimization details in Chapter 5.

Supported Windowing Elements

All four ranking functions support an optional window partition clause and a mandatory window order clause. If a window partition clause is not specified, the entire result set of the underlying query (recall the input to the *SELECT* phase) is considered one partition. As for the window ordering clause, it provides the ordering meaning for the calculation. As you can imagine, ranking rows without defining ordering has little meaning. For window ranking functions, ordering serves a different purpose than it does for functions that support framing, such as window aggregate functions. With the former, ordering is what gives logical meaning to the calculation itself. With the latter, ordering is tied to framing—namely, it serves a filtering purpose.

ROW_NUMBER

The ROW_NUMBER function computes a sequential row number starting with 1 within the respective window partition, based on the specified window ordering. Consider as an example the query in Listing 2-7.

LISTING 2-7 Query with ROW_NUMBER Function

```
SELECT orderid, val,
  ROW_NUMBER() OVER(ORDER BY orderid) AS rownum
FROM Sales.OrderValues;
```

Here's an abbreviated form of the output of this query:

```
orderid   val        rownum
--------  --------   -------
10248     440.00     1
10249     1863.40    2
10250     1552.60    3
10251     654.06     4
10252     3597.90    5
10253     1444.80    6
10254     556.62     7
10255     2490.50    8
10256     517.80     9
10257     1119.90    10
...
```

This calculation probably seems like a trivial thing, but there are a few important things to note here.

Because this query doesn't have a presentation *ORDER BY* clause, presentation ordering is not guaranteed. Therefore, you should consider presentation ordering here as arbitrary, or nondeterministic. In practice, SQL Server optimizes the query with the knowledge that absent a presentation *ORDER BY* clause, it can return the rows in any order. If you need to guarantee presentation ordering, make sure you add a presentation *ORDER BY* clause. If you want presentation ordering to be based on the calculated row number, you can specify the alias you assigned to the calculation in the presentation *ORDER BY* clause, like so:

```
SELECT orderid, val,
  ROW_NUMBER() OVER(ORDER BY orderid) AS rownum
FROM Sales.OrderValues
ORDER BY rownum;
```

But think of the row number calculation as simply generating another attribute in the result set of the query. Of course, if you like, you can have presentation ordering that is different from the window ordering, as in the following query:

```
SELECT orderid, val,
  ROW_NUMBER() OVER(ORDER BY orderid) AS rownum
FROM Sales.OrderValues
ORDER BY val DESC;
```

```
orderid   val         rownum
--------  ----------  -------
10865     16387.50    618
10981     15810.00    734
11030     12615.05    783
10889     11380.00    642
10417     11188.40    170
10817     10952.85    570
10897     10835.24    650
10479     10495.60    232
10540     10191.70    293
10691     10164.80    444
...
```

You can use the *COUNT* window aggregate to produce a calculation that is logically equivalent to the *ROW_NUMBER* function. Let *WPO* be the window partitioning and ordering specification used by a ROW_NUMBER function. Then *ROW_NUMBER() OVER(WPO)* is equivalent to *COUNT(*) OVER(WPO ROWS UNBOUNDED PRECEDING)*. As an example, following is a logical equivalent to the query presented earlier in Listing 2-7:

```
SELECT orderid, val,
  COUNT(*) OVER(ORDER BY orderid
                ROWS UNBOUNDED PRECEDING) AS rownum
FROM Sales.OrderValues;
```

As mentioned, it could be a good exercise to try and come up with alternatives to the use of window functions, never mind that the alternatives will tend to be more complicated and less efficient. With the *ROW_NUMBER* function being the focus at the moment, here's a set-based, standard alternative to the query in Listing 2-7 that doesn't use window functions:

```
SELECT orderid, val,
  (SELECT COUNT(*)
   FROM Sales.OrderValues AS O2
```

```
      WHERE O2.orderid <= O1.orderid) AS rownum
  FROM Sales.OrderValues AS O1;
```

This alternative uses a *COUNT* aggregate in a subquery to count how many rows have an ordering value (*orderid*, in our case) that is less than or equal to the current one. It's fairly simple when you have unique ordering that is based on a single attribute. Things can get tricky, though, when the ordering isn't unique, as I will demonstrate shortly when discussing determinism.

Determinism

When the window ordering is unique, as in the query in Listing 2-7, the *ROW_NUMBER* calculation is deterministic. This means that the query has only one correct result; hence, if you run it again without changing the input, you're guaranteed to get repeatable results. But if the window ordering isn't unique, the calculation is nondeterministic. The *ROW_NUMBER* function generates unique row numbers within the partition, even for rows with the same values in the window ordering attributes. Consider the following query as an example, which is followed by an abbreviated form of its output:

```
SELECT orderid, orderdate, val,
  ROW_NUMBER() OVER(ORDER BY orderdate DESC) AS rownum
FROM Sales.OrderValues;
```

```
orderid  orderdate    val       rownum
-------- -----------  --------   -------
11074    2019-05-06   232.09    1
11075    2019-05-06   498.10    2
11076    2019-05-06   792.75    3
11077    2019-05-06   1255.72   4
11070    2019-05-05   1629.98   5
11071    2019-05-05   484.50    6
11072    2019-05-05   5218.00   7
11073    2019-05-05   300.00    8
11067    2019-05-04   86.85     9
11068    2019-05-04   2027.08   10
...
```

Because the *orderdate* attribute isn't unique, the ordering among rows with the same *orderdate* value should be considered arbitrary. Technically, there's more than one correct result for this query. Take the four rows with the order date 2019-05-06 as an example. Any arrangement of the row numbers 1 through 4 in those rows is considered valid. So, if you run the query again, theoretically you can get a different arrangement than the current one—never mind the likelihood for this to happen due to implementation-specific aspects in SQL Server (optimization).

If you need to guarantee repeatable results, you need to make the query deterministic. This can be achieved by adding a tiebreaker to the window ordering specification, making it unique within the partition. As an example, the following query achieves unique window ordering by adding *orderid DESC* to the list, like so:

```
SELECT orderid, orderdate, val,
  ROW_NUMBER() OVER(ORDER BY orderdate DESC, orderid DESC) AS rownum
```

```
FROM Sales.OrderValues;

orderid   orderdate    val       rownum
--------  -----------  --------  -------
11077     2019-05-06   1255.72   1
11076     2019-05-06   792.75    2
11075     2019-05-06   498.10    3
11074     2019-05-06   232.09    4
11073     2019-05-05   300.00    5
11072     2019-05-05   5218.00   6
11071     2019-05-05   484.50    7
11070     2019-05-05   1629.98   8
11069     2019-05-04   360.00    9
11068     2019-05-04   2027.08   10
...
```

With window functions, calculating row numbers in a deterministic way is a simple thing. Trying to achieve the equivalent without window functions is trickier but doable:

```
SELECT orderdate, orderid, val,
  (SELECT COUNT(*)
   FROM Sales.OrderValues AS O2
   WHERE O2.orderdate >= O1.orderdate
     AND (O2.orderdate > O1.orderdate
          OR O2.orderid >= O1.orderid)) AS rownum
FROM Sales.OrderValues AS O1;
```

Back to the *ROW_NUMBER* function: you saw that it can be used to create nondeterministic calculations when using nonunique ordering. So, nondeterminism is allowed, but what's strange is that it's not allowed entirely. What I mean by this is that the *ORDER BY* clause is mandatory. But what if you just want to produce unique row numbers within the partition, in no particular order? You want to issue a query such as this:

```
SELECT orderid, orderdate, val,
  ROW_NUMBER() OVER() AS rownum
FROM Sales.OrderValues;
```

But as mentioned, the *ORDER BY* clause is mandatory in ranking functions, and SQL Server will produce an error:

```
Msg 4112, Level 15, State 1, Line 2
The function 'ROW_NUMBER' must have an OVER clause with ORDER BY.
```

You can try to be smart and specify a constant in the ORDER BY list, like so:

```
SELECT orderid, orderdate, val,
  ROW_NUMBER() OVER(ORDER BY NULL) AS rownum
FROM Sales.OrderValues;
```

But then SQL Server will complain and generate the following error:

```
Msg 5309, Level 16, State 1, Line 2
Windowed functions and NEXT VALUE FOR functions do not support constants as ORDER
BY clause expressions.
```

A solution exists, though, and I will present it shortly (after the "OVER Clause and Sequences" sidebar).

OVER Clause and Sequences

You might wonder what the relevance is of the *NEXT VALUE FOR* function in the error message you get when attempting to use a constant in the *OVER* clause. It's related to SQL Server's extended support for sequences compared to the SQL standard. A sequence is an object in the database used to autogenerate numbers, often to be used as keys. Here's an example for code creating a sequence object called *dbo.Seq1*:

```
CREATE SEQUENCE dbo.Seq1 AS INT MINVALUE 1;
```

You use the *NEXT VALUE FOR* function to obtain new values from the sequence. Here's an example:

```
SELECT NEXT VALUE FOR dbo.Seq1;
```

You can invoke this function as part of a query that returns multiple rows, like so:

```
SELECT orderid, orderdate, val,
    NEXT VALUE FOR dbo.Seq1 AS seqval
FROM Sales.OrderValues;
```

This code is standard. SQL Server extends the capabilities of the *NEXT VALUE FOR* function, thereby allowing you to provide ordering specification in an OVER clause similar to the one used by window functions. This way, you can provide a guarantee that the sequence values reflect the desired ordering. Here's an example using the extended *NEXT VALUE FOR* function:

```
SELECT orderid, orderdate, val,
    NEXT VALUE FOR dbo.Seq1 OVER(ORDER BY orderdate, orderid) AS seqval
FROM Sales.OrderValues;
```

The same aspects of determinism apply to the OVER clause of the *NEXT VALUE FOR* function as they do to window functions.

So, there's no direct way to get row numbers without ordering, but SQL Server is happy when given a subquery returning a constant as a window ordering element. Here's an example:

```
SELECT orderid, orderdate, val,
    ROW_NUMBER() OVER(ORDER BY (SELECT NULL)) AS rownum
FROM Sales.OrderValues;
```

```
orderid   orderdate    val       rownum
--------  -----------  --------  -------
10248     2017-07-04   440.00    1
10249     2017-07-05   1863.40   2
10250     2017-07-08   1552.60   3
10251     2017-07-08   654.06    4
10252     2017-07-09   3597.90   5
10253     2017-07-10   1444.80   6
10254     2017-07-11   556.62    7
10255     2017-07-12   2490.50   8
10256     2017-07-15   517.80    9
10257     2017-07-16   1119.90   10
...
```

Perhaps even stranger is that the following query fails:

```
SELECT orderid, orderdate, val,
  ROW_NUMBER() OVER(ORDER BY 1/1) AS rownum
FROM Sales.OrderValues;
```

It generates the following error:

```
Msg 5308, Level 16, State 1, Line 1238
Windowed functions, aggregates and NEXT VALUE FOR functions do not support
integer indices as ORDER BY clause expressions.
```

However, oddly, the following query runs successfully:

```
SELECT orderid, orderdate, val,
  ROW_NUMBER() OVER(ORDER BY 1/0) AS rownum
FROM Sales.OrderValues;
```

I'll provide more detail about computing row numbers with no ordering in Chapter 5 when discussing the optimization of window functions.

NTILE

The NTILE function allows you to arrange the rows within the window partition in roughly equally sized tiles, based on the input number of tiles and specified window ordering. For example, suppose that you want to arrange the rows from the OrderValues view in 10 equally sized tiles based on *val* ordering. There are 830 rows in the view; hence, with 10 requested tiles, the tile size is 83 (that's 830 divided by 10). So, the first 83 rows (the first tenth) based on *val* ordering will be assigned with tile number 1, the next 83 with tile number 2, and so on. Listing 2-8 shows a query calculating both row numbers and tile numbers, followed by an abbreviated form of its output.

LISTING 2-8 Query Computing Row Numbers and Tile Numbers

```
SELECT orderid, val,
  ROW_NUMBER() OVER(ORDER BY val) AS rownum,
  NTILE(10) OVER(ORDER BY val) AS tile
FROM Sales.OrderValues;
```

```
orderid   val        rownum   tile
--------  ---------  -------  -----
10782     12.50      1        1
10807     18.40      2        1
10586     23.80      3        1
10767     28.00      4        1
10898     30.00      5        1
...
10708     180.40     78       1
10476     180.48     79       1
10313     182.40     80       1
10810     187.00     81       1
11065     189.42     82       1
10496     190.00     83       1
10793     191.10     84       2
10428     192.00     85       2
10520     200.00     86       2
11040     200.00     87       2
11043     210.00     88       2
...
10417     11188.40   826      10
10889     11380.00   827      10
11030     12615.05   828      10
10981     15810.00   829      10
10865     16387.50   830      10
```

In case you're thinking that tiling is similar to paging, let me warn you not to confuse the two. With paging, the page size is a constant and the number of pages is dynamic—it's a result of the count of rows in the query result set divided by the page size. With tiling, the number of tiles is a constant, and the tile size is dynamic—it's a result of the count of rows divided by the requested number of tiles. It's obvious what the uses for paging are. Tiling is usually used for analytical purposes—ones that involve the need to distribute data to a predetermined, equally sized number of buckets based on some measure ordering.

There's no built-in function that computes page numbers in T-SQL, but it's actually easy to compute those based on row numbers. Let *rownum* be the row number of a row (computed with the *ROW_NUMBER* function) and *pagesize* be the desired page size. The page number of the row is computed as *pagenum = (rownum - 1) / pagesize + 1*, where the division operator (/) applies integer division (the default in T-SQL when the operands are integer). For example, suppose that you want to compute page numbers with a page size of 10. You use the query in Listing 2-9 to achieve this.

LISTING 2-9 Query Computing Page Numbers

```
SELECT orderid, val,
  ROW_NUMBER() OVER(ORDER BY val) AS rownum,
  (ROW_NUMBER() OVER(ORDER BY val) - 1) / 10 + 1 AS pagenum
FROM Sales.OrderValues;
```

```
orderid   val        rownum   pagenum
--------  ---------  -------  --------
10782     12.50      1        1
10807     18.40      2        1
10586     23.80      3        1
10767     28.00      4        1
10898     30.00      5        1
10900     33.75      6        1
10883     36.00      7        1
11051     36.00      8        1
10815     40.00      9        1
10674     45.00      10       1
11057     45.00      11       2
10271     48.00      12       2
10602     48.75      13       2
10422     49.80      14       2
10738     52.35      15       2
10754     55.20      16       2
10631     55.80      17       2
10620     57.50      18       2
10963     57.80      19       2
11037     60.00      20       2
10683     63.00      21       3
...
10515     9921.30    820      82
10691     10164.80   821      83
10540     10191.70   822      83
10479     10495.60   823      83
10897     10835.24   824      83
10817     10952.85   825      83
10417     11188.40   826      83
10889     11380.00   827      83
11030     12615.05   828      83
10981     15810.00   829      83
10865     16387.50   830      83
```

Back to the result of the query that calculates both row numbers and tile numbers: as you can see, the two are closely related. In fact, you could think of a tile number as a calculation that is based on a row number. Recall from the previous section that if the window ordering is not unique, the *ROW_NUMBER* function is nondeterministic. If tiling is a calculation that is conceptually based on row numbers, this means that the *NTILE* calculation is also nondeterministic if the window ordering is nonunique. This means that there can be multiple correct results for a given query. Another way to look at it is that two rows with the same ordering values can end up with different tile numbers. The same applies to our page number calculation, of course. If you need to guarantee determinism, you can follow the same recommendation I gave to produce deterministic row numbers—namely, add a tiebreaker to the window ordering, like so:

```
SELECT orderid, val,
  ROW_NUMBER() OVER(ORDER BY val, orderid) AS rownum,
  NTILE(10) OVER(ORDER BY val, orderid) AS tile
FROM Sales.OrderValues;
```

Now the query has only one correct result.

> **Note** You need to be very careful with nondeterministic windowed calculations. For example, when using such calculations within a table expression like a CTE, and the outer query has multiple references to the CTE, each reference gets inlined separately. In such a case, you can end up with different results of the computation for the same row in the different evaluations. Also, in multiple executions of the query, the same row can get different results from a nondeterministic calculation, even if the underlying data doesn't change. Therefore, it might be a good idea to always add a tiebreaker to the window ordering of calculations like *NTILE* and *ROW_NUMBER* to make them deterministic. For more details on bugs, pitfalls, and best practices related to nondeterministic calculations, see the following article: https://sqlperformance.com/2019/03/t-sql-queries/bugs-pitfalls-best-practices-determinism.

Earlier when describing the *NTILE* function, I explained that it allows you to arrange the rows within the window partition in *roughly* equally sized tiles. The reason I used the term *roughly* is because the count of rows in the underlying query might not be evenly divisible by the requested number of tiles. For example, suppose that you wanted to arrange the rows from the *OrderValues* view in 100 tiles. When you divide 830 by 100, you get a quotient of 8 and a remainder of 30. This means that the base tile cardinality is 8, but a subset of the tiles will get an extra row. The *NTILE* function doesn't attempt to evenly distribute the extra rows across the tiles with even spacing; rather, it adds one row to each tile, starting with the first, until the remainder is gone. With a remainder of 30, the cardinality of the first 30 tiles will be one greater than the base tile cardinality. So, the first 30 tiles will have 9 rows and the last 70 tiles will have 8 rows, as the query in Listing 2-10 shows.

LISTING 2-10 Query Showing Uneven Distribution of Extra Rows among Tiles

```
SELECT orderid, val,
  ROW_NUMBER() OVER(ORDER BY val, orderid) AS rownum,
  NTILE(100) OVER(ORDER BY val, orderid) AS tile
FROM Sales.OrderValues;
```

orderid	val	rownum	tile
10782	12.50	1	1
10807	18.40	2	1
10586	23.80	3	1
10767	28.00	4	1
10898	30.00	5	1
10900	33.75	6	1
10883	36.00	7	1
11051	36.00	8	1
10815	40.00	9	1
10674	45.00	10	2
11057	45.00	11	2
10271	48.00	12	2
10602	48.75	13	2
10422	49.80	14	2

10738	52.35	15	2
10754	55.20	16	2
10631	55.80	17	2
10620	57.50	18	2
10963	57.80	19	3
...			
10816	8446.45	814	98
10353	8593.28	815	99
10514	8623.45	816	99
11032	8902.50	817	99
10424	9194.56	818	99
10372	9210.90	819	99
10515	9921.30	820	99
10691	10164.80	821	99
10540	10191.70	822	99
10479	10495.60	823	100
10897	10835.24	824	100
10817	10952.85	825	100
10417	11188.40	826	100
10889	11380.00	827	100
11030	12615.05	828	100
10981	15810.00	829	100
10865	16387.50	830	100

Continuing our custom, as an exercise, try to come up with an alternative to the *NTILE* function without using window functions.

I'll show one way to achieve the task. First, here's code that calculates the tile number when given the cardinality, number of tiles, and row number as inputs:

```
DECLARE @cnt AS INT = 830, @numtiles AS INT = 100, @rownum AS INT = 42;

WITH C1 AS
(
  SELECT
    @cnt / @numtiles     AS basetilesize,
    @cnt / @numtiles + 1 AS extendedtilesize,
    @cnt % @numtiles     AS remainder
),
C2 AS
(
  SELECT *, extendedtilesize * remainder AS cutoffrow
  FROM C1
)
SELECT
  CASE WHEN @rownum <= cutoffrow
    THEN (@rownum - 1) / extendedtilesize + 1
    ELSE remainder + (((@rownum - cutoffrow) - 1) / basetilesize + 1
  END AS tile
FROM C2;
```

The calculation is pretty much self-explanatory. For the given inputs, this code returns 5 as the tile number.

Next, apply this calculation to the rows from the *OrderValues* view. Use the *COUNT* aggregate to get the result set's cardinality instead of the *@cnt* input, and use the logic presented earlier to calculate row numbers without window functions instead of the *@rownum* input, as shown in Listing 2-11.

LISTING 2-11 Query Computing Tile Numbers without the NTILE Function

```
DECLARE @numtiles AS INT = 100;

WITH C1 AS
(
  SELECT
    COUNT(*) / @numtiles AS basetilesize,
    COUNT(*) / @numtiles + 1 AS extendedtilesize,
    COUNT(*) % @numtiles AS remainder
  FROM Sales.OrderValues
),
C2 AS
(
  SELECT *, extendedtilesize * remainder AS cutoffrow
  FROM C1
),
C3 AS
(
  SELECT O1.orderid, O1.val,
    (SELECT COUNT(*)
     FROM Sales.OrderValues AS O2
     WHERE O2.val <= O1.val
       AND (O2.val < O1.val
            OR O2.orderid <= O1.orderid)) AS rownum
  FROM Sales.OrderValues AS O1
)
SELECT C3.*,
  CASE WHEN C3.rownum <= C2.cutoffrow
    THEN (C3.rownum - 1) / C2.extendedtilesize + 1
    ELSE C2.remainder + ((C3.rownum - C2.cutoffrow) - 1) / C2.basetilesize + 1
  END AS tile
FROM C3 CROSS JOIN C2;
```

As usual, don't do this at home! This exercise is a teaching aid; the performance of this technique in SQL Server is horrible compared with that of the *NTILE* function.

RANK and DENSE_RANK

The *RANK* and *DENSE_RANK* functions are calculations similar to the *ROW_NUMBER* function, only unlike the *ROW_NUMBER* function they don't have to produce unique values within the window partition. When the window ordering direction is ascending, *RANK* calculates one more than the number of rows with an ordering value less than the current one in the partition. *DENSE_RANK* calculates one more than the number of distinct ordering values that are less than the current one in the partition. When the window ordering direction is descending, *RANK* calculates one more than the number of rows with an ordering value greater than the current one in the partition. *DENSE_RANK* calculates one more than the number of distinct ordering values greater than the current one in the partition. As an example, here's a query calculating row numbers, rank, and dense rank values, all using the default window partitioning and *orderdate DESC* ordering:

```
SELECT orderid, orderdate, val,
  ROW_NUMBER() OVER(ORDER BY orderdate DESC) AS rownum,
  RANK()       OVER(ORDER BY orderdate DESC) AS rnk,
  DENSE_RANK() OVER(ORDER BY orderdate DESC) AS drnk
FROM Sales.OrderValues;
```

orderid	orderdate	val	rownum	rnk	drnk
11077	2019-05-06	232.09	1	1	1
11076	2019-05-06	498.10	2	1	1
11075	2019-05-06	792.75	3	1	1
11074	2019-05-06	1255.72	4	1	1
11073	2019-05-05	1629.98	5	5	2
11072	2019-05-05	484.50	6	5	2
11071	2019-05-05	5218.00	7	5	2
11070	2019-05-05	300.00	8	5	2
11069	2019-05-04	86.85	9	9	3
11068	2019-05-04	2027.08	10	9	3

...

The *orderdate* attribute is not unique. Still, observe that row numbers are unique. The rank and dense rank values aren't unique. All rows with the same order date—for example, *2019-05-05*—got the same *rank 5* and dense *rank 2*. *Rank 5* means that there are four rows with greater order dates (notice the ordering direction is descending), and *dense rank 2* means that there's one greater distinct order date.

The alternative to the *RANK* and *DENSE_RANK* functions that doesn't use window functions is pretty straightforward:

```
SELECT orderid, orderdate, val,
  (SELECT COUNT(*)
   FROM Sales.OrderValues AS O2
   WHERE O2.orderdate > O1.orderdate) + 1 AS rnk,
  (SELECT COUNT(DISTINCT orderdate)
   FROM Sales.OrderValues AS O2
   WHERE O2.orderdate > O1.orderdate) + 1 AS drnk
FROM Sales.OrderValues AS O1;
```

To calculate rank, you count the number of rows with a greater ordering value (remember, our example uses descending ordering) and add 1. To calculate dense rank, you count the distinct greater ordering values and add 1.

Determinism

As you might have figured out yourself, both the *RANK* and *DENSE_RANK* functions are deterministic by definition. Given the same ordering value—never mind whether they are nonunique—they produce the same ranking value. In fact, the two functions are usually interesting only when the ordering is nonunique. When the ordering is unique, both produce the same results as the *ROW_NUMBER* function.

Statistical Functions

Window statistical, or distribution, functions provide information about the distribution of data and are used mostly for statistical analysis. SQL Server supports two kinds of window distribution functions: rank distribution and inverse distribution. There are two rank distribution functions: *PERCENT_RANK* and *CUME_DIST*. And there are two inverse distribution functions: *PERCENTILE_CONT* and *PERCENTILE_DISC*.

In my examples, I will use a table called *Scores* that holds student test scores. Run the following code to present the contents of the *Scores* table:

```
SELECT testid, studentid, score
FROM Stats.Scores;

testid      studentid   score
----------  ----------  -----
Test ABC    Student A    95
Test ABC    Student B    80
Test ABC    Student C    55
Test ABC    Student D    55
Test ABC    Student E    50
Test ABC    Student F    80
Test ABC    Student G    95
Test ABC    Student H    65
Test ABC    Student I    75
Test XYZ    Student A    95
Test XYZ    Student B    80
Test XYZ    Student C    55
Test XYZ    Student D    55
Test XYZ    Student E    50
Test XYZ    Student F    80
Test XYZ    Student G    95
Test XYZ    Student H    65
Test XYZ    Student I    75
Test XYZ    Student J    95
```

Supported Windowing Elements

Window rank distribution functions support an optional window partition clause and a mandatory window order clause. Window inverse distribution functions support an optional window partition clause. There is also ordering relevance to inverse distribution functions, but it's not part of the window specification. Rather, it's in a separate clause called WITHIN GROUP, which I'll describe when I get to the details of the functions.

Rank Distribution Functions

According to the SQL standard, distribution functions compute the relative rank of a row in the window partition, expressed as a ratio between 0 and 1—what most of us think of as a percentage. The two variants—*PERCENT_RANK* and *CUME_DIST*—perform the computation slightly differently.

- Let *rk* be the *RANK* of the row using the same window specification as the distribution function's window specification.

- Let *nr* be the count of rows in the window partition.

- Let *np* be the number of rows that precede or are peers of the current one (the same as the minimum *rk* that is greater than the current *rk* minus 1, or *nr* if the current *rk* is the maximum).

Then *PERCENT_RANK* is calculated as follows: *(rk – 1) / (nr – 1)*. And *CUME_DIST* is calculated as follows: *np / nr*. The query in Listing 2-12 computes both the percentile rank and cumulative distribution of student test scores, partitioned by *testid* and ordered by *score*.

LISTING 2-12 Query Computing PERCENT_RANK and CUME_DIST

```
SELECT testid, studentid, score,
  PERCENT_RANK() OVER(PARTITION BY testid ORDER BY score) AS percentrank,
  CUME_DIST() OVER(PARTITION BY testid ORDER BY score) AS cumedist
FROM Stats.Scores;
```

Here is the output of this query:

testid	studentid	score	percentrank	cumedist
Test ABC	Student E	50	0.000	0.111
Test ABC	Student C	55	0.125	0.333
Test ABC	Student D	55	0.125	0.333
Test ABC	Student H	65	0.375	0.444
Test ABC	Student I	75	0.500	0.556
Test ABC	Student F	80	0.625	0.778
Test ABC	Student B	80	0.625	0.778
Test ABC	Student A	95	0.875	1.000
Test ABC	Student G	95	0.875	1.000
Test XYZ	Student E	50	0.000	0.100
Test XYZ	Student C	55	0.111	0.300
Test XYZ	Student D	55	0.111	0.300
Test XYZ	Student H	65	0.333	0.400
Test XYZ	Student I	75	0.444	0.500
Test XYZ	Student B	80	0.556	0.700
Test XYZ	Student F	80	0.556	0.700
Test XYZ	Student G	95	0.778	1.000
Test XYZ	Student J	95	0.778	1.000
Test XYZ	Student A	95	0.778	1.000

The output of this query was formatted for clarity.

Unless you have a statistical background, it's probably hard to make sense of the computations. Loosely speaking, try to think of the percentile rank in our example as indicating the percent of students who have a lower test score than the current score, and think of cumulative distribution as indicating the percentage of students who have a lower score or the same test score as the current score. Just remember that when calculating the two, the divisor in the former case is *(nr – 1)* and in the latter case it's *nr*.

For the sake of the exercise, calculating the percentile rank without the *PERCENT_RANK* function is pretty straightforward because *rk* can be computed with the *RANK* window function and *nr* can be calculated with the *COUNT* window aggregate function. Computing cumulative distribution is a bit trickier because the computation for the current row requires the *rk* value associated with a different row. The computation is supposed to return the minimum *rk* that is greater than the current *rk*, or *nr* if the current *rk* is the maximum one. You can use a correlated subquery to achieve this task.

Here's a query computing both percentile rank and cumulative distribution without the built-in *PERCENT_RANK* and *CUME_DIST* functions:

```
WITH C AS
(
  SELECT testid, studentid, score,
    RANK() OVER(PARTITION BY testid ORDER BY score) AS rk,
    COUNT(*) OVER(PARTITION BY testid) AS nr
  FROM Stats.Scores
)
SELECT testid, studentid, score,
  1.0 * (rk - 1) / (nr - 1) AS percentrank,
  1.0 * (SELECT COALESCE(MIN(C2.rk) - 1, C1.nr)
         FROM C AS C2
         WHERE C2.testid = C1.testid
           AND C2.rk > C1.rk) / nr AS cumedist
FROM C AS C1;
```

The reason for multiplying the numeric value 1.0 by the rest of the computation is to force implicit conversion of the integer operands to numeric ones; otherwise, you will get integer division.

As another example, the following query computes the percentile rank and cumulative distribution of employee order counts:

```
SELECT empid, COUNT(*) AS numorders,
  PERCENT_RANK() OVER(ORDER BY COUNT(*)) AS percentrank,
  CUME_DIST() OVER(ORDER BY COUNT(*)) AS cumedist
FROM Sales.Orders
GROUP BY empid;
```

empid	numorders	percentrank	cumedist
5	42	0.000	0.111
9	43	0.125	0.222
6	67	0.250	0.333
7	72	0.375	0.444

2	96	0.500	0.556
8	104	0.625	0.667
1	123	0.750	0.778
3	127	0.875	0.889
4	156	1.000	1.000

Note the mixed use of grouped aggregate functions and window rank distribution functions—that's very similar to the previously discussed mixed use of grouped aggregate functions and window aggregate functions.

Inverse Distribution Functions

Inverse distribution functions, more commonly known as *percentiles*, perform a computation you can think of as the inverse of rank distribution functions. Recall that rank distribution functions compute the relative rank of the current row in the window partition and are expressed as a ratio between 0 and 1 (percent). Inverse distribution functions accept a percentage as input and return the value from the group (or an interpolated value) that this percentage represents. Loosely speaking, given a percentage *p* as input and ordering in the group based on *ordcol*, the returned percentile is the *ordcol* value with respect to which *p* percent of the *ordcol* values are less than it. Perhaps the most known percentile is *0.5* (the fiftieth percentile), more commonly known as the *median*. As an example, given a group of values *2, 3, 7, 1759, 43112609*, the percentile *0.5* is *7*.

Recall that rank distribution functions are window functions, and it makes a lot of sense for them to be designed as such. Each row can get a different percentile rank than the others in the same partition. But inverse distribution functions are supposed to accept one input percentage, as well as ordering specification in the group, and compute a single result value per group. So, you can see that, in terms of design, it makes more sense for them to be used like grouped functions—that is, apply them to groups in the context of grouped queries, like so:

```
SELECT groupcol, PERCENTILE_FUNCTION(0.5) WITHIN GROUP(ORDER BY ordcol) AS median
FROM T1
GROUP BY groupcol;
```

Observe the *WITHIN GROUP* clause, where you define the ordering specification within the group because this is not a window function.

Sure enough, the SQL standard defines inverse distribution functions as a type of what they call an *ordered set function*, which is a type of an aggregate function and can be used as grouped aggregate functions. Alas, in SQL Server, inverse distribution functions are actually implemented only as window functions that compute the same result value for all rows in the same partition. The grouped version wasn't implemented.

In this section, I will describe the supported inverse distribution functions and provide a couple of examples for using them as window functions. However, because the more common need is to calculate those per group, I will postpone part of the coverage of the topic, including alternative methods, to Chapter 3, "Ordered Set Functions."

There are two variants of inverse distribution functions: *PERCENTILE_DISC* and *PERCENTILE_CONT*.

The *PERCENTILE_DISC* function (*DISC* for *discrete distribution model*) returns the first value in the group whose cumulative distribution (see the *CUME_DIST* function discussed earlier) is greater than or equal to the input, assuming you treat the group as a window partition with the same ordering as that defined within the group. Consider, for example, the query in Listing 2-12 from the previous section calculating the percentile rank and cumulative distribution of student test scores, and its output. Then the function *PERCENTILE_DISC(0.5) WITHIN GROUP(ORDER BY score) OVER(PARTITION BY testid)* will return the score *75* for the test named *Test ABC* because that's the score associated with the cumulative distribution *0.556*, which is the first cumulative distribution that is greater than or equal to the input *0.5*. Here's the previous output with the relevant row bolded:

```
testid      studentid  score percentrank  cumedist
----------  ---------- ----- ------------ ---------
Test ABC    Student E  50    0.000        0.111
Test ABC    Student C  55    0.125        0.333
Test ABC    Student D  55    0.125        0.333
Test ABC    Student H  65    0.375        0.444
Test ABC    Student I  75    0.500        0.556
Test ABC    Student F  80    0.625        0.778
Test ABC    Student B  80    0.625        0.778
Test ABC    Student A  95    0.875        1.000
Test ABC    Student G  95    0.875        1.000
Test XYZ    Student E  50    0.000        0.100
Test XYZ    Student C  55    0.111        0.300
Test XYZ    Student D  55    0.111        0.300
Test XYZ    Student H  65    0.333        0.400
Test XYZ    Student I  75    0.444        0.500
Test XYZ    Student B  80    0.556        0.700
Test XYZ    Student F  80    0.556        0.700
Test XYZ    Student G  95    0.778        1.000
Test XYZ    Student J  95    0.778        1.000
Test XYZ    Student A  95    0.778        1.000
```

The *PERCENTILE_CONT* function (*CONT* for *continuous distribution model*) is a bit trickier to explain. Consider the function *PERCENTILE_CONT(@pct) WITHIN GROUP(ORDER BY score)*.

- Let n be the count of rows in the group.

- Let a be $@pct*(n-1)$, let i be the integer part of a, and let f be the fraction part of a.

- Let *row0* and *row1* be the rows whose zero-based row numbers are in *FLOOR(a)*, *CEILING(a)*. Here I'm assuming the row numbers are calculated using the same window partitioning and ordering as the group and order of the *PERCENTILE_CONT* function.

Then *PERCENTILE_CONT* is computed as *row0.score + f * (row1.score – row0.score)*. This is an interpolation of the values in the two rows assuming continuous distribution (based on the fraction part of a).

As a simple, plain-English example, think of a median calculation when there is an even number of rows. You interpolate the values assuming continuous distribution. The interpolated value falls right in the middle between the two middle points, meaning that it's the average of the two middle points.

Listing 2-13 shows an example computing the median test scores using both inverse distribution functions as window functions.

LISTING 2-13 Query Computing Median Test Scores with Window Functions

```
DECLARE @pct AS FLOAT = 0.5;

SELECT testid, studentid, score,
  PERCENTILE_DISC(@pct) WITHIN GROUP(ORDER BY score)
    OVER(PARTITION BY testid) AS percentiledisc,
  PERCENTILE_CONT(@pct) WITHIN GROUP(ORDER BY score)
    OVER(PARTITION BY testid) AS percentilecont
FROM Stats.Scores;
```

testid	studentid	score	percentiledisc	percentilecont
Test ABC	Student E	50	75	75
Test ABC	Student C	55	75	75
Test ABC	Student D	55	75	75
Test ABC	Student H	65	75	75
Test ABC	Student I	75	75	75
Test ABC	Student B	80	75	75
Test ABC	Student F	80	75	75
Test ABC	Student A	95	75	75
Test ABC	Student G	95	75	75
Test XYZ	Student E	50	75	77.5
Test XYZ	Student C	55	75	77.5
Test XYZ	Student D	55	75	77.5
Test XYZ	Student H	65	75	77.5
Test XYZ	Student I	75	75	77.5
Test XYZ	Student B	80	75	77.5
Test XYZ	Student F	80	75	77.5
Test XYZ	Student A	95	75	77.5
Test XYZ	Student G	95	75	77.5
Test XYZ	Student J	95	75	77.5

Listing 2-14 shows another example computing the tenth percentile (0.1).

LISTING 2-14 Query Computing Tenth Percentile Test Scores with Window Functions

```
DECLARE @pct AS FLOAT = 0.1;

SELECT testid, studentid, score,
  PERCENTILE_DISC(@pct) WITHIN GROUP(ORDER BY score)
    OVER(PARTITION BY testid) AS percentiledisc,
  PERCENTILE_CONT(@pct) WITHIN GROUP(ORDER BY score)
    OVER(PARTITION BY testid) AS percentilecont
FROM Stats.Scores;
```

```
testid       studentid   score  percentiledisc  percentilecont
----------   ----------  -----  --------------  ----------------------
Test ABC     Student E   50     50              54
Test ABC     Student C   55     50              54
Test ABC     Student D   55     50              54
Test ABC     Student H   65     50              54
Test ABC     Student I   75     50              54
Test ABC     Student B   80     50              54
Test ABC     Student F   80     50              54
Test ABC     Student A   95     50              54
Test ABC     Student G   95     50              54
Test XYZ     Student E   50     50              54.5
Test XYZ     Student C   55     50              54.5
Test XYZ     Student D   55     50              54.5
Test XYZ     Student H   65     50              54.5
Test XYZ     Student I   75     50              54.5
Test XYZ     Student B   80     50              54.5
Test XYZ     Student F   80     50              54.5
Test XYZ     Student A   95     50              54.5
Test XYZ     Student G   95     50              54.5
Test XYZ     Student J   95     50              54.5
```

As mentioned, I will provide more details in Chapter 3 about inverse distribution functions, including alternative methods to calculate those, as part of the discussion about ordered set functions.

Offset Functions

Window offset functions include two categories of functions. One category contains functions whose offset is relative to the current row, including the *LAG* and *LEAD* functions. Another category contains functions whose offset is relative to the start or end of the window frame, including the functions *FIRST_VALUE*, *LAST_VALUE*, and *NTH_VALUE*. SQL Server supports *LAG*, *LEAD*, *FIRST_VALUE*, and *LAST_VALUE*, but it does not support *NTH_VALUE*.

Supported Windowing Elements

The functions in the first category (*LAG* and *LEAD*) support a window partition clause as well as a window order clause. The latter is the one that gives meaning to the function's offset, whether the implicit offset of 1 or an explicit offset that you mention as the function's third argument. The functions in the second category (*FIRST_VALUE*, *LAST_VALUE*, and *NTH_VALUE*) also support a window frame clause in addition to the window partition and window order clauses.

In the SQL Standard, all offset functions support indicating a *null treatment* element, where you indicate either *RESPECT NULLS* or *IGNORE NULLS*. SQL Server doesn't support this element yet. I'll explain what it means later in this section and provide an alternative that does work in SQL Server.

LAG and LEAD

The *LAG* and *LEAD* functions allow you to return a value expression from a row in the window partition that is in a given offset before (*LAG*) or after (*LEAD*) the current row. The default offset if one is not specified is 1.

As an example, the query in Listing 2-15 returns the current order value for each customer order, as well as the values of the previous and next orders by the same customer.

LISTING 2-15 Query with LAG and LEAD

```
SELECT custid, orderdate, orderid, val,
  LAG(val)  OVER(PARTITION BY custid
                ORDER BY orderdate, orderid) AS prevval,
  LEAD(val) OVER(PARTITION BY custid
                ORDER BY orderdate, orderid) AS nextval
FROM Sales.OrderValues;
```

```
custid  orderdate    orderid  val       prevval   nextval
-------  -----------  -------  --------  --------  --------
1        2018-08-25   10643    814.50    NULL      878.00
1        2018-10-03   10692    878.00    814.50    330.00
1        2018-10-13   10702    330.00    878.00    845.80
1        2019-01-15   10835    845.80    330.00    471.20
1        2019-03-16   10952    471.20    845.80    933.50
1        2019-04-09   11011    933.50    471.20    NULL
2        2017-09-18   10308    88.80     NULL      479.75
2        2018-08-08   10625    479.75    88.80     320.00
2        2018-11-28   10759    320.00    479.75    514.40
2        2019-03-04   10926    514.40    320.00    NULL
3        2017-11-27   10365    403.20    NULL      749.06
3        2018-04-15   10507    749.06    403.20    1940.85
3        2018-05-13   10535    1940.85   749.06    2082.00
3        2018-06-19   10573    2082.00   1940.85   813.37
3        2018-09-22   10677    813.37    2082.00   375.50
3        2018-09-25   10682    375.50    813.37    660.00
3        2019-01-28   10856    660.00    375.50    NULL
...
```

The output is shown here abbreviated and formatted for clarity.

Because explicit offsets weren't indicated here, the query assumes an offset of 1 by default. Because the functions partition the data by *custid*, the calculations look for relative rows only within the same customer partition. As for the window ordering, what "previous" and "next" mean is determined by *orderdate* ordering, and by *orderid* as a tiebreaker. Observe in the query output that *LAG* returns *NULL* for the first row in the window partition because there's no row before the first one and, similarly, *LEAD* returns *NULL* for the last row.

If you want to use an offset other than 1, you need to specify it after the input value expression, as in the query shown in Listing 2-16.

LISTING 2-16 Query Using LAG with an Explicit Offset

```
SELECT custid, orderdate, orderid,
  LAG(val, 3) OVER(PARTITION BY custid
                   ORDER BY orderdate, orderid) AS prev3val
FROM Sales.OrderValues;
```

```
custid  orderdate    orderid  prev3val
-------  -----------  -------  ---------
1        2018-08-25   10643    NULL
1        2018-10-03   10692    NULL
1        2018-10-13   10702    NULL
1        2019-01-15   10835    814.50
1        2019-03-16   10952    878.00
1        2019-04-09   11011    330.00
2        2017-09-18   10308    NULL
2        2018-08-08   10625    NULL
2        2018-11-28   10759    NULL
2        2019-03-04   10926    88.80
3        2017-11-27   10365    NULL
3        2018-04-15   10507    NULL
3        2018-05-13   10535    NULL
3        2018-06-19   10573    403.20
3        2018-09-22   10677    749.06
3        2018-09-25   10682    1940.85
3        2019-01-28   10856    2082.00
...
```

As mentioned, *LAG* and *LEAD* return a *NULL* by default when there's no row in the specified offset. If you want to return something else instead, for instance in situations in which a *NULL* is a valid value in a prior row, you can indicate what you want to return as the third argument to the function. For example, *LAG(val, 3, 0.00)* returns the value *0.00* if the row in offset *3* before the current one doesn't exist.

As an exercise, to implement similar calculations to *LAG* and *LEAD* without these functions, you can use the following strategy:

- Write a query that produces row numbers based on the same partitioning and ordering as needed for your calculations and define a table expression based on this query.

- Join multiple instances of the table expression as needed, representing the current, previous, and next rows.

- In the join predicate, match the partitioning columns of the different instances (current with previous/next). Also, in the join predicate, compute the difference between the row numbers of the current and previous/next instances, and filter based on the offset value that you need in your calculations.

Here's a query implementing this approach, returning for each order the current, previous, and next customers' order values:

```
WITH OrdersRN AS
(
  SELECT custid, orderdate, orderid, val,
    ROW_NUMBER() OVER(ORDER BY custid, orderdate, orderid) AS rn
  FROM Sales.OrderValues
)
SELECT C.custid, C.orderdate, C.orderid, C.val,
  P.val AS prevval,
  N.val AS nextval
FROM OrdersRN AS C
  LEFT OUTER JOIN OrdersRN AS P
    ON C.custid = P.custid
    AND C.rn = P.rn + 1
  LEFT OUTER JOIN OrdersRN AS N
    ON C.custid = N.custid
    AND C.rn = N.rn - 1;
```

Another interesting technique to compute *LAG* and *LEAD* without *LAG* and *LEAD* was created by Kamil Kosno, a former student of mine who's now working as an ETL developer at Zopa. Here's a query returning for each order the current order ID, as well as the IDs of the customer's previous and next orders:

```
WITH C AS
(
  SELECT custid, orderid,
    ROW_NUMBER() OVER(PARTITION BY custid ORDER BY orderdate, orderid) AS curid,
    ROW_NUMBER() OVER(PARTITION BY custid ORDER BY orderdate, orderid) + 1 AS
previd,
    ROW_NUMBER() OVER(PARTITION BY custid ORDER BY orderdate, orderid) - 1 AS
nextid
  FROM Sales.OrderValues
)
SELECT custid, curid, previd, nextid
FROM C
  UNPIVOT(rownum FOR rownumtype IN(curid, previd, nextid)) AS U
  PIVOT(MAX(orderid) FOR rownumtype IN(curid, previd, nextid)) AS P
WHERE curid IS NOT NULL
ORDER BY custid, curid;
```

This query generates the following output:

```
custid  curid   previd  nextid
-------  ------  -------  -------
1        10643  NULL     10692
1        10692  10643    10702
1        10702  10692    10835
1        10835  10702    10952
1        10952  10835    11011
```

```
1       11011   10952   NULL
2       10308   NULL    10625
2       10625   10308   10759
2       10759   10625   10926
2       10926   10759   NULL
3       10365   NULL    10507
3       10507   10365   10535
3       10535   10507   10573
3       10573   10535   10677
3       10677   10573   10682
3       10682   10677   10856
3       10856   10682   NULL
...
```

The inner query returns for each row its current row number (aliased as *curid*), its current row number plus 1 (aliased as *previd*, meaning that the row serves as the lag of the next row), as well as its current row number minus 1 (aliased as *nextid*, meaning that the row serves as the lead of the previous row). The outer query then unpivots the rows, generating three copies of each source row—one for *curid*, one for *previd*, and one for *nextid*. The outer query then pivots the rows, returning in each result row the IDs of the current, previous, and next rows. The filter discards the two extreme superfluous rows generated at the edges in each customer partition. Naturally, it's much easier and cheaper to achieve this with the *LAG* and *LEAD* functions, but the technique is pretty cool and interesting for the sake of the exercise.

FIRST_VALUE, LAST_VALUE, and NTH_VALUE

In the previous section, I discussed the offset functions *LAG* and *LEAD*, which allow you to specify the offset relative to the current row. This section focuses on functions that allow you to indicate the offset relative to the beginning or end of the window frame. These functions are *FIRST_VALUE*, *LAST_VALUE*, and *NTH_VALUE*, the last of which hasn't yet been implemented in SQL Server.

Recall that *LAG* and *LEAD* support window partition and window order clauses but not a window frame clause. This makes sense when the offset is relative to the current row. But with functions that specify the offset with respect to the beginning or end of the window, framing also becomes relevant. The *FIRST_VALUE* and *LAST_VALUE* functions return the requested value expression from the first and last rows in the frame, respectively. Listing 2-17 shows a query demonstrating how to return, along with each customer's order, the current order value as well as the order values from the customer's first and last orders.

LISTING 2-17 Query with FIRST_VALUE and LAST_VALUE

```
SELECT custid, orderdate, orderid, val,
  FIRST_VALUE(val) OVER(PARTITION BY custid
                        ORDER BY orderdate, orderid
                        ROWS BETWEEN UNBOUNDED PRECEDING
                                 AND CURRENT ROW) AS val_firstorder,
  LAST_VALUE(val)  OVER(PARTITION BY custid
                        ORDER BY orderdate, orderid
```

```
                      ROWS BETWEEN CURRENT ROW
                            AND UNBOUNDED FOLLOWING) AS val_lastorder
FROM Sales.OrderValues
ORDER BY custid, orderdate, orderid;

custid  orderdate    orderid  val      val_firstorder  val_lastorder
-------  -----------  -------  -------  --------------  --------------
1        2018-08-25   10643    814.50   814.50          933.50
1        2018-10-03   10692    878.00   814.50          933.50
1        2018-10-13   10702    330.00   814.50          933.50
1        2019-01-15   10835    845.80   814.50          933.50
1        2019-03-16   10952    471.20   814.50          933.50
1        2019-04-09   11011    933.50   814.50          933.50
2        2017-09-18   10308    88.80    88.80           514.40
2        2018-08-08   10625    479.75   88.80           514.40
2        2018-11-28   10759    320.00   88.80           514.40
2        2019-03-04   10926    514.40   88.80           514.40
3        2017-11-27   10365    403.20   403.20          660.00
3        2018-04-15   10507    749.06   403.20          660.00
3        2018-05-13   10535    1940.85  403.20          660.00
3        2018-06-19   10573    2082.00  403.20          660.00
3        2018-09-22   10677    813.37   403.20          660.00
3        2018-09-25   10682    375.50   403.20          660.00
3        2019-01-28   10856    660.00   403.20          660.00
...
```

You're after values from the first and last rows in the partition. With *FIRST_VALUE*, technically, you could rely on the default framing. Recall that if framing is applicable and you don't indicate a window frame clause, the default is *RANGE BETWEEN UNBOUNDED PRECEDING AND CURRENT ROW*. So, using the *FIRST_VALUE* function, you would get the first row in the partition with the default frame. However, as I explain later in the book in Chapter 5, the *RANGE* option can be more expensive for SQL Server to handle than ROWS, so it's better to be explicit with the ROWS option as demonstrated in this query.

With the *LAST_VALUE* function there is an unfortunate trap. Relying on the default framing is pointless because the last row in the frame is the current row. So, using *LAST_VALUE* and relying on the default frame will give you the wrong result. This is quite a common bug when people use the *LAST_VALUE* function for the first time. They usually indicate only the window partitioning and ordering, without an explicit frame, intuitively expecting to get the last row in the partition, but instead getting the value from the same row. Hence, this example uses an explicit frame specification with *UNBOUNDED FOLLOWING* as the upper boundary point in the frame.

Typically, you would not just return the first or last value along with all detail rows like in the last example; rather, you would apply some calculation involving a detail element and the value returned by the window function. As a simple example, the query in Listing 2-18 returns, along with each customer's order, the current order value as well as the difference between the current value and the values of the customer's first and last orders.

LISTING 2-18 Query with FIRST_VALUE and LAST_VALUE Embedded in Calculations

```
SELECT custid, orderdate, orderid, val,
  val - FIRST_VALUE(val) OVER(PARTITION BY custid
                              ORDER BY orderdate, orderid
                              ROWS BETWEEN UNBOUNDED PRECEDING
                                      AND CURRENT ROW) AS difffirst,
  val - LAST_VALUE(val)  OVER(PARTITION BY custid
                              ORDER BY orderdate, orderid
                              ROWS BETWEEN CURRENT ROW
                                      AND UNBOUNDED FOLLOWING) AS difflast
FROM Sales.OrderValues
ORDER BY custid, orderdate, orderid;
```

custid	orderdate	orderid	val	difffirst	difflast
1	2018-08-25	10643	814.50	0.00	-119.00
1	2018-10-03	10692	878.00	63.50	-55.50
1	2018-10-13	10702	330.00	-484.50	-603.50
1	2019-01-15	10835	845.80	31.30	-87.70
1	2019-03-16	10952	471.20	-343.30	-462.30
1	2019-04-09	11011	933.50	119.00	0.00
2	2017-09-18	10308	88.80	0.00	-425.60
2	2018-08-08	10625	479.75	390.95	-34.65
2	2018-11-28	10759	320.00	231.20	-194.40
2	2019-03-04	10926	514.40	425.60	0.00
3	2017-11-27	10365	403.20	0.00	-256.80
3	2018-04-15	10507	749.06	345.86	89.06
3	2018-05-13	10535	1940.8	1537.65	1280.85
3	2018-06-19	10573	2082.0	1678.80	1422.00
3	2018-09-22	10677	813.37	410.17	153.37
3	2018-09-25	10682	375.50	-27.70	-284.50
3	2019-01-28	10856	660.00	256.80	0.00

...

As mentioned, the standard *NTH_VALUE* function wasn't implemented in SQL Server. What this function allows you to do is ask for a value expression that is in a given offset in terms of a number of rows from the first or last row in the window frame. You specify the offset as a second input in addition to the value expression and *FROM FIRST* or *FROM LAST*, depending on whether you need the offset to be relative to the first row or last row in the frame, respectively. For example, the following expression returns the value from the third row from the last in the partition:

```
NTH_VALUE(val, 3) FROM LAST OVER(ROWS BETWEEN UNBOUNDED PRECEDING
                                         AND UNBOUNDED FOLLOWING)
```

As an exercise, suppose you want to create calculations similar to the *FIRST_VALUE, LAST_VALUE,* and *NTH_VALUE* without these functions. You can achieve this by using constructs such as CTEs, the *ROW_NUMBER* function, a *CASE* expression, grouping, and joining, as shown in Listing 2-19.

LISTING 2-19 Query Emulating FIRST_VALUE, LAST_VALUE, and NTH_VALUE without These Functions

```
WITH OrdersRN AS
(
  SELECT custid, val,
    ROW_NUMBER() OVER(PARTITION BY custid
                      ORDER BY orderdate, orderid) AS rna,
    ROW_NUMBER() OVER(PARTITION BY custid
                      ORDER BY orderdate DESC, orderid DESC) AS rnd
  FROM Sales.OrderValues
),
Agg AS
(
  SELECT custid,
    MAX(CASE WHEN rna = 1 THEN val END) AS firstorderval,
    MAX(CASE WHEN rnd = 1 THEN val END) AS lastorderval,
    MAX(CASE WHEN rna = 3 THEN val END) AS thirdorderval
  FROM OrdersRN
  GROUP BY custid
)
SELECT O.custid, O.orderdate, O.orderid, O.val,
  A.firstorderval, A.lastorderval, A.thirdorderval
FROM Sales.OrderValues AS O
  INNER JOIN Agg AS A
    ON O.custid = A.custid
ORDER BY custid, orderdate, orderid;
```

custid	orderdate	orderid	val	firstorderval	lastorderval	thirdorderval
1	2018-08-25	10643	814.50	814.50	933.50	330.00
1	2018-10-03	10692	878.00	814.50	933.50	330.00
1	2018-10-13	10702	330.00	814.50	933.50	330.00
1	2019-01-15	10835	845.80	814.50	933.50	330.00
1	2019-03-16	10952	471.20	814.50	933.50	330.00
1	2019-04-09	11011	933.50	814.50	933.50	330.00
2	2017-09-18	10308	88.80	88.80	514.40	320.00
2	2018-08-08	10625	479.75	88.80	514.40	320.00
2	2018-11-28	10759	320.00	88.80	514.40	320.00
2	2019-03-04	10926	514.40	88.80	514.40	320.00
3	2017-11-27	10365	403.20	403.20	660.00	1940.85
3	2018-04-15	10507	749.06	403.20	660.00	1940.85
3	2018-05-13	10535	1940.85	403.20	660.00	1940.85
3	2018-06-19	10573	2082.00	403.20	660.00	1940.85
3	2018-09-22	10677	813.37	403.20	660.00	1940.85
3	2018-09-25	10682	375.50	403.20	660.00	1940.85
3	2019-01-28	10856	660.00	403.20	660.00	1940.85
...						

In the first CTE, called *OrdersRN*, you define row numbers in both ascending and descending order to mark the positions of the rows with respect to the first and last rows in the partition. In the second CTE, called *Agg*, you use a *CASE* expression, filter only the interesting row numbers, group the data by the partitioning element (*custid*), and apply an aggregate to the result of the *CASE* expression to return the requested value for each group. Finally, in the outer query, you join the result of the grouped query with the original table to match the detail with the aggregates.

RESPECT NULLS | IGNORE NULLS

As mentioned, in the SQL standard all window offset functions support a *null treatment* option, allowing you to specify either *RESPECT NULLS* (the default) or *IGNORE NULLS*. The former, which is the default, means that you want the element in the indicated offset irrespective of whether it is *NULL*. If the element indicated in the offset is not NULL, you want to keep going in the relevant direction until you find a non-*NULL* value. Of course, if a non-NULL value can't be found, the function is supposed to return a *NULL*.

The functionality of the *IGNORE NULLS* option is actually a fairly common need, but unfortunately SQL Server doesn't support this option. It just uses *RESPECT NULLS* by default. I will provide a workaround that does work in SQL Server.

I'll use a table called T1 in my examples. Use the code in Listing 2-20 to create and populate this table.

LISTING 2-20 Code to Create and Populate T1

```
SET NOCOUNT ON;
USE TSQLV5;

DROP TABLE IF EXISTS dbo.T1;
GO

CREATE TABLE dbo.T1
(
  id INT NOT NULL CONSTRAINT PK_T1 PRIMARY KEY,
  col1 INT NULL
);

INSERT INTO dbo.T1(id, col1) VALUES
  ( 2, NULL),
  ( 3,   10),
  ( 5,   -1),
  ( 7, NULL),
  (11, NULL),
  (13,  -12),
  (17, NULL),
  (19, NULL),
  (23, 1759);
```

Suppose that this table represents an ordered stream of events based on *id* ordering, with a non-*NULL* value in an attribute like *col1* signifying the new effective attribute value. If the value doesn't change, the attribute in the event is set to *NULL*. Here, I'm showing only one attribute called *col1*, but in practice you would typically have multiple applicable attributes (say, *col2*, *col3*, and so on). You want to query *T1* and return the latest effective value of each attribute. According to the SQL standard, you would achieve this with the *LAG* function and the *IGNORE NULLS* option, like so:

```
SELECT id, col1,
  COALESCE(col1, LAG(col1) IGNORE NULLS OVER(ORDER BY id)) AS lastval
FROM dbo.T1;
```

Here's the expected result of this query:

```
id   col1   lastval
---  -----  --------
2    NULL   NULL
3    10     10
5    -1     -1
7    NULL   -1
11   NULL   -1
13   -12    -12
17   NULL   -12
19   NULL   -12
23   1759   1759
```

Getting the last non-NULL in SQL Server efficiently is doable, but not trivial. I'll show a solution that involves three steps.

In Step 1, you use a *CASE* expression to return for each row the *id* value when the *col1* value isn't *NULL*, and *NULL* otherwise, like so:

```
SELECT id, col1,
  CASE WHEN col1 IS NOT NULL THEN id END AS goodid
FROM dbo.T1;
```

This query generates the following output:

```
id    col1   goodid
----  -----  -------
2     NULL   NULL
3     10     3
5     -1     5
7     NULL   NULL
11    NULL   NULL
13    -12    13
17    NULL   NULL
19    NULL   NULL
23    1759   23
```

In Step 2, you apply the *MAX* window aggregate to the result of the *CASE* expression, ordering the window by *id*, and framing it with *ROWS UNBOUNDED PRECEDING*, like so:

```
SELECT id, col1,
  MAX(CASE WHEN col1 IS NOT NULL THEN id END)
    OVER(ORDER BY id ROWS UNBOUNDED PRECEDING) AS grp
FROM dbo.T1;
```

This query generates the following output:

```
id    col1   grp
----  -----  -----
2     NULL   NULL
3     10     3
5     -1     5
7     NULL   5
11    NULL   5
13    -12    13
17    NULL   13
19    NULL   13
23    1759   23
```

As you can see, every time *col1* gets a new value, the result *grp* attribute represents the beginning of a new group.

Finally, in Step 3, you define a CTE called *C* based on the query from Step 2, and in the outer query compute the last non-NULL *col1* value. You do so by applying the *MAX* window aggregate function to *col1*, partitioning the window by *grp*, ordering it by *id*, and framing it with *ROWS UNBOUNDED PRECEDING*. Here's the complete solution query:

```
WITH C AS
(
  SELECT id, col1,
    MAX(CASE WHEN col1 IS NOT NULL THEN id END)
      OVER(ORDER BY id
           ROWS UNBOUNDED PRECEDING) AS grp
  FROM dbo.T1
)
SELECT id, col1,
  MAX(col1) OVER(PARTITION BY grp
                 ORDER BY id
                 ROWS UNBOUNDED PRECEDING)
FROM C;
```

This query generates the desired output:

```
id   col1   lastval
---  -----  --------
2    NULL   NULL
3    10     10
5    -1     -1
7    NULL   -1
11   NULL   -1
13   -12    -12
17   NULL   -12
19   NULL   -12
23   1759   1759
```

Note You can also find a feedback item with a request to improve SQL Server by adding this feature here: *https://feedback.azure.com/forums/908035-sql-server/suggestions/32897728.*

Summary

This chapter delved into the details of the various window functions, focusing on their logical aspects. I showed both the functionality defined by the SQL standard and indicated what SQL Server supports. In cases in which SQL Server doesn't support certain functionality, I provided supported alternatives.

CHAPTER 3

Ordered Set Functions

Have you ever needed to concatenate elements of a group into one string based on some order? That's a scenario that an *ordered set function* could help address. An *ordered set function* is a type of aggregate function. What distinguishes it from a *general set function* (like *SUM*, *MIN*, *MAX*, and so on) is that there's ordering relevance to the calculation, such as the order in which you want to concatenate the elements.

In this chapter, I will discuss ordered set functions and the kinds of solutions they help with. At the date of this writing, the only ordered set function that SQL Server supports is *STRING_AGG* for string concatenation. This function was added in SQL Server 2017. There are additional ordered set functions that are defined by the SQL standard but that were not implemented yet in SQL Server. I will cover both the supported *STRING_AGG* function and the unsupported ones, and I will provide alternative solutions that do work in SQL Server for the unsupported ones.

The SQL standard defines three types of ordered set functions. One type is a string concatenation function, which the standard refers to as the *listagg* set function type; the actual function is named *LISTAGG*. SQL Server calls it *STRING_AGG* but otherwise uses the standard syntax. The other two types have very fancy, yet appropriate, names: hypothetical set functions and inverse distribution functions. When providing the specifics of each type, I will explain why they are called the way they are.

The concept of an ordered set function isn't limited to the three types of functions defined by the standard—rather, it can be extended to any aggregate function that has ordering relevance to the calculation. For instance, I'll explain why it could make a lot of sense to support offset functions like *FIRST_VALUE* and *LAST_VALUE* as ordered set functions, even though the standard doesn't support this option.

Also, it would be great if SQL Server supported the concept of Common Language Runtime (CLR) user-defined aggregates (UDAs) in the future. Naturally, if the UDA has ordering relevance to the calculation, Microsoft should follow the basic rules of the standard syntax.

You use ordered set functions in grouped queries much like you do general set functions. As for syntax, the SQL standard defines a special clause called *WITHIN GROUP* where you indicate the ordering, like so:

```
<ordered set function> WITHIN GROUP ( ORDER BY <sort specification list> )
```

Hypothetical Set Functions

Hypothetical set functions include ranking and rank-distribution functions that you're already familiar with as window functions, but they are applied to groups for an input value in a hypothetical manner. This description probably doesn't make much sense yet, but it will soon.

There are two ranking ordered set functions: *RANK* and *DENSE_RANK*. There are also two rank-distribution ordered set functions: *PERCENT_RANK* and *CUME_DIST*. There's a difference in the ordering relevance between a window function and an ordered set function. With the former, the ordering is within the window partition, and with the latter, the ordering is within the group. When used as a window function, the current row's ordering value is evaluated with respect to the ordering values in the window partition. When used as an ordered set function, the input value is evaluated with respect to the ordering values in the group. When an ordered set function is given an input value, you're asking, "What would be the result of the function for this input value if I added it as another element to the set?" Note that the use of "would be" indicates that this is hypothetical.

This is one of those topics that is best explained through examples, and this chapter provides plenty. I'll start with the *RANK* function.

RANK

Consider the following query, which uses the *RANK* window function, and its output, which is shown in abbreviated form in Listing 3-1.

LISTING 3-1 Query Using the *RANK* Window Function

```
USE TSQLV5;

SELECT orderid, custid, val,
  RANK() OVER(PARTITION BY custid ORDER BY val) AS rnk
FROM Sales.OrderValues;

orderid  custid  val      rnk
-------- ------- -------  ----
10702    1       330.00   1
10952    1       471.20   2
10643    1       814.50   3
10835    1       845.80   4
10692    1       878.00   5
11011    1       933.50   6
10308    2       88.80    1
10759    2       320.00   2
10625    2       479.75   3
10926    2       514.40   4
10682    3       375.50   1
10365    3       403.20   2
10856    3       660.00   3
10507    3       749.06   4
10677    3       813.37   5
```

```
10535   3        1940.85 6
10573   3        2082.00 7
10793   4         191.10  1
10741   4         228.00  2
10864   4         282.00  3
10743   4         319.20  4
10920   4         390.00  5
10453   4         407.70  6
10355   4         480.00  7
11016   4         491.50  8
10383   4         899.00  9
10768   4        1477.00 10
10707   4        1641.00 11
10558   4        2142.90 12
10953   4        4441.25 13
...
```

The *RANK* function ranks each customer's orders based on the order values. Can you rationalize why the rows that received rank 5 are ranked that way? If you recall from Chapter 2, "A Detailed Look at Window Functions," when using ascending ordering, *RANK* calculates one more than the number of rows in the window partition with an ordering value that is less than the current one. For example, look at customer 3. The row that got *rank 5* for customer *3* has the ordering value *813.37*. The rank was computed as *5* because there are 4 rows in the same partition with ordering values that are less than *813.37 (375.50, 403.20, 660.00, and 749.06)*.

Now suppose you want to do a kind of "what if" analysis and ask, "How would an input value *@val* rank in each customer group with respect to the other values in the *val* column?" It's as if you did the following:

1. Considered each customer group as a window partition, with window ordering based on the *val* column

2. Added a row to each partition with the input value *@val*

3. Calculated the *RANK* window function for that row in each partition

4. Returned just that row for each partition

For example, suppose that the input value *@val* is equal to *1000.00*. How would this value rank in each customer group with respect to the other values in the *val* column using ascending ordering? The result would be one more than the number of rows in each customer group that have a value less than *1000.00*. For example, for customer 3, you should get the rank 6 because there are 5 rows with values in the *val* column that are less than *1000.00 (375.50, 403.20, 660.00, 749.06, and 813.37)*.

The standard defines the following form for the *RANK* ordered set function:

```
RANK(<input>) WITHIN GROUP ( ORDER BY <sort specification list> )
```

And here's how you use it as a grouped aggregate function to address the request at hand. (Remember, this syntax is not supported by SQL Server.)

```
DECLARE @val AS NUMERIC(12, 2) = 1000.00;

SELECT custid,
  RANK(@val) WITHIN GROUP(ORDER BY val) AS rnk
FROM Sales.OrderValues
GROUP BY custid;
```

```
custid       rnk
-----------  -----------
1            7
2            5
3            6
4            10
5            7
6            8
7            6
8            3
9            9
10           7
...
```

At this point, the concept of an ordered set function should make much more sense to you.

The last example I showed demonstrates the use of the standard *RANK* ordered set function, but as mentioned, SQL Server doesn't support this syntax. It is quite simple, though, to implement the calculation without a built-in function. Use a *CASE* expression that returns some constant when the ordering value is less than the input value, and *NULL* otherwise (which is the default when an *ELSE* clause isn't specified). Apply a *COUNT* aggregate to the result of the *CASE* expression and add 1. Here's the complete query:

```
DECLARE @val AS NUMERIC(12, 2) = 1000.00;

SELECT custid,
  COUNT(CASE WHEN val < @val THEN 1 END) + 1 AS rnk
FROM Sales.OrderValues
GROUP BY custid;
```

If you're wondering about what could be a practical use case for such a calculation, one example is a marketing or sales manager working on a promotion in hopes of increasing sales and doing what-if analysis in order to determine a realistic sales target for customers.

DENSE_RANK

Recall that *DENSE_RANK*, as a window function, is similar to *RANK*, only it returns one more than the number of distinct ordering values (as opposed to number of rows) in the partition that are less than the current one. Similarly, as an ordered set function, given an input value *@val*, *DENSE_RANK* returns one more than the number of distinct ordering values in the group that are less than *@val*. Here's what the code should look like according to the standard. (Again, this is not supported by SQL Server.)

```
DECLARE @val AS NUMERIC(12, 2) = 1000.00;

SELECT custid,
  DENSE_RANK(@val) WITHIN GROUP(ORDER BY val) AS densernk
FROM Sales.OrderValues
GROUP BY custid;

custid       densernk
-----------  --------------
1            7
2            5
3            6
4            10
5            7
6            8
7            6
8            3
9            8
10           7
...
```

The alternative that is supported in SQL Server is similar to the technique used to implement *RANK*. Only instead of returning a constant from the *CASE* expression when the ordering value is less than @*val*, you return *val* and apply a *DISTINCT* clause to the aggregated expression, like so:

```
DECLARE @val AS NUMERIC(12, 2) = 1000.00;

SELECT custid,
  COUNT(DISTINCT CASE WHEN val < @val THEN val END) + 1 AS densernk
FROM Sales.OrderValues
GROUP BY custid;
```

Practical uses of the *DENSE_RANK* function are similar to using RANK, such as when doing a what-if analysis for the purpose of determining realistic sales targets. The choice between the two functions is then based on whether you need the result ranking values to reflect a count of rows or a count of distinct ordering values.

PERCENT_RANK

Very similar to ranking functions, rank distribution functions—specifically *PERCENT_RANK* and *CUME_DIST*—are also supported by the standard as hypothetical set functions. They are used mostly in statistical analysis of data. I'll start with *PERCENT_RANK* in this section and describe *CUME_DIST* in the next section.

As a reminder, *PERCENT_RANK* as a window function computes the relative rank of a row in the window partition and expresses it as a ratio between 0 and 1 (a percent). The rank is calculated as follows:

- Let *rk* be the *RANK* of the row using the same window specification as the distribution function's window specification.

- Let *nr* be the count of rows in the window partition.

- Then *PERCENT_RANK* is calculated as follows: $(rk - 1) / (nr - 1)$.

Now, think in terms of hypothetical set functions. Suppose you want to know for a given input value what its percentile rank would be in each group if it's added to all groups. For example, consider the Scores table, which holds test scores. Given an input test score (call it *@score*), you want to know what the percentile rank of the input score would be in each test if it's added as another score to all tests. According to the SQL standard, you use the *PERCENT_RANK* ordered set function as an aggregate function, like so:

```
DECLARE @score AS TINYINT = 80;

SELECT testid,
  PERCENT_RANK(@score) WITHIN GROUP(ORDER BY score) AS pctrank
FROM Stats.Scores
GROUP BY testid;
```

```
testid      pctrank
----------  ---------------
Test ABC    0.556
Test XYZ    0.500
```

To produce a percentile rank as a hypothetical set function in SQL Server, you need your own solution. One option is to generate *rk* and *nr* with *COUNT* aggregates and then compute the percentile rank as follows: $(rk - 1) / (nr - 1)$. For *rk*, you need to count the number of rows with a lower score than the input. For *nr*, simply count the number of rows and add one (for the input to be taken into consideration as part of the group). Here's the complete solution:

```
DECLARE @score AS TINYINT = 80;

WITH C AS
(
  SELECT testid,
    COUNT(CASE WHEN score < @score THEN 1 END) + 1 AS rk,
    COUNT(*) + 1 AS nr
  FROM Stats.Scores
  GROUP BY testid
)
SELECT testid, 1.0 * (rk - 1) / (nr - 1) AS pctrank
FROM C;
```

CUME_DIST

The *CUME_DIST* calculation is similar to *PERCENT_RANK*, only it's calculated slightly differently. As a window function, it is calculated as follows:

- Let *nr* be the count of rows in the window partition.

- Let *np* be the number of rows that precede or are peers of the current one.

- Then *CUME_DIST* is calculated as follows: *np / nr*.

As a hypothetical set function, *CUME_DIST* tells you what cumulative distribution an input value would get in each group if it's added to all groups. The standard version of the *CUME_DIST* function as an ordered set function applied to our Scores scenario looks like this:

```
DECLARE @score AS TINYINT = 80;

SELECT testid,
  CUME_DIST(@score) WITHIN GROUP(ORDER BY score) AS cumedist
FROM Stats.Scores
GROUP BY testid;
```

```
testid      cumedist
----------  ------------
Test ABC    0.800
Test XYZ    0.727
```

As for the version supported by SQL Server, it's quite similar to the alternative you used for the *PERCENT_RANK* function. You compute *np* as the count of rows in the group that have a score that is lower than the input, plus 1 to account for the input. You compute *nr* as a count of rows in the group, plus 1—again, to account for the input. Finally, you compute the cumulative distribution as follows: *np / nr*. Here's the complete solution:

```
DECLARE @score AS TINYINT = 80;

WITH C AS
(
  SELECT testid,
    COUNT(CASE WHEN score <= @score THEN 1 END) + 1 AS np,
    COUNT(*) + 1 AS nr
  FROM Stats.Scores
  GROUP BY testid
)
SELECT testid, 1.0 * np / nr AS cumedist
FROM C;
```

General Solution

Because SQL Server doesn't support the standard hypothetical set functions, I provided alternative methods to achieve the same calculations. The methods I provided for the different calculations were quite different from one another. In this section, I will present a more generalized solution.

All four unsupported hypothetical set functions have supported window-function counterparts. That is, SQL Server does support *RANK*, *DENSE_RANK*, *PERCENT_RANK*, and *CUME_DIST* as window functions. Remember that a hypothetical set function is supposed to return for a given input the result that the corresponding window function would return if the input value was added to the set. With this in mind, you can create a solution that works the same for all calculations. The generalized solution might not be as optimized as the specialized ones, but it is still interesting to see. The steps involved in the solution are as follows:

1. Unify the existing set with the input value.

2. Apply the window function.

3. Filter the row representing the input value to return the result.

Here's the code used for the solution:

```
SELECT P.<partition_col>, A.wf AS osf
FROM <partitions_table> AS P
  CROSS APPLY (SELECT <window_function>() OVER(ORDER BY U.<ord_col>) AS wf,
                 U.return_flag
               FROM (SELECT D.<ord_col>, 0 AS return_flag
                     FROM <details_table> AS D
                     WHERE D.<partition_col> = P.<partition_col>

                     UNION ALL

                     SELECT @input_val AS <ord_col>, 1 AS return_flag) AS U) AS A
  WHERE A.return_flag = 1;
```

The outer query is issued against the table holding the distinct partition values. Then with a *CROSS APPLY* operator, the code handles each partition separately. The innermost-derived table *U* handles the unification of the current partition's rows, which are marked with *return_flag 0*, with a row made of the input value, marked with *return_flag 1*. Then the query against *U* computes the window function, generating the derived table *A*. Finally, the outer query filters only the rows with *return_flag 1*. Those are the rows that have the computation for the input value in each partition; in other words, they're the hypothetical set calculation.

If this general form isn't clear yet, see if you can follow the logic through specific examples. The code in Listing 3-2 queries the table Customers (partitions) and the view *Sales.OrderValues* (details). It calculates both *RANK* and *DENSE_RANK* as hypothetical set calculations for an input value *@val*, with *custid* being the partitioning element and *val* being the ordering element.

LISTING 3-2 Calculating *RANK* and *DENSE_RANK*

```
DECLARE @val AS NUMERIC(12, 2) = 1000.00;

SELECT P.custid, A.rnk, A.densernk
FROM Sales.Customers AS P
  CROSS APPLY (SELECT
                 RANK() OVER(ORDER BY U.val) AS rnk,
                 DENSE_RANK() OVER(ORDER BY U.val) AS densernk,
                 U.return_flag
               FROM (SELECT D.val, 0 AS return_flag
                     FROM Sales.OrderValues AS D
                     WHERE D.custid = P.custid

                     UNION ALL
```

```
                    SELECT @val AS val, 1 AS return_flag) AS U) AS A
  WHERE A.return_flag = 1;
```

```
custid      rnk                   densernk
----------- --------------------- ---------------------
1           7                     7
2           5                     5
3           6                     6
4           10                    10
5           7                     7
6           8                     8
7           6                     6
8           3                     3
9           9                     8
11          9                     9
...
```

Similarly, the code in Listing 3-3 is issued against the tables Tests (partitions) and Scores (details). It calculates PERCENT_RANK and CUME_DIST as hypothetical set calculations for the input value @score, with *testid* being the partitioning element and *score* being the ordering element.

LISTING 3-3 Calculating *PERCENT_RANK* and *CUME_DIST*

```
DECLARE @score AS TINYINT = 80;

SELECT P.testid, A.pctrank, A.cumedist
FROM Stats.Tests AS P
  CROSS APPLY (SELECT
                PERCENT_RANK() OVER(ORDER BY U.score) AS pctrank,
                CUME_DIST() OVER(ORDER BY U.score) AS cumedist,
                U.return_flag
              FROM (SELECT D.score, 0 AS return_flag
                    FROM Stats.Scores AS D
                    WHERE D.testid = P.testid

                    UNION ALL

                    SELECT @score AS score, 1 AS return_flag) AS U) AS A
  WHERE A.return_flag = 1;
```

```
testid      pctrank               cumedist
---------- --------------------- ---------------------
Test ABC    0.555555555555556     0.8
Test XYZ    0.5                   0.727272727272727
```

Of course, there are other ways to generalize a solution for hypothetical set calculations. Here I showed just one method.

I should note that this method returns rows that appear in the partitions table even if there are no related rows in the details table. If you are not interested in those, you need to add logic to exclude them—for example, by including an *EXISTS* predicate. As an example, to exclude customers with no related orders from the query that calculates the *RANK* and *DENSE_RANK* hypothetical set calculations, use the code in Listing 3-4.

LISTING 3-4 Calculating *RANK* and *DENSE_RANK* and Excluding Empty Partitions

```
DECLARE @val AS NUMERIC(12, 2) = 1000.00;

SELECT P.custid, A.rnk, A.densernk
FROM Sales.Customers AS P
  CROSS APPLY (SELECT
                     RANK() OVER(ORDER BY U.val) AS rnk,
                     DENSE_RANK() OVER(ORDER BY U.val) AS densernk,
                     U.return_flag
                 FROM (SELECT D.val, 0 AS return_flag
                         FROM Sales.OrderValues AS D
                         WHERE D.custid = P.custid

                       UNION ALL

                       SELECT @val AS val, 1 AS return_flag) AS U) AS A
WHERE A.return_flag = 1
  AND EXISTS
    (SELECT * FROM Sales.OrderValues AS D
      WHERE D.custid = P.custid);
```

This query returns 89 rows and not 91, because only 89 out of the 91 existing customers placed orders.

Inverse Distribution Functions

Inverse distribution functions perform calculations that you can think of as the inverse of the rank distribution functions *PERCENT_RANK* and *CUME_DIST*. They are used mostly in statistical analysis of data. Rank distribution functions compute a rank of a value with respect to others in a partition or a group, expressed as a ratio in the range of 0 through 1 (a percent). Inverse distribution functions pretty much do the inverse. Given a certain percent, *@pct*, they return either a value from the partition or a calculated value that the *@pct* represents. That is, in loose terms, they return a calculated value with respect to which *@pct* percent of the values are less than. Chances are that this sentence doesn't make much sense yet, but it should be clearer after you see some examples. Inverse distribution functions are more commonly known as *percentiles*.

The standard defines two variants of inverse distribution functions: *PERCENTILE_DISC*, which returns an existing value from the population using a discrete distribution model, and *PERCENTILE_CONT*, which returns an interpolated value assuming a continuous distribution model. I explained the specifics of the two calculations in Chapter 2. As a quick reminder, *PERCENTILE_DISC* returns the first value in the group whose cumulative distribution is greater than or equal to the input. The *PERCENTILE_CONT* function identifies two rows in between which the input percent falls, and it computes an interpolation of the two ordering values assuming a continuous distribution model.

SQL Server supports only a windowed version of the functions, which I described in detail in Chapter 2. It doesn't support the more natural ordered set function versions that can be used in grouped queries. However, I will provide alternatives that are supported in SQL Server.

First, as a reminder, Listing 3-5 shows a query against the Scores table calculating the fiftieth percentile (median) of test scores, using both function variants as window functions.

LISTING 3-5 Calculating Median with *PERCENTILE_DISC* and *PERCENTILE_CONT*

```
DECLARE @pct AS FLOAT = 0.5;

SELECT testid, score,
  PERCENTILE_DISC(@pct) WITHIN GROUP(ORDER BY score)
    OVER(PARTITION BY testid) AS percentiledisc,
  PERCENTILE_CONT(@pct) WITHIN GROUP(ORDER BY score)
    OVER(PARTITION BY testid) AS percentilecont
FROM Stats.Scores;
```

```
testid      score percentiledisc percentilecont
----------  ----- -------------- ----------------------
Test ABC    50    75                 75
Test ABC    55    75                 75
Test ABC    55    75                 75
Test ABC    65    75                 75
Test ABC    75    75                 75
Test ABC    80    75                 75
Test ABC    80    75                 75
Test ABC    95    75                 75
Test ABC    95    75                 75
Test XYZ    50    75                 77.5
Test XYZ    55    75                 77.5
Test XYZ    55    75                 77.5
Test XYZ    65    75                 77.5
Test XYZ    75    75                 77.5
Test XYZ    80    75                 77.5
Test XYZ    80    75                 77.5
Test XYZ    95    75                 77.5
Test XYZ    95    75                 77.5
Test XYZ    95    75                 77.5
```

Observe that the same result percentiles are simply repeated for all members of the same partition (*test*, in our case), which is completely redundant for our purposes. You need to return the percentiles only once per group. According to the standard, you are supposed to achieve this using the ordered set versions of the functions in a grouped query, like so:

```
DECLARE @pct AS FLOAT = 0.5;

SELECT testid,
  PERCENTILE_DISC(@pct) WITHIN GROUP(ORDER BY score) AS percentiledisc,
  PERCENTILE_CONT(@pct) WITHIN GROUP(ORDER BY score) AS percentilecont
FROM Stats.Scores
GROUP BY testid;
```

However, these versions aren't yet implemented in SQL Server, so you need to figure out alternative methods to achieve this.

Because the windowed versions of the functions were implemented, one simple approach to handling the task is to use the *DISTINCT* option, like so:

```
DECLARE @pct AS FLOAT = 0.5;

SELECT DISTINCT testid,
  PERCENTILE_DISC(@pct) WITHIN GROUP(ORDER BY score)
    OVER(PARTITION BY testid) AS percentiledisc,
  PERCENTILE_CONT(@pct) WITHIN GROUP(ORDER BY score)
    OVER(PARTITION BY testid) AS percentilecont
FROM Stats.Scores;
```

testid	percentiledisc	percentilecont
Test ABC	75	75
Test XYZ	75	77.5

Another option is to assign unique row numbers to the rows in each partition, and then filter just the rows with row number 1, like so:

```
DECLARE @pct AS FLOAT = 0.5;

WITH C AS
(
  SELECT testid,
    PERCENTILE_DISC(@pct) WITHIN GROUP(ORDER BY score)
      OVER(PARTITION BY testid) AS percentiledisc,
    PERCENTILE_CONT(@pct) WITHIN GROUP(ORDER BY score)
      OVER(PARTITION BY testid) AS percentilecont,
    ROW_NUMBER() OVER(PARTITION BY testid ORDER BY (SELECT NULL)) AS rownum
  FROM Stats.Scores
)
SELECT testid, percentiledisc, percentilecont
FROM C
WHERE rownum = 1;
```

To continue the tradition in this book, as an exercise, I'll describe techniques to compute percentiles even without the windowed versions of the *PERCENTILE_DISC* and *PERCENTILE_CONT* functions. With *PERCENTILE_DISC*, you are supposed to return the first value in the group whose cumulative distribution is greater than or equal to the input percent. To calculate the cumulative distribution of each value, you need to know how many rows precede or are peers of that value (*np*) and how many rows there are in the group (*nr*). Then the cumulative distribution is *np / nr*.

Normally, to calculate *np*, you need to return one less than the minimum rank that is greater than the current one. This could involve expensive use of subqueries and the *RANK* function. Courtesy of Adam Machanic (this book's technical editor), you can achieve what you need with less effort. When peers cannot exist (that is, the ordering is unique), the *ROW_NUMBER* function returns a number that is equal to *np* for all rows. When peers can exist (the ordering isn't unique) the function returns a number that is equal to *np* for one of the peers and less than *np* for all others. Because we are talking about peers, by definition, in cases where the row number is less than *np*, the sort value is the same as the one where the row number is equal to *np*. This fact makes the *ROW_NUMBER* function sufficient for our very specific need of representing *np*. As for calculating *nr*, you can use a simple *COUNT* window function. Here's the code that implements this logic, followed by its output:

```
DECLARE @pct AS FLOAT = 0.5;

WITH C AS
(
  SELECT testid, score,
    ROW_NUMBER() OVER(PARTITION BY testid ORDER BY score) AS np,
    COUNT(*) OVER(PARTITION BY testid) AS nr
  FROM Stats.Scores
)
SELECT testid, MIN(score) AS percentiledisc
FROM C
WHERE 1.0 * np / nr >= @pct
GROUP BY testid;
```

```
testid      percentiledisc
----------  --------------
Test ABC    75
Test XYZ    75
```

As for an alternative to computing *PERCENTILE_CONT*, here's a reminder from Chapter 2 for the logic behind the computation:

- Consider the function *PERCENTILE_CONT(@pct) WITHIN GROUP(ORDER BY score)*.

- Let *n* be the count of rows in the group.

- Let *a* be *@pct*(n – 1)*, let *i* be the integer part of *a*, and let *f* be the fraction part of *a*.

- Let *row0* and *row1* be the rows whose zero-based row numbers are in *FLOOR(a)*, *CEILING(a)*. Here I'm assuming the row numbers are calculated using the same window partitioning and ordering as the group and order of the *PERCENTILE_CONT* function.

Then *PERCENTILE_CONT* is computed as *row0.score + f * (row1.score – row0.score)*. This is an interpolation of the values in the two rows assuming continuous distribution (based on the fraction part of *a*).

The code in Listing 3-6 implements this logic.

LISTING 3-6 Alternative to PERCENTILE_CONT

```
DECLARE @pct AS FLOAT = 0.5;

WITH C1 AS
(
  SELECT testid, score,
    ROW_NUMBER() OVER(PARTITION BY testid ORDER BY score) - 1 AS rownum,
    @pct * (COUNT(*) OVER(PARTITION BY testid) - 1) AS a
  FROM Stats.Scores
),
C2 AS
```

```
(
  SELECT testid, score, a-FLOOR(a) AS factor
  FROM C1
  WHERE rownum IN (FLOOR(a), CEILING(a))
)
SELECT testid, MIN(score) + factor * (MAX(score) - MIN(score)) AS percentilecont
FROM C2
GROUP BY testid, factor;
```

```
testid      percentilecont
----------  ---------------------
Test ABC    75
Test XYZ    77.5
```

Offset Functions

The SQL standard doesn't define ordered set function versions of the functions *FIRST_VALUE*, *LAST_VALUE*, and *NTH_VALUE*; rather, it defines only windowed versions, and that's also the implementation in SQL Server. As an example, the query in Listing 3-7 returns with each order the current order value, as well as the values of the first and last orders by the same customer.

LISTING 3-7 Query Using *FIRST_VALUE* and *LAST_VALUE* as Window Functions

```
SELECT custid, orderdate, orderid, val,
  FIRST_VALUE(val) OVER(PARTITION BY custid
                        ORDER BY orderdate, orderid
                        ROWS BETWEEN UNBOUNDED PRECEDING
                                     AND CURRENT ROW) AS val_firstorder,
  LAST_VALUE(val)  OVER(PARTITION BY custid
                        ORDER BY orderdate, orderid
                        ROWS BETWEEN CURRENT ROW
                                     AND UNBOUNDED FOLLOWING) AS val_lastorder
FROM Sales.OrderValues;
```

```
custid  orderdate    orderid  val      val_firstorder  val_lastorder
-------  -----------  -------  -------  --------------  --------------
1        2018-08-25   10643    814.50   814.50          933.50
1        2018-10-03   10692    878.00   814.50          933.50
1        2018-10-13   10702    330.00   814.50          933.50
1        2019-01-15   10835    845.80   814.50          933.50
1        2019-03-16   10952    471.20   814.50          933.50
1        2019-04-09   11011    933.50   814.50          933.50
2        2017-09-18   10308    88.80    88.80           514.40
2        2018-08-08   10625    479.75   88.80           514.40
2        2018-11-28   10759    320.00   88.80           514.40
2        2019-03-04   10926    514.40   88.80           514.40
3        2017-11-27   10365    403.20   403.20          660.00
3        2018-04-15   10507    749.06   403.20          660.00
3        2018-05-13   10535    1940.85  403.20          660.00
```

3	2018-06-19	10573	2082.00	403.20	660.00
3	2018-09-22	10677	813.37	403.20	660.00
3	2018-09-25	10682	375.50	403.20	660.00
3	2019-01-28	10856	660.00	403.20	660.00

...

Observe the duplication of the information in all rows by the same customer. Often that's what you want if you need to involve in the same expression both detail elements and the first, last, and *n*th values from the partition. But what if you don't? What if you need the first, last, and *n*th values only once per group?

If you think about it, there's no reason not to support grouped-aggregate, ordered-set function versions of the functions. After all, in a given group of rows, each of those functions is supposed to return only one value. In the windowed version, these functions support a window frame clause so that there can be a different applicable frame for each row in the partition and, therefore, a different result. However, often you just want the calculation applied to the entire partition or group.

You can think of ordered-set-function forms of the *FIRST_VALUE* and *LAST_VALUE* functions as being more flexible versions of the *MIN* and *MAX* functions, respectively. They're more flexible in the sense that the *MIN* and *MAX* functions treat the input as both the ordering element and the value expression to return, plus they don't support multiple ordering elements. The *FIRST_VALUE* and *LAST_VALUE* functions allow you to return one element as the value expression based on the ordering of another element, or elements. So why not support those as grouped-aggregate, ordered-set functions?

I hope this will happen in the future. In the meanwhile, you need to use alternative methods. One method, similar to what I showed with inverse distribution functions, is to invoke the windowed version of the functions, along with calculating unique row numbers within each partition. And then filter only the rows where the row number is equal to 1, as shown in Listing 3-8.

LISTING 3-8 Computing *FIRST_VALUE* and *LAST_VALUE*, Returning One Row Per Customer

```
WITH C AS
(
  SELECT custid,
    FIRST_VALUE(val) OVER(PARTITION BY custid
                          ORDER BY orderdate, orderid
                          ROWS BETWEEN UNBOUNDED PRECEDING
                                   AND CURRENT ROW) AS val_firstorder,
    LAST_VALUE(val)  OVER(PARTITION BY custid
                          ORDER BY orderdate, orderid
                          ROWS BETWEEN CURRENT ROW
                                   AND UNBOUNDED FOLLOWING) AS val_lastorder,
    ROW_NUMBER() OVER(PARTITION BY custid ORDER BY (SELECT NULL)) AS rownum
  FROM Sales.OrderValues
)
SELECT custid, val_firstorder, val_lastorder
FROM C
WHERE rownum = 1;
```

custid	val_firstorder	val_lastorder
1	814.50	933.50
2	88.80	514.40
3	403.20	660.00
4	480.00	491.50
5	1488.80	1835.70
6	149.00	858.00
7	1176.00	730.00
8	982.00	224.00
9	88.50	792.75
10	1832.80	525.00
...		

You could actually use the *ROW_NUMBER* function alone to emulate all three functions—*FIRST_VALUE*, *LAST_VALUE*, and *NTH_VALUE*. By calculating an ascending row number and filtering only the rows with row number 1, you get the equivalent of *FIRST_VALUE*. Filtering the rows with row number *n*, you get the equivalent of *NTH_VALUE FROM FIRST*. Similarly, using a row number with descending order, you produce the equivalents of *LAST_VALUE* and *NTH_VALUE FROM LAST*. Listing 3-9 shows an example implementing this logic, returning the first, last, and third order values per customer, with ordering based on *orderdate, orderid*.

LISTING 3-9 Alternatives to *FIRST_VALUE*, *LAST_VALUE*, and *NTH_VALUE*

```
WITH OrdersRN AS
(
  SELECT custid, val,
    ROW_NUMBER() OVER(PARTITION BY custid
                      ORDER BY orderdate, orderid) AS rna,
    ROW_NUMBER() OVER(PARTITION BY custid
                      ORDER BY orderdate DESC, orderid DESC) AS rnd
  FROM Sales.OrderValues
)
SELECT custid,
  MAX(CASE WHEN rna = 1 THEN val END) AS firstorderval,
  MAX(CASE WHEN rnd = 1 THEN val END) AS lastorderval,
  MAX(CASE WHEN rna = 3 THEN val END) AS thirdorderval
FROM OrdersRN
GROUP BY custid;
```

custid	firstorderval	lastorderval	thirdorderval
1	814.50	933.50	330.00
2	88.80	514.40	320.00
3	403.20	660.00	1940.85
4	480.00	491.50	407.70
5	1488.80	1835.70	2222.40
6	149.00	858.00	330.00
7	1176.00	730.00	7390.20
8	982.00	224.00	224.00
9	88.50	792.75	1549.60
10	1832.80	525.00	966.80
...			

There's another technique to handle the first-value and last-value calculations based on a carry-along-sort concept. The idea is to generate one string that concatenates first the ordering elements (*orderdate* and *orderid*, in our case), and then whichever elements you need to return. Then, by applying *MIN* or *MAX* aggregates, you get back the string holding within it the first or last value, respectively. The trick is to make sure that when you convert the original values to strings, you format them in such a way that preserves the original ordering behavior. In our case, this means converting the *orderdate* values to a *CHAR(8)* string using style 112, which produces the form *YYYYMMDD*. As for the *orderid* values, which are positive integers, you want to convert them to a fixed-sized form with leading spaces or zeros.

The following query shows the first step of the solution, where you just generate the concatenated strings:

```
SELECT custid,
  CONVERT(CHAR(8), orderdate, 112)
    + STR(orderid, 10)
    + STR(val, 14, 2)
    COLLATE Latin1_General_BIN2 AS s
FROM Sales.OrderValues;
```

custid	s
85	20170704 10248 440.00
79	20170705 10249 1863.40
34	20170708 10250 1552.60
84	20170708 10251 654.06
76	20170709 10252 3597.90
34	20170710 10253 1444.80
14	20170711 10254 556.62
68	20170712 10255 2490.50
88	20170715 10256 517.80
35	20170716 10257 1119.90
...	

Observe the use of the binary collation, which helps speed up the comparisons a bit. As for the second step, you define a CTE based on the previous query. Then, in the outer query, you apply the *MIN* and *MAX* aggregates to the string, extract the part representing the value from the result, and convert it to the original type. Here's the complete solution, followed by an abbreviated form of its output:

```
WITH C AS
(
  SELECT custid,
    CONVERT(CHAR(8), orderdate, 112)
      + STR(orderid, 10)
      + STR(val, 14, 2)
      COLLATE Latin1_General_BIN2 AS s
  FROM Sales.OrderValues
)
```

```
SELECT custid,
   CAST(SUBSTRING(MIN(s), 19, 14) AS NUMERIC(12, 2)) AS firstorderval,
   CAST(SUBSTRING(MAX(s), 19, 14) AS NUMERIC(12, 2)) AS lastorderval
FROM C
GROUP BY custid;
```

```
custid  firstorderval  lastorderval
-------  -------------  -------------
1       814.50         933.50
2       88.80          514.40
3       403.20         660.00
4       480.00         491.50
5       1488.80        1835.70
6       149.00         858.00
7       1176.00        730.00
8       982.00         224.00
9       88.50          792.75
10      1832.80        525.00
...
```

Note that I relied on the fact that the integer *orderid* values are non-negative. If you have a numeric ordering element that supports negative values, you need to add logic to make it sort correctly. This is tricky yet doable. For example, suppose that *orderid* values can be negative. To ensure that negative values sort before positive ones, you could add the letter *0* in the string before a negative value and the letter *1* before a non-negative value. To ensure that negative values sort correctly (for example, –2 before –1), you could add *2147483648* (the absolute of the minimum possible negative integer of –2147483648) to the value before converting it to a character string. Here's what the complete query would look like:

```
WITH C AS
(
  SELECT custid,
    CONVERT(CHAR(8), orderdate, 112)
      + CASE SIGN(orderid) WHEN -1 THEN '0' ELSE '1' END -- negative sorts first
      + STR(CASE SIGN(orderid)
              WHEN -1 THEN 2147483648 -- if negative add ABS(minnegative)
              ELSE 0
            END + orderid, 10)
      + STR(val, 14, 2)
      COLLATE Latin1_General_BIN2 AS s
  FROM Sales.OrderValues
)
SELECT custid,
  CAST(SUBSTRING(MIN(s), 20, 14) AS NUMERIC(12, 2)) AS firstorderval,
  CAST(SUBSTRING(MAX(s), 20, 14) AS NUMERIC(12, 2)) AS lastorderval
FROM C
GROUP BY custid;
```

When using this technique in production code, make sure you thoroughly comment the code because it isn't trivial.

String Concatenation

As mentioned, the SQL standard defines three types of ordered set functions, among which one type is called *listagg set function*. The actual standard function name is *LISTAGG*, and it uses the *WITHIN GROUP* clause to define the ordering specification. This function concatenates all strings in the input value expression based on the indicated ordering. People have been waiting to have support for such a function in SQL Server for many years, and finally, SQL Server 2017 introduced such support. The function implemented in SQL Server is called *STRING_AGG*, but otherwise it uses the standard form using the *WITHIN GROUP* clause to define order, if relevant.

For example, suppose you wanted to query the Sales.Orders table and return for each customer a string with all *orderid* values concatenated in *orderid ordering*. You use the following code to achieve this task:

```
SELECT custid,
  STRING_AGG(orderid, ',') WITHIN GROUP(ORDER BY orderid) AS custorders
FROM Sales.Orders
GROUP BY custid;
```

```
custid  custorders
-------  ---------------------------------------------------------------------------
1        10643,10692,10702,10835,10952,11011
2        10308,10625,10759,10926
3        10365,10507,10535,10573,10677,10682,10856
4        10355,10383,10453,10558,10707,10741,10743,10768,10793,10864,10920,10953,11016
5        10278,10280,10384,10444,10445,10524,10572,10626,10654,10672,10689,10733,10778,...
6        10501,10509,10582,10614,10853,10956,11058
7        10265,10297,10360,10436,10449,10559,10566,10584,10628,10679,10826
8        10326,10801,10970
9        10331,10340,10362,10470,10511,10525,10663,10715,10730,10732,10755,10827,10871,...
11       10289,10471,10484,10538,10539,10578,10599,10943,10947,11023
...
```

The *WITHIN GROUP* is optional for the *STRING_AGG* function, so if you don't care about the order for the concatenation, you simply omit this clause, like so:

```
SELECT custid,
  STRING_AGG(orderid, ',') AS custorders
FROM Sales.Orders
GROUP BY custid;
```

If you need similar functionality that is compatible with pre-SQL Server 2017 environments, you need to use an alternative solution. One of the more efficient techniques people use is based on XML manipulation using the *FOR XML* option with the *PATH* mode, like so:

```
SELECT C.custid, A.custorders
FROM Sales.Customers AS C
  CROSS APPLY (
    VALUES( STUFF(
             (SELECT ',' + CAST(O.orderid AS VARCHAR(MAX)) AS [text()]
              FROM Sales.Orders AS O
              WHERE O.custid = C.custid
              ORDER BY O.orderid
              FOR XML PATH(''), TYPE).value('.', 'VARCHAR(MAX)'),
            1, 1, '') ) ) AS A(custorders)
WHERE A.custorders IS NOT NULL;
```

The innermost applied correlated subquery filters only the *orderid* values from the Orders table (aliased as *O*) that are associated with the current customer from the Customers table (aliased as *C*). With the *FOR XML PATH('')* option, you ask to generate a single XML string out of all of the values. Using the empty string as input to the *PATH* mode means that you don't want the wrapping elements to be produced, effectively giving you a concatenation of the values without any added tags. Because the subquery specifies *ORDER BY orderid*, the *orderid* values in the string are ordered. Note that you can order by anything at all—not necessarily by the values you're concatenating. The code also adds a comma as a separator before each *orderid* value, and then the *STUFF* function removes the first comma. Finally, the outer filter removes customers without orders to make the query equivalent to the one with the *STRING_AGG* function. So, it is possible to achieve ordered string concatenation before SQL Server 2017, but it isn't pretty.

Summary

Ordered set functions are aggregate functions that have ordering relevance to the calculation. The standard defines some specific functions, but the concept is, in fact, general and can work for all kinds of aggregate calculations. I gave a few examples beyond what the standard supports, such as off-set functions. The only ordered set function that SQL Server currently supports is the *STRING_AGG* function for grouped string concatenation. I provided alternative methods to emulate the other ordered set functions. I do hope very much to see SQL Server introducing support for more ordered set functions in the future, as well as support for the standard *WITHIN GROUP* clause with *CLR* user-defined aggregate functions that have ordering relevance.

CHAPTER 4

Row-Pattern Recognition in SQL

This book is dedicated to using window functions in your T-SQL code. In large part, the book covers windowing and related analytical features that at the date of this writing have already been implemented in T-SQL. That's what you would naturally expect from a book entitled "T-SQL Window Functions." However, as you've already noticed, the book also exposes you to features that are part of the SQL standard but that have not yet been implemented in T-SQL. I find this coverage just as important. It raises awareness to what's out there, and hopefully, it will motivate you, as part of the Microsoft data platform community, to ask Microsoft to improve SQL Server and Azure SQL Database by adding such features to T-SQL. In fact, quite a few of the existing windowing features in T-SQL were added as a result of past community efforts. Microsoft is listening!

Previous chapters had mixed coverage, including both features that have already been implemented in T-SQL and of related features from the SQL standard that were not. This chapter's focus is an immensely powerful concept from the SQL standard called *row-pattern recognition*, which involves a number of features—none of which are available in T-SQL yet. Understanding that your time is valuable and that you may prefer to focus only on functionality that is already available in T-SQL, I wanted to give you a heads up so that you can elect to skip this chapter. However, if you do wish to know what is part of modern SQL but is not yet available in T-SQL, you will probably want to carry on reading this chapter.

> **Note** Once you're done, you can help improve T-SQL by casting your vote on the suggestion to "Add Support for Row-Pattern Recognition in T-SQL (SQL:2016 features R010 and R020)," which can be found at *https://feedback.azure.com/forums/908035-sql-server/suggestions/37251232-add-support-for-row-pattern-recognition-in-t-sql.*

Background

Row-pattern recognition, or RPR in short, enables you to use regular expressions to identify patterns in sequences of rows similar to the way you use regular expressions to identify patterns in character strings. You could be looking for certain patterns in stock market trading activity, time series, shipping data, material handling, DNA sequences, temperature measurements, gas emissions, and other sequences of rows. Those patterns could be meaningful to you, enabling you to derive valuable trading information, detect potentially fraudulent activity, identify trends, find gaps and islands in your data, and more. RPR uses an elegant design that makes it easy to define the patterns that you're looking for and to act on the matches with all sorts of computations.

To me, RPR is the next step in the evolution of window functions into a more sophisticated and highly flexible analytical tool. Similar to window functions, RPR uses partitioning and ordering. *Row-pattern partitioning* allows you to act on each partition of rows independently, and *row-pattern ordering defines* the order to be used for finding pattern matches in the partition. Additional elements in the RPR specification allow you to use regular expressions to define the pattern that you're looking for, and they allow you to apply computations against the matches. You can then elect to either

- Return one summary row per match, similar to grouping

- Return all rows per match, which gives you the detail rows

> **Note**   The ISO/IEC SQL 9075:2016 standard, or SQL:2016 in short, has extensive coverage of row-pattern recognition and features that use the concept. You can find the coverage in two main documents. One document is "ISO/IEC 9075-2:2016, Information technology—Database languages—SQL—Part 2: Foundation (SQL/Foundation)," which is the document containing the SQL standard's core language elements. It covers row-pattern recognition among many of the other core SQL features. This document is available for purchase at *https://www.iso.org/standard/63556.html*. Another document is a 90-page technical review called "ISO/IEC TR 19075-5," which is dedicated specifically to row-pattern recognition. This document is available for free at *https://standards.iso.org/ittf/PubliclyAvailableStandards/c065143_ISO_IEC_TR_19075-5_2016.zip*.

The SQL standard defines two main features that use row-pattern recognition:

- Feature R010, "Row-pattern recognition: *FROM* clause"

- Feature R020, "Row-pattern recognition: *WINDOW* clause"

With feature R010, you use row-pattern recognition in a table operator called *MATCH_RECOGNIZE* within the *FROM* clause. With feature R020, you use row-pattern recognition in a window specification to restrict the full window frame into a reduced window frame that is based on a pattern match. The standard also briefly mentions feature R030, "Row-pattern recognition: full aggregate support," without which an aggregate function used in row-pattern recognition shall not specify *DISTINCT* or *<filter clause>*.

This chapter covers row-pattern recognition in three main sections. The first covers feature R010, the second covers feature R020, and the third covers solutions using row-pattern recognition.

Note Oracle is an example for a database platform that implements feature R010 (introduced in version 12c). I do not know of any platform that implements feature R020 yet. Therefore, I was able to test solutions related to feature R010 on Oracle, but I could not test the solutions related to R020. In case you have access to Oracle (it's a free download for testing purposes) and wish to run the solutions from the section on feature R010, by all means, I encourage you to do so. Language features are so much better understood if you can experiment with code that uses them. Therefore, I'll provide both theoretical T-SQL code that is not runnable at the date of this writing—as well as Oracle code that is actually runnable today—or instructions for how to adapt the T-SQL code to be runnable on Oracle.

Feature R010, "Row-Pattern Recognition: FROM Clause"

Feature R010, "Row-pattern recognition: FROM clause," defines a table operator called *MATCH_RECOGNIZE*, which you use in the *FROM* clause much like you use the *JOIN*, *APPLY*, *PIVOT*, and *UNPIVOT* operators. The input is a table or table expression, and the output is a virtual table. Here's the general form of a query using the *MATCH_RECOGNIZE* operator:

```
SELECT <select list>
FROM <source table>
  MATCH_RECOGNIZE
  (
    [ PARTITION BY <partition list> ]
    [ ORDER BY <order by list> ]
    [ MEASURES <measure list> ]
    [ <row-pattern rows per match> ::=
        ONE ROW PER MATCH | ALL ROWS PER MATCH ]
    [ AFTER MATCH <skip to option> ]
    PATTERN ( <row-pattern> )
    [ SUBSET <subset list> ]
    DEFINE <definition list>
  ) AS <table alias>;
```

From a logical query processing standpoint, much like the other table operators, the *MATCH_RECOGNIZE* operator is processed as a step within the *FROM* clause. It can operate directly on an input table or table expression, or it can operate on a virtual table resulting from other table operators. Similarly, its output virtual table can be used as an input to another table operator.

The following sections describe the *MATCH_RECOGNIZE* operator and its options, illustrated through a sample task.

Sample Task

I'll illustrate the use of the *MATCH_RECOGNIZE* operator through a sample task adapted from the aforementioned technical review (called "ISO/IEC TR 19075-5"). For this purpose, I'll use a table called Ticker, with columns *symbol, tradedate,* and *price,* holding daily closing trading prices for a couple of stock ticker symbols.

Use the code in Listing 4-1 to create and populate the dbo.Ticker table in SQL Server in the sample database TSQLV5.

LISTING 4-1 Sample Data in Microsoft SQL Server

```
SET NOCOUNT ON;
USE TSQLV5;

DROP TABLE IF EXISTS dbo.Ticker;

CREATE TABLE dbo.Ticker
(
  symbol    VARCHAR(10)    NOT NULL,
  tradedate DATE           NOT NULL,
  price     NUMERIC(12, 2) NOT NULL,
  CONSTRAINT PK_Ticker
    PRIMARY KEY (symbol, tradedate)
);
GO

INSERT INTO dbo.Ticker(symbol, tradedate, price) VALUES
  ('STOCK1', '20190212', 150.00),
  ('STOCK1', '20190213', 151.00),
  ('STOCK1', '20190214', 148.00),
  ('STOCK1', '20190215', 146.00),
  ('STOCK1', '20190218', 142.00),
  ('STOCK1', '20190219', 144.00),
  ('STOCK1', '20190220', 152.00),
  ('STOCK1', '20190221', 152.00),
  ('STOCK1', '20190222', 153.00),
  ('STOCK1', '20190225', 154.00),
  ('STOCK1', '20190226', 154.00),
  ('STOCK1', '20190227', 154.00),
  ('STOCK1', '20190228', 153.00),
  ('STOCK1', '20190301', 145.00),
  ('STOCK1', '20190304', 140.00),
  ('STOCK1', '20190305', 142.00),
  ('STOCK1', '20190306', 143.00),
  ('STOCK1', '20190307', 142.00),
  ('STOCK1', '20190308', 140.00),
  ('STOCK1', '20190311', 138.00),
  ('STOCK2', '20190212', 330.00),
  ('STOCK2', '20190213', 329.00),
  ('STOCK2', '20190214', 329.00),
  ('STOCK2', '20190215', 326.00),
  ('STOCK2', '20190218', 325.00),
```

```
('STOCK2', '20190219', 326.00),
('STOCK2', '20190220', 328.00),
('STOCK2', '20190221', 326.00),
('STOCK2', '20190222', 320.00),
('STOCK2', '20190225', 317.00),
('STOCK2', '20190226', 319.00),
('STOCK2', '20190227', 325.00),
('STOCK2', '20190228', 322.00),
('STOCK2', '20190301', 324.00),
('STOCK2', '20190304', 321.00),
('STOCK2', '20190305', 319.00),
('STOCK2', '20190306', 322.00),
('STOCK2', '20190307', 326.00),
('STOCK2', '20190308', 326.00),
('STOCK2', '20190311', 324.00);

SELECT symbol, tradedate, price
FROM dbo.Ticker;
```

The last query shows the contents of the table, generating the output shown in Listing 4-2.

LISTING 4-2 Contents of *dbo*.Ticker Table

```
symbol   tradedate    price
-------  -----------  -------
STOCK1   2019-02-12   150.00
STOCK1   2019-02-13   151.00
STOCK1   2019-02-14   148.00
STOCK1   2019-02-15   146.00
STOCK1   2019-02-18   142.00
STOCK1   2019-02-19   144.00
STOCK1   2019-02-20   152.00
STOCK1   2019-02-21   152.00
STOCK1   2019-02-22   153.00
STOCK1   2019-02-25   154.00
STOCK1   2019-02-26   154.00
STOCK1   2019-02-27   154.00
STOCK1   2019-02-28   153.00
STOCK1   2019-03-01   145.00
STOCK1   2019-03-04   140.00
STOCK1   2019-03-05   142.00
STOCK1   2019-03-06   143.00
STOCK1   2019-03-07   142.00
STOCK1   2019-03-08   140.00
STOCK1   2019-03-11   138.00
STOCK2   2019-02-12   330.00
STOCK2   2019-02-13   329.00
STOCK2   2019-02-14   329.00
STOCK2   2019-02-15   326.00
STOCK2   2019-02-18   325.00
STOCK2   2019-02-19   326.00
STOCK2   2019-02-20   328.00
STOCK2   2019-02-21   326.00
STOCK2   2019-02-22   320.00
```

```
STOCK2   2019-02-25   317.00
STOCK2   2019-02-26   319.00
STOCK2   2019-02-27   325.00
STOCK2   2019-02-28   322.00
STOCK2   2019-03-01   324.00
STOCK2   2019-03-04   321.00
STOCK2   2019-03-05   319.00
STOCK2   2019-03-06   322.00
STOCK2   2019-03-07   326.00
STOCK2   2019-03-08   326.00
STOCK2   2019-03-11   324.00
```

In case you are planning to run the code samples on Oracle, use the code in Listing 4-3 to create and populate the Ticker table there.

LISTING 4-3 Sample Data in Oracle

```sql
DROP TABLE Ticker;

CREATE TABLE Ticker
(
  symbol     VARCHAR2(10) NOT NULL,
  tradedate  DATE         NOT NULL,
  price      NUMBER       NOT NULL,
  CONSTRAINT PK_Ticker
    PRIMARY KEY (symbol, tradedate)
);

INSERT INTO Ticker(symbol, tradedate, price)
  VALUES('STOCK1', '12-Feb-19', 150.00);
INSERT INTO Ticker(symbol, tradedate, price)
  VALUES('STOCK1', '13-Feb-19', 151.00);
INSERT INTO Ticker(symbol, tradedate, price)
  VALUES('STOCK1', '14-Feb-19', 148.00);
INSERT INTO Ticker(symbol, tradedate, price)
  VALUES('STOCK1', '15-Feb-19', 146.00);
INSERT INTO Ticker(symbol, tradedate, price)
  VALUES('STOCK1', '18-Feb-19', 142.00);
INSERT INTO Ticker(symbol, tradedate, price)
  VALUES('STOCK1', '19-Feb-19', 144.00);
INSERT INTO Ticker(symbol, tradedate, price)
  VALUES('STOCK1', '20-Feb-19', 152.00);
INSERT INTO Ticker(symbol, tradedate, price)
  VALUES('STOCK1', '21-Feb-19', 152.00);
INSERT INTO Ticker(symbol, tradedate, price)
  VALUES('STOCK1', '22-Feb-19', 153.00);
INSERT INTO Ticker(symbol, tradedate, price)
  VALUES('STOCK1', '25-Feb-19', 154.00);
INSERT INTO Ticker(symbol, tradedate, price)
  VALUES('STOCK1', '26-Feb-19', 154.00);
INSERT INTO Ticker(symbol, tradedate, price)
  VALUES('STOCK1', '27-Feb-19', 154.00);
INSERT INTO Ticker(symbol, tradedate, price)
  VALUES('STOCK1', '28-Feb-19', 153.00);
```

```
INSERT INTO Ticker(symbol, tradedate, price)
  VALUES('STOCK1', '01-Mar-19', 145.00);
INSERT INTO Ticker(symbol, tradedate, price)
  VALUES('STOCK1', '04-Mar-19', 140.00);
INSERT INTO Ticker(symbol, tradedate, price)
  VALUES('STOCK1', '05-Mar-19', 142.00);
INSERT INTO Ticker(symbol, tradedate, price)
  VALUES('STOCK1', '06-Mar-19', 143.00);
INSERT INTO Ticker(symbol, tradedate, price)
  VALUES('STOCK1', '07-Mar-19', 142.00);
INSERT INTO Ticker(symbol, tradedate, price)
  VALUES('STOCK1', '08-Mar-19', 140.00);
INSERT INTO Ticker(symbol, tradedate, price)
  VALUES('STOCK1', '11-Mar-19', 138.00);
INSERT INTO Ticker(symbol, tradedate, price)
  VALUES('STOCK2', '12-Feb-19', 330.00);
INSERT INTO Ticker(symbol, tradedate, price)
  VALUES('STOCK2', '13-Feb-19', 329.00);
INSERT INTO Ticker(symbol, tradedate, price)
  VALUES('STOCK2', '14-Feb-19', 329.00);
INSERT INTO Ticker(symbol, tradedate, price)
  VALUES('STOCK2', '15-Feb-19', 326.00);
INSERT INTO Ticker(symbol, tradedate, price)
  VALUES('STOCK2', '18-Feb-19', 325.00);
INSERT INTO Ticker(symbol, tradedate, price)
  VALUES('STOCK2', '19-Feb-19', 326.00);
INSERT INTO Ticker(symbol, tradedate, price)
  VALUES('STOCK2', '20-Feb-19', 328.00);
INSERT INTO Ticker(symbol, tradedate, price)
  VALUES('STOCK2', '21-Feb-19', 326.00);
INSERT INTO Ticker(symbol, tradedate, price)
  VALUES('STOCK2', '22-Feb-19', 320.00);
INSERT INTO Ticker(symbol, tradedate, price)
  VALUES('STOCK2', '25-Feb-19', 317.00);
INSERT INTO Ticker(symbol, tradedate, price)
  VALUES('STOCK2', '26-Feb-19', 319.00);
INSERT INTO Ticker(symbol, tradedate, price)
  VALUES('STOCK2', '27-Feb-19', 325.00);
INSERT INTO Ticker(symbol, tradedate, price)
  VALUES('STOCK2', '28-Feb-19', 322.00);
INSERT INTO Ticker(symbol, tradedate, price)
  VALUES('STOCK2', '01-Mar-19', 324.00);
INSERT INTO Ticker(symbol, tradedate, price)
  VALUES('STOCK2', '04-Mar-19', 321.00);
INSERT INTO Ticker(symbol, tradedate, price)
  VALUES('STOCK2', '05-Mar-19', 319.00);
INSERT INTO Ticker(symbol, tradedate, price)
  VALUES('STOCK2', '06-Mar-19', 322.00);
INSERT INTO Ticker(symbol, tradedate, price)
  VALUES('STOCK2', '07-Mar-19', 326.00);
INSERT INTO Ticker(symbol, tradedate, price)
  VALUES('STOCK2', '08-Mar-19', 326.00);
INSERT INTO Ticker(symbol, tradedate, price)
  VALUES('STOCK2', '11-Mar-19', 324.00);
```

```
COMMIT;

SELECT symbol, tradedate, price
FROM Ticker;
```

The query showing the contents of the table generates the output shown in Listing 4-4.

LISTING 4-4 Contents of Ticker Table

SYMBOL	TRADEDATE	PRICE
STOCK1	12-FEB-19	150
STOCK1	13-FEB-19	151
STOCK1	14-FEB-19	148
STOCK1	15-FEB-19	146
STOCK1	18-FEB-19	142
STOCK1	19-FEB-19	144
STOCK1	20-FEB-19	152
STOCK1	21-FEB-19	152
STOCK1	22-FEB-19	153
STOCK1	25-FEB-19	154
STOCK1	26-FEB-19	154
STOCK1	27-FEB-19	154
STOCK1	28-FEB-19	153
STOCK1	01-MAR-19	145
STOCK1	04-MAR-19	140
STOCK1	05-MAR-19	142
STOCK1	06-MAR-19	143
STOCK1	07-MAR-19	142
STOCK1	08-MAR-19	140
STOCK1	11-MAR-19	138
STOCK2	12-FEB-19	330
STOCK2	13-FEB-19	329
STOCK2	14-FEB-19	329
STOCK2	15-FEB-19	326
STOCK2	18-FEB-19	325
STOCK2	19-FEB-19	326
STOCK2	20-FEB-19	328
STOCK2	21-FEB-19	326
STOCK2	22-FEB-19	320
STOCK2	25-FEB-19	317
STOCK2	26-FEB-19	319
STOCK2	27-FEB-19	325
STOCK2	28-FEB-19	322
STOCK2	01-MAR-19	324
STOCK2	04-MAR-19	321
STOCK2	05-MAR-19	319
STOCK2	06-MAR-19	322
STOCK2	07-MAR-19	326
STOCK2	08-MAR-19	326
STOCK2	11-MAR-19	324

You're given a task to query the Ticker table and identify sequences of rows representing V shapes in the trading activity, for each symbol independently, based on trading date order. A V shape means a consecutive sequence of rows starting with any row, immediately followed by a period of strictly decreasing prices, immediately followed by a period of strictly increasing prices. We can find these sorts of price change occurrences using row-pattern recognition.

Figure 4-1 shows a visual depiction of the V-shape pattern matches that the solution query finds for STOCK1.

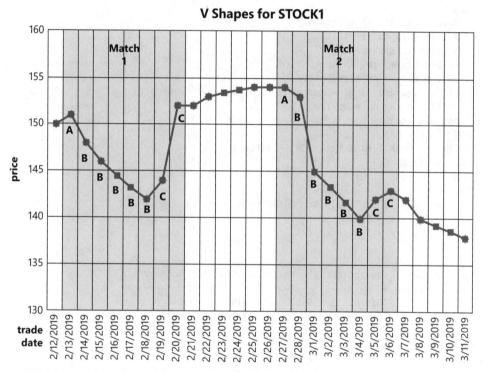

FIGURE 4-1 Visual depiction of V-shape pattern matches for STOCK1.

As part of the specification of the *MATCH_RECOGNIZE* operator, you indicate a *row-pattern rows per match* option where you indicate whether you want the output table to have one summary row per match, like in grouping, or all rows per match, where you get the detail rows. In the following sections I demonstrate both options.

ONE ROW PER MATCH

Listing 4-5 has the solution query for the sample task, showing one row per match with the summary information, followed by the query's expected output (split into two parts due to page size restrictions).

LISTING 4-5 Solution Query for Sample Task with the *ONE ROW PER MATCH* Option

```
SELECT
  MR.symbol, MR.matchnum, MR.startdate, MR.startprice,
  MR.bottomdate, MR.bottomprice, MR.enddate, MR.endprice, MR.maxprice
FROM dbo.Ticker
  MATCH_RECOGNIZE
  (
    PARTITION BY symbol
    ORDER BY tradedate
    MEASURES
      MATCH_NUMBER() AS matchnum,
      A.tradedate AS startdate,
      A.price AS startprice,
      LAST(B.tradedate) AS bottomdate,
      LAST(B.price) AS bottomprice,
      LAST(C.tradedate) AS enddate, -- same as LAST(tradedate)
      LAST(C.price) AS endprice,
      MAX(U.price) AS maxprice -- same as MAX(price)
    ONE ROW PER MATCH -- default
    AFTER MATCH SKIP PAST LAST ROW -- default
    PATTERN (A B+ C+)
    SUBSET U = (A, B, C)
    DEFINE
      -- A defaults to True, matches any row, same as A AS 1 = 1
      B AS B.price < PREV(B.price),
      C AS C.price > PREV(C.price)
  ) AS MR;
```

symbol	matchnum	startdate	startprice	bottomdate	bottomprice
STOCK1	1	2019-02-13	151.00	2019-02-18	142.00
STOCK1	2	2019-02-27	154.00	2019-03-04	140.00
STOCK2	1	2019-02-14	329.00	2019-02-18	325.00
STOCK2	2	2019-02-21	326.00	2019-02-25	317.00
STOCK2	3	2019-03-01	324.00	2019-03-05	319.00

symbol	matchnum	enddate	endprice	maxprice
STOCK1	1	2019-02-20	152.00	152.00
STOCK1	2	2019-03-06	143.00	154.00
STOCK2	1	2019-02-20	328.00	329.00
STOCK2	2	2019-02-27	325.00	326.00
STOCK2	3	2019-03-07	326.00	326.00

To run the query in Oracle, you need to apply a couple of changes. First, you can't use the AS clause to assign a table alias; you need to use a space instead. Second, instead of specifying *dbo* as the table prefix, specify the name of the user that created the table (for example, for user1, specify *FROM user1. Ticker*). If you are connected with that user, don't specify a table prefix at all (for example, *FROM Ticker*). Listing 4-6 shows the solution query for use in Oracle, followed by its output.

```
SELECT
  MR.symbol, MR.matchnum, MR.startdate, MR.startprice,
  MR.bottomdate, MR.bottomprice, MR.enddate, MR.endprice, MR.maxprice
FROM Ticker -- removed qualifier
  MATCH_RECOGNIZE
  (
    PARTITION BY symbol
    ORDER BY tradedate
    MEASURES
      MATCH_NUMBER() AS matchnum,
      A.tradedate AS startdate,
      A.price AS startprice,
      LAST(B.tradedate) AS bottomdate,
      LAST(B.price) AS bottomprice,
      LAST(C.tradedate) AS enddate,
      LAST(C.price) AS endprice,
      MAX(U.price) AS maxprice
    ONE ROW PER MATCH
    AFTER MATCH SKIP PAST LAST ROW
    PATTERN (A B+ C+)
    SUBSET U = (A, B, C)
    DEFINE
      B AS B.price < PREV(B.price),
      C AS C.price > PREV(C.price)
  ) MR; -- removed AS clause
```

SYMBOL	MATCHNUM	STARTDATE	STARTPRICE	BOTTOMDATE	BOTTOMPRICE
STOCK1	1	13-FEB-19	151	18-FEB-19	142
STOCK1	2	27-FEB-19	154	04-MAR-19	140
STOCK2	1	14-FEB-19	329	18-FEB-19	325
STOCK2	2	21-FEB-19	326	25-FEB-19	317
STOCK2	3	01-MAR-19	324	05-MAR-19	319

SYMBOL	MATCHNUM	ENDDATE	ENDPRICE	MAXPRICE
STOCK1	1	20-FEB-19	152	152
STOCK1	2	06-MAR-19	143	154
STOCK2	1	20-FEB-19	328	329
STOCK2	2	27-FEB-19	325	326
STOCK2	3	07-MAR-19	326	326

The output in Oracle shows column names in uppercase, and dates and prices in a different format than it would in SQL Server.

Let's analyze the different options in the specification of the *MATCH_RECOGNIZE* clause in the solution query.

The *row-pattern partitioning* clause (*PARTITION BY*) specifies that you want pattern matches to be handled in each partition separately. In our case, the clause is defined as *PARTITION BY symbol*, meaning that you want to handle each distinct symbol separately. This clause is optional. Absent a row-pattern partitioning clause, all rows from the input table are treated as one partition.

The *row-pattern ordering* clause (*ORDER BY*) defines the ordering based on which you want to look for pattern matches in the partition. In our query, this clause is defined as *ORDER BY tradedate*, meaning that you want to look for pattern matches based on trade date ordering. Oddly, this clause is optional. It is unlikely, though, that you will want to omit this clause since this would result in a completely nondeterministic order. From a practical standpoint, you would normally want to specify this clause.

The *DEFINE* clause defines *row-pattern variables*, each representing a subsequence of rows within a pattern match. My styling preference is to use letters like *A*, *B*, and *C* as the variable names; of course, you can use longer, more meaningful names for those if you like. This example uses the following variable names:

- *A* represents any row as a starting point (defaults to *true* when not defined explicitly but used in the *PATTERN* clause).

- *B* represents a subsequence of strictly decreasing prices *(B.price < PREV(B.price))*. As you can guess, *PREV(B.price)* returns the price from the previous row. I'll provide the functions that you can use in the *DEFINE* clause shortly.

- *C* represents a subsequence of strictly increasing prices *(C.price > PREV(C.price))*.

At least one explicit row-pattern variable definition is required, so if you need to define only one variable that is simply *true*, you will need to define it explicitly. For example, you could use *A AS 1 = 1*. In our case, we have additional row-pattern variables to define besides *A*, so you can rely on the implicit definition for *A*, which defaults to *true*.

The *PATTERN* clause uses a regular expression to define a pattern based on row-pattern variables. In our case, the pattern is *(A B+ C+)*, meaning any row, followed by one or more rows with decreasing prices, followed by one or more rows with increasing prices. Table 4-1 shows a list of quantifiers that you can use in the regular expressions, their meanings, and an example for each.

TABLE 4-1 Regular Expression Quantifiers

Quantifier	Meaning	Example
*	Zero (0) or more matches	A*
+	One (1) or more matches	A+
?	No match or one (1) match, optional	A?
{n}	Exactly n matches	A{3}
{n,}	n or more matches	A{3,}
{n, m}	Between n and m (inclusive) matches	A{1, 3}
{, m}	Between zero (0) and m (inclusive) matches	A{, 3}

Quantifier	Meaning	Example
{- Variable -}	Indicates that matching rows are to be excluded from the output (useful only if ALL ROW PER MATCH specified)	A {- B+ -} C+
|	Alternation	A | B
()	Grouping	(A | B)
^	Start of a row-pattern partition	^A{1, 3}
$	End of a row-pattern partition	A{1, 3}$

By default, quantifiers are greedy (maximize the number of matches), but by adding a question mark (?), you make a quantifier reluctant (minimize the number of matches). For example, consider the pattern A+B+ versus A+?B+. Suppose that the first item satisfying the predicate for A is found. Then when continuing to the next item, the former pattern first evaluates the item as a candidate for A, whereas the latter pattern first evaluates it as a candidate for B.

I'll demonstrate several of the above quantifiers in later examples in this chapter.

The *SUBSET* clause defines variables that represent subsets, or combinations, of variables. In our case, the clause defines the variable U representing the subset (A, B, C). Such a subset can be used as a target for a function, like an aggregate function. For instance, perhaps you want to compute the maximum stock price within a combination of the subsections represented by the variables A, B, and C. To achieve this, you apply the expression *MAX(U.price)* in the *MEASURES* clause, which I describe next.

The *MEASURES* clause defines measures that are applied to variables. Recall that each variable represents a subsequence of rows within a pattern match, or a subset of variables. The function *MATCH_NUMBER* assigns sequential integers starting with 1 for each pattern match within the partition. You can use the functions *FIRST, LAST, PREV,* and *NEXT*, as well as aggregate functions. With the *FIRST* and *LAST* functions, you can specify a nonnegative integer as a second argument representing a logical offset you want to switch to within the mapped variable. The default is zero (*0*). For example, *FIRST(A.price, 1)* means that you want to switch to the second row mapped to A (logical offset 1 from the first). By default, the offset for *PREV* and *NEXT* is one row, but you can specify a second argument with the row offset; for example, *PREV(A.price, 2)* goes two rows back compared to the current instead of just one.

The *row-pattern rows per match* option defines whether you want to return one summary row per match (*ONE ROW PER MATCH*, which is the default) or all detail rows (*ALL ROWS PER MATCH*). Our query uses the former. I'll demonstrate the latter shortly with a couple of nuances. When using the former, the output virtual table contains the row-pattern partitioning columns, as well as the measures defined in the *MEASURES* clause. When using the latter, the output virtual table contains all input table columns, as well as the measures defined in the *MEASURES* clause.

The *AFTER MATCH <skip to option>* defines where to continue looking for another match after a match is found. Our query specifies *AFTER MATCH SKIP PAST LAST ROW* (the default), meaning that after a match is found you want to skip to the row that appears immediately after the last row in the current match. You can also specify *AFTER MATCH SKIP TO NEXT* ROW, meaning the row after the first row in the current match. You can also skip to a position relative to a row-pattern variable. For example, *AFTER MATCH SKIP TO FIRST A*, or *AFTER MATCH SKIP TO LAST A*.

Armed with this knowledge, reexamine the query in Listing 4-5, as well as the visual depiction of the sample data and pattern matches in Figure 4-1, and make sure that you understand why the query generates the output that it does. Observe that since the query uses the *ONE ROW PER MATCH* option and *STOCK1* has two matches, the output shows two rows for *STOCK1*.

ALL ROWS PER MATCH

Listing 4-7 shows a slightly modified version of the query from Listing 4-5, only this time using the *ALL ROWS PER MATCH* option, followed by the expected output (again, formatted).

LISTING 4-7 Sample Query Showing *ALL ROWS PER MATCH*

```
SELECT
  MR.symbol, MR.tradedate, MR.price, MR.matchnum, MR.classy,
  MR.startdate, MR.startprice, MR.bottomdate, MR.bottomprice,
  MR.enddate, MR.endprice, MR.maxprice
FROM dbo.Ticker
  MATCH_RECOGNIZEg
  (
    PARTITION BY symbol
    ORDER BY tradedate
    MEASURES
      MATCH_NUMBER() AS matchnum,
      CLASSIFIER() AS classy,
      A.tradedate AS startdate,
      A.price AS startprice,
      LAST(B.tradedate) AS bottomdate,
      LAST(B.price) AS bottomprice,
      LAST(C.tradedate) AS enddate,
      LAST(C.price) AS endprice,
      MAX(U.price) AS maxprice
    ALL ROWS PER MATCH
    AFTER MATCH SKIP PAST LAST ROW
    PATTERN (A B+ C+)
    SUBSET U = (A, B, C)
    DEFINE
      B AS B.price < PREV(B.price),
      C AS C.price > PREV(C.price)
  ) AS MR;
```

```
symbol   tradedate    price   matchnum  classy  startdate   startprice
-------  -----------  ------- ---------- ------- ----------  ----------
STOCK1   2019-02-13   151.00  1          A       2019-02-13  151.00
STOCK1   2019-02-14   148.00  1          B       2019-02-13  151.00
STOCK1   2019-02-15   146.00  1          B       2019-02-13  151.00
STOCK1   2019-02-18   142.00  1          B       2019-02-13  151.00
STOCK1   2019-02-19   144.00  1          C       2019-02-13  151.00
STOCK1   2019-02-20   152.00  1          C       2019-02-13  151.00
```

STOCK1	2019-02-27	154.00	2	A	2019-02-27	154.00
STOCK1	2019-02-28	153.00	2	B	2019-02-27	154.00
STOCK1	2019-03-01	145.00	2	B	2019-02-27	154.00
STOCK1	2019-03-04	140.00	2	B	2019-02-27	154.00
STOCK1	2019-03-05	142.00	2	C	2019-02-27	154.00
STOCK1	2019-03-06	143.00	2	C	2019-02-27	154.00
STOCK2	2019-02-14	329.00	1	A	2019-02-14	329.00
STOCK2	2019-02-15	326.00	1	B	2019-02-14	329.00
STOCK2	2019-02-18	325.00	1	B	2019-02-14	329.00
STOCK2	2019-02-19	326.00	1	C	2019-02-14	329.00
STOCK2	2019-02-20	328.00	1	C	2019-02-14	329.00
STOCK2	2019-02-21	326.00	2	A	2019-02-21	326.00
STOCK2	2019-02-22	320.00	2	B	2019-02-21	326.00
STOCK2	2019-02-25	317.00	2	B	2019-02-21	326.00
STOCK2	2019-02-26	319.00	2	C	2019-02-21	326.00
STOCK2	2019-02-27	325.00	2	C	2019-02-21	326.00
STOCK2	2019-03-01	324.00	3	A	2019-03-01	324.00
STOCK2	2019-03-04	321.00	3	B	2019-03-01	324.00
STOCK2	2019-03-05	319.00	3	B	2019-03-01	324.00
STOCK2	2019-03-06	322.00	3	C	2019-03-01	324.00
STOCK2	2019-03-07	326.00	3	C	2019-03-01	324.00

symbol	tradedate	bottomdate	bottomprice	enddate	endprice
STOCK1	2019-02-13	NULL	NULL	NULL	NULL
STOCK1	2019-02-14	2019-02-14	148.00	NULL	NULL
STOCK1	2019-02-15	2019-02-15	146.00	NULL	NULL
STOCK1	2019-02-18	2019-02-18	142.00	NULL	NULL
STOCK1	2019-02-19	2019-02-18	142.00	2019-02-19	144.00
STOCK1	2019-02-20	2019-02-18	142.00	2019-02-20	152.00
STOCK1	2019-02-27	NULL	NULL	NULL	NULL
STOCK1	2019-02-28	2019-02-28	153.00	NULL	NULL
STOCK1	2019-03-01	2019-03-01	145.00	NULL	NULL
STOCK1	2019-03-04	2019-03-04	140.00	NULL	NULL
STOCK1	2019-03-05	2019-03-04	140.00	2019-03-05	142.00
STOCK1	2019-03-06	2019-03-04	140.00	2019-03-06	143.00
STOCK2	2019-02-14	NULL	NULL	NULL	NULL
STOCK2	2019-02-15	2019-02-15	326.00	NULL	NULL
STOCK2	2019-02-18	2019-02-18	325.00	NULL	NULL
STOCK2	2019-02-19	2019-02-18	325.00	2019-02-19	326.00
STOCK2	2019-02-20	2019-02-18	325.00	2019-02-20	328.00
STOCK2	2019-02-21	NULL	NULL	NULL	NULL
STOCK2	2019-02-22	2019-02-22	320.00	NULL	NULL
STOCK2	2019-02-25	2019-02-25	317.00	NULL	NULL
STOCK2	2019-02-26	2019-02-25	317.00	2019-02-26	319.00
STOCK2	2019-02-27	2019-02-25	317.00	2019-02-27	325.00
STOCK2	2019-03-01	NULL	NULL	NULL	NULL
STOCK2	2019-03-04	2019-03-04	321.00	NULL	NULL
STOCK2	2019-03-05	2019-03-05	319.00	NULL	NULL
STOCK2	2019-03-06	2019-03-05	319.00	2019-03-06	322.00
STOCK2	2019-03-07	2019-03-05	319.00	2019-03-07	326.00

```
symbol   tradedate    maxprice
-------  -----------  ----------
STOCK1   2019-02-13   151.00
STOCK1   2019-02-14   151.00
STOCK1   2019-02-15   151.00
STOCK1   2019-02-18   151.00
STOCK1   2019-02-19   151.00
STOCK1   2019-02-20   152.00
STOCK1   2019-02-27   154.00
STOCK1   2019-02-28   154.00
STOCK1   2019-03-01   154.00
STOCK1   2019-03-04   154.00
STOCK1   2019-03-05   154.00
STOCK1   2019-03-06   154.00
STOCK2   2019-02-14   329.00
STOCK2   2019-02-15   329.00
STOCK2   2019-02-18   329.00
STOCK2   2019-02-19   329.00
STOCK2   2019-02-20   329.00
STOCK2   2019-02-21   326.00
STOCK2   2019-02-22   326.00
STOCK2   2019-02-25   326.00
STOCK2   2019-02-26   326.00
STOCK2   2019-02-27   326.00
STOCK2   2019-03-01   324.00
STOCK2   2019-03-04   324.00
STOCK2   2019-03-05   324.00
STOCK2   2019-03-06   324.00
STOCK2   2019-03-07   326.00

(27 rows affected)
```

Observe that this time the query computes a measure called *classy* based on the function *CLASSIFIER*. This function returns a string representing the row-pattern variable that the current row is associated with, or a *NULL* if the current row is not part of a match.

By default, unmatched rows are omitted. That's why in the output of the above query all rows are associated with row-pattern variables. If you wish to include unmatched rows, you specify *ALL ROWS PER MATCH WITH UNMATCHED ROWS*, as shown in Listing 4-8.

LISTING 4-8 Query Using *ALL ROWS PER MATCH WITH UNMATCHED ROWS*

```
SELECT
  MR.symbol, MR.tradedate, MR.price, MR.matchnum, MR.classy,
  MR.startdate, MR.startprice, MR.bottomdate, MR.bottomprice,
  MR.enddate, MR.endprice, MR.maxprice
FROM dbo.Ticker
  MATCH_RECOGNIZE
  (
    PARTITION BY symbol
    ORDER BY tradedate
    MEASURES
      MATCH_NUMBER() AS matchnum,
```

```
        CLASSIFIER() AS classy,
        A.tradedate AS startdate,
        A.price AS startprice,
        LAST(B.tradedate) AS bottomdate,
        LAST(B.price) AS bottomprice,
        LAST(C.tradedate) AS enddate,
        LAST(C.price) AS endprice,
        MAX(U.price) AS maxprice
    ALL ROWS PER MATCH WITH UNMATCHED ROWS
    AFTER MATCH SKIP PAST LAST ROW
    PATTERN (A B+ C+)
    SUBSET U = (A, B, C)
    DEFINE
        B AS B.price < PREV(B.price),
        C AS C.price > PREV(C.price)
  ) AS MR;
```

symbol	tradedate	price	matchnum	classy	startdate	startprice
STOCK1	2019-02-12	150.00	NULL	NULL	NULL	NULL
STOCK1	2019-02-13	151.00	1	A	2019-02-13	151.00
STOCK1	2019-02-14	148.00	1	B	2019-02-13	151.00
STOCK1	2019-02-15	146.00	1	B	2019-02-13	151.00
STOCK1	2019-02-18	142.00	1	B	2019-02-13	151.00
STOCK1	2019-02-19	144.00	1	C	2019-02-13	151.00
STOCK1	2019-02-20	152.00	1	C	2019-02-13	151.00
STOCK1	2019-02-21	152.00	NULL	NULL	NULL	NULL
STOCK1	2019-02-22	153.00	NULL	NULL	NULL	NULL
STOCK1	2019-02-25	154.00	NULL	NULL	NULL	NULL
STOCK1	2019-02-26	154.00	NULL	NULL	NULL	NULL
STOCK1	2019-02-27	154.00	2	A	2019-02-27	154.00
STOCK1	2019-02-28	153.00	2	B	2019-02-27	154.00
STOCK1	2019-03-01	145.00	2	B	2019-02-27	154.00
STOCK1	2019-03-04	140.00	2	B	2019-02-27	154.00
STOCK1	2019-03-05	142.00	2	C	2019-02-27	154.00
STOCK1	2019-03-06	143.00	2	C	2019-02-27	154.00
STOCK1	2019-03-07	142.00	NULL	NULL	NULL	NULL
STOCK1	2019-03-08	140.00	NULL	NULL	NULL	NULL
STOCK1	2019-03-11	138.00	NULL	NULL	NULL	NULL
STOCK2	2019-02-12	330.00	NULL	NULL	NULL	NULL
STOCK2	2019-02-13	329.00	NULL	NULL	NULL	NULL
STOCK2	2019-02-14	329.00	1	A	2019-02-14	329.00
STOCK2	2019-02-15	326.00	1	B	2019-02-14	329.00
STOCK2	2019-02-18	325.00	1	B	2019-02-14	329.00
STOCK2	2019-02-19	326.00	1	C	2019-02-14	329.00
STOCK2	2019-02-20	328.00	1	C	2019-02-14	329.00
STOCK2	2019-02-21	326.00	2	A	2019-02-21	326.00
STOCK2	2019-02-22	320.00	2	B	2019-02-21	326.00
STOCK2	2019-02-25	317.00	2	B	2019-02-21	326.00
STOCK2	2019-02-26	319.00	2	C	2019-02-21	326.00
STOCK2	2019-02-27	325.00	2	C	2019-02-21	326.00
STOCK2	2019-02-28	322.00	NULL	NULL	NULL	NULL
STOCK2	2019-03-01	324.00	3	A	2019-03-01	324.00

STOCK2	2019-03-04	321.00	3	B	2019-03-01	324.00
STOCK2	2019-03-05	319.00	3	B	2019-03-01	324.00
STOCK2	2019-03-06	322.00	3	C	2019-03-01	324.00
STOCK2	2019-03-07	326.00	3	C	2019-03-01	324.00
STOCK2	2019-03-08	326.00	NULL	NULL	NULL	NULL
STOCK2	2019-03-11	324.00	NULL	NULL	NULL	NULL

symbol	tradedate	bottomdate	bottomprice	enddate	endprice
STOCK1	2019-02-12	NULL	NULL	NULL	NULL
STOCK1	2019-02-13	NULL	NULL	NULL	NULL
STOCK1	2019-02-14	2019-02-14	148.00	NULL	NULL
STOCK1	2019-02-15	2019-02-15	146.00	NULL	NULL
STOCK1	2019-02-18	2019-02-18	142.00	NULL	NULL
STOCK1	2019-02-19	2019-02-18	142.00	2019-02-19	144.00
STOCK1	2019-02-20	2019-02-18	142.00	2019-02-20	152.00
STOCK1	2019-02-21	NULL	NULL	NULL	NULL
STOCK1	2019-02-22	NULL	NULL	NULL	NULL
STOCK1	2019-02-25	NULL	NULL	NULL	NULL
STOCK1	2019-02-26	NULL	NULL	NULL	NULL
STOCK1	2019-02-27	NULL	NULL	NULL	NULL
STOCK1	2019-02-28	2019-02-28	153.00	NULL	NULL
STOCK1	2019-03-01	2019-03-01	145.00	NULL	NULL
STOCK1	2019-03-04	2019-03-04	140.00	NULL	NULL
STOCK1	2019-03-05	2019-03-04	140.00	2019-03-05	142.00
STOCK1	2019-03-06	2019-03-04	140.00	2019-03-06	143.00
STOCK1	2019-03-07	NULL	NULL	NULL	NULL
STOCK1	2019-03-08	NULL	NULL	NULL	NULL
STOCK1	2019-03-11	NULL	NULL	NULL	NULL
STOCK2	2019-02-12	NULL	NULL	NULL	NULL
STOCK2	2019-02-13	NULL	NULL	NULL	NULL
STOCK2	2019-02-14	NULL	NULL	NULL	NULL
STOCK2	2019-02-15	2019-02-15	326.00	NULL	NULL
STOCK2	2019-02-18	2019-02-18	325.00	NULL	NULL
STOCK2	2019-02-19	2019-02-18	325.00	2019-02-19	326.00
STOCK2	2019-02-20	2019-02-18	325.00	2019-02-20	328.00
STOCK2	2019-02-21	NULL	NULL	NULL	NULL
STOCK2	2019-02-22	2019-02-22	320.00	NULL	NULL
STOCK2	2019-02-25	2019-02-25	317.00	NULL	NULL
STOCK2	2019-02-26	2019-02-25	317.00	2019-02-26	319.00
STOCK2	2019-02-27	2019-02-25	317.00	2019-02-27	325.00
STOCK2	2019-02-28	NULL	NULL	NULL	NULL
STOCK2	2019-03-01	NULL	NULL	NULL	NULL
STOCK2	2019-03-04	2019-03-04	321.00	NULL	NULL
STOCK2	2019-03-05	2019-03-05	319.00	NULL	NULL
STOCK2	2019-03-06	2019-03-05	319.00	2019-03-06	322.00
STOCK2	2019-03-07	2019-03-05	319.00	2019-03-07	326.00
STOCK2	2019-03-08	NULL	NULL	NULL	NULL
STOCK2	2019-03-11	NULL	NULL	NULL	NULL

symbol	tradedate	maxprice
STOCK1	2019-02-12	NULL
STOCK1	2019-02-13	151.00

```
STOCK1   2019-02-14   151.00
STOCK1   2019-02-15   151.00
STOCK1   2019-02-18   151.00
STOCK1   2019-02-19   151.00
STOCK1   2019-02-20   152.00
STOCK1   2019-02-21   NULL
STOCK1   2019-02-22   NULL
STOCK1   2019-02-25   NULL
STOCK1   2019-02-26   NULL
STOCK1   2019-02-27   154.00
STOCK1   2019-02-28   154.00
STOCK1   2019-03-01   154.00
STOCK1   2019-03-04   154.00
STOCK1   2019-03-05   154.00
STOCK1   2019-03-06   154.00
STOCK1   2019-03-07   NULL
STOCK1   2019-03-08   NULL
STOCK1   2019-03-11   NULL
STOCK2   2019-02-12   NULL
STOCK2   2019-02-13   NULL
STOCK2   2019-02-14   329.00
STOCK2   2019-02-15   329.00
STOCK2   2019-02-18   329.00
STOCK2   2019-02-19   329.00
STOCK2   2019-02-20   329.00
STOCK2   2019-02-21   326.00
STOCK2   2019-02-22   326.00
STOCK2   2019-02-25   326.00
STOCK2   2019-02-26   326.00
STOCK2   2019-02-27   326.00
STOCK2   2019-02-28   NULL
STOCK2   2019-03-01   324.00
STOCK2   2019-03-04   324.00
STOCK2   2019-03-05   324.00
STOCK2   2019-03-06   324.00
STOCK2   2019-03-07   326.00
STOCK2   2019-03-08   NULL
STOCK2   2019-03-11   NULL

(40 rows affected)
```

This time, unmatched rows are returned (40 rows versus 27), showing *NULLs* in both result columns *matchno* and *classy*.

Note that some patterns can involve empty matches—not to confuse with unmatched rows. For instance, suppose that you define a variable *A as A.price < PREV(A.price)*, and the pattern *A+*. This pattern looks for one or more matches for A; therefore, there cannot be empty matches, but you can have unmatched rows, just like in the last example. In contrast, consider the pattern *A**, which looks for zero or more matches, and hence can have empty matches. You can specify whether to show empty matches or not. The option *SHOW EMPTY MATCHES* is the default, but you can specify *OMIT EMPTY MATCHES* if you like.

Listing 4-9 shows a query demonstrating showing empty matches (the default), followed by its expected output.

LISTING 4-9 Query Showing Empty Matches

```
SELECT
  MR.symbol, MR.tradedate, MR.matchnum, MR.classy,
  MR.startdate, MR.startprice, MR.enddate, MR.endprice, MR.price
FROM dbo.Ticker
  MATCH_RECOGNIZE
  (
    PARTITION BY symbol
    ORDER BY tradedate
    MEASURES
      MATCH_NUMBER() AS matchnum,
      CLASSIFIER() AS classy,
      FIRST(A.tradedate) AS startdate,
      FIRST(A.price) AS startprice,
      LAST(A.tradedate) AS enddate,
      LAST(A.price) AS endprice
    ALL ROWS PER MATCH -- defaults to SHOW EMPTY MATCHES
    AFTER MATCH SKIP PAST LAST ROW
    PATTERN (A*)
    DEFINE
      A AS A.price < PREV(A.price)
  ) AS MR;
```

symbol	tradedate	matchnum	classy	startdate	startprice
STOCK1	2019-02-12	1	NULL	NULL	NULL
STOCK1	2019-02-13	2	NULL	NULL	NULL
STOCK1	2019-02-14	3	A	2019-02-14	148.00
STOCK1	2019-02-15	3	A	2019-02-14	148.00
STOCK1	2019-02-18	3	A	2019-02-14	148.00
STOCK1	2019-02-19	4	NULL	NULL	NULL
STOCK1	2019-02-20	5	NULL	NULL	NULL
STOCK1	2019-02-21	6	NULL	NULL	NULL
STOCK1	2019-02-22	7	NULL	NULL	NULL
STOCK1	2019-02-25	8	NULL	NULL	NULL
STOCK1	2019-02-26	9	NULL	NULL	NULL
STOCK1	2019-02-27	10	NULL	NULL	NULL
STOCK1	2019-02-28	11	A	2019-02-28	153.00
STOCK1	2019-03-01	11	A	2019-02-28	153.00
STOCK1	2019-03-04	11	A	2019-02-28	153.00
STOCK1	2019-03-05	12	NULL	NULL	NULL
STOCK1	2019-03-06	13	NULL	NULL	NULL
STOCK1	2019-03-07	14	A	2019-03-07	142.00
STOCK1	2019-03-08	14	A	2019-03-07	142.00
STOCK1	2019-03-11	14	A	2019-03-07	142.00
STOCK2	2019-02-12	1	NULL	NULL	NULL
STOCK2	2019-02-13	2	A	2019-02-13	329.00
STOCK2	2019-02-14	3	NULL	NULL	NULL
STOCK2	2019-02-15	4	A	2019-02-15	326.00

```
STOCK2  2019-02-18  4   A     2019-02-15  326.00
STOCK2  2019-02-19  5   NULL  NULL        NULL
STOCK2  2019-02-20  6   NULL  NULL        NULL
STOCK2  2019-02-21  7   A     2019-02-21  326.00
STOCK2  2019-02-22  7   A     2019-02-21  326.00
STOCK2  2019-02-25  7   A     2019-02-21  326.00
STOCK2  2019-02-26  8   NULL  NULL        NULL
STOCK2  2019-02-27  9   NULL  NULL        NULL
STOCK2  2019-02-28  10  A     2019-02-28  322.00
STOCK2  2019-03-01  11  NULL  NULL        NULL
STOCK2  2019-03-04  12  A     2019-03-04  321.00
STOCK2  2019-03-05  12  A     2019-03-04  321.00
STOCK2  2019-03-06  13  NULL  NULL        NULL
STOCK2  2019-03-07  14  NULL  NULL        NULL
STOCK2  2019-03-08  15  NULL  NULL        NULL
STOCK2  2019-03-11  16  A     2019-03-11  324.00

symbol  tradedate   enddate     endprice  price
-------  ----------- ----------- --------- -------
STOCK1  2019-02-12  NULL        NULL      150.00
STOCK1  2019-02-13  NULL        NULL      151.00
STOCK1  2019-02-14  2019-02-14  148       148.00
STOCK1  2019-02-15  2019-02-15  146       146.00
STOCK1  2019-02-18  2019-02-18  142       142.00
STOCK1  2019-02-19  NULL        NULL      144.00
STOCK1  2019-02-20  NULL        NULL      152.00
STOCK1  2019-02-21  NULL        NULL      152.00
STOCK1  2019-02-22  NULL        NULL      153.00
STOCK1  2019-02-25  NULL        NULL      154.00
STOCK1  2019-02-26  NULL        NULL      154.00
STOCK1  2019-02-27  NULL        NULL      154.00
STOCK1  2019-02-28  2019-02-28  153       153.00
STOCK1  2019-03-01  2019-03-01  145       145.00
STOCK1  2019-03-04  2019-03-04  140       140.00
STOCK1  2019-03-05  NULL        NULL      142.00
STOCK1  2019-03-06  NULL        NULL      143.00
STOCK1  2019-03-07  2019-03-07  142       142.00
STOCK1  2019-03-08  2019-03-08  140       140.00
STOCK1  2019-03-11  2019-03-11  138       138.00
STOCK2  2019-02-12  NULL        NULL      330.00
STOCK2  2019-02-13  2019-02-13  329       329.00
STOCK2  2019-02-14  NULL        NULL      329.00
STOCK2  2019-02-15  2019-02-15  326       326.00
STOCK2  2019-02-18  2019-02-18  325       325.00
STOCK2  2019-02-19  NULL        NULL      326.00
STOCK2  2019-02-20  NULL        NULL      328.00
STOCK2  2019-02-21  2019-02-21  326       326.00
STOCK2  2019-02-22  2019-02-22  320       320.00
STOCK2  2019-02-25  2019-02-25  317       317.00
STOCK2  2019-02-26  NULL        NULL      319.00
STOCK2  2019-02-27  NULL        NULL      325.00
STOCK2  2019-02-28  2019-02-28  322       322.00
STOCK2  2019-03-01  NULL        NULL      324.00
STOCK2  2019-03-04  2019-03-04  321       321.00
```

```
STOCK2  2019-03-05  2019-03-05  319    319.00
STOCK2  2019-03-06  NULL        NULL   322.00
STOCK2  2019-03-07  NULL        NULL   326.00
STOCK2  2019-03-08  NULL        NULL   326.00
STOCK2  2019-03-11  2019-03-11  324    324.00
```

(40 rows affected)

Observe that *matchno* keeps increasing for empty matches, but classy is NULL.

Listing 4-10 shows a similar query, only this time omitting empty matches.

LISTING 4-10 Query Omitting Empty Matches

```
SELECT
  MR.symbol, MR.tradedate, MR.matchnum, MR.classy,
  MR.startdate, MR.startprice, MR.enddate, MR.endprice, MR.price
FROM dbo.Ticker
  MATCH_RECOGNIZE
  (
    PARTITION BY symbol
    ORDER BY tradedate
    MEASURES
      MATCH_NUMBER() AS matchnum,
      CLASSIFIER() AS classy,
      FIRST(A.tradedate) AS startdate,
      FIRST(A.price) AS startprice,
      LAST(A.tradedate) AS enddate,
      LAST(A.price) AS endprice
    ALL ROWS PER MATCH OMIT EMPTY MATCHES
    AFTER MATCH SKIP PAST LAST ROW
    PATTERN (A*)
    DEFINE
      A AS A.price < PREV(A.price)
  ) AS MR;
```

```
symbol  tradedate   matchnum  classy  startdate   startprice
------- ----------  --------- ------- ----------- ----------
STOCK1  2019-02-14  3         A       2019-02-14  148.00
STOCK1  2019-02-15  3         A       2019-02-14  148.00
STOCK1  2019-02-18  3         A       2019-02-14  148.00
STOCK1  2019-02-28  11        A       2019-02-28  153.00
STOCK1  2019-03-01  11        A       2019-02-28  153.00
STOCK1  2019-03-04  11        A       2019-02-28  153.00
STOCK1  2019-03-07  14        A       2019-03-07  142.00
STOCK1  2019-03-08  14        A       2019-03-07  142.00
STOCK1  2019-03-11  14        A       2019-03-07  142.00
STOCK2  2019-02-13  2         A       2019-02-13  329.00
STOCK2  2019-02-15  4         A       2019-02-15  326.00
STOCK2  2019-02-18  4         A       2019-02-15  326.00
STOCK2  2019-02-21  7         A       2019-02-21  326.00
STOCK2  2019-02-22  7         A       2019-02-21  326.00
STOCK2  2019-02-25  7         A       2019-02-21  326.00
STOCK2  2019-02-28  10        A       2019-02-28  322.00
```

```
STOCK2  2019-03-04  12         A        2019-03-04  321.00
STOCK2  2019-03-05  12         A        2019-03-04  321.00
STOCK2  2019-03-11  16         A        2019-03-11  324.00

symbol  tradedate   enddate     endprice  price
-------  ----------  ----------  --------- -------
STOCK1  2019-02-14  2019-02-14  148       148.00
STOCK1  2019-02-15  2019-02-15  146       146.00
STOCK1  2019-02-18  2019-02-18  142       142.00
STOCK1  2019-02-28  2019-02-28  153       153.00
STOCK1  2019-03-01  2019-03-01  145       145.00
STOCK1  2019-03-04  2019-03-04  140       140.00
STOCK1  2019-03-07  2019-03-07  142       142.00
STOCK1  2019-03-08  2019-03-08  140       140.00
STOCK1  2019-03-11  2019-03-11  138       138.00
STOCK2  2019-02-13  2019-02-13  329       329.00
STOCK2  2019-02-15  2019-02-15  326       326.00
STOCK2  2019-02-18  2019-02-18  325       325.00
STOCK2  2019-02-21  2019-02-21  326       326.00
STOCK2  2019-02-22  2019-02-22  320       320.00
STOCK2  2019-02-25  2019-02-25  317       317.00
STOCK2  2019-02-28  2019-02-28  322       322.00
STOCK2  2019-03-04  2019-03-04  321       321.00
STOCK2  2019-03-05  2019-03-05  319       319.00
STOCK2  2019-03-11  2019-03-11  324       324.00

(19 rows affected)
```

This time the output has 19 rows when omitting empty matches, compared to 40 rows when showing them.

RUNNING versus FINAL Semantics

In both the *DEFINE* clause and the *MEASURES* clause, you apply computations to variables representing subsequences of rows of the potential pattern match. For example, the computation *AVG(A.price)* represents the average of the prices in variable *A*. If you don't specify a variable name, such as *AVG(price)*, the calculation applies to the entire pattern match.

The *DEFINE* clause handles rows in an incremental, or *running*, manner. Therefore, all computations in the *DEFINE* clause are running computations and apply to the rows that have been processed up to that point. However, in the *MEASURES* clause you can choose whether to interact with a running computation, e.g., *RUNNING AVG(price)* or with a *final* computation of a successful pattern match, e.g., *FINAL AVG(price)*. You cannot interact with final computations in the *DEFINE* clause. By default, computations in the *MEASURES* clause are running. In the last row of a successful pattern match, running and final computations are the same, and those are the ones shown when you use the *ONE ROW PER MATCH* option.

As an example, the query in Listing 4-11 returns runs of 3+ trading days, with each row besides the last having a price that is greater than or equal to the previous price, and with the last price being greater than the first price.

```
SELECT
  MR.symbol, MR.tradedate, MR.matchno, MR.classy,
  MR.startdate, MR.startprice, MR.enddate, MR.endprice,
  MR.runcnt, MR.finalcnt, MR.price
FROM dbo.Ticker
  MATCH_RECOGNIZE
  (
    PARTITION BY symbol
    ORDER BY tradedate
    MEASURES
      MATCH_NUMBER() AS matchno,
      CLASSIFIER() AS classy,
      A.tradedate AS startdate,
      A.price AS startprice,
      FINAL LAST(tradedate) AS enddate,
      FINAL LAST(price) AS endprice,
      RUNNING COUNT(*) AS runcnt, -- default is running
      FINAL COUNT(*) AS finalcnt
    ALL ROWS PER MATCH
    PATTERN (A B* C+)
    DEFINE
      B AS B.price >= PREV(B.price),
      C AS C.price >= PREV(C.price)
          AND C.price > A.price
          AND COUNT(*) >= 3
  ) AS MR;
```

symbol	tradedate	matchno	classy	startdate	startprice
STOCK1	2019-02-18	1	A	2019-02-18	142.00
STOCK1	2019-02-19	1	B	2019-02-18	142.00
STOCK1	2019-02-20	1	B	2019-02-18	142.00
STOCK1	2019-02-21	1	B	2019-02-18	142.00
STOCK1	2019-02-22	1	B	2019-02-18	142.00
STOCK1	2019-02-25	1	B	2019-02-18	142.00
STOCK1	2019-02-26	1	B	2019-02-18	142.00
STOCK1	2019-02-27	1	C	2019-02-18	142.00
STOCK1	2019-03-04	2	A	2019-03-04	140.00
STOCK1	2019-03-05	2	B	2019-03-04	140.00
STOCK1	2019-03-06	2	C	2019-03-04	140.00
STOCK2	2019-02-18	1	A	2019-02-18	325.00
STOCK2	2019-02-19	1	B	2019-02-18	325.00
STOCK2	2019-02-20	1	C	2019-02-18	325.00
STOCK2	2019-02-25	2	A	2019-02-25	317.00
STOCK2	2019-02-26	2	B	2019-02-25	317.00
STOCK2	2019-02-27	2	C	2019-02-25	317.00
STOCK2	2019-03-05	3	A	2019-03-05	319.00
STOCK2	2019-03-06	3	B	2019-03-05	319.00
STOCK2	2019-03-07	3	B	2019-03-05	319.00
STOCK2	2019-03-08	3	C	2019-03-05	319.00

symbol	tradedate	enddate	endprice	runcnt	finalcnt	price
STOCK1	2019-02-18	2019-02-27	154.00	1	8	142.00
STOCK1	2019-02-19	2019-02-27	154.00	2	8	144.00
STOCK1	2019-02-20	2019-02-27	154.00	3	8	152.00
STOCK1	2019-02-21	2019-02-27	154.00	4	8	152.00
STOCK1	2019-02-22	2019-02-27	154.00	5	8	153.00
STOCK1	2019-02-25	2019-02-27	154.00	6	8	154.00
STOCK1	2019-02-26	2019-02-27	154.00	7	8	154.00
STOCK1	2019-02-27	2019-02-27	154.00	8	8	154.00
STOCK1	2019-03-04	2019-03-06	143.00	1	3	140.00
STOCK1	2019-03-05	2019-03-06	143.00	2	3	142.00
STOCK1	2019-03-06	2019-03-06	143.00	3	3	143.00
STOCK2	2019-02-18	2019-02-20	328.00	1	3	325.00
STOCK2	2019-02-19	2019-02-20	328.00	2	3	326.00
STOCK2	2019-02-20	2019-02-20	328.00	3	3	328.00
STOCK2	2019-02-25	2019-02-27	325.00	1	3	317.00
STOCK2	2019-02-26	2019-02-27	325.00	2	3	319.00
STOCK2	2019-02-27	2019-02-27	325.00	3	3	325.00
STOCK2	2019-03-05	2019-03-08	326.00	1	4	319.00
STOCK2	2019-03-06	2019-03-08	326.00	2	4	322.00
STOCK2	2019-03-07	2019-03-08	326.00	3	4	326.00
STOCK2	2019-03-08	2019-03-08	326.00	4	4	326.00

(21 rows affected)

Observe the different values of the running versus final row counts in the result columns *runcnt* and *finalcnt*—other than in the last row of each match. Observe that because you asked for the final last trade date and final last price in the result columns *enddate* and *endprice*, all rows that are associated with the same pattern match show the same final values in those columns.

As mentioned, when using the *ONE ROW PER MATCH* option, running and final semantics are the same, and the summery row shows the final computation. The query in Listing 4-12 demonstrates this.

LISTING 4-12 Query Demonstrating Running versus Final Semantics, Showing *ONE ROW PER MATCH*

```
SELECT
  MR.symbol, MR.matchno, MR.startdate, MR.startprice,
  MR.enddate, MR.endprice, MR.cnt
FROM dbo.Ticker
  MATCH_RECOGNIZE
  (
    PARTITION BY symbol
    ORDER BY tradedate
    MEASURES
      MATCH_NUMBER() AS matchno,
      A.tradedate AS startdate,
      A.price AS startprice,
      LAST(tradedate) AS enddate,
      LAST(price) AS endprice,
      COUNT(*) AS cnt
    PATTERN (A B* C+)
    DEFINE
```

```
        B AS B.price >= PREV(B.price),
        C AS C.price >= PREV(C.price)
             AND C.price > A.price
             AND COUNT(*) >= 3
    ) AS MR;
```

symbol	matchno	startdate	startprice	enddate	endprice	cnt
STOCK1	1	2019-02-18	142.00	2019-02-27	154.00	8
STOCK1	2	2019-03-04	140.00	2019-03-06	143.00	3
STOCK2	1	2019-02-18	325.00	2019-02-20	328.00	3
STOCK2	2	2019-02-25	317.00	2019-02-27	325.00	3
STOCK2	3	2019-03-05	319.00	2019-03-08	326.00	4

Observe that there was no need to use the *FINAL* keyword here. In fact, whether you specify *RUNNING* (the default) or *FINAL*, you get the same thing here.

Nesting FIRST | LAST within PREV | NEXT

You are allowed to nest the *FIRST* and *LAST* functions within the *PREV* and *NEXT* functions. The query in Listing 4-13 demonstrates this.

LISTING 4-13 Query Nesting the *LAST* Function within the *NEXT* Function

```
SELECT
    MR.symbol, MR.tradedate, MR.matchno, MR.classy,
    MR.startdate, MR.startprice, MR.postenddate, MR.postendprice,
    MR.cnt, MR.price
FROM dbo.Ticker
    MATCH_RECOGNIZE
    (
      PARTITION BY symbol
      ORDER BY tradedate
      MEASURES
        MATCH_NUMBER() AS matchno,
        CLASSIFIER() AS classy,
        A.tradedate AS startdate,
        A.price AS startprice,
        NEXT(FINAL LAST(tradedate), 1) AS postenddate,
        NEXT(FINAL LAST(price), 1) AS postendprice,
        RUNNING COUNT(*) AS cnt
      ALL ROWS PER MATCH
      PATTERN (A B* C+)
      DEFINE
        B AS B.price >= PREV(B.price),
        C AS C.price >= PREV(C.price)
             AND C.price > A.price
             AND COUNT(*) >= 3
    ) AS MR;
```

symbol	tradedate	matchno	classy	startdate	startprice
STOCK1	2019-02-18	1	A	2019-02-18	142.00
STOCK1	2019-02-19	1	B	2019-02-18	142.00
STOCK1	2019-02-20	1	B	2019-02-18	142.00
STOCK1	2019-02-21	1	B	2019-02-18	142.00
STOCK1	2019-02-22	1	B	2019-02-18	142.00
STOCK1	2019-02-25	1	B	2019-02-18	142.00
STOCK1	2019-02-26	1	B	2019-02-18	142.00
STOCK1	2019-02-27	1	C	2019-02-18	142.00
STOCK1	2019-03-04	2	A	2019-03-04	140.00
STOCK1	2019-03-05	2	B	2019-03-04	140.00
STOCK1	2019-03-06	2	C	2019-03-04	140.00
STOCK2	2019-02-18	1	A	2019-02-18	325.00
STOCK2	2019-02-19	1	B	2019-02-18	325.00
STOCK2	2019-02-20	1	C	2019-02-18	325.00
STOCK2	2019-02-25	2	A	2019-02-25	317.00
STOCK2	2019-02-26	2	B	2019-02-25	317.00
STOCK2	2019-02-27	2	C	2019-02-25	317.00
STOCK2	2019-03-05	3	A	2019-03-05	319.00
STOCK2	2019-03-06	3	B	2019-03-05	319.00
STOCK2	2019-03-07	3	B	2019-03-05	319.00
STOCK2	2019-03-08	3	C	2019-03-05	319.00

symbol	tradedate	postenddate	postendprice	cnt	price
STOCK1	2019-02-18	2019-02-28	153.00	1	142.00
STOCK1	2019-02-19	2019-02-28	153.00	2	144.00
STOCK1	2019-02-20	2019-02-28	153.00	3	152.00
STOCK1	2019-02-21	2019-02-28	153.00	4	152.00
STOCK1	2019-02-22	2019-02-28	153.00	5	153.00
STOCK1	2019-02-25	2019-02-28	153.00	6	154.00
STOCK1	2019-02-26	2019-02-28	153.00	7	154.00
STOCK1	2019-02-27	2019-02-28	153.00	8	154.00
STOCK1	2019-03-04	2019-03-07	142.00	1	140.00
STOCK1	2019-03-05	2019-03-07	142.00	2	142.00
STOCK1	2019-03-06	2019-03-07	142.00	3	143.00
STOCK2	2019-02-18	2019-02-21	326.00	1	325.00
STOCK2	2019-02-19	2019-02-21	326.00	2	326.00
STOCK2	2019-02-20	2019-02-21	326.00	3	328.00
STOCK2	2019-02-25	2019-02-28	322.00	1	317.00
STOCK2	2019-02-26	2019-02-28	322.00	2	319.00
STOCK2	2019-02-27	2019-02-28	322.00	3	325.00
STOCK2	2019-03-05	2019-03-11	324.00	1	319.00
STOCK2	2019-03-06	2019-03-11	324.00	2	322.00
STOCK2	2019-03-07	2019-03-11	324.00	3	326.00
STOCK2	2019-03-08	2019-03-11	324.00	4	326.00

(21 rows affected)

The expressions *NEXT(FINAL LAST(tradedate), 1)* and *NEXT(FINAL LAST(price), 1)* give you the trading date and price immediately following the last row in the current match. Remember that the offset 1 is the default for the *NEXT* function, so if you omit it in this query you get the same result. However, I wanted to add it here for clarity.

Feature R020, "Row-Pattern Recognition: WINDOW Clause"

Feature R020, "Row-pattern recognition: WINDOW clause," uses row-pattern recognition in the *WINDOW* clause. Recall from Chapter 1 that this clause allows you to reuse a window specification. In this context, RPR is used to restrict the full window frame to a reduced one. Much like the window partition reduces the input table expression (*FROM…WHERE…GROUP BY…HAVING*) and the window frame reduces the window partition, RPR further reduces the *full window frame* to a *reduced window frame* with the subset of rows representing a pattern match. The row-pattern measures that you compute in the *MEASURES* clause can then be applied in the underlying query over the defined window.

The use of RPR in a window specification is applicable only to window frames that start at the current row. It is not applicable, for example, to window frames that start with *UNBOUNDED PRECEDING*. Only one row-pattern match per full window frame is sought. Specific to using RPR with windowing, you can specify the *INITIAL* or *SEEK* options. The former means that the reduced window frame represents a pattern match only if it starts with the current row (not to be confused with the fact that the full frame must start with the current row). Otherwise, the reduced window frame is empty. The latter means that you want to search for a pattern match starting with the current row and going through to the end of the full window frame.

Remember the query shown earlier in Listing 4-1 looking for V shapes in stock trading activity. The query used the *MATCHE_RECOGNIZE* operator in the *FROM* clause, with the *ONE ROW PER MATCH* option. The query generated the following output:

symbol	matchnum	startdate	startprice	bottomdate	bottomprice	enddate	endprice	maxprice
STOCK1	1	2019-02-13	151.00	2019-02-18	142.00	2019-02-20	152.00	152.00
STOCK1	2	2019-02-27	154.00	2019-03-04	140.00	2019-03-06	143.00	154.00
STOCK2	1	2019-02-14	329.00	2019-02-18	325.00	2019-02-20	328.00	329.00
STOCK2	2	2019-02-21	326.00	2019-02-25	317.00	2019-02-27	325.00	326.00
STOCK2	3	2019-03-01	324.00	2019-03-05	319.00	2019-03-07	326.00	326.00

Listing 4-14 shows a query with a similar row-pattern specification, only this time used with windowing and followed by the query's expected output:

LISTING 4-14 Query Demonstrating Row-Pattern Recognition in *WINDOW* Clause

```
SELECT
  T.symbol, T.tradedate, T.price,
  startdate   OVER W, startprice  OVER W,
  bottomdate  OVER W, bottomprice OVER W,
  enddate     OVER W, endprice    OVER W,
```

```
    maxprice    OVER W
FROM dbo.Ticker T
WINDOW W AS
  (
    PARTITION BY symbol
    ORDER BY tradedate
    MEASURES
      A.tradedate AS startdate,
      A.price AS startprice,
      LAST(B.tradedate) AS bottomdate,
      LAST(B.price) AS bottomprice,
      LAST(C.tradedate) AS enddate,
      LAST(C.price) AS endprice,
      MAX(U.price) AS maxprice
    ROWS BETWEEN CURRENT ROW
            AND UNBOUNDED FOLLOWING
    AFTER MATCH SKIP PAST LAST ROW
    INITIAL -- pattern must start at first row of full window frame
    PATTERN (A B+ C+)
    SUBSET U = (A, B, C)
    DEFINE
      B AS B.price < PREV(B.price),
      C AS C.price > PREV(C.price)
  );
```

symbol	tradedate	price	startdate	startprice	bottomdate
STOCK1	2019-02-12	150.00	NULL	NULL	NULL
STOCK1	2019-02-13	151.00	2019-02-13	151.00	2019-02-18
STOCK1	2019-02-14	148.00	NULL	NULL	NULL
STOCK1	2019-02-15	146.00	NULL	NULL	NULL
STOCK1	2019-02-18	142.00	NULL	NULL	NULL
STOCK1	2019-02-19	144.00	NULL	NULL	NULL
STOCK1	2019-02-20	152.00	NULL	NULL	NULL
STOCK1	2019-02-21	152.00	NULL	NULL	NULL
STOCK1	2019-02-22	153.00	NULL	NULL	NULL
STOCK1	2019-02-25	154.00	NULL	NULL	NULL
STOCK1	2019-02-26	154.00	NULL	NULL	NULL
STOCK1	2019-02-27	154.00	2019-02-27	154.00	2019-03-04
STOCK1	2019-02-28	153.00	NULL	NULL	NULL
STOCK1	2019-03-01	145.00	NULL	NULL	NULL
STOCK1	2019-03-04	140.00	NULL	NULL	NULL
STOCK1	2019-03-05	142.00	NULL	NULL	NULL
STOCK1	2019-03-06	143.00	NULL	NULL	NULL
STOCK1	2019-03-07	142.00	NULL	NULL	NULL
STOCK1	2019-03-08	140.00	NULL	NULL	NULL
STOCK1	2019-03-11	138.00	NULL	NULL	NULL
STOCK2	2019-02-12	330.00	NULL	NULL	NULL
STOCK2	2019-02-13	329.00	NULL	NULL	NULL
STOCK2	2019-02-14	329.00	2019-02-14	329.00	2019-02-18
STOCK2	2019-02-15	326.00	NULL	NULL	NULL
STOCK2	2019-02-18	325.00	NULL	NULL	NULL
STOCK2	2019-02-19	326.00	NULL	NULL	NULL

```
STOCK2  2019-02-20  328.00  NULL        NULL      NULL
STOCK2  2019-02-21  326.00  2019-02-21  326.00    2019-02-25
STOCK2  2019-02-22  320.00  NULL        NULL      NULL
STOCK2  2019-02-25  317.00  NULL        NULL      NULL
STOCK2  2019-02-26  319.00  NULL        NULL      NULL
STOCK2  2019-02-27  325.00  NULL        NULL      NULL
STOCK2  2019-02-28  322.00  NULL        NULL      NULL
STOCK2  2019-03-01  324.00  2019-03-01  324.00    2019-03-05
STOCK2  2019-03-04  321.00  NULL        NULL      NULL
STOCK2  2019-03-05  319.00  NULL        NULL      NULL
STOCK2  2019-03-06  322.00  NULL        NULL      NULL
STOCK2  2019-03-07  326.00  NULL        NULL      NULL
STOCK2  2019-03-08  326.00  NULL        NULL      NULL
STOCK2  2019-03-11  324.00  NULL        NULL      NULL


symbol   tradedate    bottomprice  enddate      endprice    maxprice
-------  -----------  -----------  -----------  ----------  ----------
STOCK1   2019-02-12   NULL         NULL         NULL        NULL
STOCK1   2019-02-13   142.00       2019-02-20   152.00      152.00
STOCK1   2019-02-14   NULL         NULL         NULL        NULL
STOCK1   2019-02-15   NULL         NULL         NULL        NULL
STOCK1   2019-02-18   NULL         NULL         NULL        NULL
STOCK1   2019-02-19   NULL         NULL         NULL        NULL
STOCK1   2019-02-20   NULL         NULL         NULL        NULL
STOCK1   2019-02-21   NULL         NULL         NULL        NULL
STOCK1   2019-02-22   NULL         NULL         NULL        NULL
STOCK1   2019-02-25   NULL         NULL         NULL        NULL
STOCK1   2019-02-26   NULL         NULL         NULL        NULL
STOCK1   2019-02-27   140.00       2019-03-06   143.00      154.00
STOCK1   2019-02-28   NULL         NULL         NULL        NULL
STOCK1   2019-03-01   NULL         NULL         NULL        NULL
STOCK1   2019-03-04   NULL         NULL         NULL        NULL
STOCK1   2019-03-05   NULL         NULL         NULL        NULL
STOCK1   2019-03-06   NULL         NULL         NULL        NULL
STOCK1   2019-03-07   NULL         NULL         NULL        NULL
STOCK1   2019-03-08   NULL         NULL         NULL        NULL
STOCK1   2019-03-11   NULL         NULL         NULL        NULL
STOCK2   2019-02-12   NULL         NULL         NULL        NULL
STOCK2   2019-02-13   NULL         NULL         NULL        NULL
STOCK2   2019-02-14   325.00       2019-02-20   328.00      329.00
STOCK2   2019-02-15   NULL         NULL         NULL        NULL
STOCK2   2019-02-18   NULL         NULL         NULL        NULL
STOCK2   2019-02-19   NULL         NULL         NULL        NULL
STOCK2   2019-02-20   NULL         NULL         NULL        NULL
STOCK2   2019-02-21   317.00       2019-02-27   325.00      326.00
STOCK2   2019-02-22   NULL         NULL         NULL        NULL
STOCK2   2019-02-25   NULL         NULL         NULL        NULL
STOCK2   2019-02-26   NULL         NULL         NULL        NULL
STOCK2   2019-02-27   NULL         NULL         NULL        NULL
STOCK2   2019-02-28   NULL         NULL         NULL        NULL
STOCK2   2019-03-01   319.00       2019-03-07   326.00      326.00
STOCK2   2019-03-04   NULL         NULL         NULL        NULL
STOCK2   2019-03-05   NULL         NULL         NULL        NULL
STOCK2   2019-03-06   NULL         NULL         NULL        NULL
```

```
STOCK2   2019-03-07   NULL        NULL        NULL        NULL
STOCK2   2019-03-08   NULL        NULL        NULL        NULL
STOCK2   2019-03-11   NULL        NULL        NULL        NULL

(40 rows affected)
```

Observe that the window frame is nonempty only for rows representing the beginning of a pattern match; therefore, you get non-*NULL* results for the computations over the window. In all other rows, the results of the computations are *NULL*.

Solutions Using Row-Pattern Recognition

Row-pattern recognition can be used to solve many typical querying challenges, often in simpler and more concise ways than with more traditional tools. In this section I demonstrate only a few solutions to give you a sense, but this is just the tip of the iceberg. Note that I revisit most of the tasks that I cover in this section later in Chapter 6, demonstrating solutions using window functions without RPR.

Here I demonstrate solutions for the following groups of querying tasks:

- Top N per group

- Packing intervals

- Gaps and islands

- Specialized running sums

Note that some of the regular expression quantifiers that I use here appear for the first time in this chapter. I will naturally explain their meaning, but in addition, you will probably find it useful to revisit the information shown earlier in Table 4-1.

Top N Per Group

Top N per group is a classic task in the SQL world. It involves filtering a desired number of rows (N), typically per group, based on some order. For example, consider the Ticker table used earlier in this chapter. Suppose that you need to return only the first three trade days per stock symbol, along with the closing prices.

This is quite easy to achieve with row-pattern recognition, using the *MATCH_RECOGNIZE* operator. The advantage of doing so with RPR compared to other solutions is that the top N per group part could be just a subsection of a more sophisticated pattern. In the basic form of the task, you partition by the column *symbol*, and order by the column *tradedate*. As for measures, you can compute a running *COUNT(*)* to produce a row number (1, 2, 3). You will want to return all rows per match since you're interested in the qualifying detail rows. You need only one row-pattern variable that is always true, so define *A AS 1 = 1*. Remember that at least one row-pattern variable definition is required, so if you need only one variable representing *true*, you must be explicit. Lastly, the pattern that you need is *(^A{1, 3})*, meaning between 1 and 3 rows starting at the beginning of the partition. If you examine Table 4-1, you will notice that a leading caret symbol (^) means that the pattern match is sought at the beginning of the partition, and that curly brackets with two delimiters { n, m } means that you're looking for a number of matches between n and m.

Listing 4-15 shows the solution query followed by its expected output.

LISTING 4-15 Query Returning First Three Rows Per Symbol

```
SELECT MR.symbol, MR.rn, MR.tradedate, MR.price
FROM dbo.Ticker
  MATCH_RECOGNIZE
  (
    PARTITION BY symbol
    ORDER BY tradedate
    MEASURES COUNT(*) AS rn
    ALL ROWS PER MATCH
    PATTERN (^A{1, 3})
    DEFINE A AS 1 = 1
  ) AS MR;
```

```
symbol   rn   tradedate    price
-------  ---  -----------  -------
STOCK1   1    2019-02-12   150.00
STOCK1   2    2019-02-13   151.00
STOCK1   3    2019-02-14   148.00
STOCK2   1    2019-02-12   330.00
STOCK2   2    2019-02-13   329.00
STOCK2   3    2019-02-14   329.00
```

Similar to using a leading caret sign to indicate that you're looking for a match at the beginning of the partition, you can use a trailing $ sign to indicate that you're looking for a match at the end of the partition. For example, you would use the query in Listing 4-16 to get the last three trading days per stock symbol:

LISTING 4-16 Query Returning Last Three Rows Per Symbol

```
SELECT MR.symbol, MR.rn, MR.tradedate, MR.price
FROM dbo.Ticker
  MATCH_RECOGNIZE
  (
    PARTITION BY symbol
    ORDER BY tradedate
    MEASURES COUNT(*) AS rn
    ALL ROWS PER MATCH
    PATTERN (A{1, 3}$)
    DEFINE A AS 1 = 1
  ) AS MR;
```

```
symbol   rn   tradedate    price
-------  ---  -----------  -------
STOCK1   1    2019-03-07   142.00
STOCK1   2    2019-03-08   140.00
STOCK1   3    2019-03-11   138.00
```

```
STOCK2  1  2019-03-07  326.00
STOCK2  2  2019-03-08  326.00
STOCK2  3  2019-03-11  324.00
```

Easy peasy!

Packing Intervals

Packing intervals is a classic querying task that involves merging groups of intersecting intervals. As an example, consider a table called *Sessions* holding data for user sessions against some kind of a service.

The code in Listing 4-17 creates and populates the Sessions Table in SQL Server. Even though currently you cannot run RPR-based solutions in SQL Server, there is hope that one day you will!

LISTING 4-17 Code to Create and Populate *dbo*.Sessions in SQL Server

```
SET NOCOUNT ON;
USE TSQLV5;

DROP TABLE IF EXISTS dbo.Sessions;

CREATE TABLE dbo.Sessions
(
  id        INT          NOT NULL,
  username  VARCHAR(14)  NOT NULL,
  starttime DATETIME2(3) NOT NULL,
  endtime   DATETIME2(3) NOT NULL,
  CONSTRAINT PK_Sessions PRIMARY KEY(id),
  CONSTRAINT CHK_endtime_gteq_starttime
    CHECK (endtime >= starttime)
);

INSERT INTO Sessions(id, username, starttime, endtime) VALUES
  (1,  'User1', '20191201 08:00:00', '20191201 08:30:00'),
  (2,  'User1', '20191201 08:30:00', '20191201 09:00:00'),
  (3,  'User1', '20191201 09:00:00', '20191201 09:30:00'),
  (4,  'User1', '20191201 10:00:00', '20191201 11:00:00'),
  (5,  'User1', '20191201 10:30:00', '20191201 12:00:00'),
  (6,  'User1', '20191201 11:30:00', '20191201 12:30:00'),
  (7,  'User2', '20191201 08:00:00', '20191201 10:30:00'),
  (8,  'User2', '20191201 08:30:00', '20191201 10:00:00'),
  (9,  'User2', '20191201 09:00:00', '20191201 09:30:00'),
  (10, 'User2', '20191201 11:00:00', '20191201 11:30:00'),
  (11, 'User2', '20191201 11:32:00', '20191201 12:00:00'),
  (12, 'User2', '20191201 12:04:00', '20191201 12:30:00'),
  (13, 'User3', '20191201 08:00:00', '20191201 09:00:00'),
  (14, 'User3', '20191201 08:00:00', '20191201 08:30:00'),
  (15, 'User3', '20191201 08:30:00', '20191201 09:00:00'),
  (16, 'User3', '20191201 09:30:00', '20191201 09:30:00');
```

Use the code in Listing 4-18 to create and populate the *Sessions* table in Oracle.

LISTING 4-18 Code to Create and Populate Sessions in Oracle

```
DROP TABLE Sessions;

CREATE TABLE Sessions
(
  id        INT          NOT NULL,
  username  VARCHAR2(14)  NOT NULL,
  starttime TIMESTAMP NOT NULL,
  endtime   TIMESTAMP NOT NULL,
  CONSTRAINT PK_Sessions PRIMARY KEY(id),
  CONSTRAINT CHK_endtime_gteq_starttime
    CHECK (endtime >= starttime)
);

INSERT INTO Sessions(id, username, starttime, endtime)
  VALUES(1,  'User1', '01-DEC-2019 08:00:00', '01-DEC-2019 08:30:00');
INSERT INTO Sessions(id, username, starttime, endtime)
  VALUES(2,  'User1', '01-DEC-2019 08:30:00', '01-DEC-2019 09:00:00');
INSERT INTO Sessions(id, username, starttime, endtime)
  VALUES(3,  'User1', '01-DEC-2019 09:00:00', '01-DEC-2019 09:30:00');
INSERT INTO Sessions(id, username, starttime, endtime)
  VALUES(4,  'User1', '01-DEC-2019 10:00:00', '01-DEC-2019 11:00:00');
INSERT INTO Sessions(id, username, starttime, endtime)
  VALUES(5,  'User1', '01-DEC-2019 10:30:00', '01-DEC-2019 12:00:00');
INSERT INTO Sessions(id, username, starttime, endtime)
  VALUES(6,  'User1', '01-DEC-2019 11:30:00', '01-DEC-2019 12:30:00');
INSERT INTO Sessions(id, username, starttime, endtime)
  VALUES(7,  'User2', '01-DEC-2019 08:00:00', '01-DEC-2019 10:30:00');
INSERT INTO Sessions(id, username, starttime, endtime)
  VALUES(8,  'User2', '01-DEC-2019 08:30:00', '01-DEC-2019 10:00:00');
INSERT INTO Sessions(id, username, starttime, endtime)
  VALUES(9,  'User2', '01-DEC-2019 09:00:00', '01-DEC-2019 09:30:00');
INSERT INTO Sessions(id, username, starttime, endtime)
  VALUES(10, 'User2', '01-DEC-2019 11:00:00', '01-DEC-2019 11:30:00');
INSERT INTO Sessions(id, username, starttime, endtime)
  VALUES(11, 'User2', '01-DEC-2019 11:32:00', '01-DEC-2019 12:00:00');
INSERT INTO Sessions(id, username, starttime, endtime)
  VALUES(12, 'User2', '01-DEC-2019 12:04:00', '01-DEC-2019 12:30:00');
INSERT INTO Sessions(id, username, starttime, endtime)
  VALUES(13, 'User3', '01-DEC-2019 08:00:00', '01-DEC-2019 09:00:00');
INSERT INTO Sessions(id, username, starttime, endtime)
  VALUES(14, 'User3', '01-DEC-2019 08:00:00', '01-DEC-2019 08:30:00');
INSERT INTO Sessions(id, username, starttime, endtime)
  VALUES(15, 'User3', '01-DEC-2019 08:30:00', '01-DEC-2019 09:00:00');
INSERT INTO Sessions(id, username, starttime, endtime)
  VALUES(16, 'User3', '01-DEC-2019 09:30:00', '01-DEC-2019 09:30:00');
COMMIT;
```

The task is to pack, per user, each group of intersecting sessions into a single continuous interval. For instance, suppose that a user pays for connection time, but isn't billed multiple times for multiple concurrent sessions. So, you just want to determine the periods of time per user when the user had active sessions—never mind how many.

As an example, on December 1, 2019, *User1* had one session that started at 8:00 and ended at 8:30, another session that started at 8:30 and ended at 9:00, and another that started at 9:00 and ended at 9:30. This group of sessions should be packed together into one interval that started at 8:00 and ended at 9:30. Later, *User1* had a session that started at 10:00 and ended at 11:00, another session that started at 10:30 and ended at 12:00, and another session that started at 11:30 and ended at 12:30. This group of sessions should be packed together into one interval that started at 10:00 and ended at 12:30.

Such challenges are far from being trivial to solve with traditional SQL tools. As evidence, I cover solutions to this challenge using window functions in Chapter 6, and they are much more verbose. Here's a solution query for the task using RPR, followed by the expected output:

```
SELECT MR.username, MR.starttime, MR.endtime
FROM dbo.Sessions
  MATCH_RECOGNIZE
  (
    PARTITION BY username
    ORDER BY starttime, endtime, id
    MEASURES FIRST(starttime) AS starttime, MAX(endtime) AS endtime
    -- A* here means 0 or more matches for A
    -- B represents first item after last match in A
    PATTERN (A* B)
    DEFINE A AS MAX(A.endtime) >= NEXT(A.starttime)
  ) AS MR;
```

```
username  starttime               endtime
--------  ----------------------  ----------------------
User1     2019-12-01 08:00:00.000 2019-12-01 09:30:00.000
User1     2019-12-01 10:00:00.000 2019-12-01 12:30:00.000
User2     2019-12-01 08:00:00.000 2019-12-01 10:30:00.000
User2     2019-12-01 11:00:00.000 2019-12-01 11:30:00.000
User2     2019-12-01 11:32:00.000 2019-12-01 12:00:00.000
User2     2019-12-01 12:04:00.000 2019-12-01 12:30:00.000
User3     2019-12-01 08:00:00.000 2019-12-01 09:00:00.000
User3     2019-12-01 09:30:00.000 2019-12-01 09:30:00.000
```

You partition the rows by *username* because you need to handle each user separately. You order the rows by *starttime*, *endtime*, and *id*. The ordering starts with *starttime* to get the chronological order of the sessions. It continues with *endtime* so that among sessions that start at the same time but end at different times, a session that ends earlier will appear before a session that ends later. As for *id*, it's not really required, but I generally prefer to use deterministic order. Among sessions that start at the same time and end at the same time, *id* is used as a tiebreaker.

Now for the magic. The minimum number of sessions in a packed interval is one. Such a session is represented by the row-pattern variable *B,* which is implicitly true. This row is preceded by zero or more rows that are part of the same packed group, represented by the row-pattern variable *A.* For all those rows, the maximum end time up to the current row is greater than or equal to the start time of the next row. So, the variable *A* is based on the predicate *MAX(A.endtime) >= NEXT(A.starttime),* and the pattern is *(A* B)*. Another way to think of this pattern is that *A* represents zero or more rows that are part of the packed interval, excluding the last, and *B* represents just the last.

Eventually, you want to return one row per match, with the measures *FIRST(starttime)* as the start time of the packed interval and *MAX(endtime)* as the end time of the packed interval.

When developing solutions with RPR that are supposed to show one row per match, it's often convenient during the development process for troubleshooting purposes to show all rows per match, along with the match number and classifier, as shown in Listing 4-19.

LISTING 4-19 Looking at the Detail Rows in Packing Query

```
SELECT
  MR.id, MR.username, MR.starttime, MR.endtime, MR.matchno, MR.classy,
  MR.packedstarttime, MR.packedendtime
FROM dbo.Sessions
  MATCH_RECOGNIZE
  (
    PARTITION BY username
    ORDER BY starttime, endtime, id
    MEASURES
      MATCH_NUMBER() AS matchno,
      CLASSIFIER() AS classy,
      FIRST(starttime) AS pstart,
      MAX(endtime) AS pend
    ALL ROWS PER MATCH
    PATTERN (A* B)
    DEFINE A AS MAX(A.endtime) >= NEXT(A.starttime)
  ) AS MR;
```

id	username	starttime	endtime	matchno	classy	pstart	pend
1	User1	08:00	08:30	1	A	08:00	08:30
2	User1	08:30	09:00	1	A	08:00	09:00
3	User1	09:00	09:30	1	B	08:00	09:30
4	User1	10:00	11:00	2	A	10:00	11:00
5	User1	10:30	12:00	2	A	10:00	12:00
6	User1	11:30	12:30	2	B	10:00	12:30
7	User2	08:00	10:30	1	A	08:00	10:30
8	User2	08:30	10:00	1	A	08:00	10:30
9	User2	09:00	09:30	1	B	08:00	10:30
10	User2	11:00	11:30	2	B	11:00	11:30
11	User2	11:32	12:00	3	B	11:32	12:00
12	User2	12:04	12:30	4	B	12:04	12:30
13	User3	08:00	09:00	1	A	08:00	08:30
14	User3	08:00	08:30	1	A	08:00	09:00
15	User3	08:30	09:00	1	B	08:00	09:00
16	User3	09:30	09:30	2	B	09:30	09:30

Examine the details here and see how much easier it is to understand how the original solution got the desired summary result. Pretty cool!

Gaps and Islands

Gaps and islands are classic querying tasks where you query an ordered sequence of rows, usually with date and time entries that occur at fixed intervals. The gaps task involves identified ranges of missing values, for example, periods of inactivity. The islands task involves identifying ranges of existing values, for example, periods of activity. There could be conditions attached, like identifying periods where the stock price was greater than or equal to 150.

I'll use the *Ticker* table to demonstrate gaps and islands tasks and solutions.

As a gaps task example, suppose that you need to query the Ticker table and identify gaps in the trading activity for each symbol. A gap is found when a pair of consecutive rows based on trading date order are more than one day apart. The actual gap starts one day after the last recorded activity and ends one day before the next recorded activity. In our case, such gaps will naturally occur because of weekends and holidays when the stock market is inactive; however, in other cases, it could be related to unavailability of a service or a device.

Listing 4-20 shows a solution query for this task using RPR, followed by its expected output.

LISTING 4-20 Query Identifying Gaps

```
SELECT MR.symbol, MR.startdate, MR.enddate
FROM dbo.Ticker
  MATCH_RECOGNIZE
  (
    PARTITION BY symbol
    ORDER BY tradedate
    MEASURES
      DATEADD(day, 1, A.tradedate) AS startdate,
      DATEADD(day, -1, B.tradedate) AS enddate
    AFTER MATCH SKIP TO B
    PATTERN (A B)
    DEFINE A AS DATEADD(day, 1, A.tradedate) < NEXT(A.tradedate)
  ) AS MR;
```

```
symbol   startdate    enddate
-------  -----------  -----------
STOCK1   2019-02-16   2019-02-17
STOCK1   2019-02-23   2019-02-24
STOCK1   2019-03-02   2019-03-03
STOCK1   2019-03-09   2019-03-10
STOCK2   2019-02-16   2019-02-17
STOCK2   2019-02-23   2019-02-24
STOCK2   2019-03-02   2019-03-03
STOCK2   2019-03-09   2019-03-10
```

Like in earlier examples involving the Ticker table, naturally, partitioning is based on *symbol* and ordering is based on *tradedate*.

As for row-pattern variables, *B* represents any row (always true) and *A* represents a row preceding it, where the day after the current trade date is before the next trade date. The predicate you would use to define A with T-SQL is *DATEADD(day, 1, A.tradedate) < NEXT(A.tradedate)*. The pattern identifying a gap is then simply *(A B)*.

As for measures, you compute the day after the point before the gap (*A*) as the start of the gap; you compute the day before the point after the gap (*B*) as the end of the gap.

Can you spot an important difference between this query and all other queries shown in the chapter thus far? Until now, all queries skipped past the last row in a successful match to look for the next match. However, in our case, a trade date that appears right after one gap could potentially appear right before another gap. Therefore, this query skips to the row represented by the variable *B* after a successful match is established (*AFTER MATCH SKIP TO B*). You would get the same effect using the option *AFTER MATCH SKIP TO NEXT ROW*, but this is probably a bit less obvious than the alternative used in the query.

If you are testing the solutions in Oracle, instead of using *DATEADD(day, dt, 1)*, use *dt + INTERVAL '1' DAY*. Similarly, instead of using *DATEADD(day, dt, -1)*, use *dt - INTERVAL '1' DAY*, like so:

```
SELECT MR.symbol, MR.startdate, MR.enddate
FROM Ticker
  MATCH_RECOGNIZE
  (
    PARTITION BY symbol
    ORDER BY tradedate
    MEASURES
      A.tradedate + INTERVAL '1' DAY AS startdate,
      B.tradedate - INTERVAL '1' DAY AS enddate
    AFTER MATCH SKIP TO B
    PATTERN (A B)
    DEFINE A AS A.tradedate + INTERVAL '1' DAY < NEXT(A.tradedate)
  ) MR;
```

As for an example of an islands task, suppose that you want to pack all consecutive ranges of trading dates per symbol, assuming each consecutive point represents a one-day interval, showing when each such period started and ended. Listing 4-21 shows a solution query to handle this task, followed by its expected output.

LISTING 4-21 Query Identifying Islands

```
SELECT MR.symbol, MR.startdate, MR.enddate
FROM dbo.Ticker
  MATCH_RECOGNIZE
  (
    PARTITION BY symbol
    ORDER BY tradedate
    MEASURES
      FIRST(tradedate) AS startdate,
      LAST(tradedate) AS enddate
    PATTERN (A B*)
    DEFINE B AS B.tradedate = DATEADD(day, 1, PREV(B.tradedate))
  ) AS MR;
```

```
symbol   startdate    enddate
-------  -----------  -----------
STOCK1   2019-02-12   2019-02-15
STOCK1   2019-02-18   2019-02-22
STOCK1   2019-02-25   2019-03-01
STOCK1   2019-03-04   2019-03-08
STOCK1   2019-03-11   2019-03-11
STOCK2   2019-02-12   2019-02-15
STOCK2   2019-02-18   2019-02-22
STOCK2   2019-02-25   2019-03-01
STOCK2   2019-03-04   2019-03-08
STOCK2   2019-03-11   2019-03-11
```

As you can see, the variable *A* represents any row, and the variable *B* represents a row where the current date is equal to the previous date plus one day. The pattern (*A B**) means that a match starts with any row and continues with zero or more rows in a greedy manner, where the current date is one day after the previous date. The measures then return the first and last dates of the match. You can naturally add more measures per matching period if you like, such as starting and ending prices, minimum, maximum, average, and so on.

The solution can be easily adjusted if you need to allow more flexible intervals such as "up to 3 days" by using a less than or equal to operator (<=), and modifying the number in the *DATEADD* function to *3*, like so:

```
SELECT MR.symbol, MR.startdate, MR.enddate
FROM dbo.Ticker
  MATCH_RECOGNIZE
  (
    PARTITION BY symbol
    ORDER BY tradedate
    MEASURES
      FIRST(tradedate) AS startdate,
      LAST(tradedate) AS enddate
    PATTERN (A B*)
    DEFINE B AS B.tradedate <= DATEADD(day, 3, PREV(B.tradedate))
  ) AS MR;
```

```
symbol   startdate    enddate
-------  -----------  -----------
STOCK1   2019-02-12   2019-03-11
STOCK2   2019-02-12   2019-03-11
```

In our sample data, the effect is that we simply collapsed the weekends. However, as mentioned, this could be more meaningful with other kinds of data. For instance, consider time series data with an IoT device on the edge reporting every fixed interval of 60 seconds that it's online. You need to report periods of availability (islands). You don't have an assurance that the time recorded between consecutive entries will be precisely 60 seconds. Say you are supposed to tolerate up to a 90-second interval without considering the event as starting a new island. In the above query, you would modify the predicate for the variable *B* as *B.eventtime <= DATEADD(second, 90, PREV(B.eventtime))*.

Back to our trading data; say that you want to identify islands with 1-day interval and a price that is greater than or equal to 150. All you need to do to achieve this is to extend the original islands solution with a 1-day interval by adding the price predicate to the definitions of both variables *A* and *B*, as shown in Listing 4-22.

LISTING 4-22 Query Identifying Islands Where Price >= *150*

```
SELECT MR.symbol, MR.startdate, MR.enddate, MR.numdays
FROM dbo.Ticker
  MATCH_RECOGNIZE
  (
    PARTITION BY symbol
    ORDER BY tradedate
    MEASURES
      FIRST(tradedate) AS startdate,
      LAST(tradedate) AS enddate,
      COUNT(*) AS numdays
    PATTERN (A B*)
    DEFINE
      A AS A.price >= 150,
      B AS B.price >= 150 AND B.tradedate = DATEADD(day, 1, PREV(B.tradedate))
  ) AS MR;
```

```
symbol  startdate   enddate      numdays
------- ----------- -----------  --------
STOCK1  2019-02-12  2019-02-13   2
STOCK1  2019-02-20  2019-02-22   3
STOCK1  2019-02-25  2019-02-28   4
STOCK2  2019-02-12  2019-02-15   4
STOCK2  2019-02-18  2019-02-22   5
STOCK2  2019-02-25  2019-03-01   5
STOCK2  2019-03-04  2019-03-08   5
STOCK2  2019-03-11  2019-03-11   1
```

If you don't want weekends and holidays to be in the way, one option is to initially assign row numbers to the rows and then look for Islands with one integer interval between row numbers where the price is greater than or equal to 150, as shown in Listing 4-23.

LISTING 4-23 Query Identifying Islands of Consecutive Trading Days Where Price >= *150*

```
WITH C AS
(
  SELECT T.*, ROW_NUMBER() OVER(PARTITION BY symbol ORDER BY tradedate) AS
tradedateseq
  FROM dbo.Ticker AS T
)
SELECT MR.symbol, MR.startdate, MR.enddate, MR.numdays
FROM C
  MATCH_RECOGNIZE
  (
    PARTITION BY symbol
    ORDER BY tradedate
    MEASURES
```

```
      FIRST(tradedate) AS startdate,
      LAST(tradedate) AS enddate,
      COUNT(*) AS numdays
    PATTERN (A B*)
    DEFINE
      A AS A.price >= 150,
      B AS B.price >= 150 AND B.tradedateseq = PREV(B.tradedateseq) + 1
  ) AS MR;
```

```
symbol   startdate    enddate      numdays
-------  -----------  -----------  --------
STOCK1   2019-02-12   2019-02-13   2
STOCK1   2019-02-20   2019-02-28   7
STOCK2   2019-02-12   2019-03-11   20
```

Specialized Running Sums

Specialized running sum tasks involve applying running sums over some ordered sequence of rows, but with specialized conditions. Here I'll discuss non-negative running sums and capped sums, but there are many other variations. Some of those tasks are tricky to handle with T-SQL easily and efficiently, so people often end up resorting to cursor-based solutions. With RPR, you can handle such tasks quite easily.

I'll start with the nonnegative running sum task. I'll use a table called *T1* in my examples. Use the code in Listing 4-24 to create and populate T1 in SQL Server.

LISTING 4-24 Code to Create and Populate *dbo.T1* in SQL Server

```
SET NOCOUNT ON;
USE TSQLV5;

DROP TABLE IF EXISTS dbo.T1;

CREATE TABLE dbo.T1
(
  ordcol  INT NOT NULL,
  datacol INT NOT NULL,
  CONSTRAINT PK_T1
    PRIMARY KEY(ordcol)
);

INSERT INTO dbo.T1 VALUES
  (1,   10),
  (4,  -15),
  (5,    5),
  (6,  -10),
  (8,  -15),
  (10,  20),
  (17,  10),
  (18, -10),
  (20, -30),
  (31,  20);
```

Use the code in Listing 4-25 to create and populate *T1* in Oracle:

LISTING 4-25 Code to Create and Populate T1 in Oracle

```
DROP TABLE T1;

CREATE TABLE T1
(
  ordcol  INT NOT NULL,
  datacol INT NOT NULL,
  CONSTRAINT PK_T1
    PRIMARY KEY(ordcol)
);

INSERT INTO T1 VALUES(1,   10);
INSERT INTO T1 VALUES(4,  -15);
INSERT INTO T1 VALUES(5,    5);
INSERT INTO T1 VALUES(6,  -10);
INSERT INTO T1 VALUES(8,  -15);
INSERT INTO T1 VALUES(10,  20);
INSERT INTO T1 VALUES(17,  10);
INSERT INTO T1 VALUES(18, -10);
INSERT INTO T1 VALUES(20, -30);
INSERT INTO T1 VALUES(31,  20);
COMMIT;
```

This table represents transactions that add and subtract values in the column datacol based on ordcol ordering. These transactions could be deposits and withdrawals of monetary amounts, or they could be quantities of an item that you're adding and subtracting from a warehouse. The task is to apply a running sum of the values based on the indicated ordering, but the sum is not allowed to be negative. In such a case, you need to show a sum of zero and return a replenish value that compensates for the missing part.

Listing 4-26 shows a solution query using RPR, followed by the expected output.

LISTING 4-26 Query Computing Nonnegative Running Sum

```
SELECT
  MR.ordcol, MR.matchno, MR.datacol,
  CASE WHEN MR.runsum < 0 THEN 0 ELSE MR.runsum END AS runsum,
  CASE WHEN MR.runsum < 0 THEN - MR.runsum ELSE 0 END AS replenish
FROM dbo.T1
  MATCH_RECOGNIZE
  (
    ORDER BY ordcol
    MEASURES
      MATCH_NUMBER() AS matchno,
      SUM(datacol) AS runsum
    ALL ROWS PER MATCH
    PATTERN (A* B)
    DEFINE A AS SUM(datacol) >= 0
  ) AS MR;
```

ordcol	matchno	datacol	runsum	replenish
1	1	10	10	0
4	1	-15	0	5
5	2	5	5	0
6	2	-10	0	5
8	3	-15	0	15
10	4	20	20	0
17	4	10	30	0
18	4	-10	20	0
20	4	-30	0	10
31	5	20	20	0

The variable B represents any row. The variable A represents zero or more rows that precede B where the running sum is greater than or equal to zero, in a greedy manner. This means that B is either the point where the sum dropped below zero, or it is the last row. Therefore, the pattern (A* B) gets a match for each consecutive subsequence of rows up to and including the point where the sum becomes negative or until the last row is reached.

The outer query then uses CASE expressions to compute the nonnegative sum (when the original sum is negative then return zero, otherwise the original sum) and the replenish value (when the original sum is negative then return the additive inverse of the original sum, otherwise zero).

In Oracle, you can use the self-explanatory GREATEST and LEAST functions instead of the CASE expressions, like so:

```
SELECT
  MR.ordcol, MR.matchno, MR.datacol,
  GREATEST(MR.runsum, 0) AS runsum,
  -LEAST(MR.runsum, 0) AS replenish
FROM T1
  MATCH_RECOGNIZE
  (
    ORDER BY ordcol
    MEASURES
      MATCH_NUMBER() AS matchno,
      SUM(datacol) AS runsum
    ALL ROWS PER MATCH
    PATTERN (A* B)
    DEFINE A AS SUM(datacol) >= 0
  ) MR;
```

Another group of classic specialized running-sum tasks are capped sums. I'll use a table called T2 to demonstrate such tasks and their solutions. Use the code in Listing 4-27 to create and populate T2 in SQL Server.

LISTING 4-27 Code to Create and Populate dbo.T2 in SQL Server

```
SET NOCOUNT ON;
USE TSQLV5;

DROP TABLE IF EXISTS dbo.T2;
```

```
CREATE TABLE dbo.T2
(
  ordcol  INT NOT NULL,
  datacol INT NOT NULL,
  CONSTRAINT PK_T2
    PRIMARY KEY(ordcol)
);

INSERT INTO dbo.T2 VALUES
  (1,    10),
  (4,    15),
  (5,     5),
  (6,    10),
  (8,    15),
  (10,   20),
  (17,   10),
  (18,   10),
  (20,   30),
  (31,   20);
```

Use the code is Listing 4-28 to create and populate *T2* in Oracle.

LISTING 4-28 Code to Create and Populate *T2* in Oracle

```
DROP TABLE T2;

CREATE TABLE T2
(
  ordcol  INT NOT NULL,
  datacol INT NOT NULL,
  CONSTRAINT PK_T2
    PRIMARY KEY(ordcol)
);

INSERT INTO T2 VALUES(1,    10);
INSERT INTO T2 VALUES(4,    15);
INSERT INTO T2 VALUES(5,     5);
INSERT INTO T2 VALUES(6,    10);
INSERT INTO T2 VALUES(8,    15);
INSERT INTO T2 VALUES(10,   20);
INSERT INTO T2 VALUES(17,   10);
INSERT INTO T2 VALUES(18,   10);
INSERT INTO T2 VALUES(20,   30);
INSERT INTO T2 VALUES(31,   20);
COMMIT;
```

The first capped sum task is to apply a running sum that stops before it exceeds 50. An example would be filling containers with quantities based on the given order without exceeding their capacity. The solution using RPR is all too easy:

```
SELECT MR.ordcol, MR.matchno, MR.datacol, MR.runsum
FROM dbo.T2
  MATCH_RECOGNIZE
```

```
  (
    ORDER BY ordcol
    MEASURES
      MATCH_NUMBER() AS matchno,
      SUM(datacol) AS runsum
    ALL ROWS PER MATCH
    PATTERN (A+)
    DEFINE A AS SUM(datacol) <= 50
  ) AS MR;
```

```
ordcol   matchno   datacol   runsum
-------  --------  --------  -------
1        1         10        10
4        1         15        25
5        1         5         30
6        1         10        40
8        2         15        15
10       2         20        35
17       2         10        45
18       3         10        10
20       3         30        40
31       4         20        20
```

You define only one variable *A* based on a predicate that checks that the running sum is less than or equal to the desired cap and use the pattern *(A+)*. Remember that the + quantifier means one or more matches.

A variation of the task is stopping when the capacity reaches or exceeds 50 for the first time. The solution is just slightly more involved. It is followed by the expected output, which is shown in Listing 4-29.

LISTING 4-29 Variation to Query Computing Capped Running Sum

```
SELECT MR.ordcol, MR.matchno, MR.datacol, MR.runsum
FROM dbo.T2
  MATCH_RECOGNIZE
  (
    ORDER BY ordcol
    MEASURES
      MATCH_NUMBER() AS matchno,
      SUM(datacol) AS runsum
    ALL ROWS PER MATCH
    PATTERN (A* B)
    DEFINE A AS SUM(datacol) < 50
  ) AS MR;
```

```
ordcol   matchno   datacol   runsum
-------  --------  --------  -------
1        1         10        10
4        1         15        25
5        1         5         30
6        1         10        40
8        1         15        55
```

10	2	20	20
17	2	10	30
18	2	10	40
20	2	30	70
31	3	20	20

As you can see, the row-pattern matching logic is similar to that used in the nonnegative sum, only instead of the predicate defining *A* saying *SUM(datacol) >= 0*, it says *SUM(datacol) < 50*. The first point where you exceed the capacity, you stop, and that point is included in the match.

Summary

Row-pattern recognition is an extremely powerful concept in the SQL standard, allowing you to identify patterns in sequences of rows using regular expressions and apply computations against the matches. This chapter described the concept and the features in the SQL standard that use it. It covered feature R010, which uses RPR in a table operator called *MATCH_RECOGNIZE*, returning either a summary row or the detail rows per match. The chapter also covered feature R020, which uses RPR in a window specification to restrict the full window frame to a reduced one. The chapter concluded with solutions to practical tasks using RPR, showing how simple it is to solve many typical challenges using this tool.

If you're convinced that row-pattern recognition could be an important addition to T-SQL, make sure to cast your vote on the suggestion to "Add Support for Row-Pattern Recognition in T-SQL (SQL:2016 features R010 and R020)," which can be found at *https://feedback.azure.com/forums/908035-sql-server/suggestions/37251232-add-support-for-row-pattern-recognition-in-t-sql*.

Optimization of Window Functions

This chapter describes the optimization of window functions in Microsoft SQL Server. It assumes that you are familiar with analyzing graphical query-execution plans and with the core operators such as Index Scan, Index Seek, Sort, Nested Loops, Parallelism, Compute Scalar, Filter, Stream Aggregate, and so on.

The chapter starts with a few general aspects of optimization of window functions, such as indexing guidelines, ordering *NULLs* last, improving parallelism with *APPLY*, row-mode versus batch-mode processing, and batch mode on *columnstore* versus batch mode on *rowstore*.

The chapter then delves into the specifics of optimization of each group of window functions: ranking functions, aggregate and offset functions, and statistical (distribution) functions. For each group, the chapter starts by describing row-mode processing; then it describes batch-mode processing and the cases when it's relevant.

Note   As mentioned, part of the coverage in this chapter is about batch-mode processing and batch mode on *rowstore*. The latter was introduced in SQL Server 2019 (compatibility level 150). By default, if you are running the examples in this chapter on SQL Server 2019 or later or on Azure SQL Database, there's potential that you will get plans with batch-mode processing even when querying *rowstore* data. I typically start each section by describing row-mode processing, and later, I describe batch-mode processing. So, unless you are already connected to an earlier version of SQL Server than 2019, you will want to set your database compatibility level to 140, representing SQL Server 2017. Under compatibility levels lower than 150, batch mode on *rowstore* is disabled. Run the following code against our sample database to achieve this:

```
ALTER DATABASE TSQLV5 SET COMPATIBILITY_LEVEL = 140;
```

If you prefer to stay in compatibility level 150 or above but want to test a query under row-mode processing, you can disable batch mode using the query hint *OPTION(USE HINT('DISALLOW_BATCH_MODE'))*.

When I specifically show examples demonstrating batch mode on *rowstore*, you will then want to set your database compatibility level to a minimum of 150 to enable this optimization. Naturally, you will need to make sure that you are running those examples against SQL Server 2019 (or above) or against Azure SQL Database.

Sample Data

Most of the examples in the chapter query tables called *Accounts* and *Transactions*, which hold information about bank accounts and transactions within those accounts. For deposits, the transactions have a positive amount associated with them, and for withdrawals, they have a negative one. Run the code in Listing 5-1 to create the *Accounts* and *Transactions* tables in the *TSQLV5* sample database.

LISTING 5-1 Code to Create the Accounts and Transactions Tables

```
SET NOCOUNT ON;
USE TSQLV5;

DROP TABLE IF EXISTS dbo.Transactions;
DROP TABLE IF EXISTS dbo.Accounts;

CREATE TABLE dbo.Accounts
(
  actid   INT         NOT NULL,
  actname VARCHAR(50) NOT NULL,
  CONSTRAINT PK_Accounts PRIMARY KEY(actid)
);

CREATE TABLE dbo.Transactions
(
  actid  INT   NOT NULL,
  tranid INT   NOT NULL,
  val    MONEY NOT NULL,
  CONSTRAINT PK_Transactions PRIMARY KEY(actid, tranid),
  CONSTRAINT FK_Transactions_Accounts
    FOREIGN KEY(actid)
    REFERENCES dbo.Accounts(actid)
);
```

The code samples and performance measures I provide in the chapter assume that the tables are populated with a large set of sample data. However, if you need a small set of sample data just to test the logic of the solutions, you can use the code in Listing 5-2 to fill the tables.

LISTING 5-2 Small Set of Sample Data

```
INSERT INTO dbo.Accounts(actid, actname) VALUES
  (1,  'account 1'),
  (2,  'account 2'),
  (3,  'account 3');

INSERT INTO dbo.Transactions(actid, tranid, val) VALUES
  (1,   1,   4.00),
  (1,   2,  -2.00),
  (1,   3,   5.00),
  (1,   4,   2.00),
  (1,   5,   1.00),
  (1,   6,   3.00),
  (1,   7,  -4.00),
```

```
(1,  8, -1.00),
(1,  9, -2.00),
(1, 10, -3.00),
(2,  1,  2.00),
(2,  2,  1.00),
(2,  3,  5.00),
(2,  4,  1.00),
(2,  5, -5.00),
(2,  6,  4.00),
(2,  7,  2.00),
(2,  8, -4.00),
(2,  9, -5.00),
(2, 10,  4.00),
(3,  1, -3.00),
(3,  2,  3.00),
(3,  3, -2.00),
(3,  4,  1.00),
(3,  5,  4.00),
(3,  6, -1.00),
(3,  7,  5.00),
(3,  8,  3.00),
(3,  9,  5.00),
(3, 10, -3.00);
```

As for producing a large set of sample data, first run the following code to create a helper function called *GetNums*—more details are found in Chapter 6, "T-SQL Solutions Using Window Functions"—which generates a sequence of integers in the requested range:

```
DROP FUNCTION IF EXISTS dbo.GetNums;
GO
CREATE OR ALTER FUNCTION dbo.GetNums(@low AS BIGINT, @high AS BIGINT) RETURNS
TABLE
AS
RETURN
  WITH
    L0   AS (SELECT c FROM (VALUES(1),(1)) AS D(c)),
    L1   AS (SELECT 1 AS c FROM L0 AS A CROSS JOIN L0 AS B),
    L2   AS (SELECT 1 AS c FROM L1 AS A CROSS JOIN L1 AS B),
    L3   AS (SELECT 1 AS c FROM L2 AS A CROSS JOIN L2 AS B),
    L4   AS (SELECT 1 AS c FROM L3 AS A CROSS JOIN L3 AS B),
    L5   AS (SELECT 1 AS c FROM L4 AS A CROSS JOIN L4 AS B),
    Nums AS (SELECT ROW_NUMBER() OVER(ORDER BY (SELECT NULL)) AS rownum
               FROM L5)
  SELECT TOP (@high - @low + 1) @low + rownum - 1 AS n
  FROM Nums
  ORDER BY rownum;
GO
```

Then use the following code to fill the *Accounts* table with 100 accounts and the *Transactions* table with 20,000 transactions per account—for a total of 2,000,000 transactions:

```
DECLARE
  @num_partitions     AS INT = 100,
```

```
  @rows_per_partition AS INT = 20000;

TRUNCATE TABLE dbo.Transactions;
DELETE FROM dbo.Accounts;

INSERT INTO dbo.Accounts WITH (TABLOCK) (actid, actname)
  SELECT n AS actid, 'account ' + CAST(n AS VARCHAR(10)) AS actname
  FROM dbo.GetNums(1, @num_partitions) AS P;

INSERT INTO dbo.Transactions WITH (TABLOCK) (actid, tranid, val)
  SELECT NP.n, RPP.n,
    (ABS(CHECKSUM(NEWID()))%2)*2-1) * (1 + ABS(CHECKSUM(NEWID())%5))
  FROM dbo.GetNums(1, @num_partitions) AS NP
    CROSS JOIN dbo.GetNums(1, @rows_per_partition) AS RPP;
```

Feel free to adjust the number of partitions (accounts) and rows per partition (transactions per account) as needed, but keep in mind that I used the preceding inputs in my tests.

Indexing Guidelines

The plan operators that compute the result of a window function will be described in detail later in the chapter. For now, it suffices to say that they need the input rows to be sorted by the partitioning columns (if a window partition clause exists), followed by the ordering columns (assuming a window order clause is relevant). If no index exists that holds the data in the required order, a sort operation will be required before the window function operators can do their jobs. Involving a sort in the plan has negative implications on the scaling, response time, and throughput of the query. So, if you can avoid the need for sorting by creating the right index, it is a good thing.

POC Index

When querying *rowstore* data (the default if you didn't create a *columnstore* index), the general indexing guidelines to support window functions follow a concept I like to think of as *POC*, which is an acronym for *Partitioning*, *Ordering*, and *Covering*. A POC index's keys should be the window partition columns followed by the window order columns, and the index should include in the leaf the rest of the columns that the query refers to. The inclusion can be achieved either with an explicit *INCLUDE* clause of a nonclustered index or by means of the index being clustered—in which case, it includes all table columns in the leaf rows.

Absent a POC index, the plan includes a *Sort* operator, and with large input sets, it can be quite expensive. Sorting has $N * LOG(N)$ time complexity due to the average number of comparisons the sort algorithms perform, resulting in extra linear scaling. This means that with more rows, you pay more per row. For example, $1000 * LOG(1000) = 3000$ and $10000 * LOG(10000) = 40000$. This means that 10 times more rows results in 13 times more work, and it gets worse the further you go.

The other issue with sorting is that it's a stop-and-go, or a blocking, operation. This means that the Sort operator has to consume the entire input before it starts emitting rows to its parent operator. So, when you're querying a large input table with sorting, the response time of the query, which is the time it takes to deliver the first row to the caller, is quite long. Without sorting and other blocking operators, the response time can be virtually instant.

Moreover, sorting requires a memory grant, and if the requested memory grant is insufficient, there's always the potential for spills to *tempdb* slowing down the query execution. This issue is mitigated by intelligent query processing capabilities that support a memory grant feedback concept, which adjusts the memory grant request over multiple executions of the cached plan; however, some query executions could still experience spills.

Consider the following query, which is an example of a plan involving sorting:

```
SELECT actid, tranid, val,
  ROW_NUMBER() OVER(PARTITION BY actid ORDER BY val) AS rownum
FROM dbo.Transactions;
```

The plan for this query is shown in Figure 5-1.

FIGURE 5-1 Plan with a *Sort* operator.

The *Segment* and *Sequence Project* operators compute the row numbers. The *Segment* operator handles the window partition clause, flagging the *Sequence Project* operator when a new partition starts. In turn, the *Sequence Project* operator assigns the row number 1 if the row is the first in the partition and adds 1 if the row is not the first in the partition. These operators need to ingest the rows ordered by the partitioning and ordering elements. At the moment, there's no POC index in place. The clustered index is scanned without an ordering requirement (that is, the *Ordered* property of the scan is *False*), and then an expensive *Sort* operator is used to sort the data. The query ran for 3 seconds and used 5.8 seconds of CPU time on my system, against hot cache, and the results were discarded.

Note To discard results, open the Query Options context menu, choose Grid under Results, and select the Discard Results After Execution option.

Next, run the following code to create a POC index:

```
CREATE INDEX idx_actid_val_i_tranid
  ON dbo.Transactions(actid /* P */, val /* O */)
  INCLUDE(tranid /* C */);
```

As you can see, the first part of the key list is the window partition column (*actid*, in our case), followed by the window order columns (*val*, in our case), and then the rest of the columns referenced by the query *(tranid*, in our case). Rerun the following query:

```
SELECT actid, tranid, val,
  ROW_NUMBER() OVER(PARTITION BY actid ORDER BY val) AS rownum
FROM dbo.Transactions;
```

The plan for this query is shown in Figure 5-2.

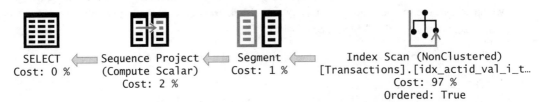

FIGURE 5-2 Plan without a *Sort* operator.

The *Sort* operator is removed. The plan performs an ordered scan of the POC index to satisfy the ordering requirement of the operators that compute the window function's result. This time, the query ran for 1.3 seconds and used 1.28 seconds of CPU time. That's less than half of the run time and less than a quarter of the CPU time compared to the previous plan with the sorting. With larger sets, the difference can be greater.

If the query also involves equality filters—for example, *WHERE col1 = 5 AND col2 = 'ABC'*—you can address both the filtering needs and the window function's ordering needs with the same index by putting the filtered columns first in the index key list. You can then think of the index as an FPOC index, with *FPO* as the key list and *C* as the include list.

If you have multiple window functions in the query, as long as they have the same window partitioning and ordering specification, they can usually rely on the same ordered data without the need to add a *Sort* operator for each. If you have more than one distinct window partitioning and ordering specification, only one can benefit from index ordering. The rest will require a sort-per-distinct specification. Also, note that when specifying multiple window functions with different window partitioning and ordering specifications (and possibly also presentation ordering), their order of appearance in the *SELECT* list can affect the number of sorts that will take place in the plan.

Merge Join (Concatenation)

Curiously, when you compute window functions against data that is unified from two tables, the optimizer has a technique called Merge Join (Concatenation) that merges rows from two sources—possibly based on index order—and provides the rows to the operators that compute the window function ordered. This means that if you create POC indexes on the two tables, you can avoid explicit sorting even though the window function is applied to the unified rows from the two tables. As an example, suppose that our bank account transactions are stored in two separate tables called *Credits* (holding the deposits) and *Debits* (holding the withdrawals). Use the following code to create and populate these tables:

```
USE TSQLV5;

DROP TABLE IF EXISTS dbo.Credits;
DROP TABLE IF EXISTS dbo.Debits;

SELECT *
INTO dbo.Credits
FROM dbo.Transactions
WHERE val > 0;

ALTER TABLE dbo.Credits
  ADD CONSTRAINT PK_Credits
    PRIMARY KEY(actid, tranid);

SELECT *
INTO dbo.Debits
FROM dbo.Transactions
WHERE val < 0;

ALTER TABLE dbo.Debits
  ADD CONSTRAINT PK_Debits
    PRIMARY KEY(actid, tranid);
```

Suppose that you want to compute row numbers similar to the ones you computed before, only this time based on the unified rows from the *Credits* and *Debits* tables. You follow the same POC guidelines like before, creating the following indexes:

```
CREATE INDEX idx_actid_val_i_tranid
  ON dbo.Credits(actid, val)
  INCLUDE(tranid);

CREATE INDEX idx_actid_val_i_tranid
  ON dbo.Debits(actid, val)
  INCLUDE(tranid);
```

As for the query, you apply the same row number calculation, only against the unified rows, like so:

```
WITH C AS
(
  SELECT actid, tranid, val FROM dbo.Debits
  UNION ALL
  SELECT actid, tranid, val FROM dbo.Credits
)
SELECT actid, tranid, val,
  ROW_NUMBER() OVER(PARTITION BY actid ORDER BY val) AS rownum
FROM C;
```

The plan for this query is shown in Figure 5-3.

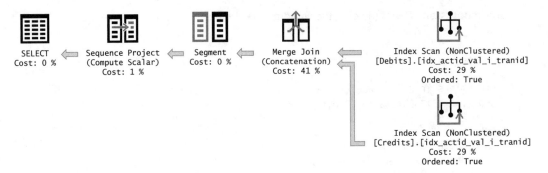

FIGURE 5-3 *Merge Join (Concatenation).*

Notice that the data is scanned from the two POC indexes ordered, merged, and ingested by the *Segment* and *Sequence Project* operators without the need for explicit sorting.

Backward Scans

The pages in the leaf level of a disk-based index are connected with a doubly linked list; that means technically, the index can be scanned either ordered forward or ordered backward. When rows need to be consumed in reverse index key order, often the optimizer will perform an ordered backward scan. However, there are curious aspects of backward scans, and the ability to rely on those to compute window functions that are interesting to know. This information can affect your choices.

The first curious aspect is that ordered forward scans can benefit from parallelism, whereas ordered backward scans cannot. Parallel backward scans are just not implemented in the storage engine at the moment. To demonstrate that forward scans can be parallelized, run the following query and request the execution plan:

```
SELECT actid, tranid, val,
  ROW_NUMBER() OVER(ORDER BY actid, val) AS rownum
FROM dbo.Transactions
WHERE tranid < 1000;
```

Figure 5-4 shows the plan for this query, showing that a parallel scan was used.

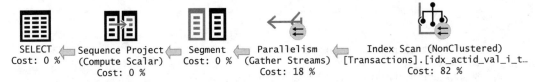

FIGURE 5-4 Parallel plan.

Next, run the following query, where the direction of the window order columns is reversed:

```
SELECT actid, tranid, val,
  ROW_NUMBER() OVER(ORDER BY actid DESC, val DESC) AS rownum
FROM dbo.Transactions
WHERE tranid < 1000;
```

The execution plan for the query is shown in Figure 5-5.

FIGURE 5-5 Serial plan.

The optimizer must make a choice between a serial-ordered backward scan of the index and a parallel unordered scan of the index, followed by explicit sorting. In this case, it chose the latter.

You might have noticed that the last two queries have only a window ordering clause but are missing a window partition clause. Still, the index created earlier satisfies the aforementioned POC guidelines; only the *P* is irrelevant here. It's not by chance that I chose not to include a window partition clause in these examples. And this leads me to the second curious aspect of optimization of window functions.

It turns out that if the function has a window partition clause, to perform an ordered scan of an index and avoid a sort, the partitioning values must be read in ascending order even though there's no logical reasoning behind it. There's an exception to this rule, but I'll get to that later.

Consider the following query, which was already used in a previous example:

```
SELECT actid, tranid, val,
  ROW_NUMBER() OVER(PARTITION BY actid ORDER BY val) AS rownum
FROM dbo.Transactions;
```

The plan for this query was shown earlier in Figure 5-2, where you saw that the POC index was scanned in an ordered fashion and a sort was avoided.

Next, try a similar query, only this time reverse the direction of the ordering column, like so:

```
SELECT actid, tranid, val,
  ROW_NUMBER() OVER(PARTITION BY actid ORDER BY val DESC) AS rownum
FROM dbo.Transactions;
```

The plan for this query is shown in Figure 5-6, where you will find a Sort operator.

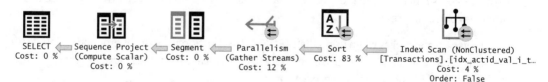

FIGURE 5-6 Plan with a *Sort* operator for descending order.

The index that was used in the previous example is used here as well because it does cover this query; however, its ordering is not relied on here. You can verify this by looking at the *Ordered* property of the *Index Scan* operator, and you will find that in this case, it is *False*, whereas in the previous case, it was *True*. That's an optimization shortcoming. The order in which the distinct partition column values are scanned shouldn't matter. What matters is that the values within each partition need to be scanned in exactly the order defined by the window order clause. So, scanning the index in backward direction should provide the values to the window function in the right order. But alas, the optimizer doesn't realize this.

There are two indexes that can prevent the need to sort: one with the key list (*actid, val DESC*) and another with the exact inverse directions (*actid DESC, val*), both with the same include list as before (*tranid*). In the former case, an ordered forward scan will be used; in the latter case, an ordered backward one will be used.

But what's even more curious is what happens if you add a presentation *ORDER BY* clause that requests to order the rows by the partitioning column in descending order. Suddenly, the operators that compute the window function are willing to consume the partitioning values in descending order and can rely on index ordering for this. So, simply adding a presentation *ORDER BY* clause with *actid DESC* to our last query removes the need for a *Sort* operator. Here's the revised query:

```
SELECT actid, tranid, val,
  ROW_NUMBER() OVER(PARTITION BY actid ORDER BY val DESC) AS rownum
FROM dbo.Transactions
ORDER BY actid DESC;
```

The plan for this query is shown in Figure 5-7.

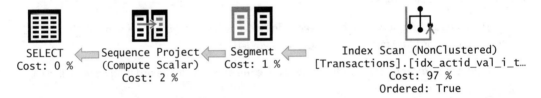

FIGURE 5-7 Plan without a *Sort* operator for descending order.

Observe that the *Sort* operator was removed. The plan performs an ordered backward scan of the index. Remember that a backward scan will not be parallelized in cases where a forward scan normally would. Still, it's remarkable to identify a case where adding a presentation *ORDER BY* clause to a query improves performance!

The very same applies when using the *STRING_AGG* function to perform grouped ordered string concatenation. The plan for the following query (*Query 1*) scans the table's clustered index in an ordered forward fashion, avoiding explicit sorting:

```
SELECT actid,
  STRING_AGG(CAST(val AS VARCHAR(MAX)), ',')
    WITHIN GROUP(ORDER BY tranid) AS amounts
FROM dbo.Transactions
GROUP BY actid;
```

The plan for the following query (*Query 2*) involves explicit sorting:

```
SELECT actid,
  STRING_AGG(CAST(val AS VARCHAR(MAX)), ',')
    WITHIN GROUP(ORDER BY tranid DESC) AS amounts
FROM dbo.Transactions
GROUP BY actid;
```

The plan for the following query (*Query 3*) scans the clustered index in an ordered backward fashion, avoiding explicit sorting:

```
SELECT actid,
  STRING_AGG(CAST(val AS VARCHAR(MAX)), ',')
    WITHIN GROUP(ORDER BY tranid DESC) AS amounts
FROM dbo.Transactions
GROUP BY actid
ORDER BY actid DESC;
```

You can find the plans for these queries in Figure 5-8.

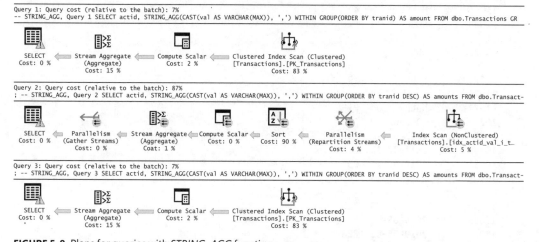

FIGURE 5-8 Plans for queries with *STRING_AGG* function.

Emulating *NULLS LAST* Efficiently

When using the *ORDER BY* clause for purposes like ordering in a window function, an ordered set function, presentation ordering, and so on, the SQL standard allows you to indicate *NULLS FIRST* or *NULLS LAST* to define whether you want *NULLs* sorted before or after non-*NULL* values, respectively. The standard does leave it to the implementation to choose the default. Microsoft chose to sort *NULLs* first when using ascending direction in SQL Server. Unfortunately, T-SQL doesn't support explicitly indicating *NULLS FIRST* or *NULLS LAST*. If you want the nondefault behavior, you must use your own programmatic solution.

The typical solution people use to get *NULLs* last (when needing ascending direction) involves using a *CASE* expression and results in explicit sorting in the plan. Here, I'll demonstrate this solution and provide an alternative that can rely on index order.

Consider the following query returning order IDs and shipped dates and computing row numbers based on ascending shipped date order:

```
SELECT orderid, shippeddate,
  ROW_NUMBER() OVER(ORDER BY shippeddate) AS rownum
FROM Sales.Orders;
```

This code generates the output shown in Listing 5-3.

LISTING 5-3 Query Output Showing *NULLs* First

```
orderid      shippeddate rownum
-----------  ----------- -------
11008        NULL        1
11019        NULL        2
11039        NULL        3
11040        NULL        4
11045        NULL        5
...
11073        NULL        17
11074        NULL        18
11075        NULL        19
11076        NULL        20
11077        NULL        21
10249        2017-07-10  22
10252        2017-07-11  23
10250        2017-07-12  24
10251        2017-07-15  25
10255        2017-07-15  26
...
11050        2019-05-05  826
11055        2019-05-05  827
11063        2019-05-06  828
11067        2019-05-06  829
11069        2019-05-06  830
```

```
(830 rows affected)
```

As you can see, in SQL Server, *NULLs* are positioned before non-*NULLs* when using ascending order.

The plan for this query is shown in Figure 5-9.

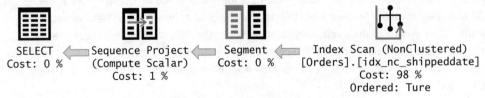

```
 SELECT    <===  Sequence Project  <===  Segment   <===  Index Scan (NonClustered)
Cost: 0 %        (Compute Scalar)       Cost: 0 %         [Orders].[idx_nc_shippeddate]
                     Cost: 1 %                                    Cost: 98 %
                                                                 Ordered: Ture
```

FIGURE 5-9 Window function computed based on index order.

Currently, there is a covering index called *idx_nc_shippeddate* on the table, with the *shippeddate* column as the leading key. As you can see in the plan, the index is scanned in key order; therefore, there's no need for explicit sorting to support the window function.

Suppose that you needed to compute the row numbers in ascending shipped date order but with *NULLs* last. According to the standard, you would simply add the *NULLS LAST* option to the window order clause, like so:

```
SELECT orderid, shippeddate,
  ROW_NUMBER() OVER(ORDER BY shippeddate NULLS LAST) AS rownum
FROM Sales.Orders;
```

As mentioned, this syntax isn't supported in SQL Server, so you need to come up with your own alternative. A typical solution people use is to start the window ordering with a *CASE* expression that returns a lower ordering value for non-*NULLs* than for *NULLs*, followed by the original ordering elements, like so:

```
SELECT orderid, shippeddate,
  ROW_NUMBER() OVER(ORDER BY CASE
                            WHEN shippeddate IS NOT NULL THEN 1
                            ELSE 2
                          END, shippeddate) AS rownum
FROM Sales.Orders;
```

This query generates the desired output with NULLs last, as shown in Listing 5-4.

LISTING 5-4 Query Output Showing NULLs Last

```
orderid     shippeddate rownum
----------- ----------- -------
10249       2017-07-10  1
10252       2017-07-11  2
10250       2017-07-12  3
10251       2017-07-15  4
10255       2017-07-15  5
...
11050       2019-05-05  805
11055       2019-05-05  806
11063       2019-05-06  807
11067       2019-05-06  808
11069       2019-05-06  809
11008       NULL        810
11019       NULL        811
11039       NULL        812
11040       NULL        813
11045       NULL        814
...
11073       NULL        826
11074       NULL        827
11075       NULL        828
11076       NULL        829
11077       NULL        830

(830 rows affected)
```

Unfortunately, though, this technique results in explicit sorting in the plan, as shown in Figure 5-10.

SELECT ⇐ Sequence Project ⇐ Segment ⇐ Sort ⇐ Compute Scalar ⇐ Index Scan (NonClustered)
Cost: 0 % (Compute Scalar) Cost: 0 % Cost: 82 % Cost: 0 % [Orders].[idx_nc_shippeddate]
                  Cost: 0 %   Cost: 17 %
                                                                     Ordered: False

FIGURE 5-10 Window function computed after explicit sorting.

There is a workaround that gets optimized without explicit sorting. You write two queries:

- One filtering non-*NULLs*, returning the constant 1 as a result column called *sortcol*

- Another filtering *NULLs*, returning the constant 2 as *sortcol*

You then unify the two queries with a *UNION ALL* operator and define a CTE based on this code. The outer query against the CTE computes the row numbers, starting with *sortcol* in the window order clause and continuing with the original ordering elements (*shippeddate* in our case). Here's the complete solution's code:

```
WITH C AS
(
  SELECT orderid, shippeddate, 1 AS sortcol
  FROM Sales.Orders
  WHERE shippeddate IS NOT NULL

  UNION ALL

  SELECT orderid, shippeddate, 2 AS sortcol
  FROM Sales.Orders
  WHERE shippeddate IS NULL
)
SELECT orderid, shippeddate,
  ROW_NUMBER() OVER(ORDER BY sortcol, shippeddate) AS rownum
FROM C;
```

This code generates the desired output with *NULLs* ordered last:

```
orderid     shippeddate rownum
----------- ----------- -------
10249       2017-07-10  1
10252       2017-07-11  2
10250       2017-07-12  3
10251       2017-07-15  4
10255       2017-07-15  5
...
11050       2019-05-05  805
11055       2019-05-05  806
11063       2019-05-06  807
11067       2019-05-06  808
11069       2019-05-06  809
11008       NULL        810
```

11019	NULL	811
11039	NULL	812
11040	NULL	813
11045	NULL	814
...		
11073	NULL	826
11074	NULL	827
11075	NULL	828
11076	NULL	829
11077	NULL	830

(830 rows affected)

The plan for this solution is shown in Figure 5-11.

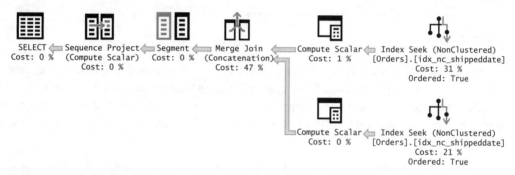

FIGURE 5-11 Window function computed based on index order and *Merge Join (Concatenation)*.

Separate *Index Seek* operators are used to get the ordered rows with the non-*NULL* shipped dates and with the *NULL* shipped dates, followed by *Compute Scalar* operators that compute *sortcol* for each of the inputs. Next, the *Merge Join (Concatenation)* operator I described earlier merges the two inputs, placing non-*NULL*s first and *NULL*s last. The Segment and Sequence Project operators get the rows ordered as needed to compute the row numbers. Notice that no explicit sorting was needed; therefore, this plan scales linearly. It also emits the first row pretty much instantaneously.

The same technique can be used with other query elements that rely on ordering, such as the *STRING_AGG* function and presentation ordering.

Improved Parallelism with *APPLY*

This section describes a technique I learned from Adam Machanic—the book's technical editor—that can sometimes improve the way parallelism is handled when optimizing queries with window functions.

Before I describe the technique, I should note that I ran the examples in this book against a system with eight logical CPUs. SQL Server does consider, among other things, the number of logical CPUs when deciding between a parallel plan and a serial plan. So, if you have fewer logical CPUs in your environment than eight, you might not get parallel plans in all the instances in which I did.

The parallel APPLY technique is mainly useful when there's a window partition clause involved, and the built-in parallelism doesn't produce an optimal result (or simply isn't used). A good example where the built-in parallel processing of window functions isn't always optimal is when Sort operators are involved, and row mode processing is used. Consider the following query as an example:

```
SELECT actid, tranid, val,
  ROW_NUMBER() OVER(PARTITION BY actid ORDER BY val) AS rownumasc,
  ROW_NUMBER() OVER(PARTITION BY actid ORDER BY val DESC) AS rownumdesc
FROM dbo.Transactions;
```

This query ran for 4 seconds on my system. The plan for this query is shown in Figure 5-12.

SELECT   Sequence Project   Segment   Parallelism   Sort   Sequence Project   Segment   Parallelism   Index Scan (NonClustered)
Cost: 0 %   (Compute Scalar)   Cost: 0 %   (Gather Streams)   Cost: 62 %   (Compute Scalar)   Cost: 0 %   (Repartition Streams)   [Transactions].[idx_actid_val_i_t…
       Cost: 0 %   Cost: 16 %   Cost: 0 %   Cost: 16 %   Cost: 6 %

FIGURE 5-12 Plan without *APPLY.*

Because two *ROW_NUMBER* functions are invoked (with different window specifications), they cannot both rely on POC indexes, even if both existed. Only one function can benefit from an ordered scan of a POC index; the other function will require a Sort operator to arrange the data in the desired order. Because a sort is involved here and the number of rows is quite large, the optimizer decides to use a parallel plan.

Parallel plans for queries with window functions need to partition the rows by the same elements as the window partitioning elements if the *Segment* and *Sequence Project* operators are in a parallel zone. If you look at the properties of the *Parallelism (Redistribute Streams)* exchange operator, it uses *Hash* partitioning and partitions the rows by *actid*. This operator redistributes the rows from the source threads used for the parallel scan of the data to the target threads that actually compute the first window function's result. Then the rows are sorted based on the ordering requirements of the second window function. A *Parallelism (Gather Streams)* exchange operator handles the gathering of the streams. Finally, the second window function's result is computed.

There are a number of bottlenecks in such a plan:

- **The repartitioning of the streams**   Moving data between threads is an expensive operation. In this case, it might have even been better if the storage engine used a serial scan and then distributed the streams directly thereafter.

- **The sort**   Currently, the DOP determines how many rows each thread will process. For example, on a DOP 8 query, each thread will process about 250,000 rows. Conversely, letting each thread work on only rows related to one account would mean 20,000 rows per sort. (Remember, there are 100 accounts, each with about 20,000 transactions.) This makes the existing sorts approximately 20 percent less efficient than they could be: $(((20000 * \log(20000)) * 100) / ((250000 * \log(250000)) * 8))$.

- **The second Segment and Sequence Project operators**   These operators are in a serial zone. Although these are not extremely expensive operators, they do have a cost, and Amdahl's

Law applies quite well. (This law states that the overall speed-up of a parallel algorithm will be limited by serial sections.)

All these bottlenecks are eliminated by the solution using the parallel *APPLY* technique, which is implemented as follows:

1. Query the table that holds the distinct partitioning values (*Accounts*, in our case).

2. Use the *APPLY* operator to apply to each left row the logic of the original query (against *Transactions*, in our case), filtered by the current distinct partitioning value.

As an example, the previous query should be rewritten as shown in Listing 5-5.

LISTING 5-5 Parallel APPLY Technique

```
SELECT C.actid, A.tranid, A.val, A.rownumasc, A.rownumdesc
FROM dbo.Accounts AS C
  CROSS APPLY (SELECT tranid, val,
                 ROW_NUMBER() OVER(ORDER BY val) AS rownumasc,
                 ROW_NUMBER() OVER(ORDER BY val DESC) AS rownumdesc
               FROM dbo.Transactions AS T
               WHERE T.actid = C.actid) AS A;
```

Observe that because the derived table A handles only one partition's rows, the window partition clause was removed from the window specification.

This query ran for 2 seconds on my system—half the run time of the previous query. The plan for the new query is shown in Figure 5-13.

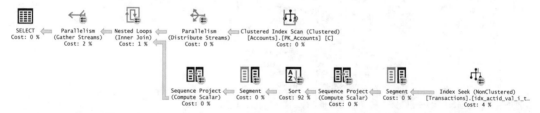

FIGURE 5-13 Plan with *APPLY*.

The plan starts by scanning the clustered index of the *Accounts* table. Then a *Parallelism (Distribute Streams)* exchange operator is used to distribute the rows to multiple threads using a basic round-robin partitioning type (next packet to next thread). So, each thread at the bottom part of the *Nested Loops* join operator gets to work on a subset of one partition's rows only but without the bottlenecks described earlier. The tradeoff is the number of index seek operations (and their associated logical reads) required to satisfy the query. When the partitioning column has very low density (for example, 200,000 partitions, each with 10 rows), you end up with a large number of seek operations. This means the *APPLY* technique is not that efficient anymore.

Note that the examples that I showed here used row execution mode. In the next section, I cover batch mode processing and explain the cases when it's applicable. With batch processing, Microsoft significantly improved the CPU efficiency and scaling—so much so that when batch processing applies, you will often get optimal handling without the need to resort to the parallel *APPLY* technique. At the end of the day, make sure that you always test the various options, especially when performance is a high priority.

When you're done, run the following code for cleanup:

```
DROP INDEX IF EXISTS idx_actid_val_i_tranid ON dbo.Transactions;
```

Batch-Mode Processing

The original (and initially, only) execution model that SQL Server had always used was a row-based execution model. With the row-based execution engine, the operators in the query plan process rows one at a time in a loop. When dealing with large numbers of rows and CPU-intensive operations, this model is not optimal. Any functions executed by an operator operate on a single row as their input. There's a cost to executing a large number of iterations. Furthermore, with this model, metadata is evaluated once per row. In short, row-mode processing tends to waste a lot of CPU cycles.

In SQL Server 2012, Microsoft introduced support for a batch-mode execution model, under which rows are processed one batch at a time. Figure 5-14 illustrates a batch.

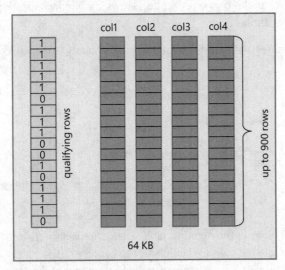

FIGURE 5-14 Batch-mode execution.

The size of a batch is 64KB, and it represents up to 900 rows. The batch has a vector (a one-dimensional array) of up to 900 cells per column that participates in the query. Figure 5-14 illustrates a batch representing four columns. The batch also has a qualifying rows vector, which marks rows that have been filtered out so that upstream operators in the plan will know to ignore them.

Under batch mode, SQL Server processes a chunk of up to 900 rows at a time. Any functions that an operator invokes operate on the batch as their input. You get significantly fewer iterations. Further-more, metadata is evaluated once per batch instead of once per row. For the right workloads—typically when there's a large number of rows involved and CPU-intensive operations—it can be much faster than row-mode processing. Batch-mode processing scales very well with multiple CPUs.

The important milestones of batch-processing support related to window functions are SQL Server 2016 and SQL Server 2019. In the first milestone, SQL Server 2016 introduced a batch-mode operator called *Window Aggregate*, which when applicable, handles windowed calculations significantly faster than before. Not only does it use batch mode, it also eliminates a lot of the inefficiencies of the older optimization of window functions. Furthermore, starting with SQL Server 2016, the *Sort* operator can use batch mode. As a reminder, window functions need the data ordered. If the data is not obtained preordered from a B-tree–based index, the plan must sort it. Columnstore indexes are not ordered, but the batch-mode *Sort* operator is really fast.

Initially, SQL Server considered using batch processing only if a *columnstore* index was present on any of the tables participating in the query. In the second milestone, SQL Server 2019 introduces support for batch mode on *rowstore*, even if there are no *columnstore* indexes present on the tables that participate in the query.

In the following sections, I demonstrate batch mode on *columnstore* and batch mode on *rowstore*. Later in the chapter, as part of the coverage of specific groups of window functions, I get into the details and conditions when the batch-mode Window Aggregate operator can and cannot be used.

Batch Mode on Columnstore

If you're running on SQL Server 2019 or later or you are running on Azure SQL Database, use the following code to set the database compatibility level to 140 (SQL Server 2017 mode), so that you don't yet enable batch mode on *rowstore*:

```
ALTER DATABASE TSQLV5 SET COMPATIBILITY_LEVEL = 140;
```

As mentioned, the first milestone in SQL Server's support for batch-mode processing with window functions was in SQL Server 2016. That's when Microsoft introduced the highly efficient batch-mode Window Aggregate and batch-mode Sort operators. However, prior to SQL Server 2019, the optimizer considered using batch-mode processing only if there was a *columnstore* index present on any of the tables participating in the query.

Columnstore indexes store the data in a column-oriented form, unlike traditional *rowstore* B-tree indexes, which store the data in a row-oriented form. The advantages of *columnstore* indexes are that they tend to highly compress the data—better than *rowstore* with compression enabled—and that SQL Server needs to physically touch only the relevant columns. This usually results in a reduced I/O footprint compared to *rowstore*. This is especially the case for extremely wide tables, such as data warehouse fact tables. The main downside of *columnstore* indexes is that they don't hold the data ordered by any usable key. Because window functions need the data ordered, the plan must involve explicit sorting when window functions are applied to data obtained from *columnstore*.

When explicit sorting needs to happen anyway (such as when you aren't able to create supporting B-tree indexes), you'll usually get better results with *columnstore*. The queries will usually involve fewer reads and take advantage of batch processing.

To demonstrate this, consider the following query:

```
SELECT actid, tranid, val,
  ROW_NUMBER() OVER(PARTITION BY actid ORDER BY val) AS rownum
FROM dbo.Transactions;
```

Currently, there's no B-tree POC index on the table to support the query. (Remember that you dropped the POC index that you used in the examples in the previous section.) There's also no *column-store* index on the table. The plan I got for this query is shown in Figure 5-15.

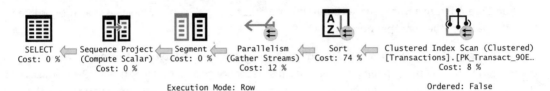

FIGURE 5-15 Plan for *ROW_NUMBER* using row mode with sort.

All operators in the plan use row-mode processing, and the plan involves explicit sorting. Here are the performance statistics that I got when executing this query on my system with results discarded:

CPU time: 5483 ms, elapsed time: 2467 ms, logical reads 6281

Next, run the following code to create a supporting B-tree POC index:

```
CREATE INDEX idx_actid_val_i_tranid
  ON dbo.Transactions(actid, val)
  INCLUDE(tranid);
```

Execute the query again:

```
SELECT actid, tranid, val,
  ROW_NUMBER() OVER(PARTITION BY actid ORDER BY val) AS rownum
FROM dbo.Transactions;
```

The plan for this execution is shown in Figure 5-16.

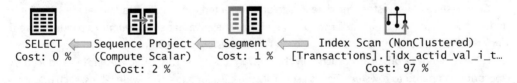

FIGURE 5-16 Plan for *ROW_NUMBER* using row mode without sort.

Observe that the index is scanned in an ordered fashion, removing the need for explicit sorting. Here are the performance statistics I got for this execution:

CPU time: 1219 ms, elapsed time: 1265 ms, logical reads 5467

CPU utilization dropped to less than one-fourth of the previous example, and run time dropped to about a half of the previous.

To test the query against *columnstore*, first run the following code to drop the POC index:

```
DROP INDEX IF EXISTS idx_actid_val_i_tranid ON dbo.Transactions;
```

Then run the following code to create a *columnstore* index:

```
CREATE NONCLUSTERED COLUMNSTORE INDEX idx_cs
  ON dbo.Transactions(actid, tranid, val);
```

Rerun the query:

```
SELECT actid, tranid, val,
  ROW_NUMBER() OVER(PARTITION BY actid ORDER BY val) AS rownum
FROM dbo.Transactions;
```

The plan for this query is shown in Figure 5-17.

```
SELECT ⟸ Parallelism ⟸Window Aggregate⟸ Sort ⟸ Columnstore Index Scan (NonCluste…
Cost: 0 %  (Gather Streams)  Cost: 0 %  Cost: 65 %     [Transactions].[idx_cs]
               Cost: 32 %                                      Cost: 2 %
    Execution Mode: Row Execution Mode: Batch Execution Mode: Batch    Ordered: False
                                                               Execution Mode: Batch
```

FIGURE 5-17 Plan for *ROW_NUMBER* using batch mode with sort.

The data is obtained from the *columnstore* index unordered. A Sort operator is required to arrange the data so that it is ordered for the windowed calculation. The batch-mode Window Aggregate operator then handles the windowed calculation using batch processing.

Here are the performance statistics that I got for this execution:

CPU time: 3485 ms, elapsed time: 1819 ms, logical reads 3787

Compared to the plan shown earlier in Figure 5-15 (using *rowstore* data but without a POC index present and requiring explicit sorting), the plan in Figure 5-17 is more optimal. It touches fewer pages (3485 versus 6281) and uses batch processing, resulting in reduced CPU time (3485 ms versus 5483 ms) and reduced elapsed time (1819 ms versus 2467 ms). However, it is slower than the plan in Figure 5-16 where a POC index is used, preventing the need for explicit sorting.

What's interesting is that if you have both *rowstore* and *columnstore* indexes on the table, the optimizer can decide to read the data from the *rowstore* index, possibly preordered if it's a POC index, and then use batch processing. As it turns out, what enables the optimizer to consider batch processing is the presence of a *columnstore* index on any table that participates in the query, even if it decides to read the data only from *rowstore* indexes.

Starting with SQL Server 2016, you can create filtered *columnstore* indexes. So, in cases where the optimal treatment is to read the data preordered from a *rowstore* POC index—but you want to enable batch processing—there is a backdoor to do so. You create a filtered *columnstore* index with two conditions that contradict each other, which triggers a contradiction detection optimization. So, the fake *columnstore* index doesn't really cost you anything—neither when you create the index, nor when you modify the table. But its presence enables batch processing.

To demonstrate the use of such a fake *columnstore* index, first drop the existing real *columnstore* index:

```
DROP INDEX IF EXISTS idx_cs ON dbo.Transactions;
```

Run the following code to create the *rowstore* POC index:

```
CREATE INDEX idx_actid_val_i_tranid
  ON dbo.Transactions(actid, val)
  INCLUDE(tranid);
```

Then use the following code to create the fake *columnstore* index:

```
CREATE NONCLUSTERED COLUMNSTORE INDEX idx_cs ON dbo.Transactions(actid)
  WHERE actid = -1 AND actid = -2;
```

Technically, now the optimizer will consider using batch processing even if it pulls the data only from *rowstore* indexes. Still, when it explores candidate plans, the plan using batch processing needs to have a lower cost than the alternatives using row processing. So, it's not guaranteed that you will get batch processing for every query. Consider our query as an example:

```
SELECT actid, tranid, val,
  ROW_NUMBER() OVER(PARTITION BY actid ORDER BY val) AS rownum
FROM dbo.Transactions;
```

As it turns out, the optimizer considers the plan that uses row mode processing as the optimal in this case; therefore, it creates the same plan shown earlier in Figure 5-16. But in other cases, there could be significant gains achieved with batch processing, and then it's more likely that it would be the preferred mode. A good example is when optimizing window aggregate functions. To demonstrate such an example, first run the following code to drop the fake *columnstore* index:

```
DROP INDEX IF EXISTS idx_cs ON dbo.Transactions;
```

Consider the following query, which computes the current bank account balance for each account, returning it alongside each of the transactions:

```
SELECT actid, tranid, val,
  SUM(val) OVER(PARTITION BY actid) AS balance
FROM dbo.Transactions;
```

There is an optimal *rowstore* POC index on the table. In fact, both the nonclustered index you created earlier and the clustered index that enforces the primary key are considered optimal POC indexes, so the optimizer could scan either one in an ordered fashion. Currently, there are no *columnstore* indexes on this table, so the optimizer can't consider using batch processing.

The plan for this query is shown in Figure 5-18.

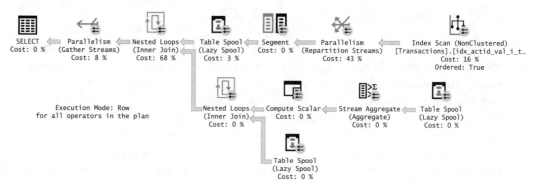

FIGURE 5-18 Plan for *SUM* using row mode without sort.

I will provide more details about how window aggregate functions get optimized later in the chapter. For now, I'll provide a fairly high-level description. All operators in the plan use row-mode processing. The plan scans the nonclustered *rowstore* POC index in an ordered fashion and doesn't involve explicit sorting. The plan then writes the data to a spool (a work table) and reads the data from the spool twice—once to compute the aggregate per account and once to get the detail rows. The plan then joins the two. This is a pretty expensive plan, especially because of the spooling that is involved. Here are the performance statistics that I got for this execution:

CPU time: 9517 ms, elapsed time = 7457 ms, logical reads: 4062569.

This plan took 7.5 seconds to execute and involved millions of reads.

Run the following code to re-create the fake filtered *columnstore* index:

```
CREATE NONCLUSTERED COLUMNSTORE INDEX idx_cs ON dbo.Transactions(actid)
  WHERE actid = -1 AND actid = -2;
```

Then rerun the following query:

```
SELECT actid, tranid, val,
  SUM(val) OVER(PARTITION BY actid) AS balance
FROM dbo.Transactions;
```

The plan for this execution is shown in Figure 5-19.

SELECT ⇐ Compute Scalar ⇐ Window Aggregate ⇐ Index Scan (NonClustered)
Cost: 0 %   Cost: 0 %   Cost: 23 %   [Transactions].[idx_actid_val_i_t...
                                                              Cost: 77 %
      Execution Mode: Batch   Execution Mode: Batch   Ordered: True
                                                       Execution Mode: Row

FIGURE 5-19 Plan for SUM using batch mode without sort.

The first shocking thing is how the plan shrank to only four operators—and that's including the root *SELECT* node! The Window Aggregate operator implements quite a few significant improvements. It completely eliminates the need for a spool. It is able to perform multiple parallel passes over the window of rows in memory. To paraphrase the boy bending spoons in *The Matrix*: There is no spool. Furthermore, it uses batch processing. And if that's not enough, observe that the data is read preordered from the *rowstore* POC index; therefore, there's no need for sorting. The index scan is done using row mode, and then the rows are converted to batches by a hidden adapter. The backdoor that enabled the use of this batch-mode operator is the fake *columnstore* index, even if it's not used.

Here are the performance statistics that I got for this execution:

CPU time: 1125 ms, elapsed time: 1220 ms, logical reads 5467

CPU time dropped to less than an eighth of the previous execution, and elapsed time dropped to less than a sixth. The number of reads dropped to a fraction of the previous (thousands instead of millions).

When you're done, run the following code to drop the fake filtered *columnstore* index:

```
DROP INDEX IF EXISTS idx_cs ON dbo.Transactions;
```

There's another backdoor that enables batch processing. You create an empty table with a *columnstore* index, like so:

```
CREATE TABLE dbo.FakeCS
(
  col1 INT NOT NULL,
  index idx_cs CLUSTERED COLUMNSTORE
);
```

You then alter your query by adding a left outer join predicate that is always false between the original table and this new table, like so:

```
SELECT actid, tranid, val,
  SUM(val) OVER(PARTITION BY actid) AS balance
FROM dbo.Transactions
  LEFT OUTER JOIN dbo.FakeCS
    ON 1 = 2;
```

The optimizer realizes that all rows from the Transactions table are qualifying rows and that there's no real need to access the *FakeCS* table at all, so it generates the same plan shown earlier in Figure 5-19. The downside of this backdoor is that it requires a code change, whereas the previous backdoor doesn't.

When you're done, run the following code to drop this dummy table:

```
DROP TABLE IF EXISTS dbo.FakeCS;
```

Make sure that you currently don't have any *columnstore* indexes on the table and that the only indexes you do have are the clustered *rowstore* index *PK_Transactions* and the nonclustered *rowstore* index *idx_actid_val_i_tranid*.

Batch Mode on Rowstore

As previously mentioned, the second major milestone in SQL Server's support for batch-mode processing with window functions was in SQL Server 2019. In this version, Microsoft introduced support for batch mode on *rowstore*. This means that in cases where you don't see the *columnstore* technology itself as beneficial to you—or perhaps you haven't tested it enough to be ready to use it, but you do see the benefit in batch-mode processing—you now have access to this technology out of the box, without the need for special backdoors. Even if the tables participating in the query don't have *columnstore* indexes—either real or fake—SQL Server will consider using batch processing.

An example where this feature can be beneficial to you is when *rowstore* indexes are more optimal for your workload. For instance, this might be true when *rowstore* indexes can provide the data preordered for your queries, but you want to benefit from newer optimization capabilities such as the batch-mode Window Aggregate operator. In general, batch processing can be beneficial when there are CPU-intensive operations in the plan. In order to enable batch mode on *rowstore*, the database compatibility needs to be 150 (SQL Server 2019 mode) or higher. Run the following code to set the compatibility mode of the TSQLV5 database to 150:

```
ALTER DATABASE TSQLV5 SET COMPATIBILITY_LEVEL = 150;
```

Let's retest the two queries we used in the previous section. Run the following code to retest the query with the *ROW_NUMBER* function:

```
SELECT actid, tranid, val,
  ROW_NUMBER() OVER(PARTITION BY actid ORDER BY val) AS rownum
FROM dbo.Transactions;
```

The plan for this query is shown in Figure 5-20.

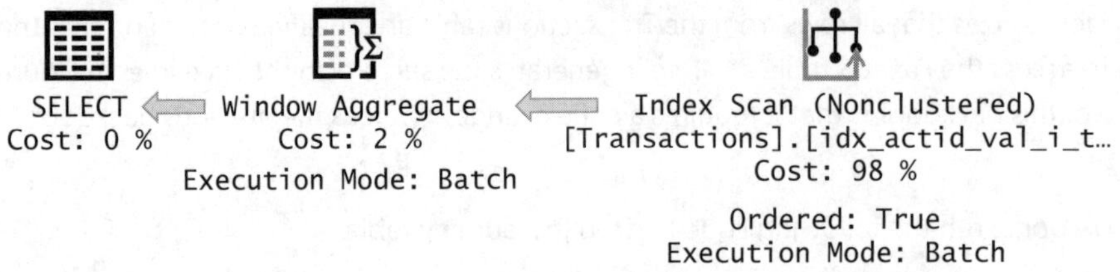

SELECT ⇐ Window Aggregate ⇐   Index Scan (Nonclustered)
Cost: 0 %   Cost: 2 %   [Transactions].[idx_actid_val_i_t...
          Execution Mode: Batch   Cost: 98 %
                                        Ordered: True
                              Execution Mode: Batch

FIGURE 5-20 Plan for *ROW_NUMBER* using batch mode on rowstore without sort.

Recall from the previous section that this query wasn't optimized with the batch-mode Window Aggregate operator when you created the fake *columnstore* index. The reason was that the candidate plan that used this operator involved a row-mode *rowstore Index Scan* operator and a hidden adapter that converts rows to batches between the *rowstore Index Scan* and the *Window Aggregate* operators. That candidate plan likely had a higher cost than the candidate plan that used row-mode processing throughout. With batch mode on *rowstore*, the *rowstore* Index Scan operator natively supports batch-mode processing without the need for an adapter, which results in a more optimal plan. This time, the candidate plan that used batch-mode processing likely had a lower cost than the candidate plan that used row-mode processing throughout. Here are the performance statistics that I got for this query:

CPU time: 750 ms, elapsed time: 798 ms, logical reads 5467

Both the CPU time and the elapsed time are less than two-thirds of the plan with the row-mode processing shown earlier in Figure 5-16.

Next, retest the query with the *SUM* aggregate:

```
SELECT actid, tranid, val,
  SUM(val) OVER(PARTITION BY actid) AS balance
FROM dbo.Transactions;
```

The plan for this execution is shown in Figure 5-21.

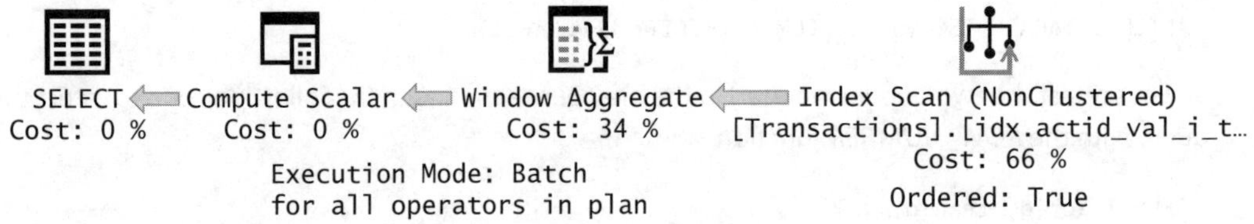

SELECT ⇐ Compute Scalar ⇐ Window Aggregate ⇐ Index Scan (NonClustered)
Cost: 0 %   Cost: 0 %   Cost: 34 %   [Transactions].[idx.actid_val_i_t...
                  Execution Mode: Batch   Cost: 66 %
                  for all operators in plan   Ordered: True

FIGURE 5-21 Plan for SUM using batch mode on rowstore without sort.

Again, observe that batch-mode processing is used throughout the plan, natively. There are no hidden adapters, and even the scanning of the *rowstore* index is done in batch mode. Here are the performance statistics that I got for this execution:

CPU time: 781 ms, elapsed time: 845 ms, logical reads: 5467

Both CPU and elapsed times are sub-second. These numbers are pretty impressive considering the fact that the numbers for the plan with the row-mode processing shown earlier in Figure 5-18 were an order of magnitude higher. These numbers also show about 20–30 percent improvement compared to when the *rowstore* index scan was done in row mode and a hidden adapter was used to convert rows to batches (the plan shown earlier in Figure 5-19).

You should be aware of a small catch though that can make the backdoor with the fake *columnstore* index still relevant in some cases, even in SQL Server 2019 and later. With the backdoor, batch mode is considered purely based on SQL Server's costing model. That is, if a candidate plan that uses batch mode has a lower cost than the rest of the explored candidate plans, the plan with batch mode will be used. With the batch mode on *rowstore* feature, SQL Server imposes additional checks based on heuristics before it enables this feature. Microsoft's concern was that without imposing any conditions other than a pure cost-based decision, some queries could experience regression if the costing formulas deem the batch processing option to have a lower cost than the row processing alternatives but in practice, would take longer to execute. So, they apply additional checks based on heuristics, raising the bar to ensure that batch processing will be used when it's really beneficial. Microsoft's official documentation says that their heuristics apply the following checks:

- An initial check of table sizes, operators used, and estimated cardinalities in the input query.

- Additional checkpoints, as the optimizer discovers new, cheaper plans for the query. If these alternative plans don't make significant use of batch mode, the optimizer stops exploring batch mode alternatives.

However, they don't really provide a lot of details and specifics about the actual heuristics they use. Dmitry Pilugin wrote an excellent article entitled "SQL Server 2019: Batch Mode on *Rowstore*," which details and demonstrates those heuristics. You can find this article at *http://www.queryprocessor.com/batch-mode-on-row-store*.

In his research, Dmitry found that at least one of the participating tables must have a minimum of 131,072 rows (2^{17}). Also, the query should be using at least one operation that will benefit from batch processing: promising join, regular aggregate, or windowed aggregate. Also, at least one of the inputs of a batch-mode operator must have a minimum of 131,072 rows. You can use the extended event *batch_mode_heuristics* to check whether and which of the heuristics' checks were met.

The reality is that some of the new optimization capabilities that Microsoft adds to SQL Server over time are implemented only in batch mode. An example is the Adaptive Join operator. If you don't meet the heuristics' checks to enable batch mode on *rowstore*, and you don't have a *columnstore* index on any of the participating tables, you won't be able to benefit from such new optimization capabilities. Using the backdoor with the fake filtered *columnstore* index, you enable batch processing purely based on costing, bypassing all the heuristics' checks. I wouldn't recommend creating such a fake index on every table, but in targeted cases, as a last resort option, I'd certainly consider using this trick.

When you're done, run the following code to switch back to compatibility level 140, to disable batch mode on *rowstore*:

```
ALTER DATABASE TSQLV5 SET COMPATIBILITY_LEVEL = 140;
```

In the upcoming sections, I go into the details of optimization of the different groups of window functions. I'll start each section with row-mode optimization and then follow with batch-mode optimization. Make sure you set your database compatibility level to 140 at the beginning of each section, and when I cover batch processing, you set it to 150 or above. If you still don't get batch processing with your database compatibility level set to level 150, you can try adding the fake filtered *columnstore* index.

Ranking Functions

This section describes the optimization of the ranking functions: *ROW_NUMBER, NTILE, RANK*, and *DENSE_RANK*. The operators computing the ranking functions need to consume the rows one partition at a time and in an order based on the window order clause. Therefore, you need to follow the POC guidelines described earlier if you want to avoid unnecessary sorts. In my examples, I'll assume that the index *idx_actid_val_i_tranid* that you created earlier in the "Batch Mode on Columnstore" section still exists. If it doesn't, make sure you create it first so that you get similar results to mine.

I'll start by describing row-mode processing of ranking functions. If you're running on SQL Server 2019 or above or Azure SQL Database, make sure you set the database compatibility to 140 to disable batch mode on *rowstore*:

```
ALTER DATABASE TSQLV5 SET COMPATIBILITY_LEVEL = 140;
```

The two key operators that help compute the ranking functions using row-mode processing are *Segment* and *Sequence Project*. *Segment* is used to handle the rows in each segment as a separate group. It has a *Group By* property that defines the list of expressions to segment by. Its output in each row is a flag called *SegmentN* (with *N* representing some number of the expression—for example, *Segment1003*) indicating whether the row is the first in the segment or not.

The *Sequence Project* operator is responsible for the actual computation of the ranking function. By evaluating the flags produced by the preceding *Segment* operators, it will reset, keep, or increment the ranking value produced for the previous row. The output of the *Sequence Project* operator holding the ranking value is named *ExpressionN* (again, with *N* representing some number of the expression—for example, *Expr1002*).

ROW_NUMBER

I'll use the following query to describe the optimization of the *ROW_NUMBER* function:

```
SELECT actid, tranid, val,
  ROW_NUMBER() OVER(PARTITION BY actid ORDER BY val) AS rownum
FROM dbo.Transactions;
```

The plan for this query is shown in Figure 5-22.

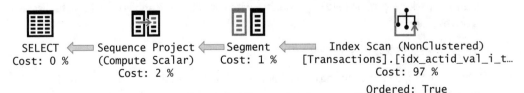

```
   SELECT          Sequence Project      Segment        Index Scan (NonClustered)
  Cost: 0 %        (Compute Scalar)     Cost: 1 %      [Transactions].[idx_actid_val_i_t...
                     Cost: 2 %                                    Cost: 97 %
                                                              Ordered: True
```

FIGURE 5-22 Plan for ROW_NUMBER.

Because there is a POC index in place, it is scanned in an ordered fashion. Without such an index, remember that an expensive *Sort* operator would be added. Next, the *Segment* operator creates groups of rows based on the partitioning column *actid*, which produces a flag (*SegmentN*) that indicates when a new partition starts. When *SegmentN* indicates that a new partition starts, the *Sequence Project* operator generates the row number value 1 (and calls it *ExprN*); otherwise, it increments the previous value by 1.

Here are the performance statistics that I got for this query:

CPU time: 1125 ms, elapsed time: 1233 ms, logical reads: 5467

There's an interesting aspect of the window ordering of ranking functions that can be an obstacle in certain cases. The window order clause of ranking functions is mandatory, and it cannot be based on a constant. Usually, it's not a problem because normally, you do need to produce ranking values based on some ordering requirements that map to some table attributes or expressions based on them. However, sometimes you just need to produce unique values in no particular order. You could argue that if ordering makes no difference, it shouldn't matter if you specify some attribute just to satisfy the requirement. However, then you need to remember that the plan will involve a *Sort* operator if a POC index doesn't exist, or the plan will be forced to use an ordered index scan if one does exist. You want to allow a scan of the data that is not required to be done in index order for potential performance improvement, and certainly you want to avoid sorting.

As mentioned, a window-order clause is mandatory, and SQL Server doesn't allow the ordering to be based on a constant—for example, *ORDER BY NULL*. But surprisingly, when passing an expression based on a subquery that returns a constant—for example, *ORDER BY (SELECT NULL)*—SQL Server will accept it. At the same time, the optimizer un-nests—or expands—the expression and realizes that the ordering is the same for all rows. Therefore, it removes the ordering requirement from the input data. Here's a complete query demonstrating this technique:

```
SELECT actid, tranid, val,
  ROW_NUMBER() OVER(ORDER BY (SELECT NULL)) AS rownum
FROM dbo.Transactions;
```

The execution plan for this query is shown in Figure 5-23.

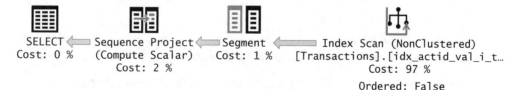

FIGURE 5-23 Plan for ROW_NUMBER with arbitrary ordering.

Observe in the properties of the *Index Scan* operator that the *Ordered* property is *False*, meaning that the operator is not required to return the data in index key order.

NTILE

As a reminder from the discussions in Chapter 2, "A Detailed Look at Window Functions," *NTILE* is a computation that is conceptually based on two elements: the row number and the count of rows in the partition. If both are known for any given row, you can then apply a formula to compute the tile number. From the previous section, you already know how a row number is computed and optimized. The tricky part is to compute the count of rows in the respective partition. I say "tricky" because a single pass over the data cannot be sufficient. This is because the partition's row count is needed for each row, and this count cannot be known until the scanning of all partition rows has been completed. To see how the optimizer handles this problem when using row-mode processing, consider the following query:

```
SELECT actid, tranid, val,
  NTILE(100) OVER(PARTITION BY actid ORDER BY val) AS rownum
FROM dbo.Transactions;
```

The plan for this query is shown in Figure 5-24.

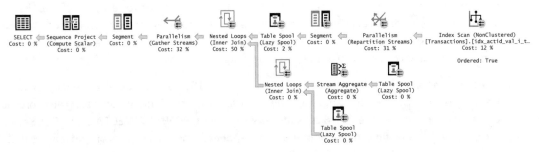

FIGURE 5-24 Plan for NTILE.

The optimizer's answer to our problem is to perform the following steps:

- Read the rows from a POC index if one exists. (One does exist, in our case.)

- Segment the rows by the partitioning element (*actid*, in our case).

- Store one partition's rows at a time in a work table (represented by the upper *Table Spool* operator in the plan).

- Read the spool twice (see the two bottom *Table Spool* operators in the plan)—once to compute the count with a *Stream Aggregate* operator and another to get the detail rows.

- Join the aggregate and detail rows to get the count and detail in the same target row.

- Segment the data again by the partitioning element (*actid*, in our case).

- Use the *Sequence Project* operator to compute the tile number.

Note that the *Table Spool* operator represents a work table in *tempdb*. Even though the percentages associated with it in the plan seem to be low, it actually has quite high overhead. To give you a sense, the same query with a *ROW_NUMBER* function ran on my system for 1.2 seconds and performed just a few thousand reads. Here are the performance statistics that I got for this query:

CPU time: 11702 ms, elapsed time: 24975 ms, logical reads: 4062569

That's 25 seconds elapsed time and millions of reads! Later in this chapter when I discuss aggregate functions without ordering and framing, I explain ways to avoid expensive spooling when using row-mode processing. Also, in the "Batch-Mode Processing" subsection for "Ranking Functions," I demonstrate the significant performance improvements you get with batch processing.

RANK and DENSE_RANK

The *RANK* and *DENSE_RANK* functions perform computations very similar to *ROW_NUMBER*, only they are sensitive to ties in the ordering values. Recall that *RANK* computes one more row than the number of rows that have a lower ordering value than the current row, and *DENSE_RANK* computes one more row than the number of distinct ordering values that are lower than the current row. So, in addition to needing the segment flag that indicates whether a new partition starts, the *Sequence Project* operator also needs to know whether the ordering value has changed. Recall that the plan shown earlier for the *ROW_NUMBER* function has a single Segment operator that is grouped by the partitioning element. The plans for *RANK* and *DENSE_RANK* are similar, but they require a second *Segment* operator that is grouped by both the partitioning and the ordering elements.

As an example, the following query invokes the *RANK* function:

```
SELECT actid, tranid, val,
  RANK() OVER(PARTITION BY actid ORDER BY val) AS rownum
FROM dbo.Transactions;
```

The plan for this query is shown in Figure 5-25.

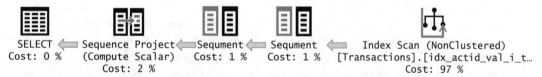

SELECT   Sequence Project   Sequement   Sequement   Index Scan (NonClustered)
Cost: 0 %   (Compute Scalar)   Cost: 1 %   Cost: 1 %   [Transactions].[idx_actid_val_i_t...
                    Cost: 2 %   Cost: 97 %

FIGURE 5-25 Plan for *RANK*.

The first Segment operator is grouped by *actid*, returning the flag *Segment1003*, and the second is grouped by *actid, val*, returning the flag *Segment1004*. When *Segment1003* indicates that the row is the first in the partition, *Sequence Project* returns a *1*. Otherwise, when *Segment1004* indicates that the ordering value has changed, *Sequence Project* returns the respective row number. If the ordering value hasn't changed, *Sequence Project* returns the same value as the previous rank.

Here are the performance statistics that I got for this query:

CPU time: 1172 ms, elapsed time: 1333 ms, logical reads: 5467

The *DENSE_RANK* function is computed in a similar way. Here's a query you can use as an example:

```
SELECT actid, tranid, val,
  DENSE_RANK() OVER(PARTITION BY actid ORDER BY val) AS rownum
FROM dbo.Transactions;
```

The plan for this query is shown in Figure 5-26.

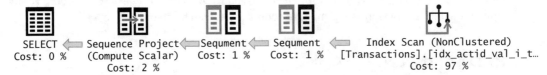

SELECT   Sequence Project   Sequment   Sequment   Index Scan (NonClustered)
Cost: 0 %   (Compute Scalar)   Cost: 1 %   Cost: 1 %   [Transactions].[idx_actid_val_i_t...
     Cost: 2 %   Cost: 97 %

FIGURE 5-26 Plan for DENSE_RANK.

The main difference here is in what the *Sequence Project* operator computes. When *Segment1004* indicates that the ordering value has changed, *Sequence Project* adds 1 to the previous dense rank value.

Here are the performance statistics that I got for this query:

CPU time: 1265 ms, elapsed time: 1351 ms, logical reads: 5467

Because the plans for *RANK* and *DENSE_RANK* are so similar to the plan for *ROW_NUMBER*, the performance you get is also very similar.

Batch-Mode Processing

To enable batch mode on *rowstore*, make sure that you're running with compatibility level 150 or above:

```
ALTER DATABASE TSQLV5 SET COMPATIBILITY_LEVEL = 150;
```

With *ROW_NUMBER*, *RANK*, and *DENSE_RANK*, and a supporting POC index in place, row-mode optimization is already quite optimal. So, the batch-mode Window Aggregate operator can improve things, but not significantly. The big-ticket item is the *NTILE* function. Remember that with row-mode processing, the high cost is involved with the spooling, which is done to compute the cardinality of the partitions. Things can be improved dramatically with the batch-mode *Window Aggregate* operator's ability to apply multiple parallel passes over the window of rows in memory and with the elimination of the need for a spool altogether.

Rerun the four queries with the four functions to test their performance using batch-mode processing:

```
-- ROW_NUMBER
SELECT actid, tranid, val,
  ROW_NUMBER() OVER(PARTITION BY actid ORDER BY val) AS rownum
FROM dbo.Transactions;

-- NTILE
SELECT actid, tranid, val,
  NTILE(100) OVER(PARTITION BY actid ORDER BY val) AS rownum
FROM dbo.Transactions;
```

```
-- RANK
SELECT actid, tranid, val,
  RANK() OVER(PARTITION BY actid ORDER BY val) AS rownum
FROM dbo.Transactions;

-- DENSE_RANK
SELECT actid, tranid, val,
  DENSE_RANK() OVER(PARTITION BY actid ORDER BY val) AS rownum
FROM dbo.Transactions;
```

The plans for these queries are shown in Figure 5-27.

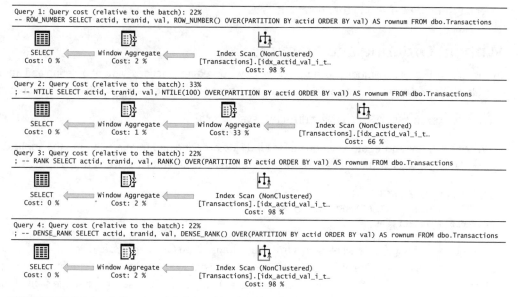

FIGURE 5-27 Batch-mode processing for ranking functions.

Notice that only one Window Aggregate operator is used to compute the *ROW_NUMBER* (first plan), *RANK* (third plan), and *DENSE_RANK* (fourth plan) functions. Two Window Aggregate operators are used to compute the *NTILE* function (second plan)—one for the count and another for *NTILE* itself.

Here are the performance statistics that I got for these queries:

- *ROW_NUMBER*: CPU time: 907 ms, elapsed time: 1062 ms, logical reads: 5467

- *NTILE*: CPU time: 968 ms, elapsed time: 1047 ms, logical reads: 5467

- *RANK*: CPU time: 860 ms, elapsed time: 1020 ms, logical reads: 5467

- *DENSE_RANK*: CPU time: 906 ms, elapsed time: 1030 ms, logical reads: 5467

Observe that they all show improvements compared to row-mode processing, but with *NTILE*, the elapsed time dropped from 25 seconds to 1 second and from millions of reads to just a few thousand. This is very similar to the performance of the other ranking functions. That's pretty impressive!

Aggregate and Offset Functions

The optimization of aggregate and offset functions varies significantly depending on whether ordering and framing are applicable. At least that's the case when using row-mode processing. Therefore, I cover the two cases separately. As usual, I start with row-mode processing and then cover batch-mode processing considerations.

Without Ordering and Framing

In this section, I cover row-mode processing of window aggregate functions without ordering and framing. Make sure you initially set the database compatibility level to 140 to disable batch mode on *rowstore*:

```
ALTER DATABASE TSQLV5 SET COMPATIBILITY_LEVEL = 140;
```

When a window aggregate function doesn't indicate ordering and framing options, the applicable frame of rows is basically the entire partition. For example, consider the following query:

```
SELECT actid, tranid, val,
  MAX(val) OVER(PARTITION BY actid) AS mx
FROM dbo.Transactions;
```

The query is asking for detail elements from each transaction (*actid*, *tranid*, and *val*) to be returned, as well as the maximum value of the current account. Both detail and aggregate elements are supposed to be returned in the same target row. As explained earlier in the "NTILE" section, a single scan of the data cannot be sufficient in this case. As you scan the detail rows, you don't know what the result of the aggregate of the partition is going to be until you finish scanning the partition. The optimizer's answer to this problem under row-mode processing is to spool each partition's rows in a work table in *tempdb* and then read the spool twice—once for the aggregate computation and again for the detail rows.

The plan for this query is shown in Figure 5-28.

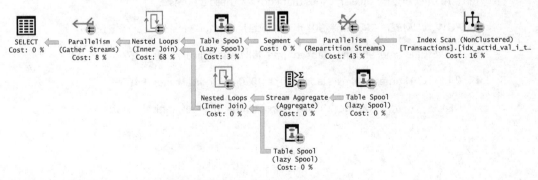

FIGURE 5-28 Plan for a window aggregate with just partitioning.

The plan performs the following steps:

■ Read the rows from the POC index.

■ Segment the rows by the partitioning element (*actid*).

■ Store one partition's rows at a time in a work table. (This step is represented by the upper *Table Spool* operator in the plan.)

■ Read the spool twice (represented by the two bottom *Table Spool* operators in the plan)—once to compute the *MAX* aggregate with a *Stream Aggregate* operator and another to get the detail rows back.

■ Join the aggregate and detail rows to get both in the same target row.

The spooling part doesn't use some kind of an optimized in-memory work table; rather, it uses an on-disk one in *tempdb*. The writes to and reads from the spool have a high overhead. Here are the performance statistics that I got for this query:

CPU time: 8671 ms, elapsed time: 6142 ms, logical reads: 4062569

If you need to filter the rows based on the result of the window function, recall that you cannot do this directly in the query's *WHERE* clause. You have to define a table expression based on the original query and then handle the filtering in the outer query, like so:

```
WITH C AS
(
  SELECT actid, tranid, val,
    MAX(val) OVER(PARTITION BY actid) AS mx
  FROM dbo.Transactions
)
SELECT actid, tranid, val
FROM C
WHERE val = mx;
```

The plan for this query is shown in Figure 5-29.

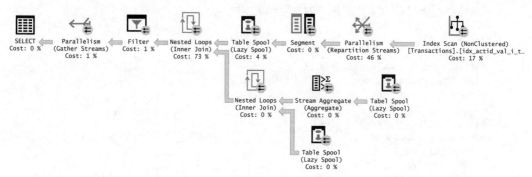

FIGURE 5-29 Plan for a window aggregate with just partitioning, plus filter.

Compared to the previous plan, this one adds a *Filter* operator prior to the gathering of the streams. I will show how to optimize the filter shortly.

Because of the high overhead of the on-disk spooling in these plans, you can actually achieve much better performance if you use a grouped query that computes the aggregate and then join its result with the base table, like so:

```
WITH Aggs AS
(
  SELECT actid, MAX(val) AS mx
  FROM dbo.Transactions
  GROUP BY actid
)
SELECT T.actid, T.tranid, T.val, A.mx
FROM dbo.Transactions AS T
  INNER JOIN Aggs AS A
    ON T.actid = A.actid;
```

The plan for this query is shown in Figure 5-30.

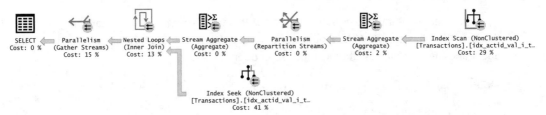

FIGURE 5-30 Plan for a grouped aggregate.

Observe that the covering index is used twice directly—once to compute the aggregate and another for the detail—and the results are joined. No spooling takes place, and this translates to a significant performance improvement. Here are the performance numbers that I got for this query:

CPU time: 2686 ms, elapsed time: 1314 ms, logical reads: 11582

Next, like before, add a filter based on the aggregate:

```
WITH Aggs AS
(
  SELECT actid, MAX(val) AS mx
  FROM dbo.Transactions
  GROUP BY actid
)
SELECT T.actid, T.tranid, T.val
FROM dbo.Transactions AS T
  INNER JOIN Aggs AS A
    ON T.actid = A.actid
    AND T.val = A.mx;
```

The plan for this query is shown in Figure 5-31.

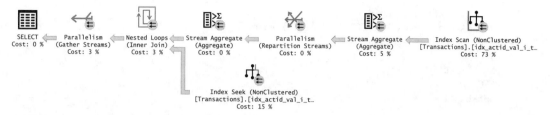

FIGURE 5-31 Plan for a grouped aggregate, plus filter.

The filter is applied as a seek predicate by the *Index Seek* operator, resulting in even better performance numbers:

CPU time: 703 ms, elapsed time: 327 ms, logical reads: 6679

Batch-Mode Processing

To enable batch mode on *rowstore*, make sure you're running with compatibility level 150 (SQL Server 2019 mode) or above:

```
ALTER DATABASE TSQLV5 SET COMPATIBILITY_LEVEL = 150;
```

Remember that if you are connected to SQL Server versions 2016 and newer, you can enable the batch-mode *Window Aggregate* operator using a fake filtered *columnstore* index.

Remember, with batch processing, there's no spooling going on, so you don't really need to resort to any tricks with more complex custom solutions. You can simply use the window function, like so:

```
SELECT actid, tranid, val,
  MAX(val) OVER(PARTITION BY actid) AS mx
FROM dbo.Transactions;
```

The plan for this query is shown in Figure 5-32.

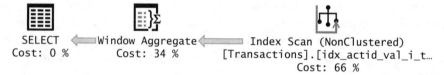

FIGURE 5-32 Plan for a window aggregate with only partitioning and using batch processing.

The plan is nice and clean. The covering index is scanned in order, and the *Window Aggregate* operator handles the *MAX* aggregate calculation without discarding the detail. Here are the performance numbers that I got for this query:

CPU time: 750 ms, elapsed time: 908 ms, logical reads: 5467

Next, test the query that adds a filter based on the aggregate:

```
WITH C AS
(
```

```
  SELECT actid, tranid, val,
    MAX(val) OVER(PARTITION BY actid) AS mx
  FROM dbo.Transactions
)
SELECT actid, tranid, val
FROM C
WHERE val = mx;
```

The plan for this query is shown in Figure 5-33.

SELECT ⇐ Parallelism ⇐ Filter ⇐ Window Aggregate ⇐ Sort ⇐ Index Scan (NonClustered)
Cost: 0 % (Gather Streams) Cost: 2 %   Cost: 2 %   Cost: 48 % [Transactions].[idx_actid_val_i_t…
         Cost: 2 %   Cost: 46 %

FIGURE 5-33 Parallel plan for a frameless window aggregate, plus filter, using batch processing.

I mentioned earlier that the new batch-mode *Window Aggregate* operator significantly improves parallelism handling and its scaling. However, with the current implementation, there is a gotcha. SQL Server isn't able to pull the data preordered from a *rowstore* index with a parallel scan and distribute it gradually and dynamically over worker threads for the *Window Aggregate* operator. It needs a mediator like a batch *Sort* operator. As explained by SQL Server developers Milan Ruzic and Vassilis Papadimos, each thread in a batch-mode window aggregate may need to know where an input batch fits in the global order. A partition may be spread among multiple threads. Beyond the global enumeration of batches, the sort producer must output batches in a way that prevents the possibility of deadlocks.

There is a fundamental difference between row-mode and batch-mode operators. Parallel plans in row-mode execution rely on generic forms of distributing data across worker threads. Generally, that is achieved via an exchange operator. In some simpler cases, a parallel scan is sufficient to split data across threads. So, the complexity of parallelism is mostly concentrated in exchange and scan operators. Other operators almost blindly operate on their own partitions of data. In batch mode, different operators have native, custom implementations of data splitting across threads. (Ignore trivial operators like *project*, *filter*, and *concatenation*.) Of course, tailored implementations are more complex, but they give far superior scalability. Also, it allows having performance that is nearly independent from the input data distribution. Compare that to row-mode execution that gets suffocated if you give it only a few big partitions.

At the date of this writing, the only operator that has custom support for such logic is the batch-mode *Sort* operator; hence, it can be used as a mediator. So, the optimizer must make a choice between a serial plan without a *Sort* operator and a parallel plan with one. As you can see, it chose the latter as it deemed it more optimal.

Here are the performance numbers that I got for this query:

CPU time: 1658 ms, elapsed time: 460 ms, logical reads: 5561

If you have a case where you believe that a serial plan is actually more optimal, you can force it with a *MAXDOP 1* hint, like so:

```
WITH C AS
(
  SELECT actid, tranid, val,
    MAX(val) OVER(PARTITION BY actid) AS mx
  FROM dbo.Transactions
)
SELECT actid, tranid, val
FROM C
WHERE val = mx
OPTION(MAXDOP 1);
```

The plan for this query is shown in Figure 5-34.

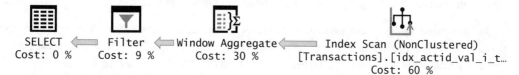

FIGURE 5-34 Serial plan for a frameless window aggregate, plus filter, using batch processing.

Here are the performance numbers that I got for this query:

CPU time: 266 ms, elapsed time: 261 ms, logical reads: 5467

Clearly, in this case, the serial option is significantly better. The lesson is that it's worthwhile experimenting with the different options, especially when there's a shortcoming in the existing optimization.

With Ordering and Framing

I'll discuss three cases of optimization with ordering and framing under row mode:

- Using a window frame extent with a lower-bound *UNBOUNDED PRECEDING*

- Expanding all frame rows

- Computing two cumulative values

I'll then describe the cases for which batch processing is applicable and demonstrate its performance advantages.

Make sure you set the database compatibility level to 140 initially to disable batch mode on *rowstore*:

```
ALTER DATABASE TSQLV5 SET COMPATIBILITY_LEVEL = 140;
```

UNBOUNDED PRECEDING: The Fast-Track Case

With row-mode processing, when you use a window frame extent with *UNBOUNDED PRECEDING* as the lower bound, the optimizer uses an optimized strategy. I refer to this case as the *fast-track* case, but I'll get to that shortly. First, let me describe the roles of the *Window Spool* and *Stream Aggregate* operators.

The purpose of the *Window Spool* operator is to expand each source row to its applicable frame rows—that's at least what happens in the worst-case scenario. For each frame row, this operator needs to generate an attribute that the subsequent operator can use for grouping and aggregation purposes. So, the *Window Spool* operator generates an attribute identifying the window frame and calls it *WindowCountN*. The *Stream Aggregate* operator then groups the rows by *WindowCountN* and computes the aggregate. Now there's a problem of where to obtain the detail row's elements once the data has been grouped; for this, the current row is always added to the *Window Spool*, and the *Stream Aggregate* operator has the logic to return the detail elements from that row.

As mentioned, each source row is expanded to all its applicable frame rows only in the worst-case scenario, and I'll get to that later. In this section, I want to discuss special optimization for cases in which the low bound of the window frame is *UNBOUNDED PRECEDING*. In such a case, instead of expanding each source row to all applicable frame rows and then grouping and aggregating, the two operators were coded with logic to just keep accumulating the values. So, for each source row, the *Window Spool* operator will have two rows—one with the cumulative information so far and another with the current row. (Remember, this is needed for the detail elements.)

For example, consider the following query:

```
SELECT actid, tranid, val,
   SUM(val) OVER(PARTITION BY actid
                 ORDER BY tranid
                 ROWS BETWEEN UNBOUNDED PRECEDING
                              AND CURRENT ROW) AS balance
FROM dbo.Transactions;
```

The plan is shown in Figure 5-35.

FIGURE 5-35 Plan for *ROWS*.

The numbers above the arrows are row counts. The rows are scanned from the POC index, in order. Then *Segment* and *Sequence Project* operators compute a row number (*RowNumberN*). This row number is used for filtering of the relevant frame rows. Our case is a straightforward one, but think of cases that aren't (for example, *ROWS BETWEEN 5 PRECEDING AND 2 FOLLOWING*). Then another *Segment* operator segments the data by *actid* for the computation of the window aggregate function. The *Window Spool* and *Stream Aggregate* operators then just keep accumulating the values within each segment. Remember that the Transactions table has 2,000,000 rows. That's the number of rows you see streaming into the *Window Spool* operator, as well as the number streaming out of the *Stream Aggregate* operator. As explained earlier, the *Window Spool* operator generates two rows for each source row in our special optimized case of *UNBOUNDED PRECEDING*—one for the cumulative value so far and another for the current row to get the detail elements. Therefore, you see 4,000,000 rows streaming from the *Window Spool* operator to the *Stream Aggregate* operator.

Also, if the conditions are right—and I'll get to the specifics shortly—the *Window Spool* operator uses an optimized, in-memory work table, without all of the usual overhead that exists with work tables in *tempdb*, such as I/O, locks, latches, and so forth. Our query did benefit from the in-memory work table, and the query used *UNBOUNDED PRECEDING*; therefore, it wasn't required to expand all frame rows. The two optimization aspects combined resulted in the following performance numbers:

CPU time: 3234 ms, elapsed time: 3355 ms, logical reads 6215.

This is not bad at all compared to any other reliable method to compute running totals. (See Chapter 6 for more details on running totals.)

A number of conditions will prevent the *Window Spool* operator from using the in-memory work table and cause it to use the far more expensive on-disk work table, with a B-tree indexed by the row number. In the next section, I'll describe those conditions in detail, and I will discuss how to check which kind of work table was used. For now, I want to mention that one of those conditions is when SQL Server cannot compute ahead of time the number of rows in the frame. An example of this is when using the *RANGE* window frame unit instead of *ROWS*.

Recall from Chapter 2 that when *using RANGE BETWEEN UNBOUNDED PRECEDING AND CURRENT ROW*, the frame of a given row can involve additional rows ahead of the current one. That's the case when the ordering values are not unique within the partition. Currently, the optimizer doesn't check whether there's uniqueness—in which case, it can theoretically convert the *RANGE* option to an equivalent *ROWS*. It just defaults to using an on-disk work table. This translates to significant performance degradation compared to the *ROWS* option.

The following query is the same as the last one, only I replaced the *ROWS* option with *RANGE*:

```
SELECT actid, tranid, val,
    SUM(val) OVER(PARTITION BY actid
                ORDER BY tranid
                RANGE BETWEEN UNBOUNDED PRECEDING
                          AND CURRENT ROW) AS balance
FROM dbo.Transactions;
```

The plan for this query is shown in Figure 5-36.

FIGURE 5-36 Plan for *RANGE*.

Nothing in the plan gives away the fact that an on-disk work table was used. In fact, it looks the same as the previous plan (minus the *Sequence Project* operator), and the same number of rows stream between the operators. The *STATISTICS IO* option is one way to tell that an on-disk work table was used. For the *ROWS* option, it reported zero reads against *'Worktable'* because it was an in-memory work table. For the *RANGE* option, it reports millions of reads. Here are the performance statistics that I got for this query:

CPU time: 17781 ms, elapsed time: 18050 ms, logical reads: 12050916

The execution time with the *RANGE* option is six times longer than with *ROWS*.

The unfortunate part is that if you indicate a window order clause without an explicit window frame clause, the default, according to the standard, is *RANGE BETWEEN UNBOUNDED PRECEDING AND CURRENT ROW*, as in the following query:

```
SELECT actid, tranid, val,
  SUM(val) OVER(PARTITION BY actid
                ORDER BY tranid) AS balance
FROM dbo.Transactions;
```

Many people use this form because they think, by default, it means *ROWS BETWEEN UNBOUNDED PRECEDING AND CURRENT ROW*; they don't realize it actually defaults to *RANGE*. This incurs the completely unnecessary performance penalty. Theoretically, in cases where there's uniqueness of the ordering values within each partition, the optimizer could first translate the *RANGE* option to *ROWS*. However, currently, there's no such logic in the optimizer. This problem doesn't exist with the batch-mode optimization because there's no use of a spool at all, as I will demonstrate shortly.

Based on the details of the preceding discussions, you can improve the parallel processing of the *RANGE* query under row-mode processing by using the parallel *APPLY* technique, like so:

```
SELECT C.actid, A.tranid, A.val, A.balance
FROM dbo.Accounts AS C
  CROSS APPLY (SELECT tranid, val,
                SUM(val) OVER(ORDER BY tranid
                              RANGE BETWEEN UNBOUNDED PRECEDING
                                            AND CURRENT ROW) AS balance
              FROM dbo.Transactions AS T
              WHERE T.actid = C.actid) AS A;
```

This query now gets a parallel plan that runs for 9 seconds—half the time of the query without *APPLY*. Still, it's much slower than the version with *ROWS*. So, you can consider it a best practice to use the *ROWS* option whenever possible—certainly when there's uniqueness and the two are conceptually equivalent.

Expanding All Frame Rows

In the previous section, I described a fast-track case that is used when the low bound of the frame is *UNBOUNDED PRECEDING*. In that case, SQL Server doesn't produce all frame rows for each source row; rather, it just keeps accumulating the values. As mentioned, the *Window Spool* operator produces only two rows for each source row—one with the accumulation of values so far and another with the base row for the detail elements.

When the low bound of the frame isn't *UNBOUNDED PRECEDING*, the fast-track case doesn't apply. In these cases, the optimizer will choose between one of two strategies. One strategy, which is the focus of this section, is to expand all frame rows for each source row. Another strategy, which is the focus of the next section, is to compute two cumulative values—*CumulativeBottom* and *CumulativeTop*—and derive the result based on the two.

To use the second strategy, the aggregate must be a cumulative one (*SUM, COUNT, COUNT_BIG, AVG, STDEV, STDEVP, VAR,* or *VARP*), and there needs to be more than four rows in the frame to justify it. If the aggregate isn't a cumulative one (*MIN, MAX, FIRST_VALUE, LAST_VALUE,* or *CHECKSUM_AGG*) or the number of rows in the frame is four or less, the first strategy (in which all frame rows are expanded for each source row) will be used.

> **Note** Internally, *LAG* and *LEAD* are converted to the *LAST_VALUE* function with only one row in the frame; therefore, I won't discuss *LAG* and *LEAD* separately. As an example, *LAG(x, 6) OVER(ORDER BY y)* is translated to *LAST_VALUE(x) OVER(ORDER BY y ROWS BETWEEN 6 PRECEDING AND 6 PRECEDING)*.

Consider the following example:

```
SELECT actid, tranid, val,
  SUM(val) OVER(PARTITION BY actid
               ORDER BY tranid
               ROWS BETWEEN 5 PRECEDING
                        AND 2 PRECEDING) AS sumval
FROM dbo.Transactions;
```

The plan for this query is shown in Figure 5-37. It took 5 seconds for the query to complete.

FIGURE 5-37 Plan expanding all frame rows.

The query uses a cumulative aggregate (*SUM*), but the frame has only four rows. Therefore, all frame rows are expanded. With four rows in each frame, plus the current row that is added for the detail elements, the *Window Spool* will produce five rows for each source row. Therefore, the plan shows that the *Window Spool* operator generates almost 10,000,000 rows out of the 2,000,000 source rows. The frames for the first few rows in each partition have fewer than four rows; hence, the plan shows that the *Window Spool* operator generates a bit less than 10,000,000 rows.

The *Window Spool* operator needs to know which target rows to store in its work table for each source row as well as generate a frame identifier in the target rows so that the *Stream Aggregate* operator has something by which to group the rows.

To figure out which rows to produce in each frame, the plan starts by computing a row number to each source row (using the first *Segment* and *Sequence Project* operators). The row number is computed using the same partitioning and ordering as those of the original window function. The plan then uses a *Compute Scalar* operator to compute for each source row the two row numbers—*BottomRowNumberN* and *TopRowNumberN*—that are supposed to bind the frame. For example, suppose that the current row has row number *10*. The row numbers of the respective frame bounds are *TopRowNumberN = 10 – 5 = 5* and *BottomRowNumber = 10 – 2 = 8*. The work table that the *Window Spool* creates is indexed by that row number. So, if the rows with the row numbers *5* through *8* already exist in the work table, they will be queried and added to the work table associated with the new frame. If some rows are missing, the plan will keep requesting more rows and feed the spool until the bottom row number is reached. The *Window Spool* operator generates for each target row an attribute it calls *WindowCountN* that identifies the frame. That's the attribute by which the *Stream Aggregate* operator groups the rows.

In addition to computing the aggregate of interest, the *Stream Aggregate* operator computes the count of rows in the frame, and then the *Compute Scalar* operator that follows will return a *NULL* if the frame is empty.

As long as the number of rows in the frame is four or fewer, regardless of which window function you use, all frame rows will be expanded. Additional examples that will be treated in this manner are the following: *2 PRECEDING AND 1 FOLLOWING*, *2 FOLLOWING AND 5 FOLLOWING*, and so on.

If the current row is one of the boundary points of the frame, the plan won't need to compute both the top and the bottom row numbers. It will compute only one row number–based boundary in addition to the existing *RowNumberN*. For example, for the frame *3 PRECEDING AND CURRENT ROW*, it will compute only *TopRowNumberN (RowNumberN – 3)*, and for the frame *CURRENT ROW AND 3 FOLLOWING*, it will compute *BottomRowNumberN (RowNumberN + 3)*. The other boundary point will simply be *RowNumberN*.

When the window function you're using is a noncumulative one (*MIN*, *MAX*, *FIRST_VALUE*, *LAST_VALUE*, or *CHECKSUM_AGG*), regardless of the number of rows in the frame, all frame rows will be expanded. Consider the following example:

```
SELECT actid, tranid, val,
  MAX(val) OVER(PARTITION BY actid
               ORDER BY tranid
               ROWS BETWEEN 100 PRECEDING
                        AND   2 PRECEDING) AS maxval
FROM dbo.Transactions;
```

The plan for this query is shown in Figure 5-38.

FIGURE 5-38 Plan for *MAX* aggregate.

Because the *MAX* aggregate is used, all frame rows get expanded. That's 99 rows per frame; multiply that by the number of rows in the table, and you end up with quite a large number of rows returned by the *Window Spool* operator (close to 200,000,000 rows). It took this query 38 seconds to complete.

You can see that SQL Server decided to use a parallel plan. I explained earlier the issues with the way parallelism is handled natively for window functions under row mode and suggested that you try using the parallel *APPLY* technique instead. Here's the parallel *APPLY* version:

```
SELECT C.actid, A.tranid, A.val, A.maxval
FROM dbo.Accounts AS C
  CROSS APPLY (SELECT tranid, val,
                MAX(val) OVER(ORDER BY tranid
                              ROWS BETWEEN 100 PRECEDING
                                       AND  2 PRECEDING) AS maxval
              FROM dbo.Transactions AS T
              WHERE T.actid = C.actid) AS A;
```

On my machine, this query finishes in 18 seconds.

The *Window Spool* operator prefers to use an optimized in-memory work table. However, if any of the following conditions is met, it will have no choice but to resort to the much slower on-disk work table with all of the associated overhead (for example, locking, latches, and I/O):

- If the distance between the two extreme points among the current, top, and bottom row numbers exceeds 10,000

- If it can't compute the number of rows in the frame—for example, when using *RANGE*

- When using *LAG* or *LEAD* with an expression as the offset

There are a couple of techniques you can use to test whether, in practice, SQL Server used an on-disk work table or an in-memory work table. The first technique is to use the *STATISTICS IO* option; the second technique is to use the *Extended Event window_spool_ondisk_warning*.

Using the *STATISTICS IO* option, you know that the in-memory work table was used when the number of reads reported against the work table is *0*. When it's greater than *0*, the on-disk one was used. As an example, the following code turns *STATISTICS IO ON* and runs two queries using the *MAX* window aggregate function:

```
SET STATISTICS IO ON;

SELECT actid, tranid, val,
  MAX(val) OVER(PARTITION BY actid
                ORDER BY tranid
                ROWS BETWEEN 9999 PRECEDING
                         AND 9999 PRECEDING) AS maxval
FROM dbo.Transactions;

SELECT actid, tranid, val,
  MAX(val) OVER(PARTITION BY actid
                ORDER BY tranid
```

```
        ROWS BETWEEN 10000 PRECEDING
                   AND 10000 PRECEDING) AS maxval
FROM dbo.Transactions;
```

The first query uses the following frame:

```
ROWS BETWEEN 9999 PRECEDING AND 9999 PRECEDING
```

The distance in terms of number of rows between the extreme points (remember, the current row is also considered for this purpose) is 10,000; hence, the in-memory work table can be used. This query finished in 3 seconds.

The second query uses the following frame:

```
ROWS BETWEEN 10000 PRECEDING AND 10000 PRECEDING
```

This time, the distance between the extreme points is 10,001; hence, the on-disk work table is used. This query finished in 18 seconds.

Here's the output of STATISTICS IO for the two queries:

```
-- 9999 PRECEDING AND 9999 PRECEDING, 3 seconds
Table 'Worktable'. Scan count 0, logical reads 0.
Table 'Transactions'. Scan count 1, logical reads 6215.

-- 10000 PRECEDING AND 10000 PRECEDING, 18 seconds
Table 'Worktable'. Scan count 2000100, logical reads 12086701.
Table 'Transactions'. Scan count 1, logical reads 6215.
```

Observe that for the first query, 0 reads are reported, whereas for the second query, 12 million reads are reported.

Before I describe the second technique, run the following code to turn the *STATISTICS IO* option to *OFF*:

```
SET STATISTICS IO OFF;
```

The second technique to identify whether an on-disk work table was used is with an *Extended Event* called *window_spool_ondisk_warning*. You can use the following code to create and start such an event session:

```
CREATE EVENT SESSION xe_window_spool ON SERVER
ADD EVENT sqlserver.window_spool_ondisk_warning
    ( ACTION (sqlserver.plan_handle, sqlserver.sql_text) );

ALTER EVENT SESSION xe_window_spool ON SERVER STATE = START;
```

You can open a Watch Live Data window for the session and rerun the preceding queries. You will find information about the queries for which an on-disk work table was used, including the plan handle and the query text.

When you're done, run the following code for cleanup:

```
DROP EVENT SESSION xe_window_spool ON SERVER;
```

Computing Two Cumulative Values

When the window function is a cumulative one (*SUM, COUNT, COUNT_BIG, AVG, STDEV, STDEVP, VAR,* or *VARP*) and there are more than four rows in the frame, the optimizer uses a specialized strategy that doesn't involve expanding all frame rows. It computes two cumulative values and then derives the result from the two. Consider the following query as an example:

```
SELECT actid, tranid, val,
  SUM(val) OVER(PARTITION BY actid
                ORDER BY tranid
                ROWS BETWEEN 100 PRECEDING
                        AND   2 PRECEDING) AS sumval
FROM dbo.Transactions;
```

The plan for this query is shown in Figure 5-39.

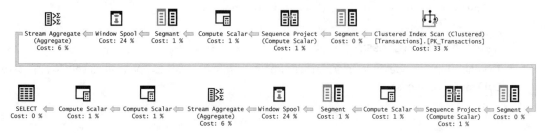

FIGURE 5-39 Plan computing two cumulative values.

Here are the performance numbers that I got for this query:

CPU time: 6578 ms, elapsed time: 6693 ms, logical reads: 6215

The optimizer decided to use a serial plan. The plan scans the POC index in key order. Then the plan uses a sequence of operators (*Segment, Sequence Project, Compute Scalar, Segment, Window Spool,* and *Stream Aggregate*) to compute the cumulative bottom *SUM* and *COUNT* aggregate values (which we'll call *CumulativeBottomSum* and *CumulativeBottomCount*). The rows that were accumulated to compute the cumulative bottom aggregates are those from the beginning of the partition up to the row with the current row number minus 2. The technique used to compute the cumulative aggregates is the one I described in the "UNBOUNDED PRECEDING: The Fast-Track Case" section. Hence, you see that the *Window Spool* operator generates only two rows for each source row—one with the accumulated values and the current row for the detail elements.

Next, the plan uses another sequence of operators (*Segment, Sequence Project, Compute Scalar, Segment, Window Spool,* and *Stream Aggregate*) to compute the cumulative top *SUM* and *COUNT* aggregate values (which we'll call *CumulativeTopSum* and *CumulativeTopCount*). The rows that were accumulated to compute those values are those from the beginning of the partition up to the row with the current row number minus 101.

Then a *Compute Scalar* operator computes the window frame *SUM* as *CumulativeBottomSum* – *CumulativeTopSum* and the window frame *COUNT* as *CumulativeBottomCount* – *CumulativeTopCount*. Finally, the last *Compute Scalar* operator evaluates the count of rows in the window frame, and if the count is 0, it returns a *NULL*.

As mentioned, this query took 6.7 seconds to complete on my system. Here, as well, you can try using the parallel *APPLY* technique, like so:

```
SELECT C.actid, A.tranid, A.val, A.sumval
FROM dbo.Accounts AS C
  CROSS APPLY (SELECT tranid, val,
                 SUM(val) OVER(ORDER BY tranid
                               ROWS BETWEEN 100 PRECEDING
                                        AND   2 PRECEDING) AS sumval
               FROM dbo.Transactions AS T
               WHERE T.actid = C.actid) AS A;
```

The run time on my system decreased to 3.4 seconds.

Batch-Mode Processing

To enable batch mode on *rowstore*, make sure you're running with compatibility level 150 (SQL Server 2019 mode) or above:

```
ALTER DATABASE TSQLV5 SET COMPATIBILITY_LEVEL = 150;
```

For window aggregate functions with a frame, currently the batch-mode Window Aggregate operator can be used only with the typical frame (*UNBOUNDED* and *CURRENT ROW* as delimiters). However, it's relevant for both *ROWS* and *RANGE*. For the offset window functions *LAG* and *LEAD*, batch-mode processing is only available with the offset of 1 (the default). Otherwise, the traditional row-mode optimization I described earlier is used. I'll demonstrate these cases with examples.

The following query applies a windowed *SUM* aggregate with the typical frame *ROWS BETWEEN UNBOUNDED PRECEDING AND CURRENT ROW* (or the shortcut *ROWS UNBOUNDED PRECEDING*), to compute a simple running total:

```
SELECT actid, tranid, val,
  SUM(val) OVER(PARTITION BY actid
                ORDER BY tranid
                ROWS BETWEEN UNBOUNDED PRECEDING
                         AND CURRENT ROW) AS balance
FROM dbo.Transactions;
```

This query gets optimized with the batch-mode Window Aggregate operator as shown in Figure 5-40.

SELECT   Compute Scalar   Window Aggregate   Clustered Index Scan (Clustered)
Cost: 0 %   Cost: 1 %   Cost: 31 %   [Transactions].[PK_Transactions]
                                                                Cost: 68 %

FIGURE 5-40 Plan for window aggregate with ROWS, using batch mode.

Here are the performance statistics that I got for this query:

CPU time: 968 ms, elapsed time: 1133 ms, logical reads: 6215

Performance is great compared to the row-mode alternative.

What's even more amazing is that since with this batch-mode operator Microsoft eliminated the need for a spool, even when using the *RANGE* option, you're getting excellent performance. Try the same query with *RANGE*:

```
SELECT actid, tranid, val,
  SUM(val) OVER(PARTITION BY actid
               ORDER BY tranid
               RANGE BETWEEN UNBOUNDED PRECEDING
                          AND CURRENT ROW) AS balance
FROM dbo.Transactions;
```

You get the plan shown in Figure 5-41.

SELECT   Compute Scalar   Window Aggregate   Clustered Index Scan (Clustered)
Cost: 0 %   Cost: 1 %   Cost: 31 %   [Transactions].[PK_Transactions]
                                                                Cost: 68 %

FIGURE 5-41 Plan for window aggregate with RANGE, using batch mode.

Here are the performance statistics that I got for this query:

CPU time: 1031 ms, elapsed time: 1154 ms, logical reads: 6215

Recall that when you don't specify the window frame unit, you're getting *RANGE* by default. The following query is a logical equivalent of the previous:

```
SELECT actid, tranid, val,
  SUM(val) OVER(PARTITION BY actid
               ORDER BY tranid) AS balance
FROM dbo.Transactions;
```

Here *RANGE* is possibly used unintentionally, but because ordering is unique within the partition, you get the right result without the performance penalty of the on-disk spool.

If you use a less typical frame, like *ROWS BETWEEN UNBOUNDED PRECEDING AND 1 PRECEDING*, SQL Server will use row-mode processing for the calculation of the aggregate. The following query demonstrates this:

```
SELECT actid, tranid, val,
  SUM(val) OVER(PARTITION BY actid
              ORDER BY tranid
              ROWS BETWEEN UNBOUNDED PRECEDING
                      AND 1 PRECEDING) AS prevbalance
FROM dbo.Transactions;
```

The plan for this query is shown in Figure 5-42.

FIGURE 5-42 Plan for window aggregate with less typical frame, using row mode.

 Note SQL Server can use batch-mode processing for the calculation of the row numbers (*Window Aggregate* operator), but not for the calculation of the aggregate itself (*Stream Aggregate operator*).

Here are the performance statistics that I got for this query:

CPU time: 3532 ms, elapsed time: 3812 ms, logical reads: 6215

As for *LAG* and *LEAD*, SQL Server can optimize those with the batch-mode *Window Aggregate* operator as long as you use an offset of 1 (the default).

Here's a query using *LAG* with the default offset 1:

```
SELECT actid, tranid, val,
  LAG(val) OVER(PARTITION BY actid
              ORDER BY tranid) AS prevval
FROM dbo.Transactions;
```

The plan for this query is shown in Figure 5-43.

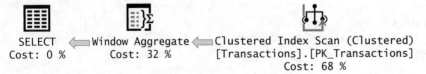

FIGURE 5-43 Plan for *LAG* with default offset.

Here are the performance statistics that I got for this query:

CPU time: 859 ms, elapsed time: 1000 ms, logical reads: 6215

Try *LAG* with a nondefault offset:

```
SELECT actid, tranid, val,
  LAG(val, 3) OVER(PARTITION BY actid
                   ORDER BY tranid) AS prevval
FROM dbo.Transactions;
```

The plan for this query uses row-mode processing for the *LAG* computation itself (via the *LAST_VALUE* function) but does use the batch-mode *Window Aggregate* operator to handle the internal row number computation, as shown in Figure 5-44.

FIGURE 5-44 Plan for *LAG* with nondefault offset.

Here are the performance statistics that I got for this query:

CPU time: 3422 ms, elapsed time: 3592 ms, logical reads: 6215

Remember, *LAG* and *LEAD* get translated behind the scenes to *LAST_VALUE* with a frame made of one row. If you use *LAST_VALUE* explicitly to emulate *LAG/LEAD* with an offset of 1, you will also get batch processing.

Distribution Functions

This section describes the optimization of statistical, or distribution, functions. I'll start with row-mode processing for rank and inverse distribution functions, and then I will cover batch-mode processing. If you don't remember the logic behind these computations, make sure you first review the section covering distribution (statistical) functions in Chapter 2.

Make sure you set the database compatibility level to 140 initially to disable batch mode on *rowstore*:

```
ALTER DATABASE TSQLV5 SET COMPATIBILITY_LEVEL = 140;
```

Rank Distribution Functions

Rank distribution functions are *PERCENT_RANK* and *CUME_DIST*. Recall that the *PERCENT_RANK* function is computed as $(rk – 1) / (nr – 1)$, where rk is the rank of the row and nr is the count of rows in the partition. Under row mode, computing the count of rows in the respective partition involves using a *Table Spool* operator, as described earlier in the chapter. Computing the rank involves using the Sequence Project operator. The plan that computes *PERCENT_RANK* simply incorporates both techniques.

Consider the following query as an example:

```
SELECT testid, studentid, score,
  PERCENT_RANK() OVER(PARTITION BY testid ORDER BY score) AS percentrank
FROM Stats.Scores;
```

The plan for this query is shown in Figure 5-45.

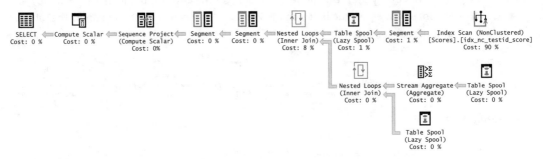

FIGURE 5-45 Plan for *PERCENT_RANK*.

The first part is scanning the data and segmenting it by *testid*. Then the partition rows are written to a spool one partition at a time, and the spool is read twice—once to compute the count (*nr*), and a second time to re-obtain the detail rows. Then the detail rows and the aggregates are joined. Next, the *Segment* and the *Sequence Project* operators are used to compute the rank (*rk*). Finally, the *Compute Scalar* operator computes the result of the *PERCENT_RANK* function as (*rk* – 1) / (*nr* – 1).

I tested this function against the larger *Transactions* table:

```
SELECT tranid, actid, val,
  PERCENT_RANK() OVER(PARTITION BY actid ORDER BY val) AS percentrank
FROM dbo.Transactions;
```

I got the following performance statistics:

CPU time: 13906 ms, elapsed time: 22972 ms, logical reads: 4062569

That's 23 seconds of run time and four million reads. This is not the most efficient performance. (I'll describe the far more optimal batch-mode optimization shortly.)

As for *CUME_DIST*, the computation is *np / nr*, where *nr* is the same as before (the count of rows in the partition) and *np* is the count of rows that precede or are peers of the current row.

Consider the following query as an example:

```
SELECT testid, studentid, score,
  CUME_DIST() OVER(PARTITION BY testid ORDER BY score) AS cumedist
FROM Stats.Scores;
```

The plan for this query is shown in Figure 5-46.

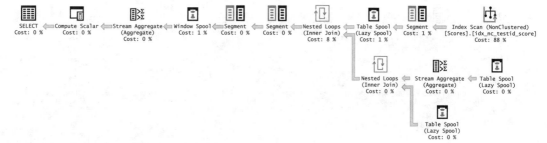

FIGURE 5-46 Plan for CUME_DIST.

The first part, which computes *nr*, is the same as in the plan for *PERCENT_RANK*. The second part is a bit trickier. To calculate *np*, SQL Server might need to look ahead of the current row. Also, the plan uses two Segment operators here—the first operator segments the rows by the partitioning element (*testid*), and the second operator segments the rows by the partitioning plus ordering elements (*testid* and *score*). However, instead of using a *Sequence Project* operator, it uses the *Window Spool* and *Stream Aggregate* operators in the fast-track mode to count the number of rows that precede or are peer of the current one. Finally, the *Compute Scalar* operator computes the *CUME_DIST* value as *np / nr*.

I tested this function against the larger *Transactions* table:

```
SELECT tranid, actid, val,
  CUME_DIST() OVER(PARTITION BY actid ORDER BY val) AS cumedist
FROM dbo.Transactions;
```

This test produced the following performance statistics:

CPU time: 19982 ms, elapsed time: 15979 ms, logical reads: 8350751

That's 16 seconds of run time and over eight million reads.

Inverse Distribution Functions

The optimization of inverse distribution functions—*PERCENTILE_CONT* and *PERCENTILE_DISC*—is more involved than that of rank distribution functions. I'll start with *PERCENTILE_DISC*. Consider the following query:

```
SELECT testid, score,
  PERCENTILE_DISC(0.5) WITHIN GROUP(ORDER BY score)
    OVER(PARTITION BY testid) AS percentiledisc
FROM Stats.Scores;
```

The plan for this query appears in Figure 5-47.

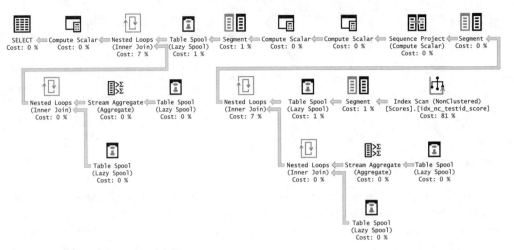

FIGURE 5-47 Plan for *PERCENTILE_DISC*.

The plan involves the following steps:

- The first set of eight operators that appear in the bottom-right section of Figure 5-47 are responsible for computing the count of rows for each row in the respective *testid* partition. The plan names this count *PartitionSizeN*.

- The *Segment* and *Sequence Project* operators that follow compute a row number within the *testid* partition based on score ordering. The plan calls this row number *RowNumberN*.

- The first *Compute Scalar* operator computes the row number of the row that holds the percentile for the partition. It does so with the expression (simplified): *CeilingTargetRowN = ceiling(@pct * PartitionSizeN)*, where *@pct* is the input percent to the function (0.5 in our case).

- The second *Compute Scalar* operator computes an expression called *PartialSumN*. This expression returns the desired percentile score if the current row's row number (*RowNumberN*) is equal to *MIN(1, CeilingTargetRowN)*; otherwise, it returns a *NULL*. In simplified terms, *PartialSumN* will have the score only if it is the desired percentile; otherwise, it returns a *NULL*.

- The last part needs to pull from each partition the non-*NULL* percentile (*PartialSumN*) and associate it with each detail row. For this, the plan again uses a *Table Spool* operator. The plan segments the data by *testid* and, one partition at a time, stores the current partition's rows in a spool. Then the plan reads the spool twice—once to retrieve the non-NULL percentile using a *MAX(PartialSumN)* aggregate (call the result *PercentileResultN*) and another time to retrieve the detail. The plan then joins the detail and the aggregates.

- The last part is checking the partition size. If it's 0, it returns *NULL*; otherwise, it returns *PercentileResultN*.

Test this function against the *Transactions* table:

```
SELECT tranid, actid, val,
  PERCENTILE_DISC(0.5) WITHIN GROUP(ORDER BY val)
    OVER(PARTITION BY actid) AS percentiledisc
FROM dbo.Transactions;
```

I got the following performance numbers for this query:

CPU time: 17418 ms, elapsed time: 13671 ms, logical reads: 8147577

As for the *PERCENTILE_CONT* function, I'll use the following query to discuss the plan:

```
SELECT testid, score,
  PERCENTILE_CONT(0.5) WITHIN GROUP(ORDER BY score)
    OVER(PARTITION BY testid) AS percentilecont
FROM Stats.Scores;
```

The plan for this query is shown in Figure 5-48.

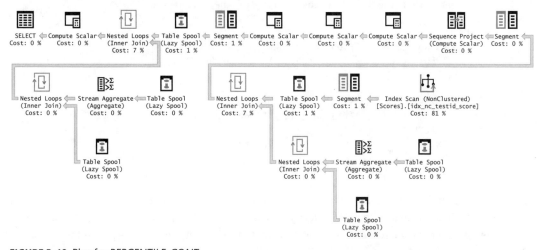

FIGURE 5-48 Plan for *PERCENTILE_CONT*.

As you can see, the general layout of the plan is similar to that for the *PERCENTILE_DISC* function. There are a couple of main differences, though. One difference is in the *Compute Scalar* operators that appear right after the computation of the row number, and the other difference is in the second *Stream Aggregate* operator. I'll start with the *Compute Scalar* operators:

- The first *Compute Scalar* operator computes the target row number, including the fraction: *TargetRowN = 1 + @pct * (PartitionSizeN – 1)*.

- The second *Compute Scalar* operator computes the floor and ceiling of *TargetRowN*, naming them *FloorTargetRowN* and *CeilingTargetRowN*, respectively.

- The third Compute Scalar operator computes an expression called *PartialSumN*. If no interpolation is needed, *PartialSumN* returns the percentile score if the current row is the target row; otherwise, 0 is returned. If an interpolation is needed, *PartialSumN* returns the parts of the interpolated score if the current row is either the floor or the ceiling of the target row; otherwise, it returns 0. The full computation of *PartialSumN* is quite convoluted; in case you have the stomach for it, here it is (simplified):

```
CASE
  -- when no interpolation is needed:
  --   return the current score if current row is target row, else 0
  WHEN CeilingTargetRowN = FloorTargetRowN AND CeilingTargetRowN = TargetRowN
    THEN CASE
           WHEN RowNumberN = TargetRowN
             THEN score
           ELSE 0
         END
  -- when interpolation is needed:
  --   return the parts of the interpolated value if current row
  --   is either the floor or the ceiling of the target row
  ELSE
    CASE
      WHEN RowNumberN = FloorTargetRowN
        THEN score * (CeilingTargetRowN - TargetRowN)
      ELSE
        CASE
          WHEN RowNumberN = CeilingTargetRowN
            THEN score * (TargetRowN - FloorTargetRowN)
          ELSE 0
        END
    END
END
```

The second difference from the plan for *PERCENTILE_DISC* is that the second *Stream Aggregate* operator in the plan uses the *SUM* aggregate instead of *MAX*. It does so because this time, more than one element could be relevant, and the parts that make the interpolated value need to be summed up.

Test this function against the larger *Transactions* table:

```
SELECT tranid, actid, val,
  PERCENTILE_CONT(0.5) WITHIN GROUP(ORDER BY val)
    OVER(PARTITION BY actid) AS percentilecont
FROM dbo.Transactions;
```

I got the following performance numbers for this query:

CPU time: 18434 ms, elapsed time: 14816 ms, logical reads: 8147577

As you can see, the row-mode processing of all four statistical functions is quite inefficient. It took the queries between a dozen and two dozen seconds to run, and they involved millions of reads. The next section describes the far more efficient batch-mode optimization.

Batch-Mode Processing

To enable batch mode on *rowstore*, make sure you're running with compatibility level 150 (SQL Server 2019 mode) or above:

```
ALTER DATABASE TSQLV5 SET COMPATIBILITY_LEVEL = 150;
```

Test the four functions against the large *Transactions* table:

```
-- PERCENT_RANK
SELECT tranid, actid, val,
  PERCENT_RANK() OVER(PARTITION BY actid ORDER BY val) AS percentrank
FROM dbo.Transactions;

-- CUME_DIST
SELECT tranid, actid, val,
  CUME_DIST() OVER(PARTITION BY actid ORDER BY val) AS cumedisc
FROM dbo.Transactions;

-- PERCENTILE_DISC
SELECT tranid, actid, val,
  PERCENTILE_DISC(0.5) WITHIN GROUP(ORDER BY val)
    OVER(PARTITION BY actid) AS percentiledisc
FROM dbo.Transactions;

-- PERCENTILE_CONT
SELECT tranid, actid, val,
  PERCENTILE_CONT(0.5) WITHIN GROUP(ORDER BY val)
    OVER(PARTITION BY actid) AS percentilecont
FROM dbo.Transactions;
```

The plans for these queries are shown in Figure 5-49.

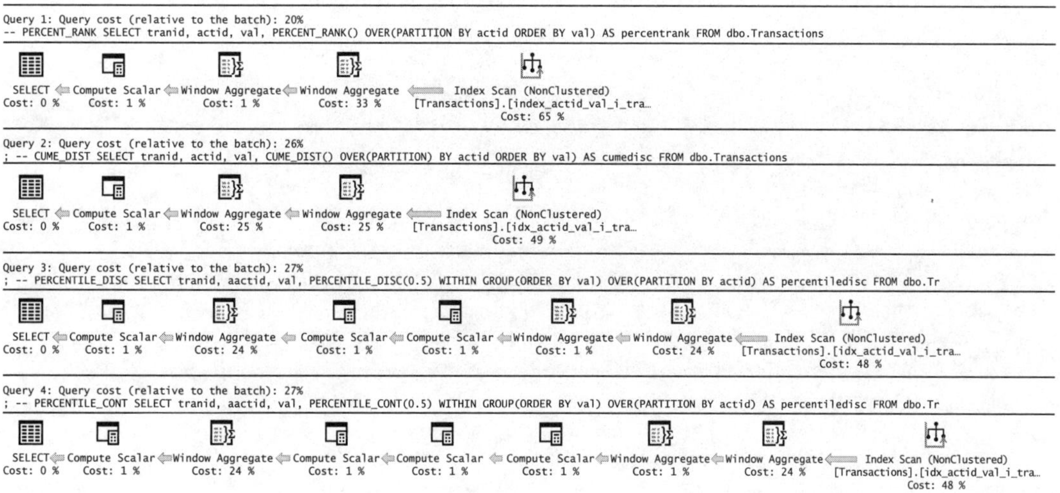

FIGURE 5-49 Plans for distribution functions using batch processing.

The plans are substantially simpler than their row-mode counterparts! If you examine the different arguments that the *Window Aggregate* operator computes and the calculations that the different *Compute Scalar* operators compute, you will see that they are similar to the ones computed under row mode processing. However, the key differences are that there's no spooling going on, and there's no need to join detail and aggregate calculations.

Here are the performance statistics that I got for these queries:

- *PERCENT_RANK*: CPU time: 937 ms, elapsed time: 1027 ms, logical reads: 5467

- *CUME_DIST*: CPU time: 891 ms, elapsed time: 983 ms, logical reads: 5467

- *PERCENTILE_DISC*: CPU time: 1219 ms, elapsed time: 1297 ms, logical reads: 5467

- *PERCENTILE_CONT*: CPU time: 1453 ms, elapsed time: 1572 ms, logical reads: 5467

These are pretty impressive numbers, considering the fact that with row-mode processing, these functions ran an order of magnitude longer and used millions of reads!

Summary

This chapter covered SQL Server's optimization of window functions. I covered both row-mode processing and batch-mode processing when applicable. Remember that if you are able to create a supporting POC index, you can avoid an expensive sort.

The next chapter gets into practical uses of window functions and, in some cases, compares solutions based on those with more traditional alternatives, demonstrating the increased efficiency of window functions.

T-SQL Solutions Using Window Functions

The first five chapters of this book described window functions in detail, including both their logical aspects and their optimization aspects. In this sixth and last chapter of the book, I'm going to show how to solve a wide range of querying tasks using window functions. What could be surprising to some is the large number of solutions that rely on the *ROW_NUMBER* function—by far the most commonly used of the bunch.

The solutions covered in this chapter are

- Virtual auxiliary table of numbers
- Sequences of date and time values
- Sequences of keys
- Paging
- Removing duplicates
- Pivoting
- Top N per group
- Emulating IGNORE_NULLS
- Mode

- Trimmed mean
- Running totals
- Max concurrent intervals
- Packing intervals
- Gaps and islands
- Median
- Conditional aggregate
- Sorting hierarchies

Note This chapter covers only a sample of solutions to show the usefulness and practicality of window functions. You will probably find many other ways to use window functions to solve tasks more elegantly and efficiently than with alternative methods.

Virtual Auxiliary Table of Numbers

An auxiliary table of numbers is a helper table filled with a sequence of integers you can use to address many different querying tasks. There are many uses for such a numbers table, such as generating sample data, generating a sequence of date and time values, and splitting separated lists of values. Normally, it is recommended to keep such a permanent table in your database, fill it with as many numbers as you will ever need, and then query it as needed. However, in some environments, you don't have an option to create and populate new tables, and you need to get by with just querying logic.

To generate a large sequence of integers efficiently using querying logic, you can use cross joins. You start off with a query that generates a result set with two rows using a table value constructor, like so:

```
SELECT c FROM (VALUES(1),(1)) AS D(c);
```

This code generates the following output:

```
c
-----------
1
1
```

Next, define a common table expression (CTE) named *L0* for *level 0* based on the previous query. Apply a cross join between two instances of the CTE to square the number of rows. This will generate four rows, like so:

```
WITH
  L0 AS(SELECT c FROM (VALUES(1),(1)) AS D(c))
SELECT 1 AS c FROM L0 AS A CROSS JOIN L0 AS B;
```

```
c
-----------
1
1
1
1
```

In a similar way, you can define a CTE named *L1* for *level 1* based on the last query. Apply a cross join between two instances of the new CTE to again square the number of rows. This will generate 16 rows, like so:

```
WITH
  L0   AS (SELECT c FROM (VALUES(1),(1)) AS D(c)),
  L1   AS (SELECT 1 AS c FROM L0 AS A CROSS JOIN L0 AS B)
SELECT 1 AS c FROM L1 AS A CROSS JOIN L1 AS B;
```

```
c
-----------
1
1
1
1
1
1
1
1
1
1
1
1
1
1
1
1
```

You can keep adding CTEs, each applying a cross join between two instances of the last CTE and squaring the number of rows. With *L* levels (starting the count with 0), the total number of rows you get is 2^{2^L} (read: two to the power of two to the power of *L*). For instance, with five levels, you get 4,294,967,296 rows. So, with five levels of CTEs aside from level *0*, this method gives you more than four billion rows. You will hardly ever need that many rows in a numbers table, but using the *TOP* or *OFFSET-FETCH* options, you can cap the number of rows based on user input. Using the *ROW_NUMBER* function with *ORDER BY (SELECT NULL)*, you can generate the actual numbers without worrying about sorting cost. Putting it all together to generate a sequence of numbers in the range *@low* to *@high*, you can use the following code:

```
WITH
   L0   AS (SELECT c FROM (VALUES(1),(1)) AS D(c)),
   L1   AS (SELECT 1 AS c FROM L0 AS A CROSS JOIN L0 AS B),
   L2   AS (SELECT 1 AS c FROM L1 AS A CROSS JOIN L1 AS B),
   L3   AS (SELECT 1 AS c FROM L2 AS A CROSS JOIN L2 AS B),
   L4   AS (SELECT 1 AS c FROM L3 AS A CROSS JOIN L3 AS B),
   L5   AS (SELECT 1 AS c FROM L4 AS A CROSS JOIN L4 AS B),
   Nums AS (SELECT ROW_NUMBER() OVER(ORDER BY (SELECT NULL)) AS rownum
            FROM L5)
SELECT TOP (@high - @low + 1) @low + rownum - 1 AS n
FROM Nums
ORDER BY rownum;
```

The beauty in this approach is that SQL Server realizes that there's no need to actually generate more rows than *@high – @low + 1*, so it short-circuits as soon as this number is reached. So, if you need a sequence of only 10 numbers, it will generate only 10 rows and stop. If you want to avoid repeating this code every time you need a sequence of numbers, you can encapsulate it in an inline table-valued function, like so:

```
USE TSQLV5;
GO
```

```
CREATE OR ALTER FUNCTION dbo.GetNums(@low AS BIGINT, @high AS BIGINT) RETURNS
TABLE
AS
RETURN
  WITH
    L0   AS (SELECT c FROM (VALUES(1),(1)) AS D(c)),
    L1   AS (SELECT 1 AS c FROM L0 AS A CROSS JOIN L0 AS B),
    L2   AS (SELECT 1 AS c FROM L1 AS A CROSS JOIN L1 AS B),
    L3   AS (SELECT 1 AS c FROM L2 AS A CROSS JOIN L2 AS B),
    L4   AS (SELECT 1 AS c FROM L3 AS A CROSS JOIN L3 AS B),
    L5   AS (SELECT 1 AS c FROM L4 AS A CROSS JOIN L4 AS B),
    Nums AS (SELECT ROW_NUMBER() OVER(ORDER BY (SELECT NULL)) AS rownum
             FROM L5)
  SELECT TOP (@high - @low + 1) @low + rownum - 1 AS n
  FROM Nums
  ORDER BY rownum;
GO
```

You could also use the *OFFSET-FETCH* filter instead, like so:

```
CREATE OR ALTER FUNCTION dbo.GetNums(@low AS BIGINT, @high AS BIGINT) RETURNS
TABLE
AS
RETURN
  WITH
    L0   AS (SELECT c FROM (VALUES(1),(1)) AS D(c)),
    L1   AS (SELECT 1 AS c FROM L0 AS A CROSS JOIN L0 AS B),
    L2   AS (SELECT 1 AS c FROM L1 AS A CROSS JOIN L1 AS B),
    L3   AS (SELECT 1 AS c FROM L2 AS A CROSS JOIN L2 AS B),
    L4   AS (SELECT 1 AS c FROM L3 AS A CROSS JOIN L3 AS B),
    L5   AS (SELECT 1 AS c FROM L4 AS A CROSS JOIN L4 AS B),
    Nums AS (SELECT ROW_NUMBER() OVER(ORDER BY (SELECT NULL)) AS rownum
             FROM L5)
  SELECT @low + rownum - 1 AS n
  FROM Nums
  ORDER BY rownum
  OFFSET 0 ROWS FETCH NEXT @high - @low + 1 ROWS ONLY;
GO
```

Both functions are optimized the same way, so performance is not a factor in determining which of the two is better to use. A factor that might matter to you is compatibility with the SQL standard. *TOP* is a proprietary feature, whereas *OFFSET-FETCH* is standard.

As an example, for using the *GetNums* function, the following code generates a sequence of numbers in the range 11 through 20:

```
SELECT n FROM dbo.GetNums(11, 20);
```

```
n
--------------------
11
```

```
12
13
14
15
16
17
18
19
20
```

To get a sense of how fast this method is, I tested it on a moderately equipped laptop after choosing the Discard Results After Execution query option from the Query Options dialog box. It took only three seconds for the following request to generate a sequence of 10,000,000 numbers:

```
SELECT n FROM dbo.GetNums(1, 10000000);
```

Compared to a physical table of numbers, like the *dbo.Nums* table in the *TSQLV5* database, in some tests, I get better performance with the *dbo.GetNums* function. Of course, with the physical table, the test result depends on whether the data is cached. I recommend you compare the performance of the two tools in any given case to see which one works better for you.

From a usability perspective, the function is easier to work with when you need a sequence that doesn't start with 1—for example, between 1,000,000,001 and 1,000,001,000.

The downside of the function is that plans for queries that use it are elaborate and can be a bit hard to follow. That's especially the case when multiple sequences are involved. Naturally, queries against a physical table of numbers produce much simpler plans.

In this chapter, you will see a number of solutions that rely on the *GetNums* function.

Sequences of Date and Time Values

Various scenarios related to data manipulation require you to generate a sequence of date and time values between some input *@start* and *@end* points, with some interval (for example, 1 day, 12 hours, and so on). Examples for such scenarios include populating a time dimension in a data warehouse, scheduling applications, and others. An efficient tool that can be used for this purpose is the *GetNums* function described in the previous section. You accept the *@start* and *@end* date and time values as inputs, and by using the DATEDIFF function, you can calculate how many intervals of the unit of interest there are between the two. Invoke the *GetNums* function with inputs *0* as *@low* and the aforementioned difference as *@high*. Finally, to generate the result date and time values, add *n* times the temporal interval to *@start*.

Here's an example for generating a sequence of dates in the range February 1, 2019 to February 12, 2019:

```
DECLARE
  @start AS DATE = '20190201',
  @end   AS DATE = '20190212';
```

```
SELECT DATEADD(day, n, @start) AS dt
FROM dbo.GetNums(0, DATEDIFF(day, @start, @end)) AS Nums;

dt
----------
2019-02-01
2019-02-02
2019-02-03
2019-02-04
2019-02-05
2019-02-06
2019-02-07
2019-02-08
2019-02-09
2019-02-10
2019-02-11
2019-02-12
```

If the interval is a product of some temporal unit—for example, 12 hours—use that unit (hour in this case) when calculating the difference between *@start* and *@end*, and divide the result by 12 to calculate *@high*; then multiply *n* by 12 to get the number of hours that need to be added to *@start* when calculating the result date and time values. As an example, the following code generates a sequence of date and time values between February 12, 2019 and February 18, 2019, with 12-hour intervals between the sequence values:

```
DECLARE
  @start AS DATETIME2 = '20190212 00:00:00.0000000',
  @end   AS DATETIME2 = '20190218 12:00:00.0000000';

SELECT DATEADD(hour, n*12, @start) AS dt
FROM dbo.GetNums(0, DATEDIFF(hour, @start, @end)/12) AS Nums;

dt
---------------------------
2019-02-12 00:00:00.0000000
2019-02-12 12:00:00.0000000
2019-02-13 00:00:00.0000000
2019-02-13 12:00:00.0000000
2019-02-14 00:00:00.0000000
2019-02-14 12:00:00.0000000
2019-02-15 00:00:00.0000000
2019-02-15 12:00:00.0000000
2019-02-16 00:00:00.0000000
2019-02-16 12:00:00.0000000
2019-02-17 00:00:00.0000000
2019-02-17 12:00:00.0000000
2019-02-18 00:00:00.0000000
2019-02-18 12:00:00.0000000
```

Sequences of Keys

In various scenarios, you might need to generate a sequence of unique integer keys when updating or inserting data in a table. SQL Server supports sequence objects, which enable you to create solutions for some of those needs. However, SQL Server will not undo the generation of sequence values if the transaction that generated them fails, meaning that you can end up with gaps between sequence values. (This is the same situation with identity.) If you need to guarantee there will be no gaps between the generated keys, you cannot rely on the sequence object. In this section, I will show you how to address a number of needs for sequence values without the sequence object.

Update a Column with Unique Values

The first scenario I'll describe involves the need to deal with data-quality issues. Run the following code to create and populate a table called *MyOrders*:

```
DROP TABLE IF EXISTS Sales.MyOrders;
GO

SELECT 0 AS orderid, custid, empid, orderdate
INTO Sales.MyOrders
FROM Sales.Orders;

SELECT * FROM Sales.MyOrders;
```

orderid	custid	empid	orderdate
0	85	5	2017-07-04
0	79	6	2017-07-05
0	34	4	2017-07-08
0	84	3	2017-07-08
0	76	4	2017-07-09
0	34	3	2017-07-10
0	14	5	2017-07-11
0	68	9	2017-07-12
0	88	3	2017-07-15
0	35	4	2017-07-16

. . .

Suppose that because of data-quality issues, the table *MyOrders* doesn't have unique values in the *orderid* attribute. You are tasked with updating all rows with unique integers starting with 1 based on *orderdate* ordering, with *custid* used as a tiebreaker. To address this need, you can define a CTE that is based on a query against *MyOrders* and that returns the *orderid* attribute as well as a *ROW_NUMBER* calculation. Then, in the outer query against the CTE, use an *UPDATE* statement that sets *orderid* to the result of the *ROW_NUMBER* calculation, like so:

```
WITH C AS
(
```

```
    SELECT orderid, ROW_NUMBER() OVER(ORDER BY orderdate, custid) AS rownum
    FROM Sales.MyOrders
)
UPDATE C
  SET orderid = rownum;
```

Query *MyOrders* after the update, and observe that the *orderid* values are now unique:

```
SELECT * FROM Sales.MyOrders;
```

orderid	custid	empid	orderdate
1	85	5	2017-07-04
2	79	6	2017-07-05
3	34	4	2017-07-08
4	84	3	2017-07-08
5	76	4	2017-07-09
6	34	3	2017-07-10
7	14	5	2017-07-11
8	68	9	2017-07-12
9	88	3	2017-07-15
10	35	4	2017-07-16
...			

At this point, it's a good idea to add a primary key constraint to enforce uniqueness in the table.

Applying a Range of Sequence Values

Suppose that you need a sequencing mechanism that guarantees no gaps. You can't rely on the identity column property or the sequence object because both mechanisms will have gaps when the operation that generates the sequence value fails or just doesn't commit. One of the common alternatives that guarantees no gaps is to store the last-used value in a table, and whenever you need a new value, you increment the stored value and use the new one.

As an example, the following code creates a table called *MySequence* and populates it with one row with the value *0* in the *val* column:

```
DROP TABLE IF EXISTS dbo.MySequence;
CREATE TABLE dbo.MySequence(val INT);
INSERT INTO dbo.MySequence VALUES(0);
```

You can then use a stored procedure such as the following when you need to generate and use a new sequence value:

```
CREATE OR ALTER PROC dbo.GetSequence
  @val AS INT OUTPUT
AS
UPDATE dbo.MySequence
  SET @val = val += 1;
GO
```

The procedure updates the row in MySequence, increments the current value by 1, and stores the incremented value in the output parameter *@val*. When you need a new sequence value, you execute the procedure and collect the new value from the output parameter, like so:

```
DECLARE @key AS INT;
EXEC dbo.GetSequence @val = @key OUTPUT;
SELECT @key;
```

If you run this code twice, you will get the sequence value *1* first and the sequence value *2* second.

Suppose that sometimes you need to allocate a whole range of sequence values—for example, for use in a multirow insertion into some table. First, you need to alter the procedure to accept an input parameter called *@n* that indicates the range size. Then the procedure can increment the *val* column in MySequence by *@n* and return the first value in the new range as the output parameter. Here's the altered definition of the procedure:

```
ALTER PROC dbo.GetSequence
  @val AS INT OUTPUT,
  @n   AS INT = 1
AS
UPDATE dbo.MySequence
  SET @val = val + 1,
      val += @n;
GO
```

You still need to figure out how to associate the individual sequence values in the range with rows in the result set of the query. Suppose that the following query returning customers from the UK represents the set you need to insert into the target table:

```
SELECT custid
FROM Sales.Customers
WHERE country = N'UK';

custid
-----------
4
11
16
19
38
53
72
```

You are supposed to generate surrogate keys for these customers and, ultimately, insert those into a customer dimension in your data warehouse. You can first populate a table variable with this result set along with the result of a *ROW_NUMBER* function that will generate unique integers starting with 1. Name this column *rownum*. Then you can collect the number of affected rows from the *@@rowcount* function into a local variable named *@rc*. Then you can invoke the procedure, passing *@rc* as the size of the range to allocate, and collect the first key in the range and put it into a local variable named *@firstkey*. Finally, you can query the table variable and compute the individual sequence values with the expression *@firstkey* + *rownum* – *1*. Here's the T-SQL code with the complete solution:

```
DECLARE @firstkey AS INT, @rc AS INT;

DECLARE @CustsStage AS TABLE
(
  custid INT,
  rownum INT
);

INSERT INTO @CustsStage(custid, rownum)
  SELECT custid, ROW_NUMBER() OVER(ORDER BY (SELECT NULL)) AS rownum
  FROM Sales.Customers
  WHERE country = N'UK';

SET @rc = @@rowcount;

EXEC dbo.GetSequence @val = @firstkey OUTPUT, @n = @rc;

SELECT custid, @firstkey + rownum - 1 AS keycol
FROM @CustsStage;

custid       keycol
-----------  -----------
4            3
11           4
16           5
19           6
38           7
53           8
72           9
```

Of course, normally, the last part inserts the result of this query into the target table. Also, observe that I use *ORDER BY (SELECT NULL)* in the window order clause of the *ROW_NUMBER* function to get an arbitrary order for the row numbers. If you need the sequence values to be assigned in a certain order (for example, *custid* ordering), make sure you revise the window order clause accordingly.

Next, run a similar process shown in Listing 6-1; this time, you are querying source customers from France.

LISTING 6-1 Adding Customers from France

```
DECLARE @firstkey AS INT, @rc AS INT;

DECLARE @CustsStage AS TABLE
(
```

```
   custid INT,
   rownum INT
);

INSERT INTO @CustsStage(custid, rownum)
  SELECT custid, ROW_NUMBER() OVER(ORDER BY (SELECT NULL)) AS rownum
  FROM Sales.Customers
  WHERE country = N'France';

SET @rc = @@rowcount;

EXEC dbo.GetSequence @val = @firstkey OUTPUT, @n = @rc;

SELECT custid, @firstkey + rownum - 1 AS keycol
FROM @CustsStage;

custid      keycol
----------- -----------
7           10
9           11
18          12
23          13
26          14
40          15
41          16
57          17
74          18
84          19
85          20
```

Observe in the result that the sequence values generated simply continued right after the end of the previously allocated range.

> **NOTE** This technique will be inherently slower than *sequence* or *identity*; also, it's more prone to blocking issues. However, it does guarantee no gaps, whereas *sequence* and *identity* don't.

When you're done, run the following code for cleanup:

```
DROP PROC IF EXISTS dbo.GetSequence;
DROP TABLE IF EXISTS dbo.MySequence;
```

Paging

Paging is a common need in applications. You want to allow the user to get one portion of rows at a time from a result set of a query so that the result can more easily fit in the target web page, UI, or screen. The two commonly used tools for paging in T-SQL are the *ROW_NUMBER* function and the *OFFSET-FETCH* filter.

Using the *ROW_NUMBER* function, you assign row numbers to the result rows based on the desired ordering and then filter the right range of row numbers based on given page-number and page-size arguments. For optimal performance, you want to have an index defined on the window ordering elements as the index keys and include in the index the rest of the attributes that appear in the query for coverage purposes. You can review what I referred to as *"POC* indexes" in Chapter 5; they are the indexing guideline for window functions.

For example, suppose you want to allow paging through orders from the *Sales.Orders* table based on *orderdate, orderid* ordering (from least to most recent), and have the result set return the attributes *orderid, orderdate, custid,* and *empid*. Following the indexing guidelines I just mentioned, you arrange the following index:

```
CREATE UNIQUE INDEX idx_od_oid_i_cid_eid
   ON Sales.Orders(orderdate, orderid)
   INCLUDE(custid, empid);
```

Then, given a page number and a page size as inputs, you use the following code to filter the correct page of rows. For example, the code shown in Listing 6-2 returns the third page with a page size of 25 rows, which means the rows with row numbers 51 through 75.

LISTING 6-2 Code Returning Third Page of Orders Using *ROW_NUMBER*

```
DECLARE
   @pagenum  AS INT = 3,
   @pagesize AS INT = 25;

WITH C AS
(
   SELECT ROW_NUMBER() OVER( ORDER BY orderdate, orderid ) AS rownum,
      orderid, orderdate, custid, empid
   FROM Sales.Orders
)
SELECT orderid, orderdate, custid, empid
FROM C
WHERE rownum BETWEEN (@pagenum - 1) * @pagesize + 1
               AND @pagenum * @pagesize
ORDER BY rownum;
```

```
orderid     orderdate  custid       empid
----------- ---------- ------------ -----------
10298       2017-09-05 37           6
10299       2017-09-06 67           4
```

10300	2017-09-09	49	2
10301	2017-09-09	86	8
10302	2017-09-10	76	4
10303	2017-09-11	30	7
10304	2017-09-12	80	1
10305	2017-09-13	55	8
10306	2017-09-16	69	1
10307	2017-09-17	48	2
10308	2017-09-18	2	7
10309	2017-09-19	37	3
10310	2017-09-20	77	8
10311	2017-09-20	18	1
10312	2017-09-23	86	2
10313	2017-09-24	63	2
10314	2017-09-25	65	1
10315	2017-09-26	38	4
10316	2017-09-27	65	1
10317	2017-09-30	48	6
10318	2017-10-01	38	8
10319	2017-10-02	80	7
10320	2017-10-03	87	5
10321	2017-10-03	38	3
10322	2017-10-04	58	7

Figure 6-1 shows the execution plan for this query.

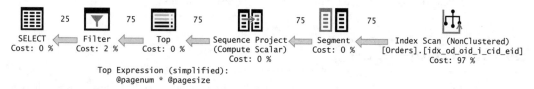

FIGURE 6-1 Execution plan for a query with *ROW_NUMBER*.

Observe that because there was an index to support the *ROW_NUMBER* calculation, SQL Server didn't really need to scan all rows from the table. Rather, using a *Top* operator based on the simplified top expression *@pagenum * @pagesize,* it filtered only the first 75 rows scanned from the index. Then, using a *Filter* operator, it further filtered the rows with row numbers 51 through 75. As you can imagine, without such an index in place, SQL Server would have no choice but to scan all rows, sort, and then filter. So, indexing here is important for good performance.

Many people like to use row numbers for paging purposes. As an alternative, you can use the *OFFSET-FETCH* filtering option. It is similar to *TOP* except that it's standard, and the *OFFSET* clause supports a skipping element that *TOP* doesn't. Here's the code you use to filter the right page of rows using the *OFFSET-FETCH* filter given the page number and page size as inputs:

```
DECLARE
  @pagenum AS INT = 3,
  @pagesize AS INT = 25;
```

```
SELECT orderid, orderdate, custid, empid
FROM Sales.Orders
ORDER BY orderdate, orderid
OFFSET (@pagenum - 1) * @pagesize ROWS FETCH NEXT @pagesize ROWS ONLY;
```

The execution plan for this query is shown in Figure 6-2.

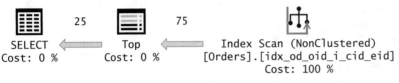

Offset Expression:
    (@pagenum - 1) * @pagesize

Top Expression: @pagesize

FIGURE 6-2 Execution plan for a query with *OFFSET-FETCH*.

Observe in the execution plan that the optimization is similar to that of the technique based on row numbers—in the sense that SQL Server scans only the first 75 rows in the index and filters the last 25. As a result, the amount of data being scanned is similar in both cases.

When you're done, run the following code for cleanup:

```
DROP INDEX IF EXISTS idx_od_oid_i_cid_eid ON Sales.Orders;
```

Removing Duplicates

De-duplication of data is a common need, especially when dealing with data-quality issues in environments that end up with duplicate rows because of the lack of enforcement of uniqueness with constraints. For example, the following code prepares sample data with duplicate orders in a table called *MyOrders*:

```
DROP TABLE IF EXISTS Sales.MyOrders;
GO

SELECT * INTO Sales.MyOrders FROM Sales.Orders
UNION ALL
SELECT * FROM Sales.Orders WHERE orderid % 100 = 0
UNION ALL
SELECT * FROM Sales.Orders WHERE orderid % 50 = 0;
```

Suppose that you need to de-duplicate the data, keeping only one occurrence of each unique *orderid* value. You mark the duplicate number using the *ROW_NUMBER* function, partitioned by what's supposed to be unique (*orderid*, in our case), and using arbitrary ordering if you don't care which row is kept and which is removed. Here's the code with the *ROW_NUMBER* function marking the duplicates:

```
SELECT orderid,
  ROW_NUMBER() OVER(PARTITION BY orderid
                      ORDER BY (SELECT NULL)) AS n
FROM Sales.MyOrders;

orderid     n
----------- ----
10248       1
10249       1
10250       1
10250       2
10251       1
...
10299       1
10300       1
10300       2
10300       3
10301       1
10302       1
...

(855 rows affected)
```

Next, you consider different options depending on the number of rows that need to be deleted and the percent they represent out of the entire table. When a small number of the rows need to be deleted, it's usually okay to use a fully logged delete operation that removes all occurrences where the row number is greater than *1*, like so:

```
WITH C AS
(
  SELECT orderid,
    ROW_NUMBER() OVER(PARTITION BY orderid
                        ORDER BY (SELECT NULL)) AS n
  FROM Sales.MyOrders
)
DELETE FROM C
WHERE n > 1;
```

If, however, you have a large number of rows that need to be deleted—especially when this number represents a large percentage of the rows in the table—the fully logged delete can prove too slow. In such a case, one of the options to consider is using a minimally logged operation, like *SELECT INTO*, to copy distinct rows (rows with row number 1) into a different table name; create constraints and indexes on the new table; truncate the original table; switch between the tables using partition-switching capabilities; then drop the new table name. Here's the code with the complete solution:

```
WITH C AS
(
  SELECT *,
    ROW_NUMBER() OVER(PARTITION BY orderid
                        ORDER BY (SELECT NULL)) AS n
```

```
    FROM Sales.MyOrders
)
SELECT orderid, custid, empid, orderdate, requireddate, shippeddate,
    shipperid, freight, shipname, shipaddress, shipcity, shipregion,
    shippostalcode, shipcountry
INTO Sales.MyOrdersTmp
FROM C
WHERE n = 1;

-- re-create indexes, constraints

TRUNCATE TABLE Sales.MyOrders;
ALTER TABLE Sales.MyOrdersTmp SWITCH TO Sales.MyOrders;
DROP TABLE Sales.MyOrdersTmp;
```

This solution is simple and straightforward, and for these reasons, it is the one that I'd recommend that you use. However, for the sake of the exercise, I wanted to discuss another solution in which you compute both *ROW_NUMBER* and *RANK* based on *orderid* ordering, like so:

```
SELECT orderid,
    ROW_NUMBER() OVER(ORDER BY orderid) AS rownum,
    RANK() OVER(ORDER BY orderid) AS rnk
FROM Sales.MyOrders;
```

orderid	rownum	rnk
10248	1	1
10248	2	1
10248	3	1
10249	4	4
10249	5	4
10249	6	4
10250	7	7
10250	8	7
10250	9	7

Observe in the result that the row number and rank are the same in only one row for each unique *orderid* value. For example, if you have a small percentage of rows to delete, you encapsulate the previous query in a CTE definition and, in the outer statement, issue a *DELETE* where the row number is different from the rank, like so:

```
WITH C AS
(
    SELECT orderid,
        ROW_NUMBER() OVER(ORDER BY orderid) AS rownum,
        RANK() OVER(ORDER BY orderid) AS rnk
    FROM Sales.MyOrders
)
DELETE FROM C
WHERE rownum <> rnk;
```

The preceding solutions are not the only solutions. For example, there are scenarios where you will want to split a large delete into batches using the *TOP* option. However, I wanted to focus here on solutions using window functions.

When you're done, run the following code for cleanup:

```
DROP TABLE IF EXISTS Sales.MyOrders;
```

Pivoting

Pivoting is a technique that aggregates and rotates data from a state of rows to a state of columns. When pivoting data, you need to identify three elements:

- The element you want to see on rows (the grouping element)

- The element you want to see on columns (the spreading element)

- The element you want to see in the data portion (the aggregation element)

For example, suppose that you need to query the *Sales.OrderValues* view and return a row for each order year, a column for each order month, and the sum of order values for each year and month intersection. In this request,

- The *on rows* (grouping element) is *YEAR(orderdate)*

- The *on cols* (spreading element) is *MONTH(orderdate)*

- The distinct spreading values are 1, 2, 3, 4, 5, 6, 7, 8, 9, 10, 11, and 12

- The *data* (aggregation) element is *SUM(val)*

To achieve pivoting, you first want to prepare a table expression, such as a CTE, where you return only the three elements that are involved in your pivoting task. Then, in the outer statement, you query the table expression and use the *PIVOT* operator to handle the pivoting logic, like so (output wrapped):

```
WITH C AS
(
  SELECT YEAR(orderdate) AS orderyear, MONTH(orderdate) AS ordermonth, val
  FROM Sales.OrderValues
)
SELECT *
FROM C
  PIVOT(SUM(val)
    FOR ordermonth IN ([1],[2],[3],[4],[5],[6],[7],[8],[9],[10],[11],[12])) AS P;

orderyear  1         2         3          4           5         6
---------- --------- --------- ---------- ----------- --------- ---------
2019       94222.12  99415.29  104854.18  123798.70   18333.64  NULL
```

```
2017       NULL      NULL      NULL       NULL        NULL      NULL
2018       61258.08  38483.64  38547.23   53032.95    53781.30  36362.82

orderyear  7         8         9          10          11        12
---------- --------- --------- ---------- ----------- --------- ---------
2019       NULL      NULL      NULL       NULL        NULL      NULL
2017       27861.90  25485.28  26381.40   37515.73    45600.05  45239.63
2018       51020.86  47287.68  55629.27   66749.23    43533.80  71398.44
```

In this case, all three pivoting elements are known, including the distinct values in the spreading element (the months). However, the spreading element often doesn't exist in the source and needs to be computed. For example, consider a request to return the order IDs of its five most recent orders for each customer. You want to see the customer IDs on rows and the order IDs in the data part, but there's nothing common to the order IDs across customers that you can use as your spreading element.

The solution is to use a *ROW_NUMBER* function that assigns ordinals to the order IDs within each customer partition based on the desired ordering—*orderdate DESC, orderid DESC,* in our case. Then the attribute representing that row number can be used as the spreading element, and the ordinals can be used as the spreading values.

First, here's the code that generates the row numbers for each customer's orders from most recent to least recent:

```
SELECT custid, val,
  ROW_NUMBER() OVER(PARTITION BY custid
                    ORDER BY orderdate DESC, orderid DESC) AS rownum
FROM Sales.OrderValues;

custid  val      rownum
------- -------- -------
1       933.50   1
1       471.20   2
1       845.80   3
1       330.00   4
1       878.00   5
1       814.50   6
2       514.40   1
2       320.00   2
2       479.75   3
2       88.80    4
3       660.00   1
3       375.50   2
3       813.37   3
3       2082.00  4
3       1940.85  5
3       749.06   6
3       403.20   7
...
```

Now you can define a CTE based on the previous query, and then in the outer query, handle the pivoting logic, with *rownum* being used as the spreading element:

```
WITH C AS
(
  SELECT custid, val,
    ROW_NUMBER() OVER(PARTITION BY custid
                      ORDER BY orderdate DESC, orderid DESC) AS rownum
  FROM Sales.OrderValues
)
SELECT *
FROM C
  PIVOT(MAX(val) FOR rownum IN ([1],[2],[3],[4],[5])) AS P;
```

```
custid  1         2         3         4         5
-------  --------  --------  --------  --------  ---------
1        933.50    471.20    845.80    330.00    878.00
2        514.40    320.00    479.75    88.80     NULL
3        660.00    375.50    813.37    2082.00   1940.85
4        491.50    4441.25   390.00    282.00    191.10
5        1835.70   709.55    1096.20   2048.21   1064.50
6        858.00    677.00    625.00    464.00    330.00
7        730.00    660.00    450.00    593.75    1761.00
8        224.00    3026.85   982.00    NULL      NULL
9        792.75    360.00    1788.63   917.00    1979.23
10       525.00    1309.50   877.73    1014.00   717.50
...
```

If you need to concatenate the order IDs of the five most recent orders for each customer into one string, you can use the *CONCAT* function, like so:

```
WITH C AS
(
  SELECT custid, CAST(orderid AS VARCHAR(11)) AS sorderid,
    ROW_NUMBER() OVER(PARTITION BY custid
                      ORDER BY orderdate DESC, orderid DESC) AS rownum
  FROM Sales.OrderValues
)
SELECT custid, CONCAT([1], ','+[2], ','+[3], ','+[4], ','+[5]) AS orderids
FROM C
  PIVOT(MAX(sorderid) FOR rownum IN ([1],[2],[3],[4],[5])) AS P;
```

```
custid      orderids
----------  ----------------------------------------------------------------
1           11011,10952,10835,10702,10692
2           10926,10759,10625,10308
3           10856,10682,10677,10573,10535
4           11016,10953,10920,10864,10793
5           10924,10875,10866,10857,10837
6           11058,10956,10853,10614,10582
```

```
7              10826,10679,10628,10584,10566
8              10970,10801,10326
9              11076,10940,10932,10876,10871
10             11048,11045,11027,10982,10975
...
```

The *CONCAT* function automatically replaces *NULL* inputs with empty strings. Alternatively, you need to use the + concatenation operator and the *COALESCE* function to replace a *NULL* with an empty string, like so:

```
WITH C AS
(
  SELECT custid, CAST(orderid AS VARCHAR(11)) AS sorderid,
    ROW_NUMBER() OVER(PARTITION BY custid
                      ORDER BY orderdate DESC, orderid DESC) AS rownum
  FROM Sales.OrderValues
)
SELECT custid,
  [1] + COALESCE(','+[2], '')
      + COALESCE(','+[3], '')
      + COALESCE(','+[4], '')
      + COALESCE(','+[5], '') AS orderids
FROM C
  PIVOT(MAX(sorderid) FOR rownum IN ([1],[2],[3],[4],[5])) AS P;
```

TOP N per Group

The Top-N-per-Group task is a common querying task that involves filtering a requested number of rows from each group, or partition, of rows, based on some defined ordering. A request to query the *Sales.Orders* table and return the three most recent orders for each customer is an example for the Top-N-per-Group task. In this case, the partitioning element is *custid*; the ordering specification is *orderdate DESC, orderid DESC* (most recent); and *N* is 3. Both the *TOP* and the *OFFSET-FETCH* filters support indicating the number of rows to filter and ordering specification, but they don't support a partition clause. Imagine how nice it would be if you could indicate both a partition clause and an order clause as part of the filter specification—something like this:

```
SELECT
  TOP (3) OVER(
    PARTITION BY custid
    ORDER BY orderdate DESC, orderid DESC)
  custid, orderdate, orderid, empid
FROM Sales.Orders;
```

Unfortunately, such syntax doesn't exist, and you have to figure out other solutions to this need.

Indexing guidelines, regardless of the solution you use, follow the POC concept. (POC stands for *Partioning, Ordering, Covering*; see Chapter 5, "Optimization of Window Functions," for more information.) The index key list is defined based on the partitioning columns (*custid,* in our case) followed by the ordering columns (*orderdate DESC, orderid DESC,* in our case), and it includes the rest of the columns that appear in the query for coverage purposes. Of course, if the index is a clustered index, all table columns are covered anyway, so you don't need to worry about the *C* part of the POC index. Here's the code to generate the POC index for our task, assuming *empid* is the only remaining column you need to return from the query other than *custid, orderdate,* and *orderid*:

```
CREATE UNIQUE INDEX idx_cid_odD_oidD_i_empid
    ON Sales.Orders(custid, orderdate DESC, orderid DESC)
    INCLUDE(empid);
```

Assuming you have a POC index in place, there are two strategies to address the task: one using the *ROW_NUMBER* function and another using the *APPLY* operator and *TOP* or *OFFSET-FETCH*. What determines which of the two is most efficient is the density of the partitioning column (*custid,* in our case). With low density—namely, a large number of distinct customers, each with a small number of orders—a solution based on the *ROW_NUMBER* function is optimal. You assign row numbers based on the same partitioning and ordering requirements as those in the request, and then you filter only the rows with row numbers that are less than or equal to the number of rows you need to filter for each group. Here's the complete solution implementing this approach:

```
WITH C AS
(
  SELECT custid, orderdate, orderid, empid,
    ROW_NUMBER() OVER(
      PARTITION BY custid
      ORDER BY orderdate DESC, orderid DESC) AS rownum
  FROM Sales.Orders
)
SELECT custid, orderdate, orderid, empid, rownum
FROM C
WHERE rownum <= 3
ORDER BY custid, rownum;
```

Figure 6-3 shows the execution plan for this query.

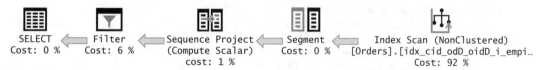

FIGURE 6-3 Execution plan for a query with low density.

What makes this strategy so efficient when the partitioning column has low density is that the plan involves only one ordered scan of the POC index and doesn't require explicit sorting. With low density, you do not want a plan that performs a seek operation in the index for each distinct partitioning value (*customer*). However, when the partitioning column has high density, a plan that performs a seek in the index for each customer becomes a more efficient strategy than a full scan of the index leaf. The way to achieve such a plan is to query the table that holds the distinct partitioning values (*Sales.Customers*, in our case) and use the *APPLY* operator to invoke a query with *TOP* or *OFFSET-FETCH* for each customer, like so:

```
SELECT C.custid, A.orderdate, A.orderid, A.empid
FROM Sales.Customers AS C
  CROSS APPLY (SELECT TOP (3) orderdate, orderid, empid
               FROM Sales.Orders AS O
               WHERE O.custid = C.custid
               ORDER BY orderdate DESC, orderid DESC) AS A;
```

The plan for this query is shown in Figure 6-4.

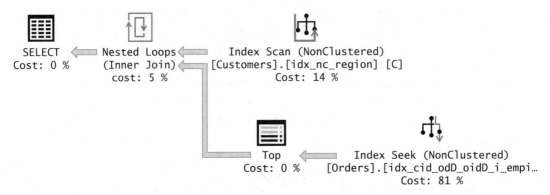

FIGURE 6-4 Execution plan for a query with high density.

Observe in the plan that an index on the *Customers* table is scanned to retrieve all customer IDs. Then the plan performs a seek operation for each customer in our POC index going to the beginning of the current customer's section in the index leaf and scans three rows in the leaf for the three most recent orders.

You can also use the alternative *OFFSET-FETCH* option instead:

```
SELECT C.custid, A.orderdate, A.orderid, A.empid
FROM Sales.Customers AS C
  CROSS APPLY (SELECT orderdate, orderid, empid
               FROM Sales.Orders AS O
               WHERE O.custid = C.custid
               ORDER BY orderdate DESC, orderid DESC
               OFFSET 0 ROWS FETCH NEXT 3 ROWS ONLY) AS A;
```

Note that to perform well, both strategies require a POC index. If you don't have an index in place and either cannot or do not want to create one, there's a third strategy that tends to perform better than the other two. However, this third strategy works only when *N* equals *1*.

At this point, you can drop the POC index:

```
DROP INDEX IF EXISTS idx_cid_odD_oidD_i_empid ON Sales.Orders;
```

The third strategy implements a *carry-along sort* technique. I introduced this technique earlier in the book in Chapter 3, "Ordered Set Functions," when discussing offset functions. The idea is to form a single string for each partition where you first concatenate the ordering attributes and then all the nonkey attributes you need in the result. It's important to use a concatenation technique that preserves the ordering behavior of the sort elements. For example, in our case, the ordering is based on *orderdate DESC* and *orderid DESC*.

The first element is a date. To get a character string representation of a date that sorts the same as the original date, you need to convert the date to the form *YYYYMMDD*. To achieve this, use the *CONVERT* function with style 112. As for the *orderid* element, it's a positive integer. To have a character string form of the number sort the same as the original integer, you need to format the value as a fixed-length string with leading spaces or zeros. You can format the value as a fixed-length string with leading spaces using the *STR* function.

The solution involves grouping the rows by the partitioning column and calculating the maximum concatenated string per group. That maximum string represents the concatenated elements from the row you need to return. Next, you define a CTE based on the last query. Then use *SUBSTRING* functions in the outer query to extract the individual elements you originally concatenated and convert them back to their original types. Here's what the complete solution looks like:

```
WITH C AS
(
  SELECT custid,
    MAX(CONVERT(CHAR(8), orderdate, 112)
        + STR(orderid, 10)
        + STR(empid, 10) COLLATE Latin1_General_BIN2) AS mx
  FROM Sales.Orders
  GROUP BY custid
)
SELECT custid,
  CAST(SUBSTRING(mx,  1,  8) AS DATETIME) AS orderdate,
  CAST(SUBSTRING(mx,  9, 10) AS INT)      AS custid,
  CAST(SUBSTRING(mx, 19, 10) AS INT)      AS empid
FROM C;
```

The query isn't pretty, but its plan involves only one scan of the data. Also, depending on size, the optimizer can choose between a sort-based and a hash-based aggregate, and it can even parallelize the work. This technique tends to outperform the other solutions when the POC index doesn't exist. Remember that if you can afford such an index, you don't want to use this solution; rather, you should use one of the other two strategies, depending on the density of the partitioning column.

Emulating IGNORE NULLS to Get the Last Non-NULL

In Chapter 2, I described the standard null treatment option for window offset functions and mentioned that SQL Server doesn't support it yet. I used a table called *T1* to demonstrate it. Use the following code to create and populate *T1* with a small set of sample data:

```
SET NOCOUNT ON;
USE TSQLV5;

DROP TABLE IF EXISTS dbo.T1;
GO

CREATE TABLE dbo.T1
(
  id INT NOT NULL CONSTRAINT PK_T1 PRIMARY KEY,
  col1 INT NULL
);

INSERT INTO dbo.T1(id, col1) VALUES
  ( 2, NULL),
  ( 3,   10),
  ( 5,   -1),
  ( 7, NULL),
  (11, NULL),
  (13,  -12),
  (17, NULL),
  (19, NULL),
  (23, 1759);
```

The idea behind the null treatment option is to allow you to control whether to respect *NULLs* (the default) or ignore *NULLs* (keep going) when requesting an offset calculation like *LAG, LEAD, FIRST_VALUE, LAST_VALUE,* and *NTH_VALUE*. For example, according to the standard, this is how you would ask for the last non-NULL *col1* value based on *id* ordering:

```
SELECT id, col1,
  COALESCE(col1, LAG(col1) IGNORE NULLS OVER(ORDER BY id)) AS lastval
FROM dbo.T1;
```

SQL Server doesn't support this option yet, but here's the expected result from this query:

```
id  col1  lastval
--- ----- --------
2   NULL  NULL
3   10    10
5   -1    -1
7   NULL  -1
11  NULL  -1
13  -12   -12
17  NULL  -12
19  NULL  -12
23  1759  1759
```

In Chapter 2, I presented the following solution (I am referring to it as *Solution 1*) that does currently work in SQL Server:

```
WITH C AS
(
  SELECT id, col1,
    MAX(CASE WHEN col1 IS NOT NULL THEN id END)
      OVER(ORDER BY id
            ROWS UNBOUNDED PRECEDING) AS grp
  FROM dbo.T1
)
SELECT id, col1,
  MAX(col1) OVER(PARTITION BY grp
                  ORDER BY id
                  ROWS UNBOUNDED PRECEDING) AS lastval
FROM C;
```

The inner query in the CTE called *C* computes for each row a result column called *grp* representing the last *id* so far that is associated with a non-NULL *col1* value. The first row in each distinct *grp* group has the last non-NULL value, and the outer query extracts it using a *MAX* window aggregate that is partitioned by *grp*.

To test the performance of this solution, you need to populate *T1* with a larger set. Use the following code to populate *T1* with 10,000,000 rows:

```
TRUNCATE TABLE dbo.T1;

INSERT INTO dbo.T1 WITH(TABLOCK)
  SELECT n AS id, CHECKSUM(NEWID()) AS col1
  FROM dbo.GetNums(1, 10000000) AS Nums
OPTION(MAXDOP 1);
```

Use the following code to test *Solution 1* using row-mode processing first:

```
WITH C AS
(
  SELECT id, col1,
    MAX(CASE WHEN col1 IS NOT NULL THEN id END)
      OVER(ORDER BY id
            ROWS UNBOUNDED PRECEDING) AS grp
  FROM dbo.T1
)
SELECT id, col1,
  MAX(col1) OVER(PARTITION BY grp
                  ORDER BY id
                  ROWS UNBOUNDED PRECEDING) AS lastval
FROM C
OPTION(USE HINT('DISALLOW_BATCH_MODE'));
```

The plan for this query is shown in Figure 6-5.

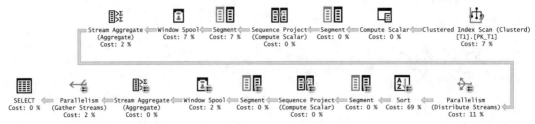

FIGURE 6-5 Execution plan for Solution 1, using row mode.

Observe that the inner window function was computed based on index order, but a sort was needed for the computation of the outer window function. Plus, there are the costs that are associated with the spooling done by the row-mode operators that compute the window aggregate functions. Here are the performance statistics that I got for this solution:

CPU time: 89548 ms, elapsed time: 40319 ms

It took 40 seconds for this solution to complete on my machine.

Test the solution again; this time, allow batch processing (must be in compatibility mode 150 or above, or have a *columnstore* index present):

```
WITH C AS
(
  SELECT id, col1,
    MAX(CASE WHEN col1 IS NOT NULL THEN id END)
      OVER(ORDER BY id
            ROWS UNBOUNDED PRECEDING) AS grp
  FROM dbo.T1
)
SELECT id, col1,
  MAX(col1) OVER(PARTITION BY grp
                ORDER BY id
                ROWS UNBOUNDED PRECEDING) AS lastval
FROM C;
```

The plan for this execution is shown in Figure 6-6.

FIGURE 6-6 Execution plan for Solution 1, using batch mode.

As I explained in Chapter 5, when the batch-mode *Window Aggregate* operator uses parallelism, it cannot rely on index order, so it needs a mediator like a parallel *Sort* operator. Therefore, you see two *Sort* operators in the plan. However, this batch-mode operator eliminates a lot of the inefficiencies of the row-mode processing, and it scales so well with multiple CPUs that the performance numbers for this plan are significantly improved:

CPU time: 11609 ms, elapsed time: 5538 ms

Run time dropped by an order of magnitude to only about 6 seconds.

This is great if you're able to benefit from batch-mode processing. However, if you can't, there's another solution that will do better in such a case. For example, you might not be able to benefit from batch-mode processing if you're running on a version of SQL Server older than 2019 and can't create a *columnstore* index—not even a fake filtered one. The second solution uses a carry-along-sort technique, similar to the one you used in the last solution for the *Top N Per Group* task. Earlier, I showed a technique that uses character string representation of the values. If you're able to use binary representation, it can be even more efficient because the binary representation tends to be more economic.

Our ordering element is the column *id*, and it's a 4-byte positive integer. Internally, SQL Server uses two's complement representation for integers. Using this format, the binary representation of positive integers preserves the original integer ordering behavior. With this in mind, you can compute a single binary string named *binstr* that concatenates the binary representation of *id* and the binary representation of *col1* (and any additional columns, if needed). In rows where *col1* is NULL, the result *binstr* is *NULL*; otherwise, it holds the binary form of the concatenated *id* and *col1* values. Then using a *MAX* window aggregate, it returns the maximum *binstr* value so far. The *col1* part of the result is the last non-NULL *col1* value. Here's the code implementing this logic:

```
SELECT id, col1, binstr,
  MAX(binstr) OVER(ORDER BY id ROWS UNBOUNDED PRECEDING) AS mx
FROM dbo.T1
  CROSS APPLY ( VALUES( CAST(id AS BINARY(4)) + CAST(col1 AS BINARY(4)) ) )
    AS A(binstr);
```

This code generates the following output against the small set of sample data:

```
id  col1  binstr              mx
--- ----- ------------------- -------------------
2   NULL  NULL                NULL
3   10    0x000000030000000A  0x000000030000000A
5   -1    0x00000005FFFFFFFF  0x00000005FFFFFFFF
7   NULL  NULL                0x00000005FFFFFFFF
11  NULL  NULL                0x00000005FFFFFFFF
13  -12   0x0000000DFFFFFFF4  0x0000000DFFFFFFF4
17  NULL  NULL                0x0000000DFFFFFFF4
19  NULL  NULL                0x0000000DFFFFFFF4
23  1759  0x00000017000006DF  0x00000017000006DF
```

All that is left is to use the *SUBSTRING* function to extract the last non-NULL *col1* value from the binary string and convert it back to *INT*, like so (forcing row-mode processing first):

```
SELECT id, col1,
  CAST( SUBSTRING( MAX( CAST(id AS BINARY(4)) + CAST(col1 AS BINARY(4)) )
                  OVER( ORDER BY id ROWS UNBOUNDED PRECEDING ), 5, 4)
```

```
          AS INT) AS lastval
FROM dbo.T1
OPTION(USE HINT('DISALLOW_BATCH_MODE'));
```

The plan for this query using row-mode processing is shown in Figure 6-7.

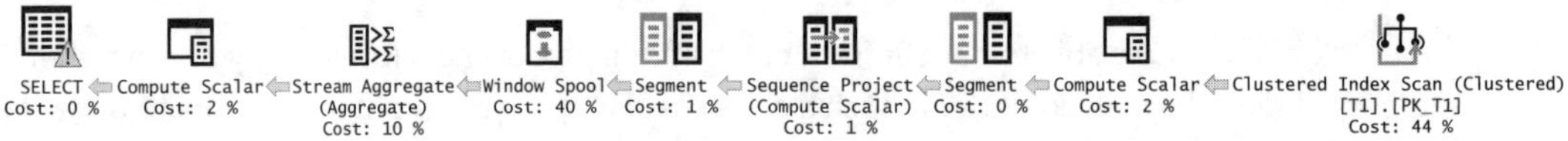

FIGURE 6-7 Execution plan for Solution 2, using row mode.

Observe that no sorting at all is needed in this plan. Here are the performance statistics that I got for this query:

CPU time: 19282 ms, elapsed time: 19512 ms

Run the query again; this time, allow batch-mode processing:

```
SELECT id, col1,
  CAST( SUBSTRING( MAX( CAST(id AS BINARY(4)) + CAST(col1 AS BINARY(4)) )
                    OVER( ORDER BY id ROWS UNBOUNDED PRECEDING ), 5, 4)
    AS INT) AS lastval
FROM dbo.T1;
```

The plan for this query using batch-mode processing is shown in Figure 6-8.

FIGURE 6-8 Execution plan for Solution 2, using batch mode.

Here are the performance statistics that I got for this query:

CPU time: 16875 ms, elapsed time: 17221 ms

This solution doesn't perform as well as *Solution 1* when using batch mode but does perform much better than when using row-mode processing.

If you're interested in additional challenges similar to the last non-NULL challenge, you can find those in the following articles:

- Previous and Next with Condition: *https://www.itprotoday.com/sql-server/how-previous-and-next-condition*

- Closest Match, Part 1: *https://sqlperformance.com/2018/12/t-sql-queries/closest-match-part-1*

- Closest Match, Part 2: *https://sqlperformance.com/2019/01/t-sql-queries/closest-match-part-2*

- Closest Match, Part 3: *https://sqlperformance.com/2019/02/t-sql-queries/closest-match-part-3*

Mode

Mode is a statistical calculation that returns the most frequently occurring value in the population. Consider, for example, the *Sales.Orders* table, which holds order information. Each order was placed by a customer and handled by an employee. Suppose you want to know, for each customer, which employee handled the most orders. That employee is the mode because he or she appears most frequently in the customer's orders.

Naturally, there is the potential for ties if there are multiple employees who handled the most orders for a given customer. Depending on your needs, you either return all ties or break the ties. I will cover solutions to both cases. If you do want to break the ties, suppose the tiebreaker is the highest employee ID number.

Indexing is straightforward here; you want an index defined on (*custid*, *empid*):

```
CREATE INDEX idx_custid_empid ON Sales.Orders(custid, empid);
```

I'll start with a solution that relies on the *ROW_NUMBER* function. The first step is to group the orders by *custid* and *empid* and then return for each group the count of orders, like so:

```
SELECT custid, empid, COUNT(*) AS cnt
FROM Sales.Orders
GROUP BY custid, empid;
```

```
custid      empid       cnt
----------- ----------- -----------
1           1           2
3           1           1
4           1           3
5           1           4
9           1           3
10          1           2
11          1           1
14          1           1
15          1           1
17          1           2
...
```

The next step is to add a *ROW_NUMBER* calculation partitioned by *custid* and ordered by *COUNT(*) DESC, empid DESC*. For each customer, the row with the highest count (and, in the case of ties, the highest employee ID number) will be assigned row number *1*:

```
SELECT custid, empid, COUNT(*) AS cnt,
  ROW_NUMBER() OVER(PARTITION BY custid
                    ORDER BY COUNT(*) DESC, empid DESC) AS rn
FROM Sales.Orders
GROUP BY custid, empid;
```

```
custid       empid        cnt          rn
-----------  -----------  -----------  --------------------
1            4            2            1
1            1            2            2
1            6            1            3
1            3            1            4
2            3            2            1
2            7            1            2
2            4            1            3
3            3            3            1
3            7            2            2
3            4            1            3
3            1            1            4
...
```

Finally, you need to filter only the rows where the row number is equal to *1* using a CTE, like so:

```
WITH C AS
(
  SELECT custid, empid, COUNT(*) AS cnt,
    ROW_NUMBER() OVER(PARTITION BY custid
                      ORDER BY COUNT(*) DESC, empid DESC) AS rn
  FROM Sales.Orders
  GROUP BY custid, empid
)
SELECT custid, empid, cnt
FROM C
WHERE rn = 1;
```

```
custid       empid        cnt
-----------  -----------  -----------
1            4            2
2            3            2
3            3            3
4            4            4
5            3            6
6            9            3
7            4            3
8            4            2
9            4            4
10           3            4
...
```

Because the window-ordering specification includes *empid DESC* as a tiebreaker, you get to return only one row per customer when implementing the tiebreaker requirements of the task. If you do not want to break the ties, use the *RANK* function instead of *ROW_NUMBER* and remove *empid* from the window order clause, like so:

```
WITH C AS
(
  SELECT custid, empid, COUNT(*) AS cnt,
    RANK() OVER(PARTITION BY custid
                ORDER BY COUNT(*) DESC) AS rk
```

```
   FROM Sales.Orders
   GROUP BY custid, empid
)
SELECT custid, empid, cnt
FROM C
WHERE rk = 1;

custid       empid        cnt
-----------  -----------  -----------
1            1            2
1            4            2
2            3            2
3            3            3
4            4            4
5            3            6
6            9            3
7            4            3
8            4            2
9            4            4
10           3            4
11           6            2
11           4            2
11           3            2
...
```

Remember that the *RANK* function is sensitive to ties, unlike the *ROW_NUMBER* function. This means that given the same ordering value—*COUNT(*)* in our case—you get the same rank. So, all rows with the greatest count per customer get rank *1*; hence, all are kept. Observe, for example, that in the case of customer 1, two different employees—with IDs 1 and 4—handled the most orders—two in number; hence, both were returned.

Perhaps you realized that the *Mode* problem is a version of the previously discussed *Top-N-per-Group* problem. And recall that in addition to the solution that is based on window functions, you can use a solution based on the carry-along-sort concept. However, this concept works only as long as *N* equals *1*, which in our case means you do want to implement a tiebreaker.

To implement the carry-along-sort concept in this case, you need to form a concatenated string with the count as the first part and the employee ID as the second part, like so:

```
SELECT custid,
   CAST(COUNT(*) AS BINARY(4)) + CAST(empid AS BINARY(4)) AS cntemp
FROM Sales.Orders
GROUP BY custid, empid;

custid       cntemp
-----------  ------------------
1            0x0000000200000001
1            0x0000000100000003
1            0x0000000200000004
1            0x0000000100000006
2            0x0000000200000003
```

```
2              0x0000000100000004
2              0x0000000100000007
3              0x0000000100000001
3              0x0000000300000003
3              0x0000000100000004
3              0x0000000200000007
...
```

Because both the count and the employee ID are positive integers, you can concatenate the binary representation of the values, which allows you to preserve their original integer ordering behavior. Alternatively, you could use fixed-length character string segments with leading spaces.

The next step is to define a CTE based on this query, and then in the outer query, group the rows by customer and calculate the maximum concatenated string per group. Finally, extract the different parts from the maximum concatenated string and convert them back to the original types, like so:

```
WITH C AS
(
  SELECT custid,
    CAST(COUNT(*) AS BINARY(4)) + CAST(empid AS BINARY(4)) AS cntemp
  FROM Sales.Orders
  GROUP BY custid, empid
)
SELECT custid,
  CAST(SUBSTRING(MAX(cntemp), 5, 4) AS INT) AS empid,
  CAST(SUBSTRING(MAX(cntemp),  1, 4) AS INT) AS cnt
FROM C
GROUP BY custid;
```

```
custid      empid       cnt
----------- ----------- -----------
1           4           2
2           3           2
3           3           3
4           4           4
5           3           6
6           9           3
7           4           3
8           4           2
9           4           4
10          3           4
...
```

As mentioned in the "TOP N per Group" section, the solution based on window functions performs well when there is an index in place, so there's no reason to use the more complicated carry-along-sort solution. But when there's no supporting index, the carry-along-sort solution tends to perform better.

When you're done, run the following code for cleanup:

```
DROP INDEX IF EXISTS idx_custid_empid ON Sales.Orders;
```

Trimmed Mean

Trimmed mean is a statistical calculation of the average of some measure after removing a certain fixed percent of the bottom and top samples, which are considered outliers.

For example, suppose that you need to query the *Sales.OrderValues* view and return the average of the order values per employee, excluding the bottom and top 5 percent of the order values for each employee. This can be done easily with the help of the *NTILE* function. Using this function, you bucketize the samples in percent groups. For instance, to arrange the orders per employee in 5-percent groups, compute *NTILE(20)*, like so:

```
SELECT empid, val,
  NTILE(20) OVER(PARTITION BY empid ORDER BY val) AS ntile20
FROM Sales.OrderValues;
```

This query generates the following output for employee 1 (abbreviated):

```
empid   val         ntile20
------  ---------   --------
1       33.75       1
1       69.60       1
1       72.96       1
1       86.85       1
1       93.50       1
1       108.00      1
1       110.00      1
1       137.50      2
1       147.00      2
1       154.40      2
1       230.40      2
1       230.85      2
1       240.00      2
1       268.80      2
...
1       3192.65     19
1       3424.00     19
1       3463.00     19
1       3687.00     19
1       3868.60     19
1       4109.70     19
1       4330.40     20
1       4807.00     20
1       5398.73     20
1       6375.00     20
1       6635.28     20
1       15810.00    20
...
```

To remove the bottom and top 5 percent of the orders per employee, place the last query in a CTE; in the outer query filter tiles 2 through 19, group the remaining rows by the employee ID. Finally, compute the average of the remaining order values per employee. Here's the complete solution query:

```
WITH C AS
(
  SELECT empid, val,
    NTILE(20) OVER(PARTITION BY empid ORDER BY val) AS ntile20
  FROM Sales.OrderValues
)
SELECT empid, AVG(val) AS avgval
FROM C
WHERE ntile20 BETWEEN 2 AND 19
GROUP BY empid;
```

This code generates the following output:

```
empid   avgval
------  ------------
1          1347.059818
2          1389.643793
3          1269.213508
4          1314.047234
5          1424.875675
6          1048.360166
7          1444.162307
8          1135.191827
9          1554.841578
```

Running Totals

Calculating running totals is a very common need. The basic idea is to keep accumulating the values of some measure based on some ordering element, possibly within partitions of rows. There are many practical examples for calculating running totals, including calculating bank account balances, tracking product stock levels in a warehouse, tracking cumulative sales values, and so on.

Without window functions, set-based solutions to calculate running totals are extremely expensive. Therefore, before window functions with a frame were introduced in SQL Server, people often resorted to iterative solutions that weren't very fast but in certain data distribution scenarios were faster than the set-based solutions. With window functions you can calculate running totals with simple set-based code that performs much better than all the alternative T-SQL solutions—set-based and iterative. I could have just showed you the code with the window function and moved on to the next topic, but to help you really appreciate the greatness of window functions and how they get optimized, I will also describe the alternatives—though inferior—and provide a performance comparison between the solutions. Feel free, of course, to read only the first section covering the window function and skip the rest if that's what you prefer.

I will compare solutions for computing bank account balances as my example for a running totals task. Listing 6-3 provides code you can use to create and populate the Transactions table with a small set of sample data.

LISTING 6-3 Create and Populate the *Transactions* Table with a Small Set of Sample Data

```
SET NOCOUNT ON;
USE TSQLV5;

DROP TABLE IF EXISTS dbo.Transactions;

CREATE TABLE dbo.Transactions
(
  actid  INT   NOT NULL,          -- partitioning column
  tranid INT   NOT NULL,          -- ordering column
  val    MONEY NOT NULL,          -- measure
  CONSTRAINT PK_Transactions PRIMARY KEY(actid, tranid)
);
GO

-- small set of sample data
INSERT INTO dbo.Transactions(actid, tranid, val) VALUES
  (1,  1,  4.00),
  (1,  2, -2.00),
  (1,  3,  5.00),
  (1,  4,  2.00),
  (1,  5,  1.00),
  (1,  6,  3.00),
  (1,  7, -4.00),
  (1,  8, -1.00),
  (1,  9, -2.00),
  (1, 10, -3.00),
  (2,  1,  2.00),
  (2,  2,  1.00),
  (2,  3,  5.00),
  (2,  4,  1.00),
  (2,  5, -5.00),
  (2,  6,  4.00),
  (2,  7,  2.00),
  (2,  8, -4.00),
  (2,  9, -5.00),
  (2, 10,  4.00),
  (3,  1, -3.00),
  (3,  2,  3.00),
  (3,  3, -2.00),
  (3,  4,  1.00),
  (3,  5,  4.00),
  (3,  6, -1.00),
  (3,  7,  5.00),
  (3,  8,  3.00),
  (3,  9,  5.00),
  (3, 10, -3.00);
```

Each row in the table represents a transaction in some bank account. When the transaction is a deposit, the amount in the *val* column is positive; when it's a withdrawal, the amount is negative. Your task is to compute the account balance at each point by accumulating the amounts in the *val* column based on ordering defined by the *tranid* column within each account independently. The desired results for the small set of sample data should look like Listing 6-4.

LISTING 6-4 Desired Results for Running Totals Task

actid	tranid	val	balance
1	1	4.00	4.00
1	2	-2.00	2.00
1	3	5.00	7.00
1	4	2.00	9.00
1	5	1.00	10.00
1	6	3.00	13.00
1	7	-4.00	9.00
1	8	-1.00	8.00
1	9	-2.00	6.00
1	10	-3.00	3.00
2	1	2.00	2.00
2	2	1.00	3.00
2	3	5.00	8.00
2	4	1.00	9.00
2	5	-5.00	4.00
2	6	4.00	8.00
2	7	2.00	10.00
2	8	-4.00	6.00
2	9	-5.00	1.00
2	10	4.00	5.00
3	1	-3.00	-3.00
3	2	3.00	0.00
3	3	-2.00	-2.00
3	4	1.00	-1.00
3	5	4.00	3.00
3	6	-1.00	2.00
3	7	5.00	7.00
3	8	3.00	10.00
3	9	5.00	15.00
3	10	-3.00	12.00

To test the performance of the solutions, you need a larger set of sample data. You can use the following code to achieve this:

```
DECLARE
    @num_partitions     AS INT = 100,
    @rows_per_partition AS INT = 10000;

TRUNCATE TABLE dbo.Transactions;
```

```
INSERT INTO dbo.Transactions WITH (TABLOCK) (actid, tranid, val)
  SELECT NP.n, RPP.n,
    (ABS(CHECKSUM(NEWID())%2)*2-1) * (1 + ABS(CHECKSUM(NEWID())%5))
  FROM dbo.GetNums(1, @num_partitions) AS NP
    CROSS JOIN dbo.GetNums(1, @rows_per_partition) AS RPP;
```

Feel free to change the inputs as needed to control the number of partitions (accounts) and number of rows per partition (transactions).

Set-Based Solution Using Window Functions

I'll start with the most optimal set-based solution that uses the SUM window aggregate function. The window specification is intuitive here; you need to partition the window by *actid*, order by *tranid*, and filter the frame of rows between no low boundary point (*UNBOUNDED PRECEDING*) and the current row. Here's the solution query:

```
SELECT actid, tranid, val,
  SUM(val) OVER(PARTITION BY actid
                ORDER BY tranid
                ROWS UNBOUNDED PRECEDING) AS balance
FROM dbo.Transactions;
```

Not only is the code simple and straightforward, it also performs very well. The plan for this query is shown in Figure 6-9.

FIGURE 6-9 Execution plan for a query using window functions.

The table has a clustered index that follows the POC guidelines that window functions can benefit from. Namely, the index key list is based on the partitioning element (*actid*) followed by the ordering element (*tranid*), and it includes for coverage purposes all the rest of the columns in the query (*val*). The plan shows an ordered scan of the index, followed by the computation of the running total with the batch-mode *Window Aggregate* operator. Because you arranged a POC index, the optimizer didn't need to add a sort operator in the plan. That's a very efficient plan. It took less than half a second to complete on my machine against a table with 1,000,000 rows, and the results were discarded. What's more, this plan scales linearly.

Set-Based Solutions Using Subqueries or Joins

Traditional set-based solutions to running totals that don't use window functions use either subqueries or joins. Using a subquery, you can calculate the running total by filtering all rows that have the same *actid* value as in the outer row and a *tranid* value that is less than or equal to the one in the outer row. Then you apply the aggregate to the filtered rows. Here's the solution query:

```
SELECT actid, tranid, val,
  (SELECT SUM(T2.val)
   FROM dbo.Transactions AS T2
   WHERE T2.actid = T1.actid
     AND T2.tranid <= T1.tranid) AS balance
FROM dbo.Transactions AS T1;
```

A similar approach can be implemented using joins. You use the same predicate as the one used in the *WHERE* clause of the subquery in the *ON* clause of the join. This way, for the *N*th transaction of account A in the instance you refer to as *T1*, you will find *N* matches in the instance *T2* with transactions *1* through *N*. The row in *T1* is repeated in the result for each of its matches, so you need to group the rows by all elements from *T1* to get the current transaction info and apply the aggregate to the *val* attribute from *T2* to calculate the running total. The solution query looks like this:

```
SELECT T1.actid, T1.tranid, T1.val,
  SUM(T2.val) AS balance
FROM dbo.Transactions AS T1
  INNER JOIN dbo.Transactions AS T2
    ON T2.actid = T1.actid
    AND T2.tranid <= T1.tranid
GROUP BY T1.actid, T1.tranid, T1.val;
```

Figure 6-10 shows the plans for both solutions.

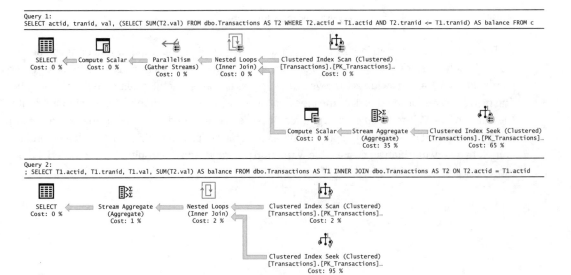

FIGURE 6-10 Execution plans for queries using subqueries and joins.

Observe that in both cases, the clustered index is scanned in full representing the instance *T1*. The plan performs a seek operation for each row in the index to get to the beginning of the current account's section in the index leaf, and then it scans all transactions where *T2.tranid* is less than or equal to *T1.tranid*. Then the point where the aggregate of those rows takes place is a bit different in the two plans, but the number of rows scanned is the same. Also, it appears that the optimizer chose a parallel plan for the subquery solution and a serial plan for the join solution.

To realize how many rows get scanned, consider the elements involved in the data. Let p be the number of partitions (accounts), and let r be the number of rows per partition (transactions). Then the number of rows in the table is roughly pr, assuming an even distribution of transactions per account. So, the upper scan of the clustered index involves scanning pr rows. But the work at the inner part of the *Nested Loops* operator is what we're most concerned with. For each partition, the plan scans $1 + 2 + ... + r$ rows, which is equal to $(r + r^2)/2$. In total, the number of rows processed in these plans is $pr + p(r + r^2)/2$. This means that with respect to partition size, the scaling of this plan is quadratic (N^2); that is, if you increase the partition size by a factor of f, the work involved increases by a factor of close to f^2. That's bad. As examples, for a partition of 100 rows, the plan touches 5,050 rows. For a partition of 10,000 rows, the plan processes 50,005,000 rows, and so on. Simply put, it translates to very slow queries when the partition size is not tiny because the squared effect is very dramatic. It's okay to use these solutions for up to a few dozen rows per partition but not many more.

As an example, the subquery solution took 10 minutes to complete on my machine against a table with 1,000,000 rows (100 accounts, each with 10,000 transactions). Remember, the query with the window function completed in less than half a second against the same data!

Cursor-Based Solution

Using a cursor-based solution to running totals is straightforward. You declare a cursor based on a query that orders the data by *actid* and *tranid*. You then iterate through the cursor records. When you hit a new account, you reset the variable holding the aggregate. In each iteration, you add the value of the new transaction to the variable; you then store a row in a table variable with the current transaction information plus the running total so far. When you're done iterating, you return the result to the caller by querying the table variable. Listing 6-5 shows the complete solution code.

LISTING 6-5 Cursor-Based Solution for Running Totals

```
DECLARE @Result AS TABLE
(
  actid   INT,
  tranid  INT,
  val     MONEY,
  balance MONEY
);

DECLARE
  @C          AS CURSOR,
  @actid      AS INT,
```

```
      @prvactid AS INT,
      @tranid   AS INT,
      @val      AS MONEY,
      @balance  AS MONEY;

  SET @C = CURSOR FORWARD_ONLY STATIC READ_ONLY FOR
    SELECT actid, tranid, val
    FROM dbo.Transactions
    ORDER BY actid, tranid;

  OPEN @C

  FETCH NEXT FROM @C INTO @actid, @tranid, @val;

  SELECT @prvactid = @actid, @balance = 0;

  WHILE @@fetch_status = 0
  BEGIN
    IF @actid <> @prvactid
      SELECT @prvactid = @actid, @balance = 0;

    SET @balance = @balance + @val;

    INSERT INTO @Result VALUES(@actid, @tranid, @val, @balance);

    FETCH NEXT FROM @C INTO @actid, @tranid, @val;
  END

  SELECT * FROM @Result;
```

The plan for the query that the cursor is based on is shown in Figure 6-11.

```
SELECT      <═══════  Clustered Index Scan (Clustered)
Cost: 0 %             [Transactions].[PK_Transactions]
                              Cost: 100 %
```

FIGURE 6-11 Execution plan for the query used by the cursor.

This plan has linear scaling because the data from the index is scanned only once, in order. Also, each fetching of a row from the cursor has a constant cost per row. If you call the cursor overhead per row o, you can express the cost of this solution as $pr + pro$. (Keep in mind that p is the number of partitions and r is the number of rows per partition.) So, you can see that if you increase the number of rows per partition by a factor of f, the work involved becomes $prf + prfo$, meaning that you get linear scaling. The overhead per row is high; however, because the scaling is linear, from a certain partition size and on this solution will perform better than the solutions based on subqueries and joins because of their quadratic scaling. Performance tests that I did show that the point where the cursor solution becomes faster is around a few hundred rows per partition.

It took the cursor solution 31 seconds to complete on my machine against a table with 1,000,000 rows.

CLR-Based Solution

One possible Common Language Runtime (CLR) solution is basically another form of a cursor-based solution. The difference is that instead of using a T-SQL cursor that involves a high amount of overhead for each fetch and slow iterations, you use a .NET *SQLDataReader* and .NET iterations, which are much faster. Furthermore, you don't need to store the result rows in a temporary table—the results are streamed right back to the caller. The logic of the CLR-based solution is similar to that of the T-SQL cursor-based solution. Listing 6-6 shows the .NET code defining the solution's stored procedure.

LISTING 6-6 CLR-Based Solution for Running Totals

```
using System;
using System.Data;
using System.Data.SqlClient;
using System.Data.SqlTypes;
using Microsoft.SqlServer.Server;

public partial class StoredProcedures
{
    [Microsoft.SqlServer.Server.SqlProcedure]
    public static void AccountBalances()
    {
        using (SqlConnection conn = new SqlConnection("context
        connection=true;"))
        {
            SqlCommand comm = new SqlCommand();
            comm.Connection = conn;
            comm.CommandText = @"" +
                "SELECT actid, tranid, val " +
                "FROM dbo.Transactions " +
                "ORDER BY actid, tranid;";

            SqlMetaData[] columns = new SqlMetaData[4];
            columns[0] = new SqlMetaData("actid"  , SqlDbType.Int);
            columns[1] = new SqlMetaData("tranid" , SqlDbType.Int);
            columns[2] = new SqlMetaData("val"    , SqlDbType.Money);
            columns[3] = new SqlMetaData("balance", SqlDbType.Money);

            SqlDataRecord record = new SqlDataRecord(columns);
            SqlContext.Pipe.SendResultsStart(record);

            conn.Open();

            SqlDataReader reader = comm.ExecuteReader();

            SqlInt32 prvactid = 0;
            SqlMoney balance = 0;

            while (reader.Read())
            {
                SqlInt32 actid = reader.GetSqlInt32(0);
```

```
    SqlMoney val = reader.GetSqlMoney(2);

    if (actid == prvactid)
    {
        balance += val;
    }
    else
    {
        balance = val;
    }

    prvactid = actid;

    record.SetSqlInt32(0, reader.GetSqlInt32(0));
    record.SetSqlInt32(1, reader.GetSqlInt32(1));
    record.SetSqlMoney(2, val);
    record.SetSqlMoney(3, balance);

    SqlContext.Pipe.SendResultsRow(record);
            }

            SqlContext.Pipe.SendResultsEnd();
        }
    }
};
```

To be able to execute the stored procedure in SQL Server, you first need to build an assembly called *AccountBalances* that is based on this code and deploy it in the TSQLV5 database.

> **NOTE**   If you're not familiar with deployment of assemblies in SQL Server, you can read about it in *T-SQL Querying* (Microsoft Press). Also, see the Microsoft article, "Deploying CLR Database Objects," at *https://docs.microsoft.com/en-us/sql/relational-databases/clr-integration/deploying-clr-database-objects*.

Assuming you called the assembly *AccountBalances*, and the path to the assembly file is *C:\AccountBalances\AccountBalances.dll*, you can use the following code to load the assembly to the database and then register the stored procedure:

```
CREATE ASSEMBLY AccountBalances FROM 'C:\AccountBalances\AccountBalances.dll';
GO
CREATE PROCEDURE dbo.AccountBalances
AS EXTERNAL NAME AccountBalances.StoredProcedures.AccountBalances;
```

After the assembly has been deployed and the procedure has been registered, you can execute the procedure using the following code:

```
EXEC dbo.AccountBalances;
```

As mentioned, a *SQLDataReader* is just another form of a cursor, only the overhead of each fetch is less than that of a T-SQL cursor. Also, iterations in .NET are much faster than iterations in T-SQL. So, the CLR-based solution also has linear scaling. In my benchmarks, this solution started performing better than the solutions using subqueries and joins at around 15 rows per partition. It took this stored procedure 3.8 seconds to complete against a table with 1,000,000 rows.

When you're done, run the following code for cleanup:

```
DROP PROCEDURE IF EXISTS dbo.AccountBalances;
DROP ASSEMBLY IF EXISTS AccountBalances;
```

Nested Iterations

So far, I have shown you solutions that are either set based or iterative. The next solution, known as *nested iterations*, is a hybrid of iterative and set-based logic. The idea is to first copy the rows from the source table (bank account transactions in our case) into a temporary table, along with a new attribute called *rownum* that is calculated by using the *ROW_NUMBER* function. The row numbers are partitioned by *actid* and ordered by *tranid*, so the first transaction in each account is assigned the row number 1, the second transaction is assigned row number 2, and so on. You then create a clustered index on the temporary table with the key list (*rownum*, *actid*). Then you use either a recursive CTE or your own loop to handle one row number at a time across all accounts in each iteration. The running total is then computed by adding the value associated with the current row number to the value associated with the previous row number.

Listing 6-7 shows the implementation of this logic using a recursive CTE.

LISTING 6-7 Solution with Recursive CTE to Running Totals

```
SELECT actid, tranid, val,
  ROW_NUMBER() OVER(PARTITION BY actid ORDER BY tranid) AS rownum
INTO #Transactions
FROM dbo.Transactions;

CREATE UNIQUE CLUSTERED INDEX idx_rownum_actid ON #Transactions(rownum, actid);

WITH C AS
(
  SELECT 1 AS rownum, actid, tranid, val, val AS sumqty
  FROM #Transactions
  WHERE rownum = 1

  UNION ALL

  SELECT PRV.rownum + 1, PRV.actid, PRV.tranid, CUR.val, PRV.sumqty + CUR.val
  FROM C AS PRV
    INNER JOIN #Transactions AS CUR
      ON CUR.rownum = PRV.rownum + 1
      AND CUR.actid = PRV.actid
)
SELECT actid, tranid, val, sumqty
```

```
FROM C
OPTION (MAXRECURSION 0);

DROP TABLE IF EXISTS #Transactions;
```

And here's the implementation of the same logic using an explicit loop:

```
SELECT ROW_NUMBER() OVER(PARTITION BY actid ORDER BY tranid) AS rownum,
  actid, tranid, val, CAST(val AS BIGINT) AS sumqty
INTO #Transactions
FROM dbo.Transactions;

CREATE UNIQUE CLUSTERED INDEX idx_rownum_actid ON #Transactions(rownum, actid);

DECLARE @rownum AS INT;
SET @rownum = 1;

WHILE 1 = 1
BEGIN
  SET @rownum = @rownum + 1;

  UPDATE CUR
    SET sumqty = PRV.sumqty + CUR.val
  FROM #Transactions AS CUR
    INNER JOIN #Transactions AS PRV
      ON CUR.rownum = @rownum
     AND PRV.rownum = @rownum - 1
     AND CUR.actid = PRV.actid;

  IF @@rowcount = 0 BREAK;
END

SELECT actid, tranid, val, sumqty
FROM #Transactions;

DROP TABLE IF EXISTS #Transactions;
```

This solution tends to perform well when there are a lot of partitions with a small number of rows per partition. This means the number of iterations is small. And most of the work is handled by the set-based part of the solution that joins the rows associated with one row number with the rows associated with the previous row number.

Using the same data with 1,000,000 rows (100 accounts, each with 10,000 transactions), the code with the recursive query took 16 seconds to complete, and the code with the loop took 7 seconds to complete.

Multirow UPDATE with Variables

The various techniques I showed so far for handling running totals are guaranteed to produce the correct result. The technique that is the focus of this section is a controversial one because it relies on observed behavior as opposed to documented behavior, and it violates relational concepts.

What makes it so appealing to some is that it is very fast, though it's still slower than a simple windowed running sum.

The technique involves using an *UPDATE* statement with variables. An *UPDATE* statement can set a variable to an expression based on a column value, as well as set a column value to an expression based on a variable. The solution starts by creating a temporary table called *#Transactions* with the *actid*, *tranid*, *val*, and *balance* attributes and a clustered index based on the key list (*actid, tranid*). Then the solution populates the temp table with all rows from the source Transactions table, setting the balance column to 0.00 in all rows. The solution then invokes an *UPDATE* statement with variables against the temporary table to calculate the running totals and assign those to the balance column. It uses variables called *@prevaccount* and *@prevbalance*, and it sets the balance using the following expression:

```
SET @prevbalance = balance = CASE
                               WHEN actid = @prevaccount
                                 THEN @prevbalance + val
                               ELSE val
                             END
```

The *CASE* expression checks whether the current account ID is equal to the previous account ID; if the account IDs are equivalent, it returns the previous balance plus the current transaction value. If the account IDs are different, it returns the current transaction value. The balance is then set to the result of the *CASE* expression and assigned to the *@prevbalance* variable. In a separate expression, the *@prevaccount* variable is set to the current account ID.

After the *UPDATE* statement, the solution presents the rows from the temporary table and then drops the table. Listing 6-8 shows the complete solution code.

LISTING 6-8 Solution Using Multirow *UPDATE* with Variables

```
CREATE TABLE #Transactions
(
  actid      INT,
  tranid     INT,
  val        MONEY,
  balance    MONEY
);

CREATE CLUSTERED INDEX idx_actid_tranid ON #Transactions(actid, tranid);

INSERT INTO #Transactions WITH (TABLOCK) (actid, tranid, val, balance)
  SELECT actid, tranid, val, 0.00
  FROM dbo.Transactions
  ORDER BY actid, tranid;

DECLARE @prevaccount AS INT, @prevbalance AS MONEY;

UPDATE #Transactions
  SET @prevbalance = balance = CASE
                                 WHEN actid = @prevaccount
                                   THEN @prevbalance + val
```

```
                        ELSE val
                    END,
        @prevaccount = actid
FROM #Transactions WITH(INDEX(1), TABLOCKX)
OPTION (MAXDOP 1);

SELECT * FROM #Transactions;

DROP TABLE IF EXISTS #Transactions;
```

The plan for this solution is shown in Figure 6-12. The first part is the *INSERT*, the second part is the *UPDATE*, and the third part is the *SELECT*.

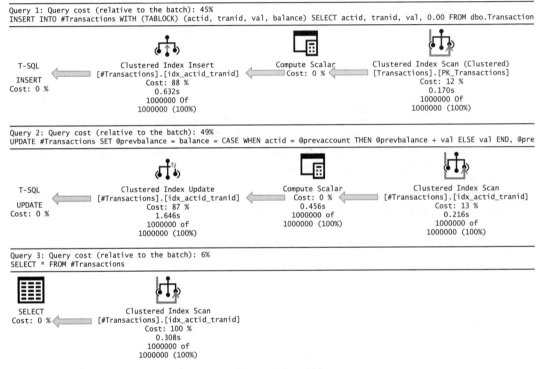

FIGURE 6-12 Execution plan for a solution using *UPDATE* with variables.

It took this solution close to 3 seconds to complete on my machine.

This solution makes an assumption that the *UPDATE* will always be optimized with an ordered scan of the clustered index, and it even uses a number of hints in an attempt to avoid situations that might prevent that—for example, parallelism. The problem is that there is no official guarantee that the optimizer will always scan the data in clustered index order. You're not supposed to make assumptions about physical processing aspects when trying to ensure the logical correctness of your code, unless there are logical elements in the code that are defined to guarantee such behavior. There's nothing in the logical aspects of the code that give any such guarantees. Of course, it's up to you to decide whether or not you want to use this technique. I think it's irresponsible to use it even if you run it a thousand times and the observed behavior is "It seems to work." The reason I'm covering it in the book is because it is being used out there in the wild, you might stumble into it, but I wanted to make sure to warn you against using it.

Fortunately, the solution using the window aggregate function is so much faster than any other solution, including this one, that it should be the preferred choice anyway.

Performance Benchmark

I ran a performance benchmark comparing the different techniques. Figures 6-13 and 6-14 show the results of that benchmark.

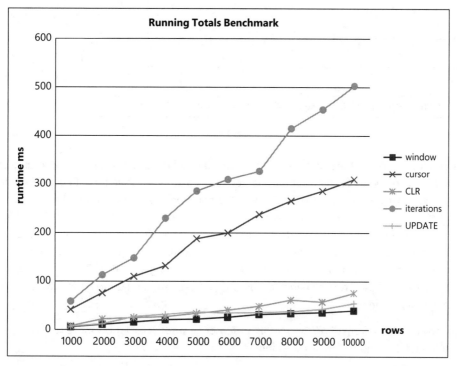

FIGURE 6-13 Benchmark of the running totals solutions, part I.

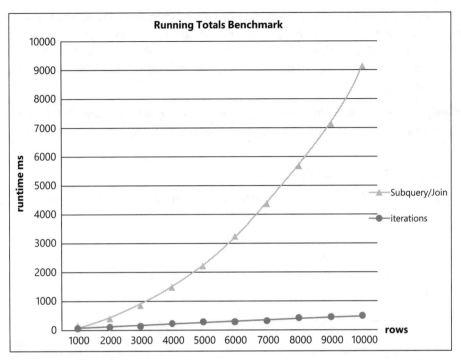

FIGURE 6-14 Benchmark of the running totals solutions, part II.

The reason for separating the results into two graphs was that the technique based on a subquery or join was so slow compared to the rest that I wanted to use a different scale for it. Regardless of the reason for doing it this way, observe that with respect to partition size, most solutions have linear scaling, and only the one based on a subquery or join has quadratic scaling. Also, you can clearly see how efficient the solution based on a window aggregate function is. The solution based on an *UPDATE* with variables is also very fast, but for the aforementioned reasons I recommended that you avoid it. The solution based on the *CLR* is also quite fast, but it involves writing all that .NET code and deploying an assembly in the database. From all perspectives, the set-based solution using a window aggregate is by far the most preferable one.

Here, I showed a basic form of running totals. In subsequent sections, I show more sophisticated uses of running totals in more complex scenarios.

Max Concurrent Intervals

Consider a set of intervals representing things such as sessions, validity periods, contract periods, drug prescription periods, and so on. There's a classic task known as *maximum concurrent intervals* where you're after the maximum number of intervals that were active concurrently. As an example, suppose that you're given a table called *Sessions* that holds data about user sessions against different applications. Your task is to write a solution that calculates, for each application, the maximum number of sessions that were active at any given point in time. If one session ends exactly when another starts, assume that you're not supposed to consider them concurrent. In other words, consider the intervals as closed-open intervals.

Here's the code to create the *Sessions* table:

```
SET NOCOUNT ON;
USE TSQLV5;

DROP TABLE IF EXISTS dbo.Sessions;

CREATE TABLE dbo.Sessions
(
  keycol    INT          NOT NULL,
  app       VARCHAR(10)  NOT NULL,
  usr       VARCHAR(10)  NOT NULL,
  host      VARCHAR(10)  NOT NULL,
  starttime DATETIME2(0) NOT NULL,
  endtime   DATETIME2(0) NOT NULL,
  CONSTRAINT PK_Sessions PRIMARY KEY(keycol),
  CHECK(endtime > starttime)
);
GO
```

Use the following code to populate the *Sessions* table with a small set of sample data to test the validity of your solution:

```
TRUNCATE TABLE dbo.Sessions;

INSERT INTO dbo.Sessions(keycol, app, usr, host, starttime, endtime) VALUES
  (2,  'app1', 'user1', 'host1', '20190212 08:30', '20190212 10:30'),
  (3,  'app1', 'user2', 'host1', '20190212 08:30', '20190212 08:45'),
  (5,  'app1', 'user3', 'host2', '20190212 09:00', '20190212 09:30'),
  (7,  'app1', 'user4', 'host2', '20190212 09:15', '20190212 10:30'),
  (11, 'app1', 'user5', 'host3', '20190212 09:15', '20190212 09:30'),
  (13, 'app1', 'user6', 'host3', '20190212 10:30', '20190212 14:30'),
  (17, 'app1', 'user7', 'host4', '20190212 10:45', '20190212 11:30'),
  (19, 'app1', 'user8', 'host4', '20190212 11:00', '20190212 12:30'),
  (23, 'app2', 'user8', 'host1', '20190212 08:30', '20190212 08:45'),
  (29, 'app2', 'user7', 'host1', '20190212 09:00', '20190212 09:30'),
  (31, 'app2', 'user6', 'host2', '20190212 11:45', '20190212 12:00'),
  (37, 'app2', 'user5', 'host2', '20190212 12:30', '20190212 14:00'),
  (41, 'app2', 'user4', 'host3', '20190212 12:45', '20190212 13:30'),
  (43, 'app2', 'user3', 'host3', '20190212 13:00', '20190212 14:00'),
  (47, 'app2', 'user2', 'host4', '20190212 14:00', '20190212 16:30'),
  (53, 'app2', 'user1', 'host4', '20190212 15:30', '20190212 17:00');
```

Here's the desired result for this small set of sample data:

```
app         mx
----------  -----------
app1        4
app2        3
```

To test the performance of your solution, you need a larger set of sample data. The following code populates the table with 1,000,000 sessions with 10 distinct applications:

```
TRUNCATE TABLE dbo.Sessions;

DECLARE
  @numrows AS INT = 1000000, -- total number of rows
  @numapps AS INT = 10;      -- number of applications

INSERT INTO dbo.Sessions WITH(TABLOCK)
    (keycol, app, usr, host, starttime, endtime)
  SELECT
    ROW_NUMBER() OVER(ORDER BY (SELECT NULL)) AS keycol,
    D.*,
    DATEADD(
      second,
      1 + ABS(CHECKSUM(NEWID())) % (20*60),
      starttime) AS endtime
  FROM
  (
    SELECT
      'app' + CAST(1 + ABS(CHECKSUM(NEWID())) % @numapps AS VARCHAR(10)) AS app,
      'user1' AS usr,
      'host1' AS host,
      DATEADD(
        second,
        1 + ABS(CHECKSUM(NEWID())) % (30*24*60*60),
        '20190101') AS starttime
    FROM dbo.GetNums(1, @numrows) AS Nums
  ) AS D;
```

Feel free to adjust the number of rows to populate the table with and the number of distinct applications according to your needs.

Before I show the efficient solutions that are based on window functions, I'll show a couple of solutions that do not use window functions and talk about their shortcomings. I'll first describe the traditional set-based solution.

Traditional Set-Based Solution

You can think of each session as being made of two events—a start event, which increases the count of active sessions, and an end event, which decreases that count. If you look at the timeline, the count of active sessions remains constant in sections between consecutive events where a session either starts or ends. What's more, because a start event increases the count of active sessions, the maximum count must fall on a start event. As an example, suppose that there were two sessions with a certain application named App1: one session started at point P1 and ended at point P3, and another session started at point P2 and ended at point P4. Here's the chronological order of events and the number of active sessions after each event:

- P1, session 1 starts, 1 active session

- P2, session 2 starts, 2 active sessions

- P3, session 1 ends, 1 active session

- P4, session 2 ends, 0 active sessions

The number of active sessions between two consecutive points remains constant. The maximum number falls on a start point—P2 in this example.

The approach taken by the traditional set-based solution relies on this logic. The solution implements the following steps:

1. Define a table expression called *TimePoints* based on a query against the *Sessions* table that returns *app* and *starttime* (aliased as *ts* for *timestamp*).

2. Use a second table expression called *Counts* to query *TimePoints* (aliased as *P*).

3. In the second table expression, use a subquery to count how many sessions you can find in the Sessions table (aliased as *S*), where *P.app* is equal to *S.app*, and *P.ts* is on or after *S.starttime* and before *S.endtime*. The subquery counts how many sessions are active during each application session's start point in time.

4. Finally, in the outer query against *Counts*, group the rows by *app* and return the maximum count for each application.

Here's the complete solution code:

```
WITH TimePoints AS
(
  SELECT app, starttime AS ts FROM dbo.Sessions
),
Counts AS
(
  SELECT app, ts,
    (SELECT COUNT(*)
     FROM dbo.Sessions AS S
     WHERE P.app = S.app
       AND P.ts >= S.starttime
       AND P.ts < S.endtime) AS concurrent
  FROM TimePoints AS P
)
SELECT app, MAX(concurrent) AS mx
FROM Counts
GROUP BY app;
```

Use the following code to create an index that supports this solution:

```
CREATE INDEX idx_start_end ON dbo.Sessions(app, starttime, endtime);
```

The solution seems straightforward, and it might not be immediately apparent that there's a performance problem with it. However, when you run it against the large set of sample data, it takes a long time to complete. To understand why it's so slow, examine the query's execution plan, as shown in Figure 6-15.

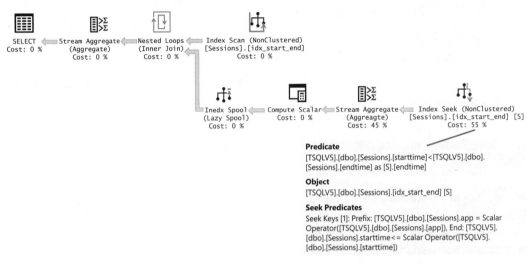

Predicate
[TSQLV5].[dbo].[Sessions].[starttime]<[TSQLV5].[dbo].
[Sessions].[endtime] as [S].[endtime]

Object
[TSQLV5].[dbo].[Sessions].[idx_start_end] [S]

Seek Predicates
Seek Keys [1]: Prefix: [TSQLV5].[dbo].[Sessions].app = Scalar
Operator([TSQLV5].[dbo].[Sessions].[app]), End: [TSQLV5].
[dbo].[Sessions].starttime<= Scalar Operator([TSQLV5].
[dbo].[Sessions].[starttime])

FIGURE 6-15 Execution plan for a traditional set-based solution.

The *Index Scan* operator in the top-right part of the plan (the outer input of the *Nested Loops* join) scans the index you created earlier (*idx_start_end*) to obtain all start points per application. Using the symbols *p* for the number of partitions (applications) and *r* for the number of rows per partition (sessions per application), this part involves scanning roughly *pr* rows. Then the inner part of the *Nested Loops* join is an *Index Seek* operator against the same index that gets executed for each row returned from the upper input. Its task is to identify the rows representing the sessions that were active for the current application during the current point in time in the outer row.

Think about the work involved in each execution of the *Index Seek* operator. For the current outer row's elements *P.app* (call it *myapp*) and *P.ts* (call it *myts*), the operator is looking for all rows where *S.app = myapp*, and *S.starttime <= myts*, and *S.endtime > myts*. The seek predicates can be applied based on any number of leading elements in the index key that appear in equality predicates (*S.app = myapp*, in our case), followed by one more element that appears in a range predicate (*S.starttime <= myts*, in our case). Only the qualifying rows that satisfy the seek predicates have to be read. However, if there are additional range predicates (*S.endtime > myts*, in our case), they are applied as residual predicates, meaning that both qualifying and nonqualifying rows have to be read, and based on the outcome of the predicate, only the qualifying rows are actually returned. Observe in Figure 6-15 that you can see which predicates are applied as *Seek Predicates* versus (residual) *Predicate* in the *Index Seek* operator's properties.

If it isn't clear by now, that's bad news. Whereas the seek predicate prevents reading nonqualifying rows, the residual predicate doesn't. I already mentioned that the *Index Scan* operator scans approximately *pr* rows. The *Index Seek* operator scans, for each row, on average about half the rows in the partition. This means that for *r* rows in a partition, it scans $r^2 / 2$ rows. In total, the number of rows being touched is $pr + pr^2 / 2$. This means that with respect to partition size, this plan has quadratic complexity. So, if the number of rows per partition increases by a factor of *f*, the work increases by a factor of close to f^2. So, beyond very small partition sizes, the query will perform very badly. It took this query more than an hour to complete on my machine with 1,000,000 rows in the table.

When you're done, run the following code to drop the index you created to support this solution:

```
DROP INDEX IF EXISTS idx_start_end ON dbo.Sessions;
```

Solutions Based on Window Functions

I'll present two solutions based on window functions—one using running totals and another using row numbers. Both solutions benefit from the following indexes that separate session start and end events:

```
CREATE UNIQUE INDEX idx_start ON dbo.Sessions(app, starttime, keycol);
CREATE UNIQUE INDEX idx_end ON dbo.Sessions(app, endtime, keycol);
```

The first solution starts by producing a chronological sequence of session start and end events, using the following code (shown here ordered):

```
SELECT keycol, app, starttime AS ts, +1 AS type
FROM dbo.Sessions

UNION ALL

SELECT keycol, app, endtime AS ts, -1 AS type
FROM dbo.Sessions

ORDER BY app, ts, type, keycol;
```

Observe that start events are marked with a *+1 event* type because they increase the count of active sessions, and end events are marked with *–1* because they decrease the count. The presentation *ORDER BY* clause is used here, for illustration purposes, to show the events in chronological order. Within each application, the events are ordered by the time stamp (*ts*), then by *type*. The reason to add *type* to the ordering is so that if one session ends exactly where another starts, the *–1* will appear before the *+1*, and this way the two will not be considered concurrent. Finally, *keycol* is added at the end of the ordering just for determinism.

This code generates the output shown in Listing 6-9 using the small set of sample data.

LISTING 6-9 Chronological Sequence of Session Start and End Events

```
keycol  app    ts                    type
-------  -----  --------------------  -----
2        app1   2019-02-12 08:30:00   1
3        app1   2019-02-12 08:30:00   1
3        app1   2019-02-12 08:45:00   -1
```

```
5       app1    2019-02-12 09:00:00    1
7       app1    2019-02-12 09:15:00    1
11      app1    2019-02-12 09:15:00    1
5       app1    2019-02-12 09:30:00    -1
11      app1    2019-02-12 09:30:00    -1
2       app1    2019-02-12 10:30:00    -1
7       app1    2019-02-12 10:30:00    -1
13      app1    2019-02-12 10:30:00    1
17      app1    2019-02-12 10:45:00    1
19      app1    2019-02-12 11:00:00    1
17      app1    2019-02-12 11:30:00    -1
19      app1    2019-02-12 12:30:00    -1
13      app1    2019-02-12 14:30:00    -1
23      app2    2019-02-12 08:30:00    1
23      app2    2019-02-12 08:45:00    -1
29      app2    2019-02-12 09:00:00    1
29      app2    2019-02-12 09:30:00    -1
31      app2    2019-02-12 11:45:00    1
31      app2    2019-02-12 12:00:00    -1
37      app2    2019-02-12 12:30:00    1
41      app2    2019-02-12 12:45:00    1
43      app2    2019-02-12 13:00:00    1
41      app2    2019-02-12 13:30:00    -1
37      app2    2019-02-12 14:00:00    -1
43      app2    2019-02-12 14:00:00    -1
47      app2    2019-02-12 14:00:00    1
53      app2    2019-02-12 15:30:00    1
47      app2    2019-02-12 16:30:00    -1
53      app2    2019-02-12 17:00:00    -1
```

Next, you compute the count of active sessions after each event using a simple running total calculation, group the result by application, and return the maximum count per application.

Here's the complete solution code:

```
WITH C1 AS
(
  SELECT keycol, app, starttime AS ts, +1 AS type
  FROM dbo.Sessions

  UNION ALL

  SELECT keycol, app, endtime AS ts, -1 AS type
  FROM dbo.Sessions
),
C2 AS
(
  SELECT *,
    SUM(type) OVER(PARTITION BY app
                   ORDER BY ts, type, keycol
                   ROWS UNBOUNDED PRECEDING) AS cnt
  FROM C1
)
```

```
SELECT app, MAX(cnt) AS mx
FROM C2
GROUP BY app;
```

Observe how simple and elegant the solution is. It is also highly efficient. Figure 6-16 shows the execution plan for this solution.

FIGURE 6-16 Execution plan for a solution using a window aggregate function.

The plan scans the indexes *idx_start* and *idx_end* to collect the session start and end events and concatenates (unifies) them. It then sorts the unified rows based on the window function's partitioning and ordering specification and applies the running total calculation with the batch-mode *Window Aggregate* operator. Finally, the plan uses a *Hash Match* aggregate to compute the maximum count per application.

I got the following performance statistics for the execution of this plan against the table with the 1,000,000 rows:

CPU time: 12172 ms, elapsed time: 3774 ms

That's less than 4 seconds of execution time compared to over an hour for the subquery-based solution.

Note that despite the fact that you arranged supporting indexes that have the start and end events preordered, the plan does not scan the indexes in order; instead, it uses a sort operator to sort the rows. This has to do with the fact that when the batch-mode *Window Aggregate* operator uses parallelism, it cannot rely on preordered data from an index without the need for a mediator like a *Sort* operator. I explained this in Chapter 5. Even with the sorting, you get excellent performance and scaling with larger volumes of data. It could be, though, that you will be able to achieve better performance, in some cases, if you force a serial plan with the MAXDOP 1 hint because this will prevent the need for the sorting. Try this query again, only this time with a hint that forces a serial plan:

```
WITH C1 AS
(
  SELECT keycol, app, starttime AS ts, +1 AS type
  FROM dbo.Sessions

  UNION ALL

  SELECT keycol, app, endtime AS ts, -1 AS type
  FROM dbo.Sessions
),
```

```
C2 AS
(
  SELECT *,
    SUM(type) OVER(PARTITION BY app
                   ORDER BY ts, type, keycol
                   ROWS UNBOUNDED PRECEDING) AS cnt
  FROM C1
)
SELECT app, MAX(cnt) AS mx
FROM C2
GROUP BY app
OPTION(MAXDOP 1);
```

The plan for this execution is shown in Figure 6-17.

FIGURE 6-17 Execution plan for a solution using a window aggregate function with MAXDOP 1 hint.

Observe that there's no *Sort* operator in the plan. The two indexes are scanned in order, and their rows are unified with an order-preserving *Merge Join (Concatenation)* operator. The *Window Aggregate* operator computes the running total, and the *Stream Aggregate* operator computes the maximum count per application—again, without requiring a sort.

I got the following performance numbers for this execution:

CPU time = 1672 ms, elapsed time = 1774 ms

Run time dropped to half, and CPU time dropped by an order of magnitude.

The second solution based on window functions relies mainly on the *ROW_NUMBER* function. I learned this elegant solution from Ben Flanaghan, who read an article that I wrote on the topic and sent his own solution. Like the previous solution, it also unifies start and end events in a chronological sequence of events, marking start events as a *+1 event* type and end events as a *–1 event* type. The only part that is handled differently is the one calculating how many intervals are active at any given point. Here's the complete solution code:

```
WITH C1 AS
(
  SELECT app, starttime AS ts, +1 AS type, keycol,
    ROW_NUMBER() OVER(PARTITION BY app ORDER BY starttime, keycol)
      AS start_ordinal
  FROM dbo.Sessions
```

```
  UNION ALL

  SELECT app, endtime AS ts, -1 AS type, keycol, NULL AS start_ordinal
  FROM dbo.Sessions
),
C2 AS
(
  SELECT *,
    ROW_NUMBER() OVER(PARTITION BY app ORDER BY ts, type, keycol)
      AS start_or_end_ordinal
  FROM C1
)
SELECT app, MAX(start_ordinal - (start_or_end_ordinal - start_ordinal)) AS mx
FROM C2
GROUP BY app;
```

The query defining the CTE *C1* generates the chronological sequence of events. It also uses the *ROW_NUMBER* function to compute start ordinals for start events (with an attribute called *start_ordinal*). The *start_ordinal* attribute represents for each start event how many intervals have started so far, irrespective of whether they've ended. For end events, the second query uses a *NULL* as a placeholder for *start_ordinal* to allow unifying the start and end events.

The query defining the CTE called *C2* queries *C1*, and it uses the *ROW_NUMBER* function to compute the *start_or_end_ordinal* attribute on top of the unified events, representing how many events—start or end—happened so far.

The magic happens in the outer query, which queries *C2*. Let *end_ordinal* be *start_or_end_ordinal – start_ordinal*. Then the count of active intervals is *start_ordinal – end_ordinal*. In other words, the count of active intervals is *start_ordinal – (start_or_end_ordinal – start_ordinal)*. As you can see, the outer query is left to group the rows from *C2* by *app* and return, for each *app*, the maximum number of active intervals.

The plan for this solution is shown in Figure 6-18.

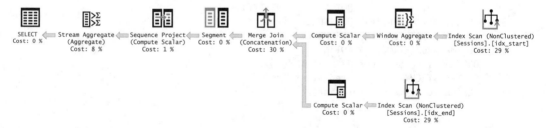

FIGURE 6-18 Execution plan for a solution using *ROW_NUMBER*.

Also, in this plan, you can see that both *ROW_NUMBER* calculations—the one computing start ordinals, as well as the one computing start or end ordinals—rely on index ordering. The same applies to the aggregate operation. Hence, not even one sort operation is required in this plan.

I got the following performance numbers for this execution:

CPU time = 1734 ms, elapsed time = 1743 ms

As you can see, this solution performs similarly to the first solution.

Packing Intervals

Packing intervals means grouping sets of intersecting intervals. Often, packing tasks in SQL involve a partitioning element (for example, a user or an application), where the packing is done for each partition independently.

The scenario I'll use involves user sessions against some application or service. Use the code in Listing 6-10 to create the *Users* and *Sessions* tables and to populate them with sample data to test the solution's validity:

LISTING 6-10 Creating and Populating Users and Sessions with Small Sets of Sample Data

```
SET NOCOUNT ON;
USE TSQLV5;

DROP TABLE IF EXISTS dbo.Sessions, dbo.Users;

CREATE TABLE dbo.Users
(
  username  VARCHAR(14)  NOT NULL,
  CONSTRAINT PK_Users PRIMARY KEY(username)
);

INSERT INTO dbo.Users(username) VALUES('User1'), ('User2'), ('User3');

CREATE TABLE dbo.Sessions
(
  id        INT          NOT NULL IDENTITY(1, 1),
  username  VARCHAR(14)  NOT NULL,
  starttime DATETIME2(3) NOT NULL,
  endtime   DATETIME2(3) NOT NULL,
  CONSTRAINT PK_Sessions PRIMARY KEY(id),
  CONSTRAINT CHK_endtime_gteq_starttime
    CHECK (endtime >= starttime)
);

INSERT INTO dbo.Sessions(username, starttime, endtime) VALUES
  ('User1', '20191201 08:00:00.000', '20191201 08:30:00.000'),
  ('User1', '20191201 08:30:00.000', '20191201 09:00:00.000'),
  ('User1', '20191201 09:00:00.000', '20191201 09:30:00.000'),
  ('User1', '20191201 10:00:00.000', '20191201 11:00:00.000'),
  ('User1', '20191201 10:30:00.000', '20191201 12:00:00.000'),
  ('User1', '20191201 11:30:00.000', '20191201 12:30:00.000'),
  ('User2', '20191201 08:00:00.000', '20191201 10:30:00.000'),
```

```
('User2', '20191201 08:30:00.000', '20191201 10:00:00.000'),
('User2', '20191201 09:00:00.000', '20191201 09:30:00.000'),
('User2', '20191201 11:00:00.000', '20191201 11:30:00.000'),
('User2', '20191201 11:32:00.000', '20191201 12:00:00.000'),
('User2', '20191201 12:04:00.000', '20191201 12:30:00.000'),
('User3', '20191201 08:00:00.000', '20191201 09:00:00.000'),
('User3', '20191201 08:00:00.000', '20191201 08:30:00.000'),
('User3', '20191201 08:30:00.000', '20191201 09:00:00.000'),
('User3', '20191201 09:30:00.000', '20191201 09:30:00.000');
```

Here's the desired result for the small set of sample data:

```
username   starttime               endtime
---------  ----------------------  ----------------------
User1      2019-12-01 08:00:00.000 2019-12-01 09:30:00.000
User1      2019-12-01 10:00:00.000 2019-12-01 12:30:00.000
User2      2019-12-01 08:00:00.000 2019-12-01 10:30:00.000
User2      2019-12-01 11:00:00.000 2019-12-01 11:30:00.000
User2      2019-12-01 11:32:00.000 2019-12-01 12:00:00.000
User2      2019-12-01 12:04:00.000 2019-12-01 12:30:00.000
User3      2019-12-01 08:00:00.000 2019-12-01 09:00:00.000
User3      2019-12-01 09:30:00.000 2019-12-01 09:30:00.000
```

Figure 6-19 is a graphical depiction of both the original intervals from the Sessions table (bars) as well as the packed intervals (arrows).

Unpacked and Packed Intervals

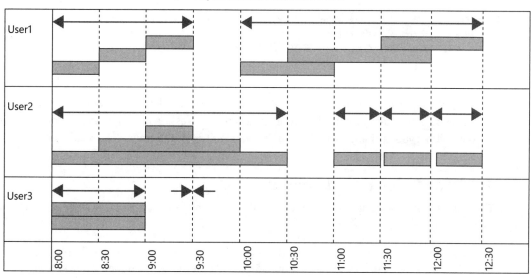

 Interval

◄──────► Packed Interval

FIGURE 6-19 Unpacked and packed intervals.

You can use the code in Listing 6-11 to populate the *Sessions* table with a large set of sample data to test the performance of the solutions.

LISTING 6-11 Code to Populate Sessions with a Large Set of Sample Data

```
DECLARE
  @num_users           AS INT        = 2000,
  @intervals_per_user AS INT        = 2500,
  @start_period       AS DATETIME2(3) = '20190101',
  @end_period         AS DATETIME2(3) = '20190107',
  @max_duration_in_ms AS INT  = 3600000; -- 60 minutes

TRUNCATE TABLE dbo.Sessions;
TRUNCATE TABLE dbo.Users;

INSERT INTO dbo.Users(username)
  SELECT 'User' + RIGHT('000000000' + CAST(U.n AS VARCHAR(10)), 10) AS username
  FROM dbo.GetNums(1, @num_users) AS U;

WITH C AS
(
  SELECT 'User' + RIGHT('000000000' + CAST(U.n AS VARCHAR(10)), 10) AS username,
      DATEADD(ms, ABS(CHECKSUM(NEWID())) % 86400000,
         DATEADD(day, ABS(CHECKSUM(NEWID())) % DATEDIFF(day, @start_period,
            @end_period), @start_period)) AS starttime
  FROM dbo.GetNums(1, @num_users) AS U
    CROSS JOIN dbo.GetNums(1, @intervals_per_user) AS I
)
INSERT INTO dbo.Sessions WITH (TABLOCK) (username, starttime, endtime)
  SELECT username, starttime,
    DATEADD(ms, ABS(CHECKSUM(NEWID())) % (@max_duration_in_ms + 1), starttime)
      AS endtime
  FROM C;
```

This code populates the *Sessions* table with 5,000,000 rows. I filled it with data for 2,000 users, each with 2,500 sessions during a period of a week and with each session lasting up to one hour. However, the code allows you to change any element that you like to test the scaling of the solutions.

Traditional Set-Based Solution

The first solution I will cover is a classic solution that does the job but very inefficiently. It will benefit from the following two indexes:

```
CREATE INDEX idx_user_start_end ON dbo.Sessions(username, starttime, endtime);
CREATE INDEX idx_user_end_start ON dbo.Sessions(username, endtime, starttime);
```

The solution's code is shown in Listing 6-12.

LISTING 6-12 Traditional Set-Based Solution to Packing Intervals

```
WITH StartTimes AS
(
  SELECT DISTINCT username, starttime
  FROM dbo.Sessions AS S1
  WHERE NOT EXISTS
    (SELECT * FROM dbo.Sessions AS S2
     WHERE S2.username = S1.username
       AND S2.starttime < S1.starttime
       AND S2.endtime >= S1.starttime)
),
EndTimes AS
(
  SELECT DISTINCT username, endtime
  FROM dbo.Sessions AS S1
  WHERE NOT EXISTS
    (SELECT * FROM dbo.Sessions AS S2
     WHERE S2.username = S1.username
       AND S2.endtime > S1.endtime
       AND S2.starttime <= S1.endtime)
)
SELECT username, starttime,
  (SELECT MIN(endtime) FROM EndTimes AS E
   WHERE E.username = S.username
     AND endtime >= starttime) AS endtime
FROM StartTimes AS S;
```

The solution can be broken down into the following steps:

- The CTE *StartTimes* isolates packed interval start times using a query that returns all interval start times for which you cannot find any interval by the same user that started before the current interval start and ended on or after the current interval start.

- The *EndTimes* CTE isolates packed interval end times using a query that returns all interval end times for which you cannot find any interval by the same user that ended after the current interval end and started on or before the current interval end.

- The outer query then matches to each packed interval start the nearest packed interval end and continues by returning the minimum end that is greater than or equal to the current start.

As mentioned, this solution is very inefficient. Left to run to completion, it should take this solution about two weeks to complete with 5,000,000 rows in the *Sessions* table.

Before continuing, run the following code to drop the indexes you created to support the last solution:

```
DROP INDEX IF EXISTS idx_user_start_end ON dbo.Sessions;
DROP INDEX IF EXISTS idx_user_end_start ON dbo.Sessions;
```

Solutions Based on Window Functions

I'll cover two solutions for packing intervals using window functions. In my testing, both solutions benefit from the trick using the fake filtered *columnstore* index that I described in Chapter 5. Here's the code to create the index:

```
CREATE NONCLUSTERED COLUMNSTORE INDEX idx_cs ON dbo.Sessions(id)
  WHERE id = -1 AND id = -2;
```

Solution 1 is based on window functions and creates a chronological sequence of session start and end events, similar to the solution for the max concurrent intervals task. Because this solution queries the start and end events separately, you want to create two separate rowstore indexes for the two kinds of events, like so:

```
CREATE UNIQUE INDEX idx_user_start_id ON dbo.Sessions(username, starttime, id);
CREATE UNIQUE INDEX idx_user_end_id ON dbo.Sessions(username, endtime, id);
```

I'll start by providing the complete solution's code, and then I'll describe its steps. Listing 6-13 shows the complete code for Solution 1.

LISTING 6-13 Solution 1 Based on Window Functions to Packing Intervals

```
WITH C1 AS
(
  SELECT id, username, starttime AS ts, +1 AS type
  FROM dbo.Sessions

  UNION ALL

  SELECT id, username, endtime AS ts, -1 AS type
  FROM dbo.Sessions
),
C2 AS
(
  SELECT username, ts, type,
    SUM(type) OVER(PARTITION BY username
                   ORDER BY ts, type DESC, id
                   ROWS UNBOUNDED PRECEDING) AS cnt
  FROM C1
),
C3 AS
(
  SELECT username, ts,
    (ROW_NUMBER() OVER(PARTITION BY username ORDER BY ts) - 1) / 2 + 1 AS grp
  FROM C2
  WHERE (type = 1 AND cnt = 1)
     OR (type = -1 AND cnt = 0)
)
SELECT username, MIN(ts) AS starttime, max(ts) AS endtime
```

```
FROM C3
GROUP BY username, grp;
```

The code in the CTE called *C1* unifies session start and end events, similar to the first step in the solution for the max concurrent intervals task.

The code in the CTE called *C2* computes a running total of the event type in chronological order to get the count of active intervals after each event; again, this is similar to the second step in the solution for the max concurrent intervals task. However, this time, the window order clause specifies type *DESC* because you do want to pack together two intervals, where one starts exactly where the other ends.

Listing 6-14 shows the output of the code in *C2*.

LISTING 6-14 Output of Code in *C2*

```
username  ts                 type   cnt
--------- ------------------ ------ ----
User1     2019-12-01 08:00   1      1
User1     2019-12-01 08:30   1      2
User1     2019-12-01 08:30   -1     1
User1     2019-12-01 09:00   1      2
User1     2019-12-01 09:00   -1     1
User1     2019-12-01 09:30   -1     0
User1     2019-12-01 10:00   1      1
User1     2019-12-01 10:30   1      2
User1     2019-12-01 11:00   -1     1
User1     2019-12-01 11:30   1      2
User1     2019-12-01 12:00   -1     1
User1     2019-12-01 12:30   -1     0
User2     2019-12-01 08:00   1      1
User2     2019-12-01 08:30   1      2
User2     2019-12-01 09:00   1      3
User2     2019-12-01 09:30   -1     2
User2     2019-12-01 10:00   -1     1
User2     2019-12-01 10:30   -1     0
User2     2019-12-01 11:00   1      1
User2     2019-12-01 11:30   -1     0
User2     2019-12-01 11:32   1      1
User2     2019-12-01 12:00   -1     0
User2     2019-12-01 12:04   1      1
User2     2019-12-01 12:30   -1     0
User3     2019-12-01 08:00   1      1
User3     2019-12-01 08:00   1      2
User3     2019-12-01 08:30   1      3
User3     2019-12-01 08:30   -1     2
User3     2019-12-01 09:00   -1     1
User3     2019-12-01 09:00   -1     0
User3     2019-12-01 09:30   1      1
User3     2019-12-01 09:30   -1     0
```

Observe that events where *type* is 1 and *cnt* is *1* mark beginnings of packed intervals, and events where *type* is –1 and *cnt* is *0* mark ends of packed intervals. The code in the CTE called *C3* filters only packed interval start and end events. After filtering, each consecutive pair of events represents a packed interval. So, the query computes a pair identifier called *grp* with the formula *grp = (rn – 1) / 2 + 1*, where *rn* is the row number.

Here's the output of the code in *C3*:

```
username   ts                  grp
---------  ------------------  ----
User1      2019-12-01 08:00    1
User1      2019-12-01 09:30    1
User1      2019-12-01 10:00    2
User1      2019-12-01 12:30    2
User2      2019-12-01 08:00    1
User2      2019-12-01 10:30    1
User2      2019-12-01 11:00    2
User2      2019-12-01 11:30    2
User2      2019-12-01 11:32    3
User2      2019-12-01 12:00    3
User2      2019-12-01 12:04    4
User2      2019-12-01 12:30    4
User3      2019-12-01 08:00    1
User3      2019-12-01 09:00    1
User3      2019-12-01 09:30    2
User3      2019-12-01 09:30    2
```

What's left for the outermost query to do is to group the rows from *C3* by *username* and *grp* and compute the beginning and end of each packed interval as the minimum *ts* and maximum *ts* values, respectively.

The plan for this solution is shown in Figure 6-20.

FIGURE 6-20 Execution plan for Solution 1 using window function.

Observe that the plan relies on ordered scans of the indexes and uses an order-preserving *Merge Join (Concatenation)* operator to unify the rows. Then without the need for explicit sorting, it computes both the running total and the row numbers using batch-mode *Window Aggregate* operators. Finally, it computes the beginning and end of each packed interval with a *Hash Match* aggregate. Because there's no need for sorting in this plan, it scales linearly.

Here are the performance numbers that I got for this query against the table with the 5,000,000 rows:

CPU time: 7094 ms, elapsed time: 7324 ms

Runtime dropped from two weeks to 7 seconds; that's not too shabby!

Before you move on to *Solution 2*, run the following code to drop the rowstore indexes that supported *Solution 1*.

```
DROP INDEX IF EXISTS idx_user_start_id ON dbo.Sessions;
DROP INDEX IF EXISTS idx_user_end_id ON dbo.Sessions;
```

Solution 2 also uses window functions, but it relies on a single scan of the data. Therefore, you need only one rowstore index to support it. Use the following code to create a rowstore index that orders the intervals by *username, starttime, endtime,* and *id*:

```
CREATE UNIQUE INDEX idx_user_start__end_id
  ON dbo.Sessions(username, starttime, endtime, id);
```

Listing 6-15 shows the complete code that implements *Solution 2*.

LISTING 6-15 *Solution 2* Based on Window Functions to Packing Intervals

```
WITH C1 AS
(
  SELECT *,
    CASE
      WHEN starttime <=
        MAX(endtime) OVER(PARTITION BY username
                          ORDER BY starttime, endtime, id
                          ROWS BETWEEN UNBOUNDED PRECEDING AND 1 PRECEDING)
        THEN 0
        ELSE 1
      END AS isstart
  FROM dbo.Sessions
),
C2 AS
(
  SELECT *,
    SUM(isstart) OVER(PARTITION BY username
                      ORDER BY starttime, endtime, id
                      ROWS UNBOUNDED PRECEDING) AS grp
  FROM C1
)
SELECT username, MIN(starttime) AS starttime, max(endtime) AS endtime
FROM C2
GROUP BY username, grp;
```

The code in the CTE called *C1* uses a *MAX* window aggregate to compute the maximum end time for all intervals up to the prior interval. Let's call this value *prevmax*. It then uses a *CASE* expression that creates a flag called *isstart* that indicates whether the current interval belongs to a previously started packed interval (when *starttime* <= *prevmax*) or not (otherwise).

Here's the output of the code in C1:

```
id    username   starttime           endtime             isstart
----  ---------  ------------------  ------------------  --------
1     User1      2019-12-01 08:00    2019-12-01 08:30    1
2     User1      2019-12-01 08:30    2019-12-01 09:00    0
3     User1      2019-12-01 09:00    2019-12-01 09:30    0
4     User1      2019-12-01 10:00    2019-12-01 11:00    1
5     User1      2019-12-01 10:30    2019-12-01 12:00    0
6     User1      2019-12-01 11:30    2019-12-01 12:30    0
7     User2      2019-12-01 08:00    2019-12-01 10:30    1
8     User2      2019-12-01 08:30    2019-12-01 10:00    0
9     User2      2019-12-01 09:00    2019-12-01 09:30    0
10    User2      2019-12-01 11:00    2019-12-01 11:30    1
11    User2      2019-12-01 11:32    2019-12-01 12:00    1
12    User2      2019-12-01 12:04    2019-12-01 12:30    1
14    User3      2019-12-01 08:00    2019-12-01 08:30    1
13    User3      2019-12-01 08:00    2019-12-01 09:00    0
15    User3      2019-12-01 08:30    2019-12-01 09:00    0
16    User3      2019-12-01 09:30    2019-12-01 09:30    1
```

The code in *C2* then computes a packed interval identifier called *grp* simply by applying a running total of the *isstart* flag.

Here's the output of the code in *C2*:

```
id    username   starttime           endtime             isstart  grp
----  ---------  ------------------  ------------------  --------  ----
1     User1      2019-12-01 08:00    2019-12-01 08:30    1         1
2     User1      2019-12-01 08:30    2019-12-01 09:00    0         1
3     User1      2019-12-01 09:00    2019-12-01 09:30    0         1
4     User1      2019-12-01 10:00    2019-12-01 11:00    1         2
5     User1      2019-12-01 10:30    2019-12-01 12:00    0         2
6     User1      2019-12-01 11:30    2019-12-01 12:30    0         2
7     User2      2019-12-01 08:00    2019-12-01 10:30    1         1
8     User2      2019-12-01 08:30    2019-12-01 10:00    0         1
9     User2      2019-12-01 09:00    2019-12-01 09:30    0         1
10    User2      2019-12-01 11:00    2019-12-01 11:30    1         2
11    User2      2019-12-01 11:32    2019-12-01 12:00    1         3
12    User2      2019-12-01 12:04    2019-12-01 12:30    1         4
14    User3      2019-12-01 08:00    2019-12-01 08:30    1         1
13    User3      2019-12-01 08:00    2019-12-01 09:00    0         1
15    User3      2019-12-01 08:30    2019-12-01 09:00    0         1
16    User3      2019-12-01 09:30    2019-12-01 09:30    1         2
```

Finally, the outermost query groups the rows by *username* and *grp* and computes the beginning and end of each packed interval as the minimum start time and maximum end time, respectively.

The plan for this solution is shown in Figure 6-21.

FIGURE 6-21 Execution plan for Solution 2 using window function.

Because the windowed *MAX* aggregate ends with *1 PRECEDING*, it cannot use the batch mode *Window Aggregate* operator, other than to compute the row numbers that it uses internally. The actual *MAX* aggregate uses row-mode processing.

Here are the performance numbers that I got for this solution:

CPU time: 10016 ms, elapsed time: 10393 ms

It's a bit slower than *Solution 1*, but it does have an advantage in that it requires only one rowstore index instead of two. The run times of both solutions dwarf compared to the original solution with the subquery, which takes about two weeks to complete.

There are many variations of interval packing tasks. You can find a couple of additional examples for such tasks here:

- Packing intervals with priorities: *https://www.itprotoday.com/sql-server/ packing-intervals-priorities*

- Identifying existence of intersections in intervals: *https://www.itprotoday.com/sql-server/ identifying-existence-intersections-intervals*

Also, if you haven't done so already, make sure to check out what the solution for packing would look like using row-pattern recognition in Chapter 4.

Gaps and Islands

Gaps and Islands are classic tasks in SQL that manifest themselves in practice in many forms. The basic concept is that you have some sort of sequence of numbers or date and time values where there's supposed to be a fixed interval between the entries, but some entries could be missing. Then the gaps task involves identifying all ranges of missing values in the sequence, and the islands task involves identifying all ranges of existing values. To demonstrate techniques to identify gaps and islands, I'll use a table called *T1* with a numeric sequence in a column called *col1* with an interval of *1* integer and a table called *T2* with a date and time sequence in a column called *col1* with an interval of 1 day. Listing 6-16 shows code to create T1 and T2 and fill them with some sample data.

LISTING 6-16 Code to Create and Populate Tables *T1* and *T2*

```
SET NOCOUNT ON;
USE TSQLV5;

-- dbo.T1 (numeric sequence with unique values, interval: 1)
DROP TABLE IF EXISTS dbo.T1;

CREATE TABLE dbo.T1
(
  col1 INT NOT NULL
    CONSTRAINT PK_T1 PRIMARY KEY
);
GO

INSERT INTO dbo.T1(col1)
  VALUES(2),(3),(7),(8),(9),(11),(15),(16),(17),(28);

-- dbo.T2 (temporal sequence with unique values, interval: 1 day)
DROP TABLE IF EXISTS dbo.T2;

CREATE TABLE dbo.T2
(
  col1 DATE NOT NULL
    CONSTRAINT PK_T2 PRIMARY KEY
);
GO

INSERT INTO dbo.T2(col1) VALUES
  ('20190202'),
  ('20190203'),
  ('20190207'),
  ('20190208'),
  ('20190209'),
  ('20190211'),
  ('20190215'),
  ('20190216'),
  ('20190217'),
  ('20190228');
```

Because these sample tables are so small, SQL Server will not consider using batch-mode processing on *rowstore* by default. Obviously with larger, more realistic volumes, it would. Use the following code to create fake filtered *columnstore* indexes on these tables to enable batch processing even with our small volumes (details on this trick in Chapter 5):

```
CREATE NONCLUSTERED COLUMNSTORE INDEX idx_cs ON dbo.T1(col1)
  WHERE col1 = -1 AND col1 = -2;

CREATE NONCLUSTERED COLUMNSTORE INDEX idx_cs ON dbo.T2(col1)
  WHERE col1 = '00010101' AND col1 = '00010102';
```

Gaps

As mentioned, the gaps task involves identifying the ranges of missing values in the sequence. Using our sample data, here are the desired results for the numeric sequence in T1:

```
rangestart   rangeend
-----------  -----------
4            6
10           10
12           14
18           27
```

And here are the desired results for the temporal sequence in T2:

```
rangestart   rangeend
----------   ----------
2019-02-04   2019-02-06
2019-02-10   2019-02-10
2019-02-12   2019-02-14
2019-02-18   2019-02-27
```

The *LAG* and *LEAD* window functions are very handy to solve tasks involving identifying gaps. Using the *LEAD* function, you can return for each current *col1* value (call it *cur*) the next value in the sequence (call it *nxt*). Then you can filter only pairs where the difference between the two is greater than the interval. Then add one interval to *cur* and subtract one interval from *nxt* to produce the actual gap information. Here's the complete solution with the numeric sequence followed by its execution plan (in Figure 6-22):

```
WITH C AS
(
  SELECT col1 AS cur, LEAD(col1) OVER(ORDER BY col1) AS nxt
    FROM dbo.T1
)
SELECT cur + 1 AS rangestart, nxt - 1 AS rangeend
FROM C
WHERE nxt - cur > 1;
```

FIGURE 6-22 Plan for a solution to the gaps task.

Observe how efficient the plan is, performing only one ordered scan of the index defined on *col1*. To apply the same technique to the temporal sequence, you simply use the *DATEDIFF* function to compute the difference between *cur* and *nxt*, and you use *DATEADD* to add or subtract an interval, like so:

```
WITH C AS
(
  SELECT col1 AS cur, LEAD(col1) OVER(ORDER BY col1) AS nxt
```

```
    FROM dbo.T2
)
SELECT DATEADD(day, 1, cur) AS rangestart, DATEADD(day, -1, nxt) rangeend
FROM C
WHERE DATEDIFF(day, cur, nxt) > 1;
```

Islands

The islands task involves identifying ranges of existing values. Here's the desired output against the numeric sequence:

```
start_range end_range
----------- -----------
2           3
7           9
11          11
15          17
28          28
```

And here's the desired output against the temporal sequence:

```
start_range end_range
----------- ----------
2019-02-02  2019-02-03
2019-02-07  2019-02-09
2019-02-11  2019-02-11
2019-02-15  2019-02-17
2019-02-28  2019-02-28
```

One of the most efficient solutions to the islands task involves using ranking calculations. You use the DENSE_RANK function to create a sequence of integers in *col1* ordering, and you calculate the difference between *col1* and the dense rank, like so:

```
SELECT col1,
  DENSE_RANK() OVER(ORDER BY col1) AS drnk,
  col1 - DENSE_RANK() OVER(ORDER BY col1) AS diff
FROM dbo.T1;

col1  drnk  diff
----- ----- -----
2     1     1
3     2     1
7     3     4
8     4     4
9     5     4
11    6     5
15    7     8
16    8     8
17    9     8
28    10    18
```

Observe that within an island the difference is the same, and that difference is unique for each island. That's because within an island, both *col1* and *drnk* keep advancing by the same interval. As soon as you jump to the next island, *col1* increases by more than one interval, whereas *drnk* keeps increasing by one. Therefore, the difference in each island is greater than the previous island's difference. Because this difference is the same within an island and unique for each island, you can use it as a group identifier. So, what's left is just to group the rows by this difference and return the minimum and maximum *col1* values in each group, like so:

```
WITH C AS
(
  SELECT col1, col1 - DENSE_RANK() OVER(ORDER BY col1) AS grp
  FROM dbo.T1
)
SELECT MIN(col1) AS start_range, MAX(col1) AS end_range
FROM C
GROUP BY grp;
```

The plan for this solution is shown in Figure 6-23.

SELECT   Hash Match   Compute Scalar   Window Aggregate   Clustered Index Scan (Clustered)
Cost: 0 %   (Aggregate)   Cost: 0 %   Cost: 0 %   [T1].[PK_T1]
         Cost: 35 %   Cost: 65 %

FIGURE 6-23 Plan for a solution to the islands task.

The plan is very efficient because the computation of the dense rank value can rely on the ordering of the index on *col1*.

You might be wondering why we use the *DENSE_RANK* function and not *ROW_NUMBER*. This has to do with needing support for cases where the sequence values are not guaranteed to be unique. Using the *ROW_NUMBER* function, the technique works only when the sequence values are unique (which happens to be the case in our sample data), but it fails when duplicates are allowed. Using the *DENSE_RANK* function, the technique works both with unique and nonunique values; hence, I prefer to always use *DENSE_RANK*.

The technique can even work with temporal intervals, but it might not immediately be apparent how to adjust it for this case. Remember that the technique involves producing a group identifier—namely, a value that is the same for all members of the same island and different from the values produced for other islands. With the temporal sequence, the *col1* values and dense rank values use different types of intervals—one uses an interval of 1 integer, and the other uses an interval of 1 day. To make the technique work, simply subtract from the *col1* value as many times the temporal interval as the dense rank value. You need to use the *DATEADD* function to achieve this. Then you will get a date and time value as a result that is the same for all members of the same island and different from the values produced for other islands. Here's the complete solution code:

```
WITH C AS
(
```

```
    SELECT col1, DATEADD(day, -1 * DENSE_RANK() OVER(ORDER BY col1), col1) AS grp
    FROM dbo.T2
)
SELECT MIN(col1) AS start_range, MAX(col1) AS end_range
FROM C
GROUP BY grp;
```

As you can see, instead of directly subtracting the result of the dense rank function from *col1*, you use *DATEADD* to subtract the dense rank multiplied by one day from *col1*.

There many examples of querying tasks where you need to use the islands technique, such as availability reports, periods of activity, and others. Earlier I demonstrated that you can even use the islands technique to handle interval packing.

There are versions of the islands task that are more complicated than the fundamental one. For example, say you are supposed to ignore gaps of up to a certain size—for example, in our date sequence, say you are supposed to ignore gaps of up to 2 days. Then the desired output would be the following:

```
rangestart  rangeend
----------  ----------
2019-02-02  2019-02-03
2019-02-15  2019-02-17
2019-02-28  2019-02-28
2019-02-07  2019-02-11
```

Observe that the dates in February 2019 with the day units 7, 8, 9, and 11 are all part of one island starting with 7 and ending with 11. The gap between 9 and 11 is ignored because it isn't greater than 2.

You can use the LAG and SUM window functions to handle this task. You first define a CTE called *C1* based on a query against T2 computing an attribute called *isstart*. This attribute is a flag whose value is *0* when the current value isn't the first in the island and *1* when it is. If the difference between the current *col1* value and the previous value (obtained using the LAG function) is less than or equal to 2 days, the value is not the first value in the island; otherwise, it is the first value in the island.

Next, the code defines a CTE called *C2* that computes a running total of the *isstart* flag, resulting in a unique value per island that you can use as a group identifier.

Finally, the outer query groups the rows from *C2* by the island identifier and returns the minimum start time and maximum end time as the island boundaries.

Here's the complete solution code:

```
WITH C1 AS
(
  SELECT col1,
    CASE
      WHEN DATEDIFF(day, LAG(col1) OVER(ORDER BY col1), col1) <= 2
        THEN 0
```

```
      ELSE 1
    END AS isstart
  FROM dbo.T2
),
C2 AS
(
  SELECT *,
    SUM(isstart) OVER(ORDER BY col1 ROWS UNBOUNDED PRECEDING) AS grp
  FROM C1
)
SELECT MIN(col1) AS rangestart, MAX(col1) AS rangeend
FROM C2
GROUP BY grp;
```

The execution plan for this query is shown in Figure 6-24.

FIGURE 6-24 Plan for a solution to the islands task ignoring gaps up to two days.

This plan is highly efficient, applying one ordered scan of the data, and avoiding the need for sorting altogether.

This technique where you create a flag that tells you whether the current event starts a new island after obtaining data from the previous row using *LAG*, and then apply a running total calculation to produce an island identifier, is very powerful. It can be used to solve almost any kind of islands task that you can think about.

Here's another example. Use the following code to generate a new table called *T1* and fill it with sample data:

```
DROP TABLE IF EXISTS dbo.T1;

CREATE TABLE dbo.T1
(
  id  INT         NOT NULL PRIMARY KEY,
  val VARCHAR(10) NOT NULL
);
GO

INSERT INTO dbo.T1(id, val) VALUES
  (2,  'a'),
  (3,  'a'),
  (5,  'a'),
  (7,  'b'),
  (11, 'b'),
  (13, 'a'),
  (17, 'a'),
```

```
(19, 'a'),
(23, 'c'),
(29, 'c'),
(31, 'a'),
(37, 'a'),
(41, 'a'),
(43, 'a'),
(47, 'c'),
(53, 'c'),
(59, 'c');
```

The task in this case is to identify consecutive ranges of IDs where the value in the *val* attribute remains the same. Observe that there can be multiple islands associated with the same value in *val*. Here's the desired output for the given sample data:

```
rangestart   rangeend      val
-----------  -----------   ----------
2            5             a
7            11            b
13           19            a
23           29            c
31           43            a
47           59            c
```

Here's the solution that applies our flexible technique to handle this task:

```
WITH C1 AS
(
  SELECT id, val, CASE WHEN val = LAG(val) OVER(ORDER BY id) THEN 0 ELSE 1 END
    AS isstart
  FROM dbo.T1
),
C2 AS
(
  SELECT *,
    SUM(isstart) OVER(ORDER BY id ROWS UNBOUNDED PRECEDING) AS grp
  FROM C1
)
SELECT MIN(id) AS rangestart, MAX(id) AS rangeend, val
FROM C2
GROUP BY grp, val;
```

The query in the CTE called *C1* computes the *isstart* flag, setting it to 0 when the value in the current and previous rows are the same, otherwise to 1. The query in the CTE called *C2* computes a running total of the *isstart* flag, resulting in an island, or group, identifier called *grp*. The outer query then groups the rows from C2 by *grp* and *val* and returns the minimum ID and maximum ID as the island boundaries.

Gaps and islands tasks can also be solved very elegantly using row pattern recognition. Make sure that you check out Chapter 4 to see how.

Median

In Chapters 2 and 3, I discussed how to compute percentiles. I mentioned that the 50th percentile—commonly known as the median—represents, loosely speaking, the value in the population that 50 percent of the values are less than. I provided solutions to calculating any percentile. Here, I'll just remind you of the solution using the *PERCENTILE_CONT* function (*CONT* for the continuous distribution model) and then, for the sake of the exercise, show additional interesting solutions specific to the median calculation without using the built-in function.

For sample data, I'll use the *Stats.Scores* table, which holds student test scores. Suppose your task was to compute, for each test, the median score assuming continuous distribution model. If there's an odd number of student test scores for a given test, you're supposed to return the middle score. If there's an even number, you're supposed to return the average of the two middle scores. Here's the desired output for the given sample data:

```
testid      median
----------  -------
Test ABC    75
Test XYZ    77.5
```

As already mentioned in this book, the function *PERCENTILE_CONT* is used to compute percentiles assuming a continuous distribution model. However, this function wasn't implemented as a grouped ordered set function; rather, it was implemented as a window function. This means that you can use it to return a percentile along with all detail rows but to return it only once per group, you need to add a *DISTINCT* clause, like so:

```
SELECT DISTINCT testid,
  PERCENTILE_CONT(0.5) WITHIN GROUP(ORDER BY score) OVER(PARTITION BY testid) AS median
FROM Stats.Scores;
```

It's a little bit awkward, but it works.

As an exercise, to compute median without the built-in *PERCENTILE_CONT* function, you have to be more creative. One solution is to compute, for each row, a position within the test based on score ordering (call it *pos*) and the count of scores in the respective test (call it *cnt*). To compute *pos*, you use the *ROW_NUMBER* function, and to compute *cnt*, you use the COUNT window aggregate function. Then you filter only the rows that are supposed to participate in the median calculation—namely, the rows where *pos* is either equal to *(cnt + 1) / 2* or *(cnt + 2) / 2*. Note that the expressions use integer division, so any fraction is truncated. When there is an odd number of elements, both expressions return the same middle point. For example, when there are 9 elements in the group, both expressions return 5. When there is an even number of elements, the expressions return the two middle points. For example, when there are 10 elements in the group, the expressions return 5 and 6. After you filter the right rows, what's left is to group the rows by the test ID and return for each test the average score. Here's the complete solution query:

```
WITH C AS
(
  SELECT testid, score,
    ROW_NUMBER() OVER(PARTITION BY testid ORDER BY score) AS pos,
    COUNT(*) OVER(PARTITION BY testid) AS cnt
  FROM Stats.Scores
)
SELECT testid, AVG(1. * score) AS median
FROM C
WHERE pos IN( (cnt + 1) / 2, (cnt + 2) / 2 )
GROUP BY testid;
```

Another interesting solution involves computing two row numbers—one in ascending *score*, *studentid* ordering (*studentid* added for determinism), and another in descending ordering. Here's the code to compute the two row numbers followed by its output:

```
SELECT testid, score,
  ROW_NUMBER() OVER(PARTITION BY testid ORDER BY score, studentid) AS rna,
  ROW_NUMBER() OVER(PARTITION BY testid ORDER BY score DESC, studentid DESC)
    AS rnd
FROM Stats.Scores;
```

testid	score	rna	rnd
Test ABC	95	9	1
Test ABC	95	8	2
Test ABC	80	7	3
Test ABC	80	6	4
Test ABC	75	5	5
Test ABC	65	4	6
Test ABC	55	3	7
Test ABC	55	2	8
Test ABC	50	1	9
Test XYZ	95	10	1
Test XYZ	95	9	2
Test XYZ	95	8	3
Test XYZ	80	7	4
Test XYZ	80	6	5
Test XYZ	75	5	6
Test XYZ	65	4	7
Test XYZ	55	3	8
Test XYZ	55	2	9
Test XYZ	50	1	10

Can you generalize a rule that identifies the rows that need to participate in the median calculation?

Observe that when there's an odd number of elements, the median is where the two row numbers are the same. When there's an even number of elements, the median elements are where the absolute difference between the two row numbers is equal to 1. To merge the two rules, the median elements are in the rows where the absolute difference between the two row numbers is less than or equal to 1. Here's the complete solution code that relies on this rule:

```
WITH C AS
(
  SELECT testid, score,
    ROW_NUMBER() OVER(PARTITION BY testid ORDER BY score, studentid) AS rna,
    ROW_NUMBER() OVER(PARTITION BY testid ORDER BY score DESC, studentid DESC)
      AS rnd
  FROM Stats.Scores
)
SELECT testid, AVG(1. * score) AS median
FROM C
WHERE ABS(rna - rnd) <= 1
GROUP BY testid;
```

The last two solutions perform quite well when the group element (the test ID in our case) has low density. When it has high density, a different solution tends to be more optimal. It's a solution that uses a combination of the *APPLY* operator and *OFFSET-FETCH* filter.

The idea is to handle each group separately. You use one query to identify the groups with their relevant parameters and another to handle each group. The first query is a grouped query that based on the count of test scores per test ID computes parameters for an *OFFSET-FETCH* filter. The second query is an applied correlated query that skips and filters the right number of test scores for the current test ID. You use the following formulas to compute the offset value (call it *ov*) and fetch value (call it *fv*) columns:

- ov = (COUNT(*) - 1) / 2

- fv = 2 - COUNT(*) % 2

The calculation of *ov* uses integer division since the count is an integer. The % sign is used as a modulo operator; it tells you whether the count is odd or even.

Once you have your grouped query compute the *ov* and *fv* columns, you define a CTE named C based on it and have the outer query against C use *CROSS APPLY* to apply an *OFFSET-FETCH* query that skips and fetches the right number of rows, group the result by *testid*, and compute the average of the returned scores.

Here's the complete solution query:

```
WITH C AS
(
  SELECT testid, (COUNT(*) - 1) / 2 AS ov, 2 - COUNT(*) % 2 AS fv
  FROM Stats.Scores
  GROUP BY testid
)
```

```
SELECT C.testid, AVG(1. * A.score) AS median
FROM C CROSS APPLY ( SELECT S.score
                     FROM Stats.Scores AS S
                     WHERE S.testid = C.testid
                     ORDER BY S.score
                     OFFSET C.ov ROWS FETCH NEXT C.fv ROWS ONLY ) AS A
GROUP BY C.testid;
```

You do want to make sure that you have an index on the key list (*testid*, *score*) to support all of the presented solutions.

Conditional Aggregate

Our next task involves computing a running total that always returns a non-negative value. That is, if the running total is negative at a point, return zero instead. Then, when you move to the next item in the sequence, you proceed from *0*. The practical use case is processing transactions that consume quantities from some stock, and when the stock level drops below zero, you replenish the stock from elsewhere. For sample data, use the following code, which creates and populates a table called *T1*:

```
USE TSQLV5;

DROP TABLE IF EXISTS dbo.T1;
GO

CREATE TABLE dbo.T1
(
  ordcol  INT NOT NULL PRIMARY KEY,
  datacol INT NOT NULL
);

INSERT INTO dbo.T1 VALUES
  (1,    10),
  (4,   -15),
  (5,     5),
  (6,   -10),
  (8,   -15),
  (10,   20),
  (17,   10),
  (18,  -10),
  (20,  -30),
  (31,   20);
```

According to the description of the task, here's the desired output for the given sample data, computing a non-negative sum of *datacol* (representing the quantity of the transaction) based on *ordcol* ordering (representing chronological order):

```
ordcol        datacol        nonnegativesum replenish
-----------   -----------    --------------- -----------
1             10             10              0
4             -15            0               5
5             5              5               0
6             -10            0               5
8             -15            0               15
10            20             20              0
17            10             30              0
18            -10            20              0
20            -30            0               10
31            20             20              0
```

I'll present an elegant solution that uses window functions. Listing 6-17 shows the complete solution code, followed by its output (adding the intermediate computations *partsum* and *adjust* to help explain the solution):

LISTING 6-17 Solution for Nonnegative Running Sum Task

```
WITH C1 AS
(
  SELECT ordcol, datacol,
    SUM(datacol) OVER (ORDER BY ordcol
                       ROWS UNBOUNDED PRECEDING) AS partsum
  FROM dbo.T1
),
C2 AS
(
  SELECT *,
    MIN(partsum) OVER (ORDER BY ordcol
                       ROWS UNBOUNDED PRECEDING) as mn
  FROM C1
)
SELECT ordcol, datacol, partsum, adjust,
  partsum + adjust AS nonnegativesum,
  adjust - LAG(adjust, 1, 0) OVER(ORDER BY ordcol) AS replenish
FROM C2
  CROSS APPLY(VALUES(CASE WHEN mn < 0 THEN -mn ELSE 0 END)) AS A(adjust);
```

```
ordcol  datacol  partsum  adjust  nonnegativesum replenish
------- -------- -------- ------- -------------- ----------
1       10       10       0       10             0
4       -15      -5       5       0              5
5       5        0        5       5              0
6       -10      -10      10      0              5
8       -15      -25      25      0              15
10      20       -5       25      20             0
17      10       5        25      30             0
18      -10      -5       25      20             0
20      -30      -35      35      0              10
31      20       -15      35      20             0
```

The code defining the CTE called *C1* creates an attribute called *partsum* that computes a plain running total of *datacol* based on *ordcol* ordering. This *partsum* attribute can be negative because the values in *datacol* can be negative. Then the code defining the CTE called *C2* queries *C1*, creating an attribute called *adjust* that is the additive inverse of the minimum *partsum* value when negative up to the current point. The outer query then computes the nonnegative sum by adding *adjust* to *partsum*, and the replenish quantity by subtracting the *adjust* value of the previous row, if present, from the current row's *adjust* value.

It can take a few rounds of going over this output to see that the logic works, but it does!

 NOTE This and similar capped sum tasks can be handled very easily and elegantly using row pattern recognition. Make sure to check such solutions in Chapter 4.

Sorting Hierarchies

Suppose that you need to present information from some hierarchy in a sorted fashion. You're supposed to present a parent before its descendants. Also, you need to be able to control the order among siblings. For sample data, use the code in Listing 6-18, which creates and populates a table called *dbo.Employees*. (This is not to be confused with the existing HR.Employees table that has different data.)

LISTING 6-18 Code to Create and Populate the Employees Table

```
USE TSQLV5;

DROP TABLE IF EXISTS dbo.Employees;
GO
CREATE TABLE dbo.Employees
(
  empid   INT         NOT NULL
    CONSTRAINT PK_Employees PRIMARY KEY,
  mgrid   INT         NULL
    CONSTRAINT FK_Employees_mgr_emp REFERENCES dbo.Employees,
  empname VARCHAR(25) NOT NULL,
  salary  MONEY       NOT NULL,
  CHECK (empid <> mgrid)
);

INSERT INTO dbo.Employees(empid, mgrid, empname, salary) VALUES
  (1,  NULL, 'David'  , $10000.00),
  (2,  1,    'Eitan'  , $7000.00),
  (3,  1,    'Ina'    , $7500.00),
  (4,  2,    'Seraph' , $5000.00),
  (5,  2,    'Jiru'   , $5500.00),
  (6,  2,    'Steve'  , $4500.00),
  (7,  3,    'Aaron'  , $5000.00),
  (8,  5,    'Lilach' , $3500.00),
```

```
(9,   7,   'Rita'   ,  $3000.00),
(10, 5,   'Sean'   ,  $3000.00),
(11, 7,   'Gabriel',  $3000.00),
(12, 9,   'Emilia' ,  $2000.00),
(13, 9,   'Michael',  $2000.00),
(14, 9,   'Didi'   ,  $1500.00);

CREATE UNIQUE INDEX idx_unc_mgrid_empid ON dbo.Employees(mgrid, empid);
```

Suppose that you need to present employees in hierarchical order—always presenting the manager before subordinates—and sorting siblings by *empname*. To achieve this task, you can use two main tools: the *ROW_NUMBER* function and a recursive CTE. You define a regular CTE called *EmpsRN* first, where you compute an attribute called *n* representing a row number partitioned by *mgrid* and ordered by *empname, empid* (*empid* added for determinism):

```
WITH EmpsRN AS
(
  SELECT *,
    ROW_NUMBER() OVER(PARTITION BY mgrid ORDER BY empname, empid) AS n
  FROM dbo.Employees
)
SELECT * FROM EmpsRN;
```

empid	mgrid	empname	salary	n
1	NULL	David	10000.00	1
2	1	Eitan	7000.00	1
3	1	Ina	7500.00	2
5	2	Jiru	5500.00	1
4	2	Seraph	5000.00	2
6	2	Steve	4500.00	3
7	3	Aaron	5000.00	1
8	5	Lilach	3500.00	1
10	5	Sean	3000.00	2
11	7	Gabriel	3000.00	1
9	7	Rita	3000.00	2
14	9	Didi	1500.00	1
12	9	Emilia	2000.00	2
13	9	Michael	2000.00	3

Next, you define a recursive CTE called *EmpsPath*, where you iterate through the employees one level at a time, starting with the root (CEO), then to direct subordinates, then to subordinates of subordinates, and so on. You construct a binary path for each employee that starts as an empty path for the root, and in each level of subordinates, you concatenate the manager's path with the binary form of *n* (the row number). Note that to minimize the size of the path, you need only enough bytes to cover the maximum number of direct subordinates a single manager can have. For example, a single byte is sufficient for up to 255 direct subordinates, two bytes are sufficient for up to 32,767 direct subordinates, and so on. Let's assume that we need two bytes in our case. You can also compute the level of the employee in the tree (the distance from the root) by assigning the level *0* to the root, and for a subordinate, you add 1 to the manager's level. Listing 6-19 shows the code that computes both the sort path (*sortpath*) and the level (*lvl*).

LISTING 6-19 Code Computing *sortpath* and *lvl*

```
WITH EmpsRN AS
(
  SELECT *,
    ROW_NUMBER() OVER(PARTITION BY mgrid ORDER BY empname, empid) AS n
  FROM dbo.Employees
),
EmpsPath
AS
(
  SELECT empid, empname, salary, 0 AS lvl,
    CAST(0x AS VARBINARY(MAX)) AS sortpath
  FROM dbo.Employees
  WHERE mgrid IS NULL

  UNION ALL

  SELECT C.empid, C.empname, C.salary, P.lvl + 1,
    P.sortpath + CAST(n AS BINARY(2)) AS sortpath
  FROM EmpsPath AS P
    INNER JOIN EmpsRN AS C
      ON C.mgrid = P.empid
)
SELECT *
FROM EmpsPath;
```

```
empid  empname  salary    lvl   sortpath
------ -------- --------- ----  ------------------
1      David    10000.00  0     0x
2      Eitan    7000.00   1     0x0001
3      Ina      7500.00   1     0x0002
7      Aaron    5000.00   2     0x00020001
11     Gabriel  3000.00   3     0x000200010001
9      Rita     3000.00   3     0x000200010002
14     Didi     1500.00   4     0x0002000100020001
12     Emilia   2000.00   4     0x0002000100020002
13     Michael  2000.00   4     0x0002000100020003
5      Jiru     5500.00   2     0x00010001
4      Seraph   5000.00   2     0x00010002
6      Steve    4500.00   2     0x00010003
8      Lilach   3500.00   3     0x000100010001
10     Sean     3000.00   3     0x000100010002
```

What's left to do to guarantee that the employees are presented in the desired order is to order the rows by *sortpath*. You can also achieve indentation in the output based on the employee's level in the hierarchy by replicating a string *lvl* times. Listing 6-20 provides the complete solution code.

LISTING 6-20 Sorting Employee Hierarchy with Siblings Sorted by *empname*

```
WITH EmpsRN AS
(
  SELECT *,
    ROW_NUMBER() OVER(PARTITION BY mgrid ORDER BY empname, empid) AS n
  FROM dbo.Employees
),
EmpsPath
AS
(
  SELECT empid, empname, salary, 0 AS lvl,
    CAST(0x AS VARBINARY(MAX)) AS sortpath
  FROM dbo.Employees
  WHERE mgrid IS NULL

  UNION ALL

  SELECT C.empid, C.empname, C.salary, P.lvl + 1,
    P.sortpath + CAST(n AS BINARY(2)) AS sortpath
  FROM EmpsPath AS P
    INNER JOIN EmpsRN AS C
      ON C.mgrid = P.empid
)
SELECT empid, salary, REPLICATE(' | ', lvl) + empname AS empname
FROM EmpsPath
ORDER BY sortpath;
```

Observe in the output of this solution that a manager always appears before his or her subordinates, and that siblings are sorted by *empname*:

```
empid        salary                  empname
----------   ---------------------   --------------------
1            10000.00                David
2            7000.00                 | Eitan
5            5500.00                 | | Jiru
8            3500.00                 | | | Lilach
10           3000.00                 | | | Sean
4            5000.00                 | | Seraph
6            4500.00                 | | Steve
3            7500.00                 | Ina
7            5000.00                 | | Aaron
11           3000.00                 | | | Gabriel
9            3000.00                 | | Rita
14           1500.00                 | | | Didi
12           2000.00                 | | | Emilia
13           2000.00                 | | | Michael
```

If you need siblings to be sorted differently—say, by salary—simply change the *ROW_NUMBER* function's window ordering clause, accordingly, as shown in Listing 6-21.

LISTING 6-21 Sorting Employee Hierarchy with Siblings Sorted by *salary*

```
WITH EmpsRN AS
(
  SELECT *,
    ROW_NUMBER() OVER(PARTITION BY mgrid ORDER BY salary, empid) AS n
  FROM dbo.Employees
),
EmpsPath
AS
(
  SELECT empid, empname, salary, 0 AS lvl,
    CAST(0x AS VARBINARY(MAX)) AS sortpath
  FROM dbo.Employees
  WHERE mgrid IS NULL

  UNION ALL

  SELECT C.empid, C.empname, C.salary, P.lvl + 1,
    P.sortpath + CAST(n AS BINARY(2)) AS sortpath
  FROM EmpsPath AS P
    INNER JOIN EmpsRN AS C
      ON C.mgrid = P.empid
)
SELECT empid, salary, REPLICATE(' | ', lvl) + empname AS empname
FROM EmpsPath
ORDER BY sortpath;
```

Here's the output of this query:

```
empid        salary                 empname
-----------  ---------------------  --------------------
1            10000.00               David
2            7000.00                | Eitan
6            4500.00                | | Steve
4            5000.00                | | Seraph
5            5500.00                | | Jiru
10           3000.00                | | | Sean
8            3500.00                | | | Lilach
3            7500.00                | Ina
7            5000.00                | | Aaron
9            3000.00                | | | Rita
14           1500.00                | | | | Didi
12           2000.00                | | | | Emilia
13           2000.00                | | | | Michael
11           3000.00                | | | Gabriel
```

Summary

I can't keep myself from admiring the beautiful design of window functions. They're engineered to overcome a number of shortcomings of more traditional SQL constructs, and they lend themselves to excellent optimization. You saw in this book that there are so many querying tasks that can be handled both elegantly and efficiently with window functions. I hope you will think of what you saw as just the start, and that you will find interesting and creative ways of your own to use them.

Standard SQL sees the great value in window functions and therefore, keeps adding more and more functions and functionality. Let's hope we see more powerful analytical capabilities added to SQL Server in the future, such as row-pattern recognition and additional windowing support.

Index

Symbols

Plug into learning at

MicrosoftPressStore.com

The Microsoft Press Store by Pearson offers:

- Free U.S. shipping

- Buy an eBook, get three formats – Includes PDF, EPUB, and MOBI to use with your computer, tablet, and mobile devices

- Print & eBook Best Value Packs

- eBook Deal of the Week – Save up to 50% on featured title

- Newsletter – Be the first to hear about new releases, announcements, special offers, and more

- Register your book – Find companion files, errata, and product updates, plus receive a special coupon* to save on your next purchase

 Pearson